SIX-GUN LAW

The Westerns of Randolph Scott, Audie Murphy, Joel McCrea and George Montgomery

Randolph Scott

SIX-GUN LAW

The Westerns of Randolph Scott, Audie Murphy, Joel McCrea and George Montgomery

BY BARRY ATKINSON

MIDNIGHT MARQUEE PRESS, INC.
BALTIMORE, MARYLAND, USA; LONDON, UK

Copyright © 2015 Barry Atkinson
Interior layout: Gary J. Svehla
Cover design: A. Susan Svehla
Copy Editor: Linda J. Walter

Midnight Marquee Press, Inc., Gary J. Svehla and A. Susan Svehla do not assume any responsibility for the accuracy, completeness, topicality or quality of the information in this book. All views expressed or material contained within are the sole responsibility of the author.

Without limiting the rights under copyright reserved above, no part of this publication may be reproduced, stored in or introduced into a retrieval system, or transmitted, in any form, or by any means (electronic, mechanical, photocopying, recording or otherwise), without the prior written permission of the copyright owner or the publishers of the book.

ISBN 13: 978-1-936168-54-5
Library of Congress Catalog Card Number 2015909291
Manufactured in the United States of America

First Printing by Midnight Marquee Press, Inc., September 2015

Dedication

🐎 TO THE HORSE ... 🐎

What that noblest of animals had to put up with over the course of an average 85-minute Western sometimes beggars belief. Whatever was asked of them, they undertook to do it, with only the occasional whinny or snort betraying any sort of discomfort on their part. We fans salute them for their perseverance and faithful natures. They epitomize the spirit of the Old West.

TABLE OF CONTENTS

8	Chapter 1: Last Sunset: The Decline of the Western
12	Chapter 2: Four Western Heroes
15	Chapter 3: Randolph Scott: The Man from Virginia
18	Chapter 4: Audie Murphy: All-American War Hero
21	Chapter 5: Joel McCrea: Easy Does It
25	Chapter 6: George Montgomery: The Glamour Cowboy
29	Chapter 7: Scott: The Virginian and the Zane Grey "Bs" 1929-1935
40	Chapter 8: McCrea Earns His Spurs, 1937-1949
56	Chapter 9: Montgomery: Republic to Fox, 1935-1948
62	Chapter 10: Scott: The Westerner, 1936-1949
101	Chapter 11: 1950: Murphy Makes It Big

110	Chapter 12: Scott at Columbia and Warner Bros., 1950-1957
145	Chapter 13: McCrea in the 1950s
176	Chapter 14: Montgomery at Columbia and United Artists 1950-1955
202	Chapter 15: Murphy: The Universal Years, 1951-1959
229	Chapter 16: Scott: The Budd Boetticher Westerns, 1956-1960
245	Chapter 17: Montgomery: 1956-1959
259	Chapter 18: Scott and McCrea at MGM, 1962
264	Chapter 19: Murphy: 1960-1969
286	Chapter 20: Final Roundup: McCrea and Montgomery, 1965-1976
294	Chapter 21: Filmography
318	Bibliography and Acknowledgment

Chapter 1
Last Sunset:
The Decline of the Western

When did the Western genre die out, and why? By the mid-1960s, new trends in violence and a changing moral climate in the cinema had filtered over into the "cowboy flick," pushing aside refinements in plot, characterization and the overall feel of what had been, after all, cinema's earliest crowd-pleaser, an oeuvre that 99 times out of 100 was a sure-fire guarantee to pull in the punters and set cash registers ringing on a Saturday night. Sergio Leone's highly stylized *Dollar* trilogy redefined and revitalized the Old West as well as becoming an homage to it, the director sourcing his material by drawing on countless actioners of the previous decades and then artfully molding the end product into something uniquely his own, thus changing an audience's perception of what a Western should now look like. However, Clint Eastwood's taciturn antihero, the Man With No Name in *A Fistful of Dollars*, was no different than John Wayne's coldly detached antihero, Ethan Edwards, in John Ford's *The Searchers*, or Randolph Scott's relentless bounty hunter, Ben Brigade, in Budd Boetticher's *Ride Lonesome*. The big difference lay in the no-holds-barred depiction of dispassionate bloodletting and "non-characters" at the expense of the previous elegiac portrayal of the West: Children and horses shot, women brutalized and raped, fistfights far more sadistic than they ever were, bullets slamming into bodies and prolonged scenes of torture and crimson carnage.

In Britain, following the release of Leone's trailblazer in 1967, it seemed every Western going out on the circuits carried an "A" or "X" certificate, each tailor-made specifically for an adult audience, the censor's office condoning this violence to a certain degree but ensuring that the younger moviegoing age group should not be a part of it. One of the first of these new "let's ban the kids" Westerns to actually appear before Leone's in-your-face saga to stir up the censorial waters was Universal's *He Rides Tall* in 1964, directed by R.G. Springsteen. Springsteen, a director of the old school, bowed to current public needs by throwing in two semi-rape scenes and a touch more viciousness than usual from veteran player Dan Duryea, spicing up an otherwise drab and forgettable oater. A few of the more extreme examples were shown in London only and banned outright from the provinces, or presented in heavily edited versions: Ralph Nelson's graphically filmed attack on an Indian camp in the final stages of *Soldier Blue* ensured that the director's rather mundane feature, gaining notoriety from this one sequence alone, received the prohibitive "X London" certificate in 1970, while Sam Peckinpah's choreographed blood

and guts that splattered the screen in *The Wild Bunch* (1969) caused no end of censorship problems; like *Soldier Blue*, it was vetoed in many parts of the United Kingdom. Westerns, even those made in the 1950s, were renowned for their roughhouse set pieces, but not to this extent. It was very hard to recall the sublime homespun poetry of Alan Ladd riding across the wide open prairie in *Shane* when sitting through *Ulzana's Raid*'s bloodbath or *Chato's Land*'s savagery, two X-rated reactionary oaters from the 1970s that were crude additions to the genre, neither displaying the frontier tale style so magisterially put across in George Stevens' 1953 sagebrush masterpiece. Unquestionably, it was during the 1970s that the much-loved, fondly remembered Western, for those of us who had sat through scores of them during the genre's golden age, the 1950s, sank into a self-parodied mire exemplified in 1972's *Dirty Little Billy*: Stan Dragoti's mud-plastered countercultural take on the Billy the Kid legend summed up just how low the once exalted horse opera had descended, the very antithesis of Kurt Neumann's beautifully observed *The Kid from Texas* (1950) starring a fresh-faced Audie Murphy as the wayward outlaw. Everything and everybody had to wallow in filth in the name of so-called realism. It made unattractive, somewhat depressing, viewing for Western diehards everywhere.

In 1964 *He Rides Tall* featured two semi-rape sequences, heralding the increasing violent nature of the Western.

Attempts have been made over the past few years to rejuvenate, or reinvent, the Western by promoting its past cultural values and virtues, hauling the product back on the big screen by the scruff of the neck and tailoring it to suit a newer audience. By and large, this has met with failure. A glance at the current releases on offer to the masses in May 2014 shows *Godzilla*, *Dawn of the Planet of the Apes*, *Dinosaur 13* and *Edge of Tomorrow* as the box-office attractions—not a Western in sight, and none appearing on the horizon, either. Clint Eastwood is (or was) about the only modern-day actor determined that the Western should not die out, with a succession of near-classics to his name, as both star and director: *High Plains Drifter* (1973), *The Outlaw Josey Wales* (1976) and *Pale Rider* (1985). But even his output has petered out. *Dances with Wolves* (1990), Eastwood's *Unforgiven* (1992) and *Open Range* (2003) are three latter-day examples of movie-making that have admirably preserved within their bodywork time-honored traits found in the

By the late 1960s, the Euro-Spaghetti Western was replacing the American Western genre.

glorious Westerns of the '40s and '50s, the undoubted halcyon period for such fare. But are the studios flogging (figuratively speaking) a dead horse? More to the point, are audiences interested in Westerns anymore? The answer has to be a resounding *No*.

Let's look at the statistics. From 1890 to 1919, a total of around 200 Westerns were made in Hollywood (this figure, and all others, are approximations). From 1920 to 1929, the figure rose to 260. During the 1930s, it steadied at 300. The 1940s were the peak years, a colossal 800 Westerns produced, but this figure is inflated by the Western serial; around 20 were in operation throughout the decade, contributing scores of chapterplays to the genre: *The Cisco Kid*, *The Durango Kid*, *Range Busters*, *Trail Blazers*, *The Texas Rangers*, *Sunset Carson*, *The Lone Rider*, *Cheyenne Davis*, *Rough Riders*, *The Canadian Mountie* and *Red Ryder*, among others. The 1950s, the real heyday of the low- to big-budget adult outdoor Western, saw a further 600 released, a more impressive total as serials had died out, the B- to medium-budget cowboy picture taking precedence and issued by the score as second-feature material and program fillers, a lot of the product real dime-a-dozen stuff. From this heady era, 1890 to 1959, we are talking traditional-style cowboy films: sheriffs, marshals, desperadoes, hard-working lasses, bar girls, bar bums, cattle drives, ranch hands, trail wranglers, outlaws, gringos, town tamers, despotic town owners, rustlers, horse thieves, cow punchers, crooked saloon owners, devious town officials, covered wagons, land-grabbers, heroes riding off into the sunset, wild horses on the open range, forts, cavalry and Indians on the warpath. 1960 onwards witnessed a gradual decline setting in: 190 Westerns during the decade, a figure that includes inroads made by the European Spaghetti Western. To their detriment, even non-American actors were beginning to be hired as headliners in Westerns—Terence Stamp, Sean Connery and Oliver Reed, to name but three; quaint, maybe, perhaps novel in a way, but all decidedly out of their territory, and out of their depth, to boot. The drop-off continued throughout the 1970s, 95 including Spaghetti outings, but the rot really set in during the 1980s: Spoof Westerns, horror Westerns, sci-fi Westerns, comedy Westerns, racial Westerns, sex Westerns, contemporary Westerns, anything *but* the good old traditional Western we were used to seeing. Taking all this into consideration, the number of what you would actually categorize as *true* traditional Westerns sunk to around 20 between the years 1980 to 1989. From 1990 to 1999, buffs were treated to a paltry 11 "proper" Westerns, while from 2000 up to and including 2013, only 20 having the sense and good grace to give a nod in the direction of conventional classics (most of these have been remakes, such as 2007's *3:10 to Yuma*) have graced the big screen among the mostly unwatchable welter of oddities, curios, clunkers and bastardizations released under the Western banner. And the 21st-century Western (those few that *are* made) is so intent on portraying the West as it *really* was that the end product comes across as a tedious, dimly photographed exercise in grime, gloom and doom, earnestness equating with dullness, so alien in concept to true lovers of the orthodox cowboy movie. Compare 2004's turgid rendition of *The Alamo* to John Wayne's vibrant, flag-waving epic of 1960, and you'll see what I mean. Westerns of the 1940s, 1950s and early 1960s may not have been entirely accurate in their depiction of the Old West, but they moved like wildfire and entertained prewar and postwar audiences by the millions.

Perhaps not always historically accurate, but John Wayne's *The Alamo* represents a more vibrant approach to American mythology.

Yes, the classic American Western which formed a major part of the diets of an entire generation of cinemagoers prior to 1970 no longer exists; the genre's death knell sounded when studios decided to ditch the Western from their production schedules around 40 years ago, reasoning that they no longer had a role to play in the cinematic scheme of things, being out of vogue with public taste, leading to dwindling audiences. No one connected with the film industry these days appears to mourn its passing. The great Western hero actors of the past—John Wayne, Gary Cooper, James Stewart, Kirk Douglas, Burt Lancaster, Henry Fonda—have holstered their six-shooters and ridden off into the fading sunset, never to be replaced in fans' affections. But what these hombres and their contemporaries have left behind is a vast body of work that has preserved, frame by frame, the mythology of the Old West and one that continues to bring pleasure and enjoyment to many, many fans of a certain age, and maybe even (one would like to think) a few younger members who wish to enroll as members of the classic Western club. After all, the cinema industry as a whole was founded on the cowboy and Indians movie over 120 years ago. Which is where certain Messrs. Randolph Scott, Audie Murphy, Joel McCrea and George Montgomery quite literally step into the picture.

Chapter 2
Four Western Heroes

My father was a bona fide Western movie fan, always had been since a young lad, and, from 1954 to 1959, took me to see many a cowboy adventure at the old Crescent cinema in Leatherhead, our local watering hole. I had to accompany him, whether I liked it or not—along with horror, I was totally hooked on Western pictures. They were my passion, as they were with the vast majority of English school kids at that time. But the main stumbling block to us watching them came in the form of The British Board of Film Censors; an awful lot released in the United Kingdom were awarded "A" classifications by the censor's office, including the countless Universal, Warner Bros. and Columbia Westerns churned out during the 1950s and screened as co-features. This meant a blanket ban on under-14s unless a grown-up felt kindly disposed to take you in, which my father did, on numerous occasions. Very often, the U.K.'s strict censorial code somewhat limited our viewing pleasures to the less-meaty U-rated Westerns along the lines of *Davy Crockett*, *The Charge at Feather River*, *White Feather* and *The Light in the Forest*. However, with parental help, I managed to get in and sit through *Shane, Yellow Sky, The Gunfighter, The Naked Spur, Vera Cruz, The Indian Fighter, Distant Drums, The Big Country, Gunfight at the O.K. Corral, Broken Arrow, Gun Fury, Night Passage, The Searchers, Garden of Evil, The Kentuckian, Warlock, Drum Beat, The Man from Laramie, The Last Command, The Far Country, The Law and Jake Wade, Horizons West, The Violent Men, Gunman's Walk, The Big Sky* and *The Tin Star*. All must-sees and all carrying an "A" certificate. Dad would often say to me in the evening, "We're off to see a John Wayne Western Friday night," or "There's a Gary Cooper cowboy film on Saturday," or (to my mother) "I'm taking Barry to see James Stewart's latest." But *never* a Randolph Scott, Joel McCrea, George Montgomery or Audie Murphy Western (*Night Passage* is the Murphy exception, but Dad classed it as a James Stewart Western, not one of Murphy's. The only other Murphys I ever caught in a cinema were *Seven Ways from Sundown*, on a double bill with *This Island Earth* in 1962, and *Destry*, playing with Mario Bava's *Hercules in the Haunted World*, in 1963). The aforementioned 26 films were the main attractions wher-

As a child my father always manged to take me to see the top-of-the-line Westerns ...

ever they were screened, classed as grade-A productions. Scott, Murphy, McCrea and Montgomery's Westerns were for the most part issued in England as the supporting program and mistakenly regarded by the great British public as B-movies, so perhaps the major presentation they appeared with never appealed to my father, this being the reason why I never caught one. Later in life, Dad found consolation in this remiss on his part by ordering DVD releases of the cowboy quartet's better movies and wondering why he had never bothered with them at the cinema in the first place.

In hindsight, my father, by ignoring the flicks made by these four heroic stalwarts, was, without realizing it, robbing himself of the chance to see some of the choicest of Westerns ever committed to celluloid. In the hierarchy of Western actors, and of the Western genre per se, Scott and his compadres are up there with the best. Putting aside the founding cowboy giants of the silent era such as Hoot Gibson and Tom Mix, who helped formulate the genre for mass audiences (between them, these two Western megastars featured in over 200 Westerns), and Roy Rogers' total of 104, Gene *The Singing Cowboy* Autry's 93, Tex Ritter's 74 and Hopalong Cassidy's 66 (all four are generally classed as novelty, or children's matinee, acts and certainly don't fall into what fans might discern as the serious Western category), we have diminutive cowboy actor Bob Steele. Steele chalked up 163 Westerns in a career spanning four decades, but many of his '30s and '40s flicks were bottom-of-the-bill low-budget fodder with running times of an hour or less, and they have long since faded in memory. The same could be said of the early output of Johnny Mack Brown—127 Westerns, the majority serials and program fillers. On behalf of the "Big Guns," John Wayne came in with 84 Westerns under his leather belt, but many of his '30s and '40s offerings were grade-B efforts with hour-long running times. The Duke's formidable total is almost equaled by Randolph Scott, who racked up a highly respectable 64 and *never* acted in a Western serial. Scott's repertoire is not all that far off George Montgomery's 58. However, Montgomery's tally includes 26 un-credited roles and a *Lone Ranger* serial; his true figure, as leading man/co-star, is 31. Next, we have Allan "Rocky" Lane (51), Jack

Seven Ways from Sundown **was one of the few Audie Murphy Westerns I saw in a movie theater.**

Rory Calhoun, though he appeared in some good Westerns, lacked the charisma to attract a cult following.

Holt (44, including 20 silents), Gary Cooper (40), Tom Keane (38), Tim Holt (35), Audie Murphy (33), Joel McCrea (31), Robert Mitchum (30), Rory Calhoun (29), Robert Ryan (25), Rod Cameron (21), Henry Fonda (21), Sterling Hayden (21), James Stewart (19), Richard Widmark (19), Kirk Douglas (18), Dale Robertson (18), Burt Lancaster (16), Stephen McNally (16), John Payne (16), Alan Ladd (14), Jeff Chandler (14), Philip Carey (13), Rock Hudson (13), Robert Taylor (13) and Gregory Peck (12). George "Gabby" Hayes appeared in over 60 Westerns, but mostly as a sidekick to the headliners, as did character actor Walter Brennan, with 49; likewise, the totals of Lee Van Cleef (53), Jack Elam (46), Edgar Buchanan (45), Ward Bond (38), Lee Marvin (25), Leo Gordon (28) and Hugh O'Brian (22) are remarkable, but again, many of their roles were as support to the leads, mostly as the bad guy.

So what have Scott, Murphy, McCrea and Montgomery got in common over the other stars listed above and why choose to feature their respective careers in the saddle above so many other Western actors? The key answer principally lies in the 1950s, the Western's finest hour, and this particular foursome's finest hour also. Scott strolled onto the Western '50s stage looking and acting more like a cowboy than the other three, having starred in 36 oaters, able to bring a certain amount of dexterity into the roles he played. McCrea, like Scott, had appeared in a wide number of parts and was able to bring his undoubted acting knowhow to the table. Montgomery, not a leading man in the same league as Scott and McCrea and nowhere near as versatile, had nevertheless sharpened his teeth as an un-credited extra in a run of Republic Western potboilers and a *Lone Ranger* serial so was ready, willing and able to make a name for himself in whatever Western setup suited him. On the other hand, although Murphy's career only kicked off in 1950, he made such a big impression in such a short space of time that he quickly rose above the ranks, firmly establishing his credentials as a Western actor of some note. Although Rory Calhoun, Sterling Hayden, Dale Robertson, Rod Cameron, Stephen McNally, Jeff Chandler et al. made some darned fine cowboy pictures, they never connected with the fans on a mass scale as did Scott, Murphy, McCrea and Montgomery and didn't possess the same charisma or screen presence. In England and America during the 1950s, you paid to go and see a Scott Western, a Murphy Western, a McCrea Western and a Montgomery Western; you didn't, for example, pay to go see a Rory Calhoun Western. That was the big difference; all four rode very similar trails, which is why this book will focus on those four stars alone.

Chapter 3
Randolph Scott:
The Man from Virginia

George Randolph Scott, the second of six children, was born into a well-to-do family on January 23, 1898, in Orange County, Virginia, of Scottish/American descent. Spending his childhood in Charlotte, North Carolina, young Scott, known as "Randy" to his friends, showed prowess in most sports at a succession of private schools and at the Georgia Institute of Technology, including football, swimming and horse racing. In April 1917, when America entered World War I, he joined the 2nd Trench Mortar Battalion and elected to stay on in France after hostilities had ended, enrolling in an artillery school. In 1919, Scott returned to the States and at one time harbored ambitions to become an American football player, but a persistent back injury put paid to that, so he continued his education at the University of North Carolina, graduating with a degree in textile engineering and then leaving to work in the textile trade with Scott Senior. In 1927, the theater and stage acting took his fancy; via his father, Scott was introduced to none other than the celebrated eccentric moviemaker Howard Hughes in 1928, scoring, as a result, a small slot in the romantic comedy, *Sharp Shooters*. More walk-ons followed in *The Far Call*, *Weary River*, *The Black Watch* (all 1928) and *Dynamite* and *Sailor's Holiday* (1929). His career in the Western genre dates a long way back, to this early talkie era of 1929, when he had a bit part in Paramount's *The Virginian*, hired as voice coach to iron out leading man Gary Cooper's thick Southern intonation and also getting a basically insignificant part riding a horse as a bonus; this fleeting moment establishes Victor Fleming's outdoor actioner as Randolph Scott's very first Western, albeit in a "blink and you'll miss him" role.

Randolph Scott in a 1930s publicity pose for Paramount

Progressing through a series of Zane Grey B-programmers in the early '30s, he finally, after years of honing his skills as a co-star, found his footing top billed in 1946's *Abilene Town*. From this point on, Scott made a series of Westerns produced on modest budgets, put together by jobbing directors, every bit as good as those featuring Wayne,

Randolph Scott in a publicity photo taken during the 1940s

Cooper, Fonda and Stewart (all handled for the most part by Hollywood's top directors), frequently epitomizing the fearless frontier lawman standing stoically by the code and ethics of the Old West. Scott's collaboration with director Budd Boetticher, between 1956 and 1960, produced seven gleaming, sharp-edged sagebrush sagas that have since been re-evaluated and recognized by critics as being superlative examples of the minimalist Western genre. A multi-millionaire through canny investments in oil, the leather-faced actor unexpectedly bowed out of the film industry on a high note in 1962 with Sam Peckinpah's *Ride the High Country*, sharing top billing with Joel McCrea, leaving behind a raft of movies that are essential items on any Western aficionado's list of must-haves.

Could the man act? Well, Gary Cooper won the 1953 Best Actor Oscar for his role in *High Noon* and his facial expressions remained almost immobile throughout, matching his one-tone delivery. One snooty critic even had the audacity to state that Cooper's performance was "wooden." But that didn't matter: "Coop" didn't have to act the part of Will Kane; he *was* the part. His magnetism oozed from the screen, audiences totally identifying with his "A man's gotta do what a man's gotta do" characteristic creed, rooting for his betrayed marshal, proud and alone, having to face up to four gunslingers, the town's faint-hearted citizens and new wife Grace Kelly having deserted him in his hour of need. Audie Murphy (his Universal Westerns ran neck-and-neck with Scott's during the 1950s) and George Montgomery were another pair whose strength of personality and star quality compensated for what purists might conceive as a limited acting range. McCrea, out of the four featured in this book, was the more accomplished and expressive actor; Scott was marginally more gifted than Murphy and Montgomery. Watch his impassive features: a flicker of a smile here, a narrowing of the eyes there, the delivery a softly spoken Southern drawl tinged with an underlying forcefulness. Scott, much like Cooper, Montgomery and Murphy, possessed strength of character by the bucket-load. When he looked at us with those flinty eyes, we knew he meant business. Overstatement and overacting didn't come into it. Underrated by some at the time, Scott was a deceptively fine performer *of his type*, a natural who made a plethora of outstanding pictures over a 33-year period, as we shall see in the following chapters.

Scott's six-foot-two and a half-inch lean, rangy build—allied with sun-burnished, rugged good looks and disarming, laconic disposition—perfectly suited the Western milieu which was to become his specialty; the strong silent type so loved by cowboy fans and women, and so feared by the bad guys (although the actor would play a few bad guys himself along the trail as well). Scott, like all great Western heroes, was a gentleman of integrity possessing a quiet deadliness, able to stop an aggressor squarely in his tracks and then switch on the charm as though nothing had happened. While his opponents felt nervous in his presence, women felt safe, which is why, in most of Scott's pre-1950s Westerns, he had two of them vying for his attention. Perhaps his films lack the gloss of those featuring Wayne and Stewart, relying on workhorse directors such as Ray Enright, Edwin L. Marin, André De Toth and Budd Boetticher rather than big hitters Anthony Mann and John Ford, but in that respect, they're probably grittier, meaner and a touch more authentic as a result of their lower origins. Take Universal's *Man Without a Star* (1955), directed by King Vidor and starring Kirk Douglas. Big budget, big star and big director—but no better in many ways than De Toth's *Man in the Saddle* (1951) or Roy Huggins' *Hangman's Knot* (1952). Make no mistake about it; Scott's Westerns are just as important to the genre as those made by the more illustrious Hollywood stars and form a vital body of work that enriches the cinema of the Old West. A Randolph Scott Western is right up there alongside a John Wayne Western, even more so in a lot of cases.

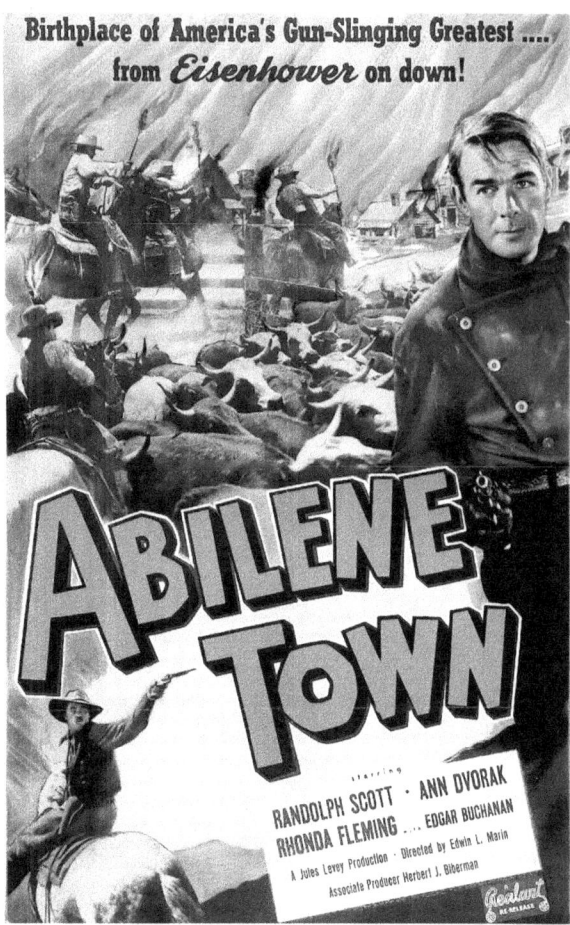

Randolph Scott received top billing in *Abilene Town*.

Note the signet ring on the little finger of Scott's left hand, which he sported in practically every movie he starred in. A love token from roommate Cary Grant, dating from the time they shared a beach house ("Bachelor Hall") in Malibu in the 1930s. Some film writers and Hollywood gossip columnists have suggested as such, hinting at a sexual relationship between the two, but Scott was a man who kept his personal life private and we will probably never know the truth. In fact, he married twice: to Marianna (Marion) DuPont in 1936, and Patricia Stillman in 1944.

Chapter 4
Audie Murphy:
All-American War Hero

Audie Leon Murphy came into the world on June 20, 1925, born in Kingston, Hunt County, Texas, the sixth of 12 children (only nine survived to adulthood), raised by poor Texan sharecroppers of Irish descent. An orphan in all but name only at the age of 16 (his father had fled the family roost in 1939; his mother died in 1941), Murphy took it upon himself to support his siblings by shooting live game for their supper and working on neighboring farms in the Greenville and Farmersville areas to scrape a dollar; he dropped out of elementary school in Celeste because of these family commitments, a loner with a short fuse and an almighty grudge. Not an auspicious start, then, for a slight, baby-faced, unschooled farm boy who would go on to become America's most decorated war hero, a tally of 33 awards earned for a series of bloody confrontations with German troops on the battlefields of Europe during 1943 (Murphy played himself in the biopic of his exploits, *To Hell and Back*, released by Universal in 1955). After the Japanese attack on Pearl Harbor on December 7, 1941, Murphy had tried to enlist in the army but was rejected because of his age (15) and deficiency in weight and height (five-foot-five-inches). In June 1942, he falsified his birth certificate with the help of his sister Corrine and was accepted into the services, supposedly aged 18 (but, in fact, 17); just over a year later, a military legend was born.

On his discharge from the army in September 1945, weighed down with medals but nowhere to go, Murphy appeared in full glory on the front cover of *Life* magazine and was invited to Hollywood by James Cagney and his brother William, whose production company paid for Murphy's acting, dancing and voice coaching lessons. Like Scott and McCrea (but certainly not Montgomery), farming boy Murphy didn't go overboard for the glossy Hollywood lifestyle. It was too far removed from his roots and he often used to query precisely why he ever took up acting as a career at all. But Cagney was convinced that the boyish-looking, five-foot-eight-inch ex-sergeant with all those medals of distinction, the man who had personally killed around 240 Germans, had something going for him. Their brief association ended in 1947 after a series of disagreements, the Cagneys reaching the conclusion that Murphy didn't have what it took to become an actor.

At a loose end, broke and sleeping rough, Murphy finally managed to get bit roles in two movies during 1948 through the help of his friend, writer David McClure: *The Girl from Texas* (Robert S. Golden Prods.) and Paramount's *Beyond Glory*, starring Alan Ladd. Neither film did a thing for Murphy's stuttering new career and their failure only added to his self-doubt, brought on (although not recognized at the time) by Post-Traumatic Stress Disorder, or in plain language, "Battle Fatigue." His third feature film, *Bad Boy* (1949), was the one that did it for him. Theater owners Paul Short and James Cherry badgered Allied Artists/Monogram into allowing their young protégée to play the lead in Kurt Neumann's social drama (that same year, Murphy married actress Wanda Hendrix); he starred as a juvenile delinquent sent to a ranch in lieu of prison to sort himself out. The movie bombed at the box-office, but Murphy's assured performance

Audie Murphy managed to acquire a bit role in *Beyond Glory*, starring Alan Ladd, in 1948, but the role failed to ignite his film career.

caught the eyes of Universal-International executives who were on the lookout for a new cowboy star to headline their proposed string of sagebrush sagas as the '50s cowboy flick began to gain momentum and pull in the postwar crowds. He was signed up in 1950 at $12,000 a picture, a figure that would greatly increase as his popularity with the public took hold. (A note concerning Murphy's conflicting height. In 1940, records show him as being five-foot-five inches. In 1942, he had increased by half an inch. By 1945, he was five-foot-eight. He had grown another half an inch at the start of his Universal career in 1950. In the '60s, his height topped five-foot-10 inches! Murphy joked that he was so malnourished as a youngster that once he was on a proper Hollywood diet, he never stopped growing. For the purposes of this book, we will put him at five-foot-eight, which is how he appeared on screen against his frequently taller support cast.)

Murphy wasn't by any stretch of the imagination your Joe-average Western hero, in fact far from it. He was a good few inches shorter than most rangy cowboy stars but well-built, his complexion ruddy rather than rugged and perpetually looking a decade younger than he really was (which he found to be a hindrance to his career later on, complaining that critics wouldn't take him seriously). But this new quietly spoken, fresh-faced kid on the block packed a punch in more ways than one. Succinctly described by one officer during the war as thus, "Don't be fooled by that baby face. Murphy is one tough son-of-a-bitch," the young actor could out-ride, out-draw, out-shoot and out-fight all of his co-stars. An expert horseman and dead shot by the age of 11, he firmly refused to use stunt doubles when tearing around on horseback, much to Universal's

"That kid can pull a trigger on you faster than anyone I've seen."

consternation. As for his shooting skills, Dan Duryea remarked after working with Murphy on *Ride Clear of Diablo*: "That kid can pull a trigger on you faster than anyone I've seen," particularly alarming as live ammunition was sometimes used on set instead of blanks. Murphy's renowned fistfights were over-vigorous to the point of punishing. Bob Steele came on the receiving end of Murphy's trademark storming, two-fisted pummeling while filming *Drums Across the River* and had to receive medical treatment afterwards to repair the damage. Murphy had wised up and learned to look after himself after the war and it carried over into his movie work. Being America's most decorated war hero had its drawbacks. He was a target for every half-drunk bar bum who thought that *they* could beat him in a fight. They never did. Murphy never lost a fight in his life and if invariably his protagonist was taller than himself, a short length of lead pipe soon sorted out that problem.

So this unrestrained bundle of energy, who slept with a loaded revolver under his pillow at night and possessed an explosive temper, brought a different kind of charisma to the big screen. Many critics remark on Murphy's acting style, or perceived lack of one. It's true that in a lot of his movies, he simply stares at the camera, purses his lips and does very little else, remaining almost expressionless. He certainly wasn't what you would call a born actor. But did he have to resort to acting his socks off? Murphy tended to act as himself—he was what directors call "a natural." Again, like Scott and Montgomery in particular, it's all about screen presence and how to carry a production on that presence alone. Murphy could do it, could fill the screen with that soft-spoken but murderous bearing, which is why, in the '50s, his films were so well liked, directed with pace by the likes of Nathan Juran, Don Siegel, Jesse Hibbs, the great Jack Arnold and Budd Boetticher. So at the start of 1950, following his breakthrough success as Billy the Kid in *The Kid from Texas*, we had the Audie Murphy Western competing with the Randolph Scott Western, the Joel McCrea Western and the George Montgomery Western. A splendid time was guaranteed by all!

CHAPTER 5
JOEL MCCREA: EASY DOES IT

Star of over 130 movies, six-foot-three Joel McCrea sometimes made it look all so easy. Like Scott, he appeared in a wide variety of roles, displaying an offhand, sincere charm and wholesome good looks that even the Master of Suspense took a shine to, headlining Hitchcock's definitive espionage wartime thriller *Foreign Correspondent* (Walter Wanger Productions 1940). From 1946 onwards (the same year that Scott decided where *his* career path lay), he concentrated on Westerns, saying he felt comfortable in the saddle wearing a hat and boots, becoming somewhat disillusioned with the whole Hollywood star system. He wanted things simple, and the then fashionable cowboy picture provided that simplicity. He was without doubt a bigger name in movies than Scott and Montgomery during the late '30s/early '40s, but not in Westerns (he made only 11 from 1933 to 1949 as opposed to Scott's extensive 36 and Montgomery's 32, including bit parts). It was from 1950 that their career paths merged, as they would do so with Audie Murphy's: The 1950s was the period in which McCrea made his reputation as a dependable star of medium-budget Westerns.

Joel Albert McCrea was born on November 5, 1905 in South Pasadena, California, one of three children. His grandparents had traveled to the far West in a wagon train, fighting Indians on the long journey, so McCrea had the pioneering family heritage to back up his credentials as a leading Western hero. Father Thomas P. McCrea was an

Joel McCrea (second from the left) stands with Laraine Day and George Sanders in Alfred Hitchcock's *Foreign Correspondent* (1940).

Joel McCrea protects Fay Wray from the horrors created by the crazed hunter in *The Most Dangerous Game*.

executive with the Los Angeles Gas and Electric Company, moving to Hollywood when the company opened up an office there. As a paper boy, McCrea's route brought him within touch of the rich and famous, including Cecil B. DeMille, and it appears that he caught the acting bug while watching D.W. Griffith filming *Intolerance* in 1916 (coincidentally the year George Montgomery was born). Attending first Hollywood High School and then Pomona College in 1928 to study the ranching business, he took part in stage plays, enrolled in an acting and public speaking course and appeared at the Pasadena Community Playhouse, as had Scott and many other actors in their formative years. Hanging around on film sets, his rangy, tough frame stood him in good stead as a stunt double and horse tamer in a few cheapo program fillers starring Tom Mix and William S. Hart, and he picked up a handful of un-credited parts in MGM's *Torrent* (1926), *The Enemy* (1927) and *The Fair Co-Ed* (1927). MGM decided to sign him up permanently in 1928 after he graduated from the University of California. McCrea's first major role was in 1929's *The Jazz Age*, followed by fifth billing in DeMille's *Dynamite* (conversely, one Randolph Scott was way down on the cast list, playing a coal miner).

McCrea moved over to RKO-Radio in 1930 after being rejected for the main role in Raoul Walsh's *The Big Trail* in favor of John Wayne, his first-ever lead for the company playing Boyd Emerson in *The Silver Horde* (1930). At RKO, he quickly made his name as a rugged, handsome ladies' man, causing a furor in his semi-nude scenes with screen siren Dolores del Rio in *Bird of Paradise* (1932) and charging around the old *King Kong* jungle set with Fay Wray in *The Most Dangerous Game* (1932). McCrea had a walk-on part in a solitary Western in 1933, *Scarlet River*, astutely investing in land deals if, as he thought

at the time, his acting career didn't work out (he eventually became a multi-millionaire through these deals). It did, Paramount, Sam Goldwyn, Warner Bros. and RKO using McCrea for all kinds of roles, from doctor (*Private Worlds*, 1935) to social climber (*Splendor*, 1935), as a gauche gold miner (*Barbary Coast*, 1935) and a comedian (*Banjo on My Knee*, 1937). McCrea also became the first screen Doctor Kildare in Paramount's *Interns Can't Take Money* (1937.) The actor found himself in the clutches of some stunning screen sirens in his films from this period: Constance Bennett (*Rockabye*, 1932), Irene Dunne (*The Silver Cord*, 1933), Barbara Stanwyck (*Gambling Lady*, 1934), Merle Oberon and Miriam Hopkins (*These Three*, 1936) and Ginger Rogers (*Primrose Path*, 1940). He married actress Frances Dee in 1933, the two starring together in his first Western proper, *Wells Fargo* (Paramount 1937) and probably reached his non-Western peak as an actor in the early 1940s: Hitchcock's *Foreign Correspondent*, Preston Sturges' *Sullivan's Travels* (Paramount 1941) and George Stevens' *The More the Merrier* (Columbia 1943) are three classics from Hollywood's golden age, big prestige pictures as durable today as they ever were. But McCrea had little time for Hollywood and all its gossip and intrigue, feeling that his personal life was more important, one of the reasons why perhaps he stuck to Westerns (with one exception, the British thriller *Rough Shoot* in 1952) after filming a remake of *The Virginian* in 1946.

McCrea was a fine actor, arguably better than Scott, Montgomery and Murphy, but in his Westerns, he steadfastly refused to play an all-out bad guy, unlike the other three; he could be a tad virtuous at times, too darned nice for his own good, a description one could never level at Scott, Murphy or Montgomery, coming across like someone's favorite uncle. On the occasions he *was* cast as someone on the wrong side of the law,

Edgar G. Robinson, Miriam Hopkins and Joel McCrea in *Barbary Coast* (1935)

his heart was always in the right place and he usually turned from villain to hero halfway through the action. His own code of ethics decreed that audiences, used to seeing him perform heroics in other films, should continue to see him as the hero in his sagebrush sagas. Therefore, as a Western actor, it limited somewhat his variety of roles and he came down to, if that is not too unkind an expression, the level of Scott, Montgomery and Murphy, even eclipsed by them in many movies, particularly by Scott's more finely-tuned mean attitude, Murphy's youthful brio and Montgomery's boldness. His Westerns could be less hard-bitten than the other three's, staid even, leaving one with a sense of frustration and contemplating, "If only …"

As was the case with his three fellow actors, McCrea was directed by a number of less illustrious but nevertheless extremely competent filmmakers, in his time as a Western star, from Joseph M. Newman to B-movie regular Charles Marquis Warren. From 1949 onwards, he was never afforded a high-powered director such as Anthony Mann or John Ford but didn't suffer as a consequence, spending most of his '50s career with United Artists, Allied Artists and Universal. Men like Ray Enright, Kurt Neumann and George Sherman were quite capable of turning out a decent oater and more than able to capitalize on McCrea's laid-back approach to the genre. In hindsight, Scott, Murphy, McCrea and Montgomery, in their string of medium-budget, trail-bustin' outings, epitomized the Hollywood cowboy *and* the Hollywood cowboy picture a great deal more than a lot of major players ever did, yet their movies continue to be submerged under the likes of *The Searchers*, *Warlock*, *Shane*, *High Noon*, *Vera Cruz* and other highly acclaimed big-star Westerns. They were *not* pretenders to the throne, far from it, and the aim of this book is to redress that situation.

Chapter 6
George Montgomery:
The Glamour Cowboy

The youngest of 15 children, George Montgomery Letz (he later dispensed with his surname on instructions from Fox producer Darryl F. Zanuck in 1938) was born of Ukrainian immigrant parents on August 29, 1916 in Brady, Pondera County, northern Montana. Reared on a ranch during the Depression years, he endured a tough upbringing, becoming an expert rider, cattle handler and a dead shot with a rifle when he was a youngster not out of his teens. From his boyhood years, he displayed exceptional craftsmanship in carpentry, painting, design and sculpture, which he put to professional use in later years, sculpting bronze models of, among other people, John Wayne, Ronald Reagan and Clint Eastwood. After attending Great Falls High School, Letz studied law and ended up majoring in interior design at the University of Montana where he became boxing champion; like so many other youths of that period, he got hooked on the movies at a very early age, particularly Westerns (fellow Montanan Gary Cooper was his hero) after watching a Harry Carey cowboy movie as a seven year old. Dropping out of further university studies, he left the wilds of Montana for Hollywood, fame and excitement in 1935 with $46 in his back pocket ("A wild goose chase," commented his father). Letz was offered a bit part in Republic's *The Singing Vagabond* but that was the sum total of his endeavors and he went back home, chastened by the experience. However, George Letz didn't abandon his dream; he returned to the film capital in 1937 and, within two days, a friend fixed him with a job as a stunt Cossack horseman (one of a hundred) on the set of MGM's *Conquest*, starring Greta Garbo and Charles Boyer; he was spotted by talent scouts and snapped up by Republic, mainly on account of his good looks. Letz was tall (six-foot-three), attractive to the opposite sex, an ex-boxer, athletic, spoke in a rich, deep tone with unusually precise pronunciation (very noticeable in his '50s features) and

George Montgomery appeared in the 1938 Republic serial, *The Lone Ranger*.

Ginger Rogers sweeps George Montgomery off his feet in *Roxie Hart*, one of Montgomery's early hits that brought him notice.

was a skilled horse rider. This personable bona fide Montana cowboy was ideal material to place in any number of the company's "roll-'em-out quick and cheap" Westerns, if nothing else.

Between 1937 and 1939, Montgomery/Letz cut his Western teeth on 25 low-budget 60-minute oaters starring Gene Autry, Roy Rogers and John Wayne, including Republic's early serial version of *The Lone Ranger*, plus a stand-in role in Universal's *The Road to Reno*. Montgomery didn't receive a single credit in any of these movies apart from the *Lone Ranger* 15-episode serial (as George Letz; a condensed 69-minute film version of the serial was released in 1940), hired as an extra to play cowhands, henchmen, riders, rustlers and used extensively for stunt work, doubles and stand-ins. Montgomery in the late 1930s was quintessential male Hollywood beefcake, described by *Life* magazine as "Six-foot-three inches tall, weighs 200 pounds, rides a horse well and is superlatively handsome." Offered a contract by 20th Century Fox in 1940 after making an impact in 1939's *The Cisco Kid and the Lady*, he scored his first big motion picture hit in *Roxie Hart*, appearing opposite Ginger Rogers, and was one of the movie gossip column's pinup boys at the time (the "Glamour Cowboy" and "The Hottest New Hero"), embracing Hollywood's café society like a kid let loose in a sweet shop, photographed cavorting with a bevy of lovelies in one nightclub after another. Liaisons with Rogers (rumor spread that they were to be married at one point) and screen goddesses Hedy Lamarr, Lana Turner, Kay Williams, K.T. Stevens, Sonja Henie and Carole Landis did nothing to dent his reputation as an out-and-out ladies' man (Landis was another prospective Mrs. Montgomery), even when he married singer Dinah Shore in 1943 (they divorced

George Montgomery as Philip Marlowe, with Nancy Guild, in *The Brasher Doubloon* (aka *The High Window* in Great Britain).

in 1963). It was shortly after his marriage that he enlisted in the U.S. Army Air Corps, remaining with them until the end of the war when he returned to Hollywood to pick up where he had left off in the movie business.

Big prestige pictures weren't to come Montgomery's way, even though reviews of his films were uniformly exceptional; his popularity was growing and Fox chief Zanuck rated the deep-voiced heartthrob actor highly enough to offer him a new seven-year contract, Montgomery's agent stipulating that the star's salary should begin at $3,750 per week, climbing to $10,000 per week. Great things were therefore expected when he took on the role of Philip Marlowe in *The High Window* (Fox 1947), but the critics unfairly compared his lukewarm performance with that of Humphrey Bogart's definitive Marlowe in Howard Hawks' *The Big Sleep* (Warner Bros. 1946) and found it lacking in depth. It wasn't the career break he had hoped for; Montgomery couldn't shake off his image as a cowboy actor in all those Republic oaters and probably, somewhere along the line gave up trying to compete with Hollywood's higher echelon, torn between movieland's glitz and putting his undoubted skills in architecture, house design and furniture making to good use (he ran his own furniture business as a sideline, constructing tables, chairs and cabinets for a host of Hollywood stars). In 1948, after lengthy arbitration hearings, he was released from his Fox contract, having had a major quarrel with Zanuck over salary. The Fox boss, annoyed at being dictated to on the subject of payment terms, threatened career ruination by insisting that Montgomery be allowed only one take per scene, whatever the outcome, even going so far as to veto close-ups of that finely chiseled profile. He signed up with the MCA agency, which hired him out to United Artists and

George Montgomery's performance earned him a contract with 20th Century Fox

Columbia, where he stayed until 1955, earning between $15,000 and $25,000 a week (less than Scott and McCrea, more on a par with Murphy). So Montgomery, like Scott and McCrea, fell back on the core Western as his vocational niche, his trail converging with Scott, McCrea and Murphy's in the 1950s where, for 10 years, he was thrust to the forefront of the low- to medium-budget, no-nonsense B-Western.

Like Scott, Murphy and McCrea, Montgomery embraced the cowboy way of life, on set and off; having been brought up on ranches with animals, he had an affinity with horses and liked nothing better than to gallop off into the wilderness to escape the rigors of filming (John Wayne's idea of relaxation was to pack food and water and hitch up with actor Ben Johnson. The two would disappear with their horses into canyon country, living rough for a week). Note the caring attitude these stars had toward their steeds in many of their scenes: A gentle "whoa" here, a reassuring pat on the neck when dismounting there. Man and horse as one, an almost ethereal melding of human and animal not witnessed in today's techno-mad cinema.

Montgomery, it has to be said, was not the most expressive of actors on the Hollywood backlot. He had the sex appeal, the commanding physique, a stronger than usual vocal delivery and that all-important presence, but not a great deal of acting ability. This is why he involved himself with B-movie directors from 1950 onwards: William Castle, Lesley Selander, Sidney Salkow, Phil Karlson and Ray Nazarro, among them. These jobbing filmmakers brought out the best in Montgomery's sparse, matter-of-fact delivery, which ranged from stern looking to moderately happy (he very rarely smiled in his films), but always forceful—like Murphy, he also preferred to perform his own stunts. When he stood up against the bad guys, he didn't evade the issue, getting stuck straight in, unlike McCrea and Scott who would often talk their way out of a threatening situation. Some state that even Montgomery's color movies were black-and-white affairs with very little in the way of shade. Maybe that was the case in some instances, but at least he made his emphatic stance clear to all: "Mess with me and you'll pay." Even his below-average Westerns (*Pawnee*; *Fort Ti*) received favorable reviews, a sign that the critics always took kindly to a Montgomery oater, despite its defects—and they all made money. In that respect, if audiences are in the mood for a straightforward, decent Western high on gunplay and fistfights, with a commendable shortfall on sermonizing and deep thought, look no further than a George Montgomery Western. They're that good.

CHAPTER 7
SCOTT: THE VIRGINIAN AND THE ZANE GREY "Bs" 1929-1935

In 1929, Randolph Scott appeared as an extra in Paramount's groundbreaking *The Virginian*, directed by Victor Fleming, an early and significant talkie produced by the company to promote the talents of Gary Cooper, and *not* a Randolph Scott Western. But it has to be included because of his involvement in the production: A Southerner like Cooper, he was hired to smooth out the leading man's thick Montanan drawl, sitting with his back to the actor in some scenes with lines of dialogue pinned to his shirt; for his pains, he received a "now you see him, now you don't" part, playing a rider in long shot (you would have to trawl through the print one frame at a time with a magnifying lens to spot his brief showing). Notwithstanding Scott's absence, *The Virginian* (remade in 1946 with McCrea in the lead role) still stands up as a pretty authentic snapshot of frontier life and a classic of its type, Cooper's gangly, awkward but tough cowpoke offset by Mary Brian's perky, naïve schoolteacher and Walter Huston's bully-boy cattle rustler. Coop stars as a cattle foreman having to face up to the local bad man on the eve of his wedding to a newly appointed schoolmarm. The good guys wear white hats; Huston and his gang all wear black outfits; troublemakers are "no-good ornery polecats" and friends are greeted with "you son-of-a-gun." "This country ain't big enough to hold the two of us," growls Huston to Cooper, a legendary one-liner getting its premiere airing. And, as a portent of things to come, location filming took place around California's Lone

Pine region, an area that would play a prominent part in future Randolph Scott sagebrush sagas, if not Cooper's. Yes, Scott's first Western is one where it is almost impossible to locate him. Nevertheless, it must still be officially classed as his first-ever foray into the Old West, however perfunctory it turned out to be, a humble introduction to the world of the Western.

Following a stint at the Pasadena Playhouse and Hollywood's Vine Street Theater, Scott was spotted by Hollywood talent scouts, undertook a number of screen tests and was offered a seven-year contract with Paramount in 1932, although the company wasn't averse to loaning him out to other studios. Before the signing, he had another un-credited part in 20th Century Fox's *Born Reckless* (1930), leading to his first role proper, Headline Picture's *Women Men Marry* (1931); 1932's *Sky Bride* was his first Paramount picture. Between 1932 and 1935, he cut his acting teeth in a variety of roles, branching out into comedy (*A Successful Calamity*; Warner Bros. 1932), musical (*Hello, Everybody!*; Paramount 1933), mild horror (*Murders in the Zoo*; Paramount 1933), mystery thriller (*Supernatural*; Paramount 1933), romance (*Cocktail Hour*; Columbia 1933) and fantasy adventure (*She*; RKO-Radio 1935). He even appeared in the Fred Astaire/Ginger Roberts musical, *Roberta* (RKO-Radio 1935). However, it was from starring in 10 B-Westerns produced by Paramount/Unity and Paramount/Favorite Films, all loosely adapted from the pulp novels of Zane Grey who co-wrote the scripts, that the actor was to discover his true vocation. Seven of the movies were directed by Henry Hathaway, later to become one of Hollywood's most reputable directors of top-flight Westerns (*How the West Was Won*; *The Sons of Katie Elder*; *True Grit*), and it was these films, above all others, that molded Scott into the authoritative Westerner he would later become recognized for in his Columbia and Warner Bros. classics of the 1950s. As of the time of writing (2013), four of the Zane Grey "Bs" remain commercially unavailable; it is not certain, in fact, whether there are any surviving prints: *Wild Horse Mesa* (1932); *Sunset Pass* (1933); *The Last Round-Up* (1934) and *Home on the Range* (aka *Code of the West*, 1935).

Randolph Scott in *Wild Horse Mesa* (1932), from the Zane Grey B-Western series.

Viewed 80 years on, these vintage, historical Zane Grey Westerns appear antiquated and rough-around-the-edges, their simplistic unified themes assembled with zeal, if not a great deal of finesse, over the course of 60 to 70 minutes. The bad guy cherishes the good guy's ranch/land, regardless of who gets in the way; Scott, the lone wolf, intervenes and successfully defeats the villains, ending up with the leading lady who invariably is tagging along, under duress, with the baddies' outfit. Unsophisticated they may well be, but the Zane Grey low-budgeters allow one the chance to observe

Kathleen Burke and Randolph Scott in *Rocky Mountain Mystery* (1935)

Scott in his younger days, developing from a somewhat gauche, callow youth in *Heritage of the Desert* to a more mature, commanding figure in *Rocky Mountain Mystery*. Rarely thought of today, or even looked at, these early Paramount throwbacks to a distant era of filmmaking were the fascinating period pieces that put Scott on the Western map and he acknowledged as such in interviews. They were to become his 10 individual stepping-stones, leading to a distinguished run of sagebrush sagas that are as enjoyable today as they were on first release.

1932's *Heritage of the Desert* (aka *When the West Was Young*) was the springboard for Scott's long, rewarding career in the saddle, taking place in 1890: Land-grabbers, horse thieves and cattle rustlers, led by a crooked cattle baron, are making life hell for a rancher who steadfastly refuses to allow them to drive stolen livestock through his property. "How did you know I was a stranger?" These words, addressed to a dance hall girl 10 minutes into Henry Hathaway's directorial debut, marked the modest start to Randolph Scott's 33-year employment in the Western genre as a headliner. Primitive-looking even for the year it was made, akin in parts to a silent movie (there's no backing soundtrack), rancher J. Farrell MacDonald is at loggerheads with corrupt David Landau who's not only stealing his cattle and horses but is in cahoots with the rancher's son, Gordon Wescott. Wescott owes considerable gambling debts to Landau and is willing to sacrifice his father's ranch in order to settle them. Scott ambles into the scenario, a surveyor by the name of Jack Hare, hired to mark out boundary lines bordering Zion Canyon to legally enforce MacDonald's land rights. As quick as a flash, he falls in love with petite Sally Blane, Westcott's intended bride. Jilting Wescott on their wedding day because she feels the same toward Scott, an all-out war is set in motion between the surveyor

Randolph Scott's first major role in a motion picture, *Heritage of the Desert* (1932), showed his cinematic charisma.

and the enraged bridegroom, with gunfights and fistfights galore as Landau, dimwitted henchman Guinn "Big Boy" Williams and his mob clash with MacDonald's boys. Scott gets Blane to himself in the end after Landau murders Westcott; MacDonald exacts his revenge, shooting down Landau and Williams in a blazing, all-guns finale.

Filmed around California's Red Rock Canyon State Park locale, as many Westerns would be in the coming years, *Heritage of the Desert* portrayed a young Randolph Scott full of self-confidence, handling his action scenes with aplomb. He looked good in the saddle, spoke his few words with authority and seemed blessed with a charisma that the rest of the cast didn't possess. Low-key as Westerns go, perhaps, but a promising beginning for Scott who appeared to have found his feet pretty quickly, considering this was his first major role in a motion picture.

Heritage of the Desert was swiftly followed by *Wild Horse Mesa* (1932), Scott playing Chane Weymer, a cowpoke up against a gang of horse rustlers led by Fred Kohler, who are stealing herds from the Indians and corralling them in barbed wire enclosures. A remake of the Jack Holt/Famous Players' 1925 silent, the story resurfaced for a third time in RKO-Radio's 1947 version, starring Holt's son Tim in the title role. Issued on tape in Denmark (*Den Vilda Horde*) and Spain (*El Paso del Ocaso*) several years back, this movie is one of four Zane Grey adaptations featuring Scott that, at present, appears to be lost.

An action-packed outdoor Western filmed with real zest, 1933's *Buffalo Stampede* (aka *The Thundering Herd*) remains one of the better of the early Scott/Hathaway trail-

Randolph Scott and Kathleen Burke in *Sunset Pass* (1933). In this one Scott plays a villain and is shot dead at the finale.

blazing sagas, as rousing today as it was 80 years ago, the movie pitting Harry Carey's wranglers against Noah Beery's scalawags. Carey is plundering the buffalo herds by the thousand for their skins, Scott (Tom Doan) leading the hunters; Beery is content to rob Carey's outfit, plus others, for the hides without resorting to hunting. Their joint actions are provoking the Indian tribes to declare war because of this mass slaughter. Frisky Judith Allen provides the love interest but she's with Beery's camp and Beery has designs on the gal, despite witch-like Blanche Friderici hovering in the background, longing for the brawny ruffian to hold her in his arms. On the eve of Scott's wedding to Allen, she's abducted by Beery, so our hero has to get her back while dealing with those "pesky Injuns" who are planning an uprising.

Shot against a backdrop of the snow-capped California Sierras and Lone Pine's craggy bluffs, Hathaway lays on an exciting stagecoach chase at the beginning and a rip-roaring climax when Carey's men are attacked by Indians, a group of settlers coming to the rescue in their covered wagons. Footage of the Indian tribes and buffalo stampedes was filched from 1925's silent *The Thundering Herd*, which also starred Beery. Scott, hair darkened and complete with pencil-thin mustache (the idea was to make him look like silent cowboy star Jack Holt), saves Allen from being trampled by a stampeding herd. The Indians are routed and evil Friderici shoots Beery in the back after killing two of his confederates. Raymond Hatton shines as a grizzled hunter, and heavies Buster Crabbe and Barton MacLane make up a first-rate supporting cast. Hathaway composes his shots with care, taking full advantage of that splendid scenery, filming with vigor; there's

Randolph Scott and Verna Hillie in *Man of the Forest* (1933)

even snatches of background music to add spice to the proceedings. Of the 10 Zane Grey adaptations, *Buffalo Stampede* appears to have stood the test of time more so than the others, with Scott a dashing leading man; the print is in pristine condition as well.

Sunset Pass, released in 1933, saw Scott as Ash Preston, a rancher blackmailed into helping a gang of outlaws rustle cattle. He has a dark family history involving his supposed sister Kathleen Burke; Harry Carey, leader of the rustlers, has threatened to reveal all if Scott doesn't get involved. The film was remade by RKO-Radio in 1946 with James Warren playing the Scott part. This becomes the only Scott/Zane Grey movie where Scott is shot dead at the end—he also plays a heavy. Tapes issued in Portugal (*Na Pista do Criminoso*) and Austria (*Flammenre Iter*) are no longer available, and it is doubtful whether this movie will ever surface to appease all those Scott lovers who wish to have everything in their collections.

The third of Scott's four 1933 Westerns, *Man of the Forest* (aka *Challenge of the Frontier*), wasn't one of the better of the Scott/Zane Grey actioners. Scott's Brett Dale is a trapper who foils a greedy land-grabber's scheme to steal the permits to a lake owned by an honest rancher, coming up against burly Noah Beery who kidnaps Harry Carey's niece (Verna Hillie) to force the rancher to sign over his land. Scott, who comes to Hillie's rescue, is later implicated in Carey's murder (Beery is the culprit), escapes from jail and ends up playing house with the damsel in distress on her uncle's ranch. Beery gets his just desserts, shot by spurned landlady Blanche Friderici (just as he was in *Buffalo Stampede*) for making eyes at Hillie under her nose. Apart from Beery's heavyweight presence, the cast is bolstered by a bevy of sidewinders: Barton MacLane, Guinn "Big Boy" Williams,

Randolph Scott and Jack La Rue (wearing all black) in *To the Last Man* (1933)

Buster Crabbe, Vince Barnett, plus a family of friendly mountain lions. There's not a great deal of gunplay or fighting apart from one lively sequence when Scott is holed up in a warehouse, at the mercy of Beery's gunslingers. The part where Scott takes Hillie to his cabin, the two indulging in flirting games, is strung out to the point of tedium (the spanking scene is a hoot, though), while a couple of comic interludes involving a frisky ass and a trio of exuberant lion cubs might be a tad cutesy for Western diehards. The good guys wear wide chaps and white, 10-gallon Stetsons, giving the film a turn-of-the-century look; Hillie, as wholesome as apple pie, puts one in mind of a '20s "IT" girl; and Scott, still sporting that pencil-thin mustache, bears an uncanny resemblance to a young Errol Flynn. Current DVD releases have been unable to overcome the numerous jumps in the print, leading to a loss of quality in the first 15 minutes. A lackluster fifth Zane Grey outing for Scott who, give him his due, soldiers on with a certain amount of quiet charm through the hackneyed plot.

To the Last Man (aka *Law of Vengeance*) was a distinct improvement on the flaccid *Man of the Forest*. In 1866, following the end of the Civil War, two families from Kentucky head out west to Nevada, continuing a feud that dates back 15 years, the self-proclaimed Colby-Hayden war. Scott (as Lynn Hayden) doesn't appear until 25 minutes have rolled by in an oater that boasts not only a fine retinue of early '30s heavies in Noah Beery, Jack La Rue, Barton MacLane and Buster Crabbe (Beery, MacLane and Crabbe were retained from *Man of the Forest*), but also a fleeting glimpse of toddler-cum-future child star Shirley Temple. Available DVD issues show the existing print to be in a lamentable state, so be prepared for a hailstorm of scratches, blips and uneven sound balance. After

Sexual tension seems to be the order of the day for Randolph Scott and Barbara Fritchie (billed as Barbara Adams) in *The Last Round-Up* (1934).

shooting dead Scott's grandpa (when Scott was a little boy), brutish Beery is jailed for 15 years. On his release, he vows to kill rival rancher Egon Brecher, who informed the authorities of the murder; for starters, he rustles cattle from Brecher's herds to supplement his own stock and steals his horses in an act of provocation, including Scott's favorite steed White Cloud. Beery's feisty daughter, Esther Ralston, is lusted after by La Rue (dressed entirely in black), but it is Scott who tames her wild instincts; once in his caring arms, La Rue's rough and ready approach refuses to hold any appeal for the lass. Indistinguishable in plot to *Heritage of the Desert*, La Rue simmers at Ralston's fondness for Scott and, wanting to run things his way, manages to wipe out most of the cast in a landslide; boss Beery is shoved off a cliff and shot. Homing in on the blonde tomboy in her cabin and tussling with her, La Rue is stabbed to death by Scott, alive but injured in the rock fall; the final frame sees him and Ralston happily wedded.

Location shooting took place in the picturesque Big Bear Lake region of California and there was a stronger storyline plus more inventiveness than *Man of the Forest* managed to display, hence the longer running time. The picture, though, has dated badly, crying out for a suitable score to add flavor. Scott evinced a softer side to his nature, not headlining the production, which tended to concentrate a great deal on Beery and La Rue's black-hearted villainy. Slowly but surely, the unassuming actor was making the grade as a man of action who always grabs the girl in the end.

1934's *The Last Round-Up*, the last of the Hathaway Zane Greys, starred Scott as Jim Cleve, a cowpoke caught up in a bandit gang, the Border Legion, led by Monte

Blue, who are robbing stagecoaches of their bullion, following a gold rush in Utah. Tapes released in Spain as *El Ultimo Rodeo* and Austria as *Todesiego* are no longer on the market, and all prints appear to have vanished.

Charles Barton took over the directorial reins in 1934's *Wagon Wheels* (aka *Caravans West*), producing the finest (with *Buffalo Stampede*) of the Scott/Zane Grey screen adaptations. Scott (as Clint Belmet) played a scout leading a wagon train from Missouri to Oregon, pursued by a treacherous landowner who invokes the Indian tribes to attack, thereby preventing the settlers from setting up a community. The actor, now more fully grown in looks and demeanor, strode effortlessly through a slight storyline in which baddie Monte Blue, half Indian, shadows a wagon train over the Rocky Mountains to Oregon; he doesn't want colonizers setting up camp on land that he covets. Basically a harsh portrait of pioneers migrat-

ing to a better life in 1844, admirably cutting down on the sentiment, this low-budget remake of Gary Cooper's expensive *Fighting Caravans* (1931) is a well-balanced Western that contains an endearing four-year-old (Billy Lee) who latches on to Scott (as does his mother, Gail Patrick); three catchy songs: "Wagon Wheels," "Under the Daisies" and "Estrellita"; a tremendous Indian attack at Powder River in the final 10 minutes (stock footage from *Fighting Caravans*); two amiable sidekicks in Raymond Hatton and Olin Howland and a somewhat clichéd script ("Injuns! The varmints are closing in on us!"). There's even a rousing score by an un-credited John Leipold to boost the cowboys versus hostiles sequences. During the mass charge, scowling Blue, in Indian garb, is shot while in a struggle with Scott and the Redskins retreat, the scout blowing up a raft full of powder kegs to frighten them off; even young Billy Lee joins in with his catapult!

Scott's marked self-assurance was beginning to shine through at this juncture of his early career; bigger and better things were beckoning just around the corner, but he was still contracted to make two more Zane Greys before tackling something different. *Wagon Wheels*, along with *Buffalo Stampede*, represents the pinnacle of these now long-forgotten oaters featuring a future Westerner in his embryonic stage.

Home on the Range (aka *Code of the West*, 1935) remains unavailable as at the time of writing. A trio of swindlers from Alaska, now owners of a hotel in Nevada, employ underhand tactics in an attempt to wrest a ranch from horse trainer Tom Hatfield, played by Scott; complications arise when one of the trio, Evelyn Brent, falls in love

Now a seemingly lost print, *Home on the Range* (1935) featured Randolph Scott (second from the right) as a horse trainer.

with the ranch owner. A Portuguese tape entitled *A Lei do Oeste* cannot be traced, and celluloid prints are either languishing in vaults or are non-existent.

Scott's final Zane Grey picture, released in 1935, was a real curio, *Rocky Mountain Mystery* (aka *The Fighting Westerner*), adapted from Grey's novel *Golden Dreams*, giving him ample opportunity to demonstrate his acting chops, rather than charge around on a horse shooting the bad 'uns. More talkative mystery than action cowboy movie, like *The Old Dark House* out West, it boasts the series' best title theme (composer: Rudolph G. Kopp). Scott played mining engineer Larry Sutton, investigating the mysterious death of Adolph Borg, engineer and caretaker of the Jim Ballard Ranch, becoming involved in a family intrigue to gain control of the radium mine situated on the property. In tandem with grizzled deputy sheriff Charles "Chic" Sale, he has to decide who is accountable for the murder. Suspects are to be found among the strange family residing on the site: Bedridden George Marion, Sr.; grim-faced housekeeper Leslie Carter; his two nieces and nephew who, up until now, have never met him and Carter's son. All hover round his bed like vultures, waiting for him to expire. Is Willie Fung, the Chinese handyman, also involved? Marion, Sr.'s nephew, Howard Wilson, is found crushed under a noisy stamps machine, niece Kathleen Burke is stabbed with a razor and Scott, attacked from behind, narrowly avoids being flattened under the crusher himself. Borg's corpse also disappears. There are three wrongdoers here: First, Marion, Sr. isn't, in fact, an invalid; he's Adolph Borg, himself killing off former partner Ballard to gain control of the mine. Second, Carter has taken on the mantle of Borg's wife since his divorce 30 years back, and has been skulking around in a hat and cloak like a character out of a '30s horror film, perpetrating the foul deeds by disposing of the Ballard heirs to the will. The third guilty party, doting son James C. Eagles, is in on the act as well. It takes a visit from the original Mrs. Ballard to uncover this nest of vipers ("He's not my husband!" she exclaims when setting eyes on Marion, Sr.). The impersonator falls to his death from a mine building in the final reel, leaving Scott to set up house with the surviving niece (lovely Ann Sheridan in an early role) in Hawaii. Crusty old Sale is promoted to sheriff for uncovering the conspiracy with, it has to be said, a great deal of help from his six-foot-plus partner who towers over the cast, radiating good-natured bonhomie. "Good entertainment," wrote *Variety*.

Oddly enough, a gramophone player, car and telephones figure in some scenes, leaving one to question in which period all this was supposed to be taking place, even though our sturdy leading man packs a hefty gun on his belt. Two snippets of dialogue in this convoluted drama sum up Scott to perfection: Sheridan describes his smile as "Slow and easy." This could very well apply itself to Scott's acting technique. And the final line is an omen of what was to come: "We're sitting on top of the world." For Scott, if not exactly "sitting on top of the world," having served his Zane Grey apprenticeship with honors, now larger, more highly esteemed (and profitable) parts in big-budget pictures were his for the taking.

Compared to other Western fare made in the early to mid-1930s, Scott's 10 contributions don't come off all that badly. At least he was a leading man, albeit a fairly unknown one to the public. Following his role in Raoul Walsh's $2,000,000 *The Big Trail* (Fox 1930), John Wayne returned to low-budget fare because of the film's failure at the box-office, churning out hour-long Westerns (*Two-Fisted Law*, *Riders of Destiny*, *The Trail Beyond*, *Lawless Range*), yet to make his mark as a Western lead; the days of the big-budget Western, appealing to mass audiences, were still some way off. Cowboy films produced during these years were very much '20s in look and design, populated by the likes of Bob Steele, William Haines, Ken Maynard, Bob Custer, Buck Jones, Lane Chandler, Tim McCoy and Kermyt Maynard, with titles including *The Nevada Buckaroo*, *Way Out West*, *Hell Fire Austin*, *Law of the Rio Grande*, *Range Feud*, *Texas Tornado*, *Fighting Shadows* and *The Fighting Trooper*. These are lost productions consigned to Western folklore, directed by a host of long-forgotten hacks such as John P. McCarthy, Fred Niblo, Forrest Sheldon, Bennett Ray Cohen, D. Ross Lederman, Oliver Drake, David Selman and Ray Taylor, names that have vanished from cinemagoers' memories forever, as have the Poverty Row production outfits they worked for: Empire Films, Conn Pictures, G.A. Durham Productions, Willis Kent Productions, Quadruple Films, Argosy, Supreme Pictures, K.B.S. Productions. Therefore, in the overall scheme of things, Scott was making *his* mark in a slow and steady manner with more noteworthy directors and major Hollywood companies probably without realizing, at that moment in time, how important he was to become to the Western genre. 1936 would be the year when, for him, big things would start to happen.

Chapter 8
McCrea Earns His Spurs, 1937-1949

RKO-Radio's *Scarlet River*, released in 1933 (directed by Otto Brower), was a modern-day Western concerning a film crew searching for a suitable location to shoot their leading man's next opus, a film-within-a-film scenario starring Tom Keane (complete with customary 10-gallon Stetson) in the lead. Lon Chaney, Jr., billed as Creighton Chaney, was the bad guy, a ranch foreman up to no good, proving to be a pain in the butt for owner Dorothy Wilson by, among other things, poisoning her cattle. At 57 minutes long, this anarchic black-and-white farce really belonged to the silent era, more famous than anything else for stuntman Yakima Canutt breaking his shoulder while performing his "crawling under the wagon" routine. After six-and-a-half minutes, Joel McCrea makes his 25th movie appearance, playing himself, emerging suited and booted from a restaurant packed with the stars of the day (including Bruce Cabot, taking a break from *King Kong?*) greeting Keane; the scene lasts a paltry 18 seconds.

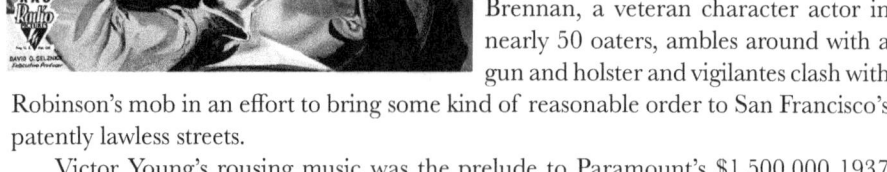

McCrea's slight brush with the Western genre could also be applied to Samuel Goldwyn's period drama *Barbary Coast* (1935), in which he received third billing behind Edward G. Robinson and Miriam Hopkins. Directed by Howard Hawks and set in the California gold rush days of 1849, McCrea's gold miner (Jim Carmichael) was a poem-spouting milksop, a complete contrast to Robinson's snarling, reptilian gambling house boss allied to Brian Donlevy's black-clad assassin. What feisty blonde Hopkins ever saw in him, one is never quite sure, but this murky evocation of the period was a fine, if studio-bound, drama of the kind Hollywood ceased to make many moons ago. The movie just misses out on being loosely termed a Western, even if Walter Brennan, a veteran character actor in nearly 50 oaters, ambles around with a gun and holster and vigilantes clash with Robinson's mob in an effort to bring some kind of reasonable order to San Francisco's patently lawless streets.

Victor Young's rousing music was the prelude to Paramount's $1,500,000 1937 production *Wells Fargo*, directed with vigor by Frank Lloyd, the man behind two of the '30s biggest hits, *Cavalcade* (1933) and *Mutiny on the Bounty* (1935). Trimmed by 18 minutes from the original running time of 115 minutes, Lloyd brought his trademark epic approach to the saga of the Wells Fargo Company and the man who helped map out the freight routes, Ramsay MacKay, played by McCrea. Beginning in the 1840s and spanning a 25-year period, the movie saw McCrea traipsing from the East Coast to San Francisco and back again with partner Bob Burns and his Pawnee Indian crony, Bernard Siegel, at the expense of his marriage to Frances Dee (the two were real-life husband and wife). It was the couple's stormy on/off relationship that Lloyd chose to predominantly focus upon, no doubt to appease '30s audiences hooked on romance, and subsequently, the pace got bogged down, especially when McCrea is charged by Abe Lincoln to transport $2,000,000 in gold over the Rocky Mountains to the Union army during the Civil War; Dee is a Southern sympathizer and, after several heated confrontations with McCrea, informs the Confederates about the plan. Led by her ex-beau, the Confederates clash with McCrea's troops on the plains, leading to the only slice of action on display. McCrea and Dee are reconciled in the final reel, the Wells Fargo overland mail express now well and truly established.

Lloyd's frenetic style, all noise, hustle and bustle, hasn't aged well, while McCrea, in his first major movie role, carries the picture with ease, if not a great deal of steel. But that was *his* style—the all-round regular guy who breezes through one incident after another, a dependable, good-looking leading man who perhaps lacked, at this early stage of his Western career, the gravitas that Scott in particular already possessed at this juncture in *his* career. He would get a lot tougher as his Western films took off; for now, Joel McCrea was a typical product of the era: easygoing, light on his feet, humorous, heroic and attractive enough in physique and looks for the ladies to swoon over.

Never let it be said that Cecil B. DeMille didn't know how to put on an epic show. Big sets, big cast and big action sequences, with a stirring score (Sigmund Krumgold, John Leipold) the icing on the cake; one of cinema's greatest exponents of over-the-top pageantry for the masses lavished a million and a half dollars on *Union Pacific*, cramming into its 135-minutes rival train companies, murderous villains, corrupt politicians, marauding Redskins, two spectacular train wrecks, a fiery Irish heroine and McCrea at last looking as though he meant business, an engineer turned troubleshooter tasked with preventing Brian Donlevy from halting progress on the Union Pacific railroad, due to meet up with the Central Pacific line at Ogden. A huge hit for Paramount in 1939, DeMille's saga (it was his last black-and-white picture) cut down on the corn and moved as fast as one of the steam locomotives it so heavily featured. It ranks as one of

Joel McCrea (left) plays an engineer turned troubleshooter who must see that the railroad is built in *Union Pacific* (1939). Sultry Barbara Stanwyck stands in the middle.

the flamboyant director's more noteworthy pieces of work: *Variety* raved: "Socko spectacular," while *Photoplay* chipped in with "Melodramatic and breathtaking."

Although classed by Congress as a "monumental folly," President Lincoln gives the go-ahead for a rail link from the East Coast to the West, meeting with the Central Pacific line's own set of tracks just east of San Francisco. Devious banker Henry Kolker hits on a way to get rich by dabbling in Union Pacific shares, profiting from their collapse if Donlevy and his group of dishonest buckaroos, owners of a portable saloon, can divert the workers' attention to liquor and gals instead of hard, honest labor. In steps McCrea (as Jeff Butler) to maintain order, dressed in black, twin guns on hips with butts turned outwards, his stern expression boding ill for Donlevy (fast making a name for himself as a reliable Western heavy). Their first encounter on a train is a classic of Western macho tension, McCrea, glaring, striding toward camera and hurling one of Donlevy's henchman out of the carriage after a bruising fistfight. McCrea has his own pair of bodyguards, unkempt ruffians Akim Tamiroff and Lynne Overman, a marvelous double-act, amusing without plunging into silliness. Lovely Barbara Stanwyck plays the engineer's daughter, a tomboy postmistress who falls for McCrea but has promised herself to gambler Robert Preston (his first major role). Snag is, Preston is not only an old war buddy of McCrea's but sides with Donlevy, leading to complications and incidents galore when he robs a train of its $200,000 payroll. Divided loyalties rear their ugly head as Stanwyck marries Preston on condition that McCrea isn't murdered, and Mc-

Crea furtively assists Preston to escape a hanging. All this plus a prolonged, exciting Indian attack on one of the hated Iron Horses, the train derailed, the braves scavenging like wolves among the spilled belongings, McCrea, Preston and Stanwyck holed up in a busted carriage short on ammunition; Donlevy's Big Tent saloon trashed by an angry workforce; a locomotive having to rush over a burning bridge; McCrea dealing with Robert Barrat's grizzly bear-type thug, hired to cause mischief; Tamiroff using his skills on the whip to lethal effect; Stanwyck (one can forgive her questionable Irish accent in so measured a performance) torn between McCrea and Preston and another spectacular train crash at the end on a snowbound cliff (how DeMille loved those train wrecks: His Oscar-winning *The Greatest Show on Earth* [1952] climaxed with one). This was '30s Hollywood pizzazz done in the grand manner, and audiences loved every minute of it.

Walter de Leon, C. Gardner Sullivan and Jesse Lasky, Jr.'s script is just as high-tuned as the action. "That Jeff Butler doesn't have all his brains in his holster," observes Stanwycks's father on first seeing the tall stranger, while Stanwyck flashes her eyelashes, cooing, "Did you never know that flirting gets into a woman's blood like fighting gets into a man's." McCrea, confronting Anthony Quinn who has just cold-bloodedly shot an innocent player at a cards table, warns him, "If you're not out of this town in an hour, one of us will be keeping his mouth shut for a long time," and when McCrea turns and guns down Quinn, Overman drily remarks, "When Jeff shoots, they don't need a doctor, they need an undertaker," telling a group of heavies, "Now you boys has got your options of getting out in 30 seconds or being buried in 30 minutes." Following the disclosure of Preston's alliance with Donlevy, McCrea states, "I'm afraid we're in different armies now," a foretaste of differences to come between them. In the final minutes, Donlevy shoots Preston dead ("I'm just a busted flush," the gambler gasps to McCrea) before tobaccy-chewing Overman puts a thoroughly deserved bullet into the saloon boss. DeMille closes his film with the two rail companies meeting, McCrea and Stanwyck framed cheek-to-cheek and a shot of a modern-day express hurtling down the route those early pioneers sweated over for years to construct across America's hostile badlands.

DeMille was over fond of utilizing back-projection in his movies, sometimes to the detriment of the finished product; he does so in *Union Pacific*, the scene in which McCrea gallops after Preston, firing at his back, clumsily handled. But this, in a film of such

scope and imagination, is a minor gripe. *Union Pacific* is loud, brash, highly watchable and extremely well acted and directed, the pace pitch-perfect. Although only McCrea's second Western, it still remains, over 70 years later, one of the best he ever starred in.

Between *Union Pacific* and his next Western for Paramount, *The Great Man's Lady* in 1942, McCrea chalked up two resounding smashes, Hitchcock's *Foreign Correspondent* and Preston Sturges' *Sullivan's Travels*, cementing his standing as one of Hollywood's more exceptional leading players. Barbara Stanwyck took the principal role in *The Great Man's Lady*, playing 100-year-old Hannah Sempler, who reminisces to biographer Katharine Stevens about her eventful life spent with Ethan Hoyt (McCrea), philanthropist and founding father of Hoyt City, whose imposing statue has just been erected in the city square. What reporters want to know is this: Was Sempler married to Hoyt and if so, as rumor suggests, why the change in name? All is revealed in flashback over the course of a sometimes-tortuous plotline saturated in bathos and mostly shot at night, thus giving the production a gloomy, slightly somber air. McCrea, first seen in buckskins in 1848, whisks coquettish Stanwyck away from her soon-to-be-husband (Lloyd Corrigan) and weds her himself during a thunderstorm, promising her a bright future. Idealistic to a fault, he plans to open up the Old West and build a city, financed by gold he reckons is waiting to be discovered in the mountains. Eight years later, with love-struck gambler Brian Donlevy hovering in the background, aching for Stanwyck's loving touch, McCrea is a drifter and a loser, down on his luck through broken land deals; in the meantime, his wife, unbeknown to him, has lost her twin babies in a flooded river, a harrowing sequence guaranteed not to leave a dry eye in the house. In a drunken temper, McCrea shoots his rival, thinks he's dead as well as Stanwyck, remarries and reaches the

heights as a senator. Stanwyck's father, robber baron Thurston Hall, finding out that his daughter is alive and working as a croupier in Donlevy's gambling den, lays his cards on the table: "I want you to remain dead, legally. Change your name. Do it for Ethan." Hall has thrown in his political lot with McCrea and doesn't want any scandal upsetting the gravy train. Stanwyck divorces McCrea officially, refuses Donlevy's hand for a final time and arranges an unexpected rendezvous with McCrea while he is battling his fellow politicians over the rights and wrongs of allowing the Western Railroad Company to drive a line to Hoyt City, built on the riches obtained from the region's silver mines. The film ends with McCrea's protracted death scene and Stanwyck tearing up her marriage certificate on the statue's steps to the refrains of Victor Young's beautiful, melancholy score.

The Great Man's Lady is Stanwyck's show, every single minute of it, a part tailor-made for her talents. One of Hollywood's most accomplished actresses of the day, she's a delight to watch, whether flirting with McCrea in her early scenes, warding off frisky Donlevy, mourning the loss of her infants, reuniting with McCrea as a grieving lost soul or, heavily made-up, narrating her tale to Stevens. Under William A. Wellman's direction, she radiates the kind of wholesome charm that's sadly no longer in evidence in today's gadget-mad cinematic climate. McCrea once stated that she was his favorite leading lady (they made six films together) and it's apparent here. As for McCrea, it has to be said that he comes off second-best to Donlevy's more interesting, and more charismatic, gambler. His character becomes increasingly effete as the story progresses, certainly a stark contrast to his all-action role in *Union Pacific*. A Western variation on Jeanette MacDonald's melodramatic *Maytime* (1937), *The Great Man's Lady*, containing

impressive, almost Gothic, set design by A. Earl Hedrick and Hans Dreier, has dated badly and one would have thought that, judging by his humdrum performance in this picture, Joel McCrea had little to offer the Western genre. He was getting there, but slowly, as was his style, both on and off screen.

20th Century Fox's *Buffalo Bill* (1944) was shot in glorious Technicolor amid the rugged buffs of Arizona's House Rock Canyon, with Leon Shamroy responsible for the pristine cinematography (Shamroy chalked up four Oscars in his career, including one for the Burton/Taylor epic, *Cleopatra*, in 1963); David Buttolph's blistering score added spice to a picture that moved like wildfire in the first hour, thanks to William A. Wellman's well-paced direction. A fairly accurate account of the life of William Frederick Cody, the movie came in two parts: the Indian wars of 1877 and Cody's fall from grace in Washington, followed by his Wild West Show that traveled the world to great success. Part one is stirring stuff, the Cheyenne, led by Anthony Quinn, and the Sioux (the costume design is fantastically colorful) depicted as noble savages at the mercy of the white man's greed for land and buffalo hides. McCrea plays the buckskin-clad scout coming to the rescue of Maureen O'Hara and Edgar Buchanan in the opening minutes from a bunch of drunken braves, while back at the fort, squaw Linda Darnell, a teacher, eyes him from afar in unrequited love.

Ten minutes into the movie, it could be said that McCrea, with long hair, mustache and goatee beard, doesn't seem all that comfortable in a role crying out for the gutsy swagger Errol Flynn would have brought to the part. It's a bit on the tame side when you consider that this man and his exploits became as famous as General Custer and *his* exploits in the press and periodicals. McCrea displays genuine regard for the tribes ("Indians are good people if you leave them alone.") but O'Hara, once wedded to the scout, declares her hatred for the frontier life and the native Indians, desperately wishing to return East. "Savages! Brutes! Fiends!" she cries. "Why did I ever come to this nightmare of a country?" After 25 minutes, the peace treaty is broken, Quinn and McCrea's friendship is in tatters and the Cheyenne and Sioux join forces, buoyed up by their success at Custer's defeat at the Little Bighorn. The 10-minute battle at War Bonnet Gorge, cavalry and Indians charging at each other head-on through a shallow river basin, is one of the Western's greatest-ever adrenalin-pumping action sequences, brilliantly orchestrated by Wellman, muddy water splashing over camera lenses to create maximum impact, a toning down of intrusive music heightening the effect of

Joel McCrea (as Buffalo Bill, left), Thomas Mitchell and Maureen O'Hara in *Buffalo Bill* (1944)

mass slaughter. After this pulsating set piece (Quinn is drowned in the river by McCrea and Darnell is killed), the movie drastically changes course (and mood) into family melodrama: McCrea is summoned to Washington for a medal, his infant son dies from diphtheria, he's discredited in the press and has to earn his living as a sharpshooter in a sideshow. Blaming O'Hara for their son's death by moving East ("A disease of civilization"), the couple is eventually reunited after the success of his Wild West Show, returning West to start a new life.

At just under 90 minutes, *Buffalo Bill* was too short to be a thorough biopic and seems rushed in some areas. That first hour really grabs the attention and probably took care of a huge chunk of the picture's $1,000,000 budget. The remaining 30 minutes pales by comparison, with McCrea looking uneasy in many of his scenes. But it wouldn't be that long before the actor pledged himself to the Western genre full-time with *The Virginian* in 1946, coincidentally the very same year that Randolph Scott established himself as one of the Western's foremost leading players in *Abilene Town*.

Paramount's adaptation of Owen Wister's 1902 Western potboiler, *The Virginian*, was the fourth time the tale had been filmed. None have bettered Gary Cooper's 1929 version, and McCrea's stab at taking on the amiable eponymous title character was no exception. The familiar story is paper-thin: Posh Easterner Barbara Britton ditches her fiancé and moves out West to take up schoolteacher duties in Medicine Bow; McCrea and pal Sonny Tufts are rivals for her affections and black-clad baddie Brian Donlevy rustles everybody's cattle. Lazily shot by Stuart Gilmore in bright Technicolor, with an

alarming paucity of action, *The Virginian* is dull fare. McCrea seems to sum up the lackluster enterprise by failing to put the required quota of energy into the part, drifting through the movie's 90 minutes with a slight look of boredom creasing his features; there's little depth to his character, even though the narrative is built around him. The infamous lynching scene, where Tufts and two others are strung up for rustling, Tufts leaving a note for his friend who has sanctioned the hanging, is short on emotional impact and lines of dialogue are lifted wholesale from Cooper's flick, such as McCrea facing Donlevy: "When you call me that, smile." "With a gun in my belly, I always smile," retorts the future *Quatermass* star. In fact, Donlevy steals the show, the only one on set to display any signs of animation (Tufts isn't all that bad, either), even though his black-dressed villain looks as though he has stepped straight out of a 1920s cowboy serial. And as McCrea is rightly referred to as "The Virginian," what, pray, does Britton call herself when she eventually weds the cowpoke? Perhaps, as one reviewer suggested, *The Virginian*, showing signs of tiredness both in plot and execution, should have been put out to pasture a long time back.

Despite its lack of originality and air of sameness, plus a critical backlash, *The Virginian* was McCrea's career turning point: It was at this stage that he decided that his acting path lay in Westerns, which, with one exception, he concentrated on for the rest of his moviemaking days. But, unlike Scott's breakthrough role as Marshal Dan Mitchell in Edwin L. Marin's *Abilene Town*, McCrea was still finding his spurs, due in part to his extensive and successful role-playing in other categories of cinema, mostly as a romantic hero. He hadn't yet established himself in the public mind as a rugged Western man of action, low on the intrinsic toughness and authority evident in Scott's nailed-to-the-wall performances. Enterprise/United Artists' *Ramrod*, released in 1947, went a long way to changing all of that.

Ramrod is a rare example of '40s Western *noir*, directed with spunky determination by André De Toth, then married to the film's leading lady, screen siren Veronica Lake.

Joel McCrea, along with Veronica Lake (playing a woman possessed), only adds to the film noir tone of the Western *Ramrod* (1947).

Full credit to De Toth and the production team in ditching the conventional route by not spelling out the plot machinations from the outset: So opaque are the opening scenes that a full 10 minutes passes by before all is more or less made clear. Lake is a woman possessed, brimming with hatred, revenge, greed and ambition, prepared to use her feminine wiles to get what she wants: "From now on, I'm going to make a life of my own. And, being a woman, I won't have to use guns," she declares to those around her. What is the reason for her pugnacious attitude? Lake's intended fiancé, sheep farmer Ian MacDonald, is driven out of town by her bully of a father, cattleman Charles Ruggles, and his henchman Preston Foster. Sheep, they state, are not wanted on cattle property. Lake hires reformed drunk McCrea (playing Dave Nash) as her ranch foreman, seeing him as the man to fight Foster and her father to the bitter end. Very soon, McCrea, a too-honest cowpoke tormented by the death of his wife and son in a cabin fire and who has a thing going with Arleen Whelan, becomes aware of femme fatale Lake's deviousness in manipulating men to carry out her bidding, all falling under the spell of those peek-a-boo eyes and blonde sexual allure. The vamp teases every male in sight, switching her attention from one to the other; when Foster burns her ranch to the ground, she organizes the stampeding of her own herd, placing the blame on Foster who, in a confrontation with Sheriff Donald Crisp, shoots the lawman dead. McCrea has enlisted the aid of an old friend, Don DeFore, a loutish, slightly psychopathic loose cannon who carries out his own agenda of killings before sacrificing himself to give McCrea, wounded in a gunfight, time to finish Preston off with a shotgun blast in the final reel. "It's all over now. You've got what you wanted," is his parting shot to Lake before he falls into the welcoming arms of Whelan.

Ramrod is unremittingly violent for its time, with a high body count and much emphasis on physical slapping, beating and fighting, a lot of it quite bloody. Added to this are the betrayal of friendships and absence of humor, and we are left with an adult, densely plotted Western that reflected the changing face of the genre as the 1950s approached. Adolph Deutsch's score complemented the stark canyon scenery of Utah's Zion National Park, photographed in clear-cut monochrome by Russell Harlan, particularly effective in the picture's last quarter when Foster and his gang stalk McCrea, Lake and DeFore through endless rocky defiles. It seems strange that in later years, both McCrea and De Toth had little to commend this excellent movie, the director claiming that he thought Gary Cooper more suitable for the role; McCrea could underplay as well as Cooper, but Coop was firmly lodged in the cinemagoing public's psyche as a major Hollywood Western star. McCrea hadn't yet reached that point in his career. When he'd shaken off that sorrowful, hound-dog demeanor, he was now beginning to look the part instead of appearing to simply act it, even though his six-foot-three-inch frame, towering over Lake's four-foot-11-inches, made their joint scenes appear awkward. (McCrea didn't rate Lake in her role, even though they had scored a hit together in *Sullivan's Travels*. In all probability, Barbara Stanwyck would have been his ideal choice.) *Ramrod* wasn't quite his *Abilene Town* or *Stagecoach* moment, but was near enough for him to be shrugging off that wholesome romantic image and deftly taking on the persona of a Westerner, edging toward audience acceptance as a cowboy star. In all respects, it was a vast improvement on the lukewarm *The Virginian* and it told on McCrea's more vigorous performance.

The second Enterprise/United Artists Western, *Four Faces West* (also released as *They Passed This Way*) has become famous for being the only cowboy movie where not

Joel McCrea (right) in *Four Faces West* (1948), a movie that helped to cement his persona as a Western hero, even though not one shot is fired.

one single shot is fired; there are no fistfights either. On the face of it, this spells a recipe for disaster. It's not, far from it. Released in 1948, Alfred E. Green's chase Western is highly unusual and engrossing, featuring *noir*-ish overtones in its tale of cowhand Ross McEwen (McCrea) who relieves a bank of $2,000 and is relentlessly hunted by lawman Pat Garrett (Charles Bickford) and his posse, the bank robber finding salvation, and love, as he's pursued. Set amid New Mexico's arid Gallup area, photographed in glistening black-and-white by Russell Harlan, *Four Faces West*, along with *Ramrod*, cemented McCrea's persona as an all-round Westerner; it's ironic that it took two outings from a minor film studio to mold the actor into the role he was to be identified with from then on, but that's just what Enterprise achieved before folding in late 1948.

McCrea holds up the bank in Santa Maria at the same moment that Bickford is being inaugurated as the new sheriff. Apart from a note to his father, we are never allowed to know why he commits this against-type robbery (in doing so, McCrea almost plays a bad guy, but only almost!). What follows is a long pursuit over rugged territory, by horse, foot, train and, at one point, a steer that McCrea ropes in. Saloon owner Joseph Calleia (sounding just like Anthony Quinn), crossing paths on a train with McCrea, becomes his *de facto* guardian angel; he suspects McCrea of the crime and is tempted by the $3,000 bounty but chooses to help the loner instead, forming an attachment to him. Also suspicious is the radiant Mrs. Joel McCrea, Frances Dee, a nurse who falls head over heels for the lanky drifter, even to the extreme of quitting her post and galloping after him into the rocky wilds. When McCrea stumbles across a rancher (Calleia's uncle) and his family, sick with diphtheria, he elects to stay and help them out,

Joel McCrea and Dorothy Malone in *South of St. Louis* (1949)

emptying his entire cartridge belt of bullets to obtain the necessary sulfur with which to revive the two children. Thanks to his administrations, the family survives, and it's this act of kindness, plus the fact that McCrea has paid back some of the money he stole, that opens Bickford's eyes to the man's true character; he's not the hardened criminal everyone takes him for. Promising to wed Dee on his return, McCrea rides off with Bickford to begin a lenient prison sentence for his misdeed, his name etched on the towering Inscription Rock (the El Morro National Monument in New Mexico) as one of many who have "passed this way."

Adapted from Eugene Manlove Rhodes' pulp novel *Paso poy Aqui*, *Four Faces West* manages to serve up suspense, drama, tension, romance and the great outdoors without gunfire and brawls, a remarkable feat in itself. McCrea is marvelous in the role, bringing to the fore all of his expertise gained in a wide variety of roles spread over the 68 pictures preceding this one. The rest of the cast also put in equally good performances while a special salute must be given to Paul Sawtell's brilliant score. Sawtell's soundtrack, in all its various forms, nuances and shades, is a virtual blueprint of how a Western score should be effectively written. It's a real pleasure to listen to, as *Four Faces West* is a real pleasure to watch.

Director Ray Enright, one of Hollywood's most underrated talents, was more than capable of serving a tasty Western dish containing lashings of verve to appease both cowboy-mad kids and adults alike, and he did precisely that with 1949's *South of St. Louis*, a noisy actioner that doesn't let up for a single second, in perfect tune with Max Steiner's thunderous score. Warner Bros. chose to remake the Cagney/Bogart 1939 gangster thriller *The Roaring Twenties* as a Western: McCrea (as Kip Davis) took on the Cagney role, playing a good guy driven to drink when Douglas Kennedy steals his girl (Dorothy Malone); and Zachary Scott became the Bogart character, one part of the trio of friends who turns downright bad.

Set in the Civil War, Enright, in the opening sequence, focuses his camera on three sets of jingling spurs as the self-proclaimed "The Three Bells" (McCrea, Scott and Kennedy) stroll into Union-held Brownsville's saloon, intent on redress and facing up to snarling guerrilla leader Victor Jory, a second-rate Quantrill whose outfit has just burned down their ranch. What follows is a bruising fistfight between McCrea and Jory, McCrea the victor spitting at Jory: "Get outta Texas and don't come back." But the trio's loyalties are put to the test when Kennedy decides to join up with the Confederates; Malone, betrothed to McCrea but disagreeing with him over his revengeful outlook on life, moves to Edenton to work in a hospital and McCrea and Scott decide to ferry guns and powder over the Mexican border to Matamoras in direct opposition to Jory's identical activities. Poisoned dwarf Bob Steele, enlisted by Scott against his partner's wishes, flits from one side to the other, stirring up trouble, while ravishing saloon singer Alexis Smith is the tart with a heart of gold, a direct contrast to Malone's self-righteous, home-loving nurse; both love McCrea, but which gal will he finally choose.

Belgian poster for *South of St. Louis*

Enright concocts an invigorating brew, each and every frame drenched in Karl Freund's deep rich Technicolor hues, a delight to the eye. The incident-packed action is fast and furious, shifting mainly between Brownsville and Matamoras on the Mexican border. Malone rebels against McCrea's dealings in contraband and turns to Kennedy for succor; Smith hankers after McCrea, who hits the tequila bottle when Malone rejects his marriage proposal, and Scott turns nasty, wanting to boss the outfit himself. Jory is killed in an ambush set up by traitor Steele, the war ends and Kennedy becomes a Texas Ranger, forcing him to curb McCrea and Scott's lucrative gun-running. "We were always going to be together. You took Deb away and Charlie tried to kill me," laments McCrea to Kennedy; Scott then threatens to shoot Kennedy if he doesn't leave Brownsville. The final showdown doesn't disappoint. The camera again focuses on two sets of shiny spurs as McCrea and Kennedy confront Scott and his gunmen in Matamoras. Scott, spying a sniper in an upstairs window, ready to put a bullet in McCrea's back, blasts him dead and springs into action with his two former buddies,

Joel McCrea and Virginia Mayo as doomed lovers in *Colorado Territory*

an artful shot showing *three* sets of spurs retreating backwards. Steele guns down Scott before McCrea dispatches him, and McCrea does the sensible thing by getting hitched to glamorous Smith, the two riding their buggy into the newly built Three Bell Ranch.

South of St. Louis was a critical and commercial winner and McCrea, now firmly entrenched in moviegoers' minds as a cowboy star, was on a roll. His next, Warner Bros.' *Colorado Territory* (1949), was originally offered to John Wayne, but Wayne had other obligations and McCrea eventually got the part after numerous other actors were tested ("I get the parts Wayne, Cooper and Stewart turn down," joked McCrea in interviews at the time). One of Hollywood's most accomplished action directors, Raoul Walsh, was at the helm of what was virtually a revamp of Humphrey Bogart's *High Sierra* (1941), also directed by Walsh, a man who certainly knew how to put the word "move" into movie. *Colorado Territory* rattles along at a frantic pace; together with stupendous location work at Gallup, New Mexico and Arizona's Sedona area, plus a great score from Warner regular David Buttolph, the picture proved to be the high with which McCrea desired to finish out his 1940s film repertoire. This masculine, rough-tough oater remains one of his best-remembered pieces of work.

Bank robber Wes McQueen (McCrea), after busting out of jail with the help of his aunt, has a final job to do before quitting and leading the quiet life, a train heist which will net him and his confederates $100,000. After meeting rancher Henry Hull and daughter Dorothy Malone on a stage, he's quickly decided that doe-eyed Malone is the girl for him and plans to settle down with her after the robbery. But McCrea hasn't accounted for sultry half-breed Virginia Mayo's attentions; she's holed up in the ruined town of Todos Santos, situated in the mountains, with argumentative John Archer and James Mitchell all aware of McCrea's plans. Bully-boy Archer wants to kill McCrea when the job is over, jealous of his reputation and the fact that Mayo is smitten with him, while unbeknown to all four, train guard Ian Wolfe, revealing details of where the payroll is kept, is in fact in cahoots with the law, planning a double-cross to collect the ransom on McCrea's head. There's a quarrel to see who is top dog, with McCrea hitting Archer on the jaw. "Get outta line again and I'll kill both of you," he snaps at him and Mitchell. The robbery is then carried out, a prolonged and exciting sequence aboard a Rio Grande Railroad locomotive, superbly constructed by Walsh. Archer and Mitchell are manacled by McCrea for trying to outwit him (they're eventually hanged), McCrea's old partner Basil Ruysdael, due to receive a cut of the loot, is murdered and Malone, far from being the future wife he imagined, reveals a poisonous, uncaring side to her nature. Realizing that Mayo is far more suitable as a buddy, the two hightail it back to the ruined township with the stolen cash, a posse of 22 men, led by Marshal Morris Ankrum, in hot pursuit. What follows is a Western Shakespearean tragedy played out against awesome rock formations, wonderfully photographed by Sidney Hickox in the kind of needle-sharp black-and-white that may never again be experienced in modern-day cinema auditoriums.

"What is it, Wes. What does it mean," says a worried Mayo, spotting smoke signals on the horizon. "Means we're a couple of fools in a dead village, dreaming about something that'll probably never happen," replies McCrea with resignation. You know the lovers are doomed from this moment on, even when McCrea splits and heads for the scenically splendid Canyon of Death after hiding the cash inside a chapel—they've booked a one-way ticket to nowhere and are going to pay for it. A superb, almost poetic, finale sees Ankrum and his men closing in on McCrea, hiding in an abandoned Indian pueblo (City of the Moon) high up on an enormous cliff face while Mayo, on foot, hurries frantically across the rocky wastes to his aid. Wounded by an Indian marksman on the opposite ridge, McCrea staggers down the rocky slope to his woman who is armed with two pistols. Both guns blazing, the pair advance toward Ankrum's posse and are mowed down in a hail of lead, clasping hands as they expire in the dust, an ending as startlingly violent as it is moving (Walsh topped this off with James Cagney's classic demise in *White Heat*, released the same year, an explosive [literally!] scene that has gone down in history as one of cinema's greatest-ever climaxes.)

The 1940s had come to a close; McCrea had earned his spurs and was now fully able to line up on the starting block with Scott, Murphy and Montgomery and a host of others during the cowboy crazy '50s, without doubt the genre's golden period. For lovers of horse operas everywhere, it promised to be an exhilarating and enjoyable ride.

Chapter 9
Montgomery:
Republic to Fox, 1935-1948

George Montgomery's first appearance in a motion picture was an un-credited part as a soldier in Republic's *The Singing Vagabond* (1935). Four years and 37 movies later, he bagged his first major credited role, that of Tommy Bates in Fox's 1939 addition to O. Henry's *Cisco Kid* saga, *The Cisco Kid and the Lady*, Cesar Romero starring as the dashing, womanizing bandit (Romero and Chris-Pin Martin, playing sidekick Gordito, made four more Cisco Kid adventures between 1940 and 1941: *Viva Cisco Kid, Lucky Cisco Kid, The Gay Caballero* and *Ride on Vaquero*).

Twenty-seven years before Clint Eastwood, Eli Wallach and Lee Van Cleef searched for a fortune in buried gold, each possessing partial clues as to its whereabouts, in Sergio Leone's masterful *The Good, the Bad and the Ugly*, Romero, Martin and bad guy Robert Barrat searched for a rich mine, each only knowing a third of the location; Romero has rolled up his portion of the map and smoked it, Martin has swallowed his bit while Barrat still retains his third. The map's owner dies in a wagon holdup, leaving the cutest of cute babies behind, so we are now in pre-*Three Godfathers* territory on top of everything else. Watch out for that alarming scene when the baby crawls out onto the trail and is nearly run over by a stagecoach; shot without back projection, this would have guaranteed all mothers leaping from their seats in absolute horror. Romero and Martin ride into town with the baby and hand the gurgling infant over to schoolmarm Marjorie Weaver; Romero flirts with her *and* saloon gal Virginia Field and Barrat joins forces with Romero, then doesn't; he finally disguises himself as the Cisco Kid, gunned down in the street by soldiers for his foolhardy impersonation of one of the West's most wanted men ("All that time posing as a respectable citizen!" say the bemused townsfolk, standing over his dead body). The mine is eventually discovered, Romero and Martin handing it over to Weaver and the baby before riding off into the sunset with Field in tow.

Where does 23-year-old Montgomery fit into this madcap Western frolic? In the 28th minute, he steps from a stage in black duds, looking mighty fancy, and makes a beeline for Weaver, his fiancée. Enraged at Romero's overtures toward his intended, he gets drunk, winds up in jail with the two bandits, breaks free with them and is reunited with Weaver, who plans to bring up the baby and live on the mine's proceeds. Beautifully filmed around Lone Pine's Alabama Hills region by Barney McGill in sharply defined monochrome, and blessed with Frances Hyland's amusing script, *The Cisco Kid and the Lady* is a ridiculously enjoyable movie that will have audiences grinning as much as Romero does if we don't take it too seriously. "Dashing and amusing," agreed *Daily Variety*. The showy actor, flashing his gleaming teeth at every given opportunity, makes a memorable Cisco Kid and Martin's rotund gun-happy bandit is a hoot. As for Montgomery, audiences would never, in a million years, foresee on this showing that this round-faced dude was destined to become a key figure in the '50s B-Western movie revival. Scott looked rugged from the outset; McCrea  also had that cowboy persona about him, and Murphy was so utterly different in appearance, almost verging on unique, that he was accepted as Western material, albeit unusual material, from the word go. Montgomery, in 1939, had matinee-idol good looks, at odds with the tough oaters he would star in several years later. However, he'd completed the spadework in all those Gene Autry/Roy Rogers/John Wayne potboilers made between 1935 and 1939 and the critics and public took to him. It only remained for the right material to come his way for him to become one of the Western's more notable lead role-players.

Two years later, having lost some of his baby fat, a leaner-looking Montgomery turned up as rodeo star Lank Garrett in Fox's 1941 screwball Western comedy *The Cowboy and the Blonde*. Ray McCarey's frenetic version of *The Taming of the Shrew* would have been the ideal vehicle for Clark Gable and Jean Harlow to take on; Montgomery and Mary Beth Hughes didn't figure in that higher stratosphere inhabited by the likes of

Gable, but they did a fair job in this little-seen picture. Pampered diva Hughes flounces around on set, and off it, like Queen Bitch, leaving exasperated Consolidated Pictures' owner Alan Mowbray no choice but to bring in Montgomery as her next leading man ("A new Western discovery."), hopefully to calm her down, despite his inexperience. The blonde's new picture is going to be a Western, so who better to star opposite her than a famous rodeo star, even if he can't act. What follows is a light, breezy romantic farce of the type Hollywood specialized in so well during the '30s and '40s: Montgomery just about scrapes through his screen test, Hughes falls for him and wants to quit acting, the cowboy reckons she's stringing him along for her own purposes and wisecracking buddy Fuzzy Knight spits out salacious comments every time a perky starlet crosses his path ("Well cut my legs off and call me shorty," he exclaims at one point, an example of William Brent and Walter Bullock's humorous script). "You beautiful dope," Hughes continually calls Montgomery, clinging to him like a leech and smothering him with kisses (the two had a dalliance at the time of filming and it shows), the six-foot-three hunk doing his best not to appear too embarrassed. They end up getting hitched after a series of misunderstandings, leave the movie industry behind and go to live on the rodeo rider's ranch, the Gila Valley.

In 1941, Fox shot back-to-back movie adaptations of two Zane Grey pulp novels, both of which had previously been filmed three times: *Last of the Duanes* and *Riders of the Purple Sage*, a determining moment when buffs will state, "This is where Montgomery's career in Westerns really started." Fox's fourth screen versions had the fledgling cowboy star following in the exalted footsteps of those who had rode these trails before: William Farnum (1919/1920), Tom Mix (1924/1925) and George O'Brien (1930/1931). Farnum had a small role in *Duanes*, playing the head Ranger. Coming in at just under an hour, these primitive efforts, resembling 1930s serials more than Fox feature films, gave audiences a chance to sum up Montgomery's claim to be a top Western box-office draw—"Has leading man potentialities" wrote *Daily Variety*. Despite the obvious low budgets, he did an okay job, his suave looks and flashing smile probably delighting the females in the theater at the time, while men could appreciate his prowess on horseback, the belligerent, hard-nosed way in which he stood up to the bad guys and his lightning trigger finger on the draw.

Given top billing in *Last of the Duanes*, Montgomery's smooth features and halting performance (as Buck Duane) just about carry the day in a fast-paced actioner that had its parentage very much in the realms of the still-marketable Western serial. We're in Texas, 1870: Jettisoning vital parts of Grey's story (Montgomery's father is killed, but this is skimmed over, as is the hurried conclusion), the revengeful cowpoke, fine and dandy in wide-brimmed black hat, black kerchief and freshly laundered shirt, hits the Lone Pine wilds after he shoots a deputy, a posse of Texas Rangers on his tail. Hitching up with grizzled outlaw Francis Ford, the plot twists and turns like one of those Lone Pine trails: Ford is shot and fatally wounded; Montgomery takes his horse into Rimrock to hand over to George E. Stone and he has a run-in with town heavy Joe Sawyer. Damsel-in-distress Lynne Roberts, an old childhood friend of Montgomery's, is rescued from Don Costello's bunch of outlaws (Roberts was given second billing but disappears after a couple of short scenes); he then joins the Rangers to go undercover and flush out the ringleader of a criminal gang. Saloon girl Eve Arden, siding with villain Truman Bradley, the ringleader, flutters her eyelashes at the handsome cowboy, but to no avail

and, after gunning down Bradley, he's pardoned for his original crime and heads off to locate his father's murderer.

Last of the Duanes is an unsubtle, 57-minute oater that looks very rough-hewn for the year it was made, featuring a catchy score by an un-credited David Buttolph and passable direction/photography. There's no doubting Montgomery's screen presence, however naïve he occasionally appears. He rides well, handles a gun with rapid ease, rattles off his terse lines with intent and charms the ladies. What more could you wish for in a Western hero? But it would be some time yet before the 25-year-old with the looks of a male model became molded into the much harder character that, along with Scott, Murphy and McCrea, spearheaded the B-Western movie revival of the 1950s.

Like *Last of the Duanes*, much of Grey's convoluted storyline was streamlined in *Riders of the Purple Sage* to fit in with the 58-minute running time. Once audiences had managed to get their head round the tortuous plot, we could sit back, relax and watch black-clad Montgomery (as Jim Lassiter) gallop across the Lone Pine landscape, dishing out lead and fists at the drop of a Stetson. The cowboy arrives in Cottonwood, Arizona seeking satisfaction: Years back, a man abducted his sister and her baby; his sister died, so Montgomery wants to find out who the man was and what happened to the child. Meanwhile, ranch owner Mary Howard and her cute adopted orphan, Patsy Patterson, are being terrorized by corrupt Judge Robert Barrat's vigilante gang, trying to drive her off her prime farmland because he wants to own the territory lock, stock and barrel. Rustling her cattle is just one of his underhand tactics. Howard also knows the name of the person who abducted Montgomery's sister. It was Barrat; the masked rider seen with his mob is the baby who grew up to be Lynne Roberts, an outlaw. Roberts is captured and taken to a hidden valley by Howard's foreman, James Gillette, where they unexpectedly fall

in love. After much skullduggery (Howard burns down her ranch to prevent Barrat laying his hands on it), Montgomery finishes off the judge in his own courtroom and baddies Richard Lane and Kane Richmond are shot. The whole kit and caboodle climaxes in nihilistic fashion with Montgomery, having rescued young Patterson from Barrat's mob, clambering up a steep mountain slope and pushing a colossal boulder onto the heads of the pursuing vigilantes; they perish to a man under an avalanche of rocks. The curtain closes with hero Montgomery, Howard and Patterson setting up home together in Surprise Valley.

Too involved for its own low-budget trappings, *Riders of the Purple Sage* is fascinating to view nowadays because, alongside *Last of the Duanes* (both are in need of an official DVD release), it gives one the opportunity to study a youthful George Montgomery in his formative Western stage, playing a hard-ridin', hard-shootin' cowboy whose prettyboy looks belie a toughness we wouldn't expect. Certainly his opponents in these two grade-B oaters don't catch on—he polishes them off without batting an eyelid. Not a rugged Westerner like Scott, nowhere near the accomplished actor that McCrea was, yet George Montgomery, like Murphy, was somehow different enough to make a visual impression in the genre. *Hollywood Motion Picture Review* noted: "George Montgomery is excellent as the cowboy hero." Above all else, he possessed the right attitude for the job. But he still hadn't chosen to go down the Western movie route full-time and Fox, unsure of his talent, didn't appear to be grooming him as a future cowboy star anyway; a further 11 pictures were to pass before his next Western appeared, *Belle Starr's Daughter*, released by Fox in 1948, the year that he acrimoniously left them behind: Nine for Fox, one for Columbia (*Lulu Belle*, 1948) and one for United Artists (*The Girl from Manhattan*, 1948). In his Fox movies, he was sometimes billed as the lead (*Orchestra Wives*, 1942), second-placed (*Three Little Girls in Blue*, 1946) or third (*Roxie Hart*, 1942). These movies, along with *Ten Gentleman from West Point* (1942), *Coney Island* (1943) and *Bomber's Moon* (1943), were immensely popular during the war years and Montgomery was looked upon as a staunch male lead, if low on true star magnitude. He was capable enough in whatever he appeared in, but was short of the quality that propels some actors into becoming Hollywood screen legends.

Belle Starr's Daughter is a serviceable oater, one of many in the cycle of "famous outlaw" movies made in the 1940s. Isabel Jewell played Starr, the Bandit Queen of Cherokee Flats (as she did in Scott's 1946 feature *Badman's Territory*), shot to death during an argument in the opening few minutes by one of her own men, Rod Cameron, busy trying to romance her daughter, Ruth Roman, behind her back. The fragile peace treaty between Starr's outlaw territory and the nearby town of Antioch is shattered, Cameron takes on the guise of notorious outlaw Bittercreek, robbing stages, and Roman goes to work in Antioch where Marshal Tom Jackson (Montgomery) falls for her. Cameron rides into town, leads her astray and she is now the Rose of Cimarron, joining up with Cameron's gang and fending off his leering advances. Roman thinks Montgomery killed her mother, unaware that Cameron is the real murderer; old-timer Wallace Ford knows about Cameron, but he's shot before he has the chance to spill the beans to Roman—it's left to fatally wounded William Phipps, dismayed at Cameron's callous treatment of him, to tell Roman the truth. In a frantic finale, Cameron and Montgomery shoot it out; there are no prizes as to who gets the upper hand and Roman in the bargain. The marshal promises to wait for her while she serves a possible five-year prison sentence.

Plenty of horse riding and shooting, plus standoffs in saloons—*Belle Starr's Daughter* was standard, no frills '40s Western fare, directed with pace by Lesley Selander, spoiled somewhat by a strange, non-Western-type score from classical pianist Edward Kilenyi. Montgomery, back in the saddle after a spell of seven years out of it, displayed that characteristically direct, no-nonsense stance that was to become a trait of his in his '50s oaters; he certainly doesn't pussyfoot around with his opponents. "Get those guns off," he barks at Cameron's boys at one point with a fixed stare and later repeats it to another bunch: "Take those guns off and get outta town." It's a more-than-adequate way with which to finish off the decade; moreover, Montgomery had probably decided that it was the Western or bust for him from now on. Out of the 28 pictures he was to make in the 1950s, 24 were Westerns, and it was with these 24 films that Montgomery secured his reputation as a sober, stern-faced man of action, not as refined as Scott or McCrea, and not as exuberant as Murphy, but a central character nonetheless in the medium-budget Western that was to predominate in the new decade.

Chapter 10
Scott: The Westerner, 1936–1949

Between 1936 and 1945, Randolph Scott starred in 30 motion pictures, only 14 of which were Westerns; *The Road to Reno* (Universal 1938) and *Susannah of the Mounties* (20th Century Fox, 1939) could, at a pinch, be classed as pseudo-Westerns and are included in that total. Still on loan to other film companies by Paramount (his contract with them ended in 1938; he then began freelancing), Scott's roll call of movies from this frenetic period was, like the title of his 1937 musical Western, "High, Wide, and Handsome," taking in drama, musicals, crime, war, romance, historical actioner and two Shirley Temple outings: *Rebecca of Sunnybrook Farm* (20th Century Fox, 1938) and the aforementioned *Susannah of the Mounties*. *Follow the Fleet* (RKO-Radio, 1936—his second Astaire/Rogers vehicle), *Go West, Young Man* (Major Pictures, 1936, with Mae West), *Coast Guard* (Columbia, 1939), *My Favorite Wife* (RKO-Radio, 1940), *Paris Calling* (Universal, 1941), *Pittsburgh* (Universal, 1942), *To the Shores of Tripoli* (20th Century Fox, 1942), *Bombardier* (RKO-Radio, 1943), *Corvette K-225* (Universal, 1943), *Gung Ho!* (Universal, 1943) and a swashbuckler, *Captain Kidd* (Miracle, 1945). This transitional, fruitful period of filmmaking was the bedrock on which journeyman actor Scott honed his craft, slotting seamlessly into any number of characters and emerging with his growing reputation intact, firmly establishing himself as a popular star with audiences of the day (he also narrowly missed out on the role of Ashley Wilkes in MGM's mammoth *Gone with the Wind*, the part eventually given to Leslie Howard). Most of these features are now beyond recall—it is those dozen or so serviceable Westerns he made that shaped Scott into the all-round Western hero, a part he felt so comfortable with that, from 1946 onwards, at age 48 but looking years younger, he concentrated (with two exceptions) on cowboy movies to the exclusion of everything else.

United Artists' *The Last of the Mohicans* (1936) was the fifth film adaptation of James Fenimore Cooper's notable 1826 period adventure novel detailing the conflict between the English and French to gain control of the North American colonies. An obscure 1912 production, two from the 1920s (including Luna-Film's German silent starring Bela Dracula Lugosi as Chingachgook!) and Harry Carey's 1932 serial are

Robert Barrat's glum-looking Chingachgook consults with Randolph Scott's Hawkeye, in *The Last of the Mohicans* (1936).

the others. Scott's first major role in a grade-A production proved to be an unqualified success, his tough but principled Hawkeye deemed by most to be a step up from other actors' interpretation of the character. Moreover, there wasn't a vast amount of Western opposition around in 1936 to dent Scott's flowering career; Cecil B. DeMille's $1,000,000 production for Paramount, *The Plainsman*, stabilized Gary Cooper's star presence on the Western front, but apart from that, the rock-bottom budget oater reigned supreme, a genre that Scott never once dipped his toes into, proof enough that he was looked upon by those that mattered as being suitable for far more superior material. Against Scott's sturdy Hawkeye, Robert Barrat's glum-looking Chingachgook didn't amount to much; in the Indian stakes, Bruce Cabot's fearsome Magua upstaged him by a mile. The story, set in 1757, should be familiar to all by now: The English Redcoats march to the aid of Fort William Henry, heinous scout Cabot and his Huron buddies siding with the French; Chingachgook's son, Uncas (Philip Reed), falls for winsome Heather Angel ("Got squaw fever," mutters Barrat, disapproving of their relationship); at the same time, colonel's daughter Binnie Barnes eyes up handsome Scott in his buckskins and coonskin cap, shunning Major Henry Wilcoxon's clumsy, stiff overtures; Scott and his two Mohican chums are imprisoned for treason following a 10-day assault on the fort; the two women are abducted by Cabot and his warriors; Reed is killed by Cabot and Angel jumps over a cliff to her doom, joining her Indian lover in death; Barrat gets even with Cabot, drowning him in a river; and Scott is saved from burning at the stake by the infantry, kissing Barnes in the final few seconds with the approval of rejected suitor Wilcoxon.

Irene Dunne and Randolph Scott in *High, Wide, and Handsome* (1937)

Fine outdoor photography amidst California's forested Big Bear Lake region and nonstop subsidiary set pieces directed at a rattling pace by George B. Seitz ensured that this large-scale recreation of Cooper's Boy's-Own tale still ranks highly with fans, particularly as it showcased Scott as a daring man of action with a caring, thoughtful side to him, the actor's emerging skill beginning to reap dividends. And although the score is credited to Roy Webb, soundtrack buffs with a keen ear will detect several sequences utilizing Max Steiner's music from *King Kong*, notably in the canoe chase, the storming battle scenes and the Indian attack on the fort. Bruce Cabot, the other *Kong* connection, must have really felt at home!

After the critical and commercial success of *The Last of the Mohicans*, Scott returned to Paramount in 1937 for *High, Wide, and Handsome*, directed by Rouben Mamoulian, second on the bill to Irene Dunne. The action took place in Titusville, Western Pennsylvania, in the 1870s, oilman Peter Cortlandt (Scott) going head-to-head with a corrupt railroad official who does his utmost to sabotage plans to have the precious black liquid transported to refineries via a pipeline. Mamoulian brought his trademark flamboyant touch to one of the 1930s' most least-remembered Western musical dramas, a roistering mix of romance, music, cornball comedy and conflict that, in some instances, didn't quite come off. With music and lyrics by Jerome Kern and Oscar Hammerstein II, a cast that included not only Scott but also songbird Dunne (fresh from her 1936 triumph, *Show Boat*), Alan Hale, Akim Tamiroff, Charles Bickford and Dorothy Lamour, it seems hard to understand why this delightful movie has sunk without a trace over the years.

Randolph Scott, as oilman Peter Cortlandt, sits at the table with roughneck Alan Hale in *High, Wide, and Handsome* (1937).

Granted, it should have been produced in Technicolor; perhaps by appearing to be three different types of film in one package and ultimately failing to fully coalesce, audiences couldn't identify with twee sentiment and brawling action rubbing shoulders.

At $2,000,000, Mamoulian's rip-roaring feature was Scott's biggest budget film to date. Hair much longer than normal and beefed up to manly proportions (he filled a shirt nicely!), he romances Dunne, a singer with Raymond Walburn's traveling medicine show, and strikes oil on his property on their wedding day. Mamoulian paints a picture of rural bliss in the first half: panoramic vistas, meadows filled with daisies, the apple blossom much in evidence as Dunne warbles the heart-achingly poignant "The Folks Who Live On the Hill" to her soppy beloved who plans to build a home for them on his own private hill. But when roughneck Alan Hale decides to up railroad rates and freeze out Scott and his workers, Dunne is rudely cast aside as her work-mad husband bypasses the railway and goes all out to connect pipes to the nearby refinery, despite constant disruption from Hale and henchman Charles Bickford. Feeling neglected, Dunne runs off to join Bower's Carnival, taking up her old singing role. The astonishing climax sees an entire circus, complete with elephants, coming to the aid of Scott and his workforce, busy hauling pipes up a cliff face and harassed by Bickford and his whip-wielding mob. As in all good Hollywood films of that period, Scott and Dunne are reunited in love.

A barnstorming jamboree, fistfights on a shanty boat, sultry Dorothy Lamour singing a couple of memorable tunes ("The Things I Want" and "Allegheny Al"), double-dealing with shady saloon owner Tamiroff over land deals and Elizabeth Patterson chewing the scenery as Scott's feisty grandma—*High, Wide, and Handsome* is more of a drama

Randolph Scott from *The Texans*

incorporating musical interludes than, by definition, a straightforward musical, a vintage pleasure to be savored from Hollywood's golden age. By redirecting his talents from *The Last of the Mohicans* to this, Scott showed both his versatility and evolvement as an all-round performer. More importantly, as a future Western star, nobody else was attempting this kind of material in 1937, which says a lot for Scott and his acting chops. There was little sign yet of the hard-nosed Westerner he was to become; that was nine years away (there's a solitary gunshot at 74 minutes, and that's it); Scott was still in the process of perfecting his craft and, by the look of it, enjoying himself (he doesn't, by the way, sing a single note!). Those dusty frontier town dramas would have to wait just a little while longer.

It was back to basics for *The Texans* (Paramount 1938), a rather unsatisfactory "end of Civil War" oater directed by James P. Hogan. It's Texas, 1865: Victorious Yankee soldiers are treating the defeated Confederates like scum, forcing a rebel ranch owner to drive her cattle herds to Abilene on the Chisholm Trail in an attempt to make peace with those "up north." Tough trail boss Kirk Jordan (Scott) is sick of fighting the Bluecoats and persuades blonde gunrunner Joan Bennett to lead her steers to the Kansas border instead of Mexico as she intends; the gal wants to join forces with Emperor Maximilian's army and overthrow the Yankees. A promising scenario based on the opening up of the Old West floundered in this fitful period Western adventure (a forerunner to Howard Hawks' classic cattle-driving opus *Red River*) which saw Scott, billed second to Bennett, back in buckskins, teamed up with bewhiskered Walter Brennan playing his trademark trigger-happy hayseed. Bennett was woefully miscast as the headstrong rancher, looking spotless throughout; this role demanded more of a "Calamity Jane" approach, Hogan spending too much time focusing his camera on the actress' fine bone structure. Many sequences were studio-bound, the Achilles heel of outdoor action pictures because of the obvious use of back-projection footage. Scott, in his early scenes set in Indianola, appeared ill at ease, only relaxing when he was hitting the trail and pantomime villain Robert Barrat veered from buffoon to snarling oaf with a lack of conviction. Even Robert Cummings, the supposed male romantic lead, fell by the wayside, Bennett switching her affections to Scott in the blink of an eyelash. It was left to veteran actress May Robson, Bennett's grandmother, to act everyone else off the screen, a crotchety performance to relish.

A romantic portrait of Randolph Scott and Hope Hampton from *The Road to Reno*

A thundering Comanche attack, scheming carpetbaggers, wagons stuck in quagmires, a prairie fire, stampeding cattle, fistfights, a dust storm, hardships, Yankees versus Rebels—it was all there, but disappointingly welded together, one of the few early Scott Westerns where the verdict is: "It's nothing special." In fact, the movie presents a shambling mishmash of styles: One gets the impression that it could have been more cohesive in all departments and perhaps stretched out to the two-hour epic mark; it's a little *too* sprawling for a 90-minute picture and remains undoubtedly one of Scott's lesser efforts from the '30s.

That "lesser effort" was followed, in the same year, by possibly Scott's poorest-ever Western, Universal's little-seen *The Road to Reno* (aka *The Ranger and the Lady*). Every actor is entitled to an off day—*The Road to Reno* was undoubtedly Scott's! S. Sylvan Simon clumsily directed an obscure musical contemporary Western masquerading as a '30s screwball comedy, not boding well for Randolph Scott fans hoping to see their hero out on the open range, gun strapped to his waist; from the moment Hope Hampton screeches her way through a snippet from Puccini's *La Boheme* during the first three minutes, we know we're in for a rough ride in a positively weird picture that is certainly no cause for celebration. Just about squeezing itself into the Western category (after all, Scott *does* play a rancher/cowboy), Hampton travels west, wanting a divorce from estranged husband Scott (as Steve Fortness) but unable to obtain one because the Fortness Dude Ranch is divided by the California/Nevada border line; what's legal in one state isn't legal in the other. Accompanying Hampton is flighty man-eater pilot Glenda Farrell, determined to grab Scott once he's free. Then Hampton, reckoning that hunky

Scott isn't such a bad catch after all, decides to ditch boyfriend Alan Marshal, hoping to get back with her hubby, who then changes *his* mind by announcing that *he* now wants a divorce. Aunt Helen Broderick fusses around in the background, as does bumbling sidekick David Oliver, trying to provide light comedy relief in a stodgy confection veering between slapstick farce and musical lowlights, with an over-emphasis on clumsy back-projected scenes. Humm … what are the two most embarrassing moments among many? Horsemen riding through the dusk after a hard day's work on the prairie, all singing their heads off to the tune of "Ridin' Home." And Hampton and Scott lying side-by-side in a cabin, the camera zooming in on their faces: Hampton, looking blissful, warbling "I Gave My Heart Away," Scott looking desperate, wishing (no doubt) that his next film venture would do far more for his reputation than this clunker would ever achieve (it did—see *Jesse James* below). It all ends in a protracted court scene crammed with misunderstandings, Hampton and Scott back in each other's arms, Farrell waltzing off with discarded Marshal. At one point, Hampton (her part would have suited sassy Alice Faye down to the ground) asks Scott: "Well? Have you had enough?" By then, you would have had more than enough of this hilariously awful debacle which, among the 64 Westerns that Scott logged up in his career, has disappeared off the face of the earth and has never been given an official DVD release. That's probably just as well!

A little-known side note: George Montgomery was a stand-in for Alan Marshal in the bronco busting sequence (at 45 minutes), an obscure fact that many film compendiums fail to mention (*The Years of George Montgomery*, written by the man himself. Sagebrush Press 1981).

Jesse James (20th Century Fox, 1939) was a fictionalized account of the life and times of the notorious outlaw, with Scott playing Marshal Will Wright, sympathetic to the bank robber's cause. Fox's expensive first attempt at presenting scrumptious-looking male star of the day Tyrone Power as a serious actor, not just a pinup boy fit only for the movie magazines, resulted in a critical and commercial winner, a "box-office smacko,"

in the words of *Variety*. Teamed with Henry Fonda, Fox's romanticized take on the Jesse James myth, produced on a $2,000,000 budget, is a spanking good Super Western, one of the '30s best and most expensive. Scott received fourth billing behind Power, Fonda and Nancy Kelly, it was his first Western in color (as it was Power's) and, although not appearing on the scene until 24 minutes had elapsed, his smartly dressed lawman more than held its own against the magnetic pairing of Power and Fonda. After gunning down unscrupulous railroad boss man Brian Donlevy for inadvertently causing the death of his mother, Missouri farmer Power, now a wanted man, stages a series of train and bank holdups with brother Fonda and their masked gang. Kelly supplies the romance, marrying Power and having his baby, while Scott (who also longs for Kelly) more or less falls in with the James gang when the head of the new Iron Horse Company reneges on a lenient prison sentence after Power turned himself in. Nunnally Johnson's pithy script chose to play fast and loose with historical fact concerning the outlaw's criminal way of life, concentrating on all-out action and, in the process, converting Jesse James from a hardened gunslinger into a Robin Hood-type figure; the Hollywood Production Code, America's answer to British censorship, dictated that audiences shouldn't be allowed to commiserate with a wrongdoer, however honorable his motives were, so Fox, by necessity, had to soften the James persona to meet the Code's requirements.

A stellar cast included Henry Hull as an irascible newspaper editor, veteran Jane Darwell as the James boys' mother and John Carradine as the coward Bob Ford who shoots the outlaw leader in the back. The vibrant photography was a joy, a color palette to dazzle the senses; the blazing Northfield Bank shoot-out a thrilling bullet-strewn sequence and the plight of Power and Kelly, forever on the run like a Western Bonnie

and Clyde, movingly put across, with patient Scott hovering on the sidelines ("He's no good," he states to Kelly. "You can't love him. Nobody can."). Hull's eulogy at the end, spoken over the bandit's tombstone, summed up the folk hero facet which still remains part of the Jesse James image, even though history states that the man was far from being the saintly do-gooder portrayed in the film, a film that did no harm to Scott's expanding curriculum vitae whatsoever, even though, compared to the rest of the players, his character was a little on the subdued side. But he above all others was getting the juicy parts that mattered in big-budget Westerns, competing this particular year with Errol Flynn in Michael Curtiz's *Dodge City* (Warner Bros.), Fonda in John Ford's *Drums Along the Mohawk* (Fox), Joel McCrea in DeMille's $1,500,000 *Union Pacific* (Paramount) and James Stewart in *Destry Rides Again* (Universal). Even John Wayne, after languishing in B-Westerns for years, finally hit the big time with *Stagecoach* (Walter Wanger Prods.), rounding off an influential and highly productive year for Western addicts. It can therefore be seen that Scott was more than holding his own against his more illustrious contemporaries, showing true flexibility in taking on role-rotation, although not quite yet lodged in the public mind as a Western "great."

Scott's adaptability came to the fore again in Fox's *Susannah of the Mounties*, released the same year as *Jesse James* but poles apart in every aspect. A vehicle for the fading box-office charms of Shirley Temple, the curly headed moppet starred as a young girl who survives an Indian massacre, only to take on the role of peacemaker in an impending outbreak of war between the Mounted Police and the Blackfoot tribes. The movie opens with Mounties led by Inspector Angus "Monty" Montague (Scott) encountering the smoldering remains of wagons, arrow-riddled bodies sprawled amid the embers—and then up pops Temple from under a barrel, grinning and shaking her unruly locks. A disconcerting mix of full-blooded Indian versus cavalry engagements and cutesy-pie Temple antics, this was the third instance that Scott and Temple's paths had crossed. Despite reports that he didn't particularly enjoy working with children, Scott's scenes with the 11-year-old child superstar come off well enough, even in the potentially embarrassing interlude where the little minx teaches him the waltz. While Scott attempts to romance radiant Margaret Lockwood, Temple becomes a blood brother to the chief's

Randolph Scott, as Wyatt Earp, becomes the new marshal when Ward Bond (middle) gives up the position, in *Frontier Marshal* (1939).

son (Martin Good Rider), learns how to smoke a pipe (which makes her a tad queasy), handles a pony, performs a war dance and allows herself to be called "Squaw." The youngsters eventually avert a bloodbath caused by villainous Blackfoot Victor Jory, who is fanning the flames of discontent by selling stolen horses to the railroaders. The old "Indians against the Iron Horse" standby constitutes the main thrust of the plot, Temple's wide-eyed innocence not sitting comfortably with bloodthirsty Redskins on the warpath, who are attacking a fort and killing indiscriminately. The movie wasn't a success at the time (a few prints were issued in Sepiatone), even with Temple devotees, and Scott, in some scenes, looked as though he wished he were somewhere else. His next effort would be a whole lot more rewarding than this one.

Fox's *Frontier Marshal* (1939) saw Scott (as Wyatt Earp) back on the lawless Old West streets of Tombstone, Arizona, and looking all the better for it. Allan Dwan's 71-minute essay into the Wyatt Earp myth is said to be the inspiration behind John Ford's rambling classic *My Darling Clementine* (1946). Not sticking too closely to historical truth (very few Westerns did!), the director's more compact contribution to the legend, a remake of Fox's 1934 movie with the corresponding title (George O'Brien played Earp), is a robust little B-programmer, a great deal more forthright and straightforward in execution than Ford's more leisurely, character-driven approach. Scott's in top form in this noisy, action-filled drama, hooked up with Cesar Romero's ailing, self-destructive Doc (named "Halliday" in this version); Romero's performance, give the actor credit, easily equals that of Victor Mature's Doc in the Ford oater. Rival saloons The Bella Union and The Palace of Pleasure are at loggerheads over customers and profits: Brassy dance hall singer

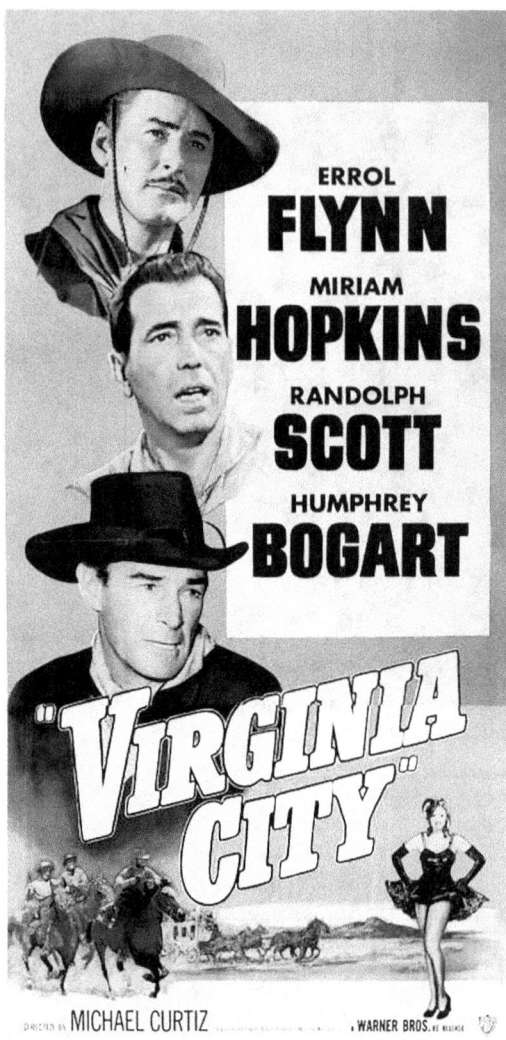

Binnie Barnes is in cahoots with Joe Sawyer's gang, who are busy robbing stages of silver bullion on instructions from cadaverous saloon owner John Carradine; hardheaded dame Barnes is also in love with Romero, as is ex-girlfriend Nancy Kelly, who comes looking for him, leading to frequent sparring sessions between the two women.

However, there is no room for romantic attachments or sentiment in Scott's life, even though he secretly admires Barnes' pushiness; from the moment he drags an outlaw's wounded body out into the street like a sack of potatoes, we know that this is a man who shoots first and asks questions later. He wants troublemaker Barnes out of town, closes down Carradine's joint, slays Lon Chaney, Jr. and his gunslinging gorillas in a street battle and goes it alone at the O.K. Corral, wiping out Sawyer's boys without the aid of Romero, who has been killed in an ambush (Barnes finishes off Sawyer). The final shot is of Boot Hill Cemetery, John Halliday's (Doc Holliday's) tombstone framing the foreground, the distant Lone Pine hills shimmering in the heat as Barnes leaves Tombstone for good.

A novelty here was the inclusion of goofy Eddie Foy, Jr. taking on the part of his father, famous vaudevillian comedy star Eddie Foy, Sr., his brief revue sketch providing light relief in a somber but cracking picture, endowed with gleaming black-and-white photography by Charles G. Clarke. *Frontier Marshal* showed Scott coming to the fore, taking on the casehardened persona that was to typify his work from 1946 onwards; it remains one of his most satisfying 1930s Westerns.

Entering into a new decade, the Western began casting off its outmoded '20s and '30s image, becoming a force to be reckoned with. Serials continued to be all the rage, boosting the decade's overall total to a staggering 800 Westerns, but the cowboy film was beginning to grow up and get serious, with big stars to match the big budgets. Warner Bros.' *Virginia City* (1940) was a case in point, featuring one of Hollywood's major players, Errol Flynn, and directed by top action specialist Michael Curtiz. Scott was in it, billed third behind Flynn and Miriam Hopkins, but at least he was cast in a

Miriam Hopkins and Randolph Scott from *Virginia City* (1940)

leading role where others had been overlooked, another sign that he was reaching the heights; rival Wayne, on the other hand, returned to B-Western fodder following the success of *Stagecoach* because of contractual commitments, his career in the big action oater stalling as a result.

In 1864 during the last days of the American Civil War, Confederate officer Vance Irby (Scott) is charged with the task of smuggling $5,000,000 worth of gold bullion out of Virginia City, Nevada ("The richest, roughest town on the face of the Earth") and transporting it 1,200 miles to Richmond, Virginia in a last-ditch attempt to help the ailing Rebel cause. Yes, with one of Hollywood's most accomplished action directors at the helm, a rousing Max Steiner score, glistening monochrome photography by Sol Polito and Flynn in mesmerizing form, *Virginia City* possessed the appropriate credentials to become a revered classic, but it failed to hit the mark in some areas. Miscasting was one major problem: Hopkins, playing a Southern rebel spy posing as a song and dance gal in Union-held Virginia City, looked far too prissy for the role; the part called for a more upfront, assertive actress along the lines of Binnie Barnes or Ann Sheridan. And Humphrey Bogart's Mexican bandit chief proved conclusively that Bogie was completely out of his depth in Westerns, as was his old sparring partner James Cagney. Scott (Ronald Reagan was first put forward for the part) appeared ever so slightly uneasy, locking horns with a flamboyant Flynn on full throttle (why Flynn didn't make more Westerns—only eight in his career—is a mystery). Compared to his

Randolph Scott and Humphrey Bogart hand off the money in *Virginia City*.

assertive Wyatt Earp in *Frontier Marshal*, Scott's unsympathetic role seemed muted and stilted, as though the actor was aware that little personal headway was being made in the genre he was to dominate in future movies. Besides, Flynn and Curtiz had already scored five massive box-office smashes with *Captain Blood* (1935), *The Charge of the Light Brigade* (1936), *The Adventures of Robin Hood* (1938), *The Private Lives of Elizabeth and Es*sex (1939) and *Dodge City* (1939), each budgeted at between $1,300,000 and $2,000,000. This big-scale, equally expensive Western was Flynn's show; he was the bankable movie star here and Scott, like other cast members, knew it.

Scott travels to boomtown Virginia City to ferry out a fortune in gold from under the noses of the Yankees. Hopkins is there to spy on Union activities and Flynn, an intelligence officer recently escaped from Libby Prison in Richmond (where he met Scott), also turns up with partners Alan Hale and Guinn "Big Boy" Williams (a great double-act from these two stalwarts). Hopkins falls for Flynn (what actress didn't at the time!) and Scott yearns for the girl as well; meanwhile, Bogart and his guerrillas are enlisted by the Rebels to attack the Union garrison as a diversion for 10 wagons masquerading as an immigrant train to leave town, the gold hidden on a couple of them. The middle section of *Virginia City* becomes bogged down in a series of dance hall routines, the endeavors of Flynn to discover the Rebels' hideout and their plans for the gold, plus the on-off romance between Flynn and Hopkins, and Hopkins and Scott. Once the wagons are on the move, Curtiz picks up the pace, we are in the great outdoors, and it's a case of whether Scott and the Rebels can make it to Richmond with both the Union soldiers and Bogart's gang in pursuit. In a thundering climax, Scott is shot dead when Bogart

and his bandits attack the wagons; Flynn buries the gold under tons of rock, having a degree of sympathy with the Confederates; and Bogart is gunned down as the Union cavalry come to the rescue of the wagon train. Court-martialed for perceiving to change sides, Flynn avoids execution when Hopkins pleads his case with Abraham Lincoln, by which time the war is over. In the closing moments, Flynn and Hopkins (who finally looks happy, having bagged the man of her dreams) are reunited to start a new life together.

Admittedly, there's action and incident a'plenty in *Virginia City* (originally released in Sepiatone), but viewed as a whole, the picture does have its share of lumpy moments. For Flynn worshippers, the film is top-notch fare, no two ways about it; for Scott buffs, be content to see the actor play second fiddle to a true Hollywood legend and be happy with that.

Scott was back to top billing in Universal's *When the Daltons Rode* (1940), directed by George Marshall, playing lawyer Tod Jackson, a childhood friend of the Dalton family who becomes embroiled in their infamous exploits when the gang embarks on a series of train and bank robberies. Not sporting a gun and holster, not firing a single shot, slugged without putting up much of a show *and* wearing a suit throughout, one might be forgiven for thinking that Scott, in this movie, had gone soft on us. Not only that, but his character is absent a lot of the time in the picture's second half, the dynamic pairing of Broderick Crawford and Brian Donlevy, two of the Dalton brothers, taking center stage. Universal's unofficial riposte to Fox's *Jesse James* suffered from the standard '40s malaise of introducing a wealth of quirky characters in the first 20 minutes at the expense of action, including bumbling buffoon Andy Devine, plagued by woman trouble, the Dalton boys' old Ma (Mary Gordon), Edgar Buchanan in a bit role as narrator and two gals, one good-time, the other bad-time. Once the Daltons go on a rampage and

Scott becomes smitten by Crawford's girlfriend (Kay Francis), the pace heats up, with plenty of stunt-work (Yakima Canutt perfecting his "crawling under a moving stagecoach" turn) and blazing gunplay. Scott not only has to fend off a bruising Crawford for stealing his girl, but also find out who is the brains behind the Kansas Land and Development Company, busy grabbing land from the farmers, a catalyst for the Daltons becoming outlaws. Crooked George Bancroft is the culprit, shot by Crawford in a blood and thunder climax when the gang are ambushed and wiped out to a man, while robbing Coffeyville's First National Bank. Scott, in the end, marries Francis.

When the Daltons Rode, in some ways, didn't play to Scott's best strengths—it was burly Crawford who dominated the proceedings, upstaging all around him (with the exception of Donlevy). In addition, the movie was a might disorganized in the middle section (as in the brawling courtroom scene), Scott flitting in and out of the scenario, odd when you consider he received top billing. But it's still a stirring, old-fashioned '40s horse opera and would have looked even better in color. It's just a pity that, in this instance, Randy wasn't allowed to flaunt his true mettle.

Fritz Lang's *Western Union* (Fox 1941) had Scott teaming up with Robert Young in a story set in 1861. The Western Union Company is building a telegraph line between Omaha, Nebraska and Salt Lake City, Utah, hampered by Sioux Indians and rustlers. Fresh from his triumph with Fox's *The Return of Frank James* (1940), German/Austrian director Lang directed this exciting Zane Grey opus soaked in cinematographer Edward Cronjager's rich Technicolor hues, making the most of Arizona's eye-catching House Rock Canyon formations and Utah's arresting Kanab area. Scott was second billed to Robert Young and felt hard-done by, a travesty in his book; this was his picture, redeeming himself after his wishy-washy showing in *When the Daltons Rode* and playing a much stronger character than Young's dandyish surveyor. Scott is Vance Shaw, a tough bank robber looking for a new chance in life, joining with Dean Jagger's outfit, which is attempting to supply a telegraph line over country plagued by marauding Sioux. He soon falls under the spell of Jagger's perky blonde sister, Virginia Gilmore, as does Young, leading to a friendly rivalry between the pair.

Randolph Scott (middle) and Robert Young (right) wait nervously in *Western Union* **(1941).**

Among a strong cast, Chill Wills plays the foreman responsible for keeping his rowdy workforce in check, John Carradine stars as a doctor and old-timer Slim Summerville is a hoot as a cowardly cook, petrified of Redskins and forced to go along for the ride. To add to the troubles, Scott's brother in the movie, glowering Barton MacLane, whose character participated in the bank robbery involving Scott, is inciting trouble by getting his gang to masquerade as Indians, rustling horses and selling them back to Jagger at a profit; the outlaw is also a Confederate sympathizer, training his cohorts in guerrilla tactics and planning to burn the Western Union main depot to the ground out of spite. A potent, escapade-packed brew indeed, concocted with a great deal of panache by Lang, the movie benefiting enormously from David Buttolph's bombastic score.

Western Union was the first occasion that Scott had bumped into producer Harry Joe Brown, later to take up an important position in the actor's future projects. Here, the Scott image as recognized by the moviegoing public was getting nearer to the hard-as-nails roles that he would perfect from *Abilene Town* onward; unusually in a Scott Western, he dies, shot by MacLane in a street gunfight before his evil brother is finished off by Young. The film ends with an exquisite sunset panoramic shot of a line of telegraph poles fading into the distant Utah hills, a fitting final frame to a glorious, somewhat brushed-aside '40s Technicolor Western that deserves further recognition.

Scott's next Western, *Belle Starr*, was produced by Fox in 1941 in an attempt to capitalize on up-and-coming screen queen Gene Tierney's sultry sex appeal; he shared top billing with her. However, the actress, in her fourth film, must have spent too much time studying Vivien Leigh's melodramatic Oscar-winning performance as Scarlett

O'Hara in *Gone with the Wind*; her over-theatrical playing as Southern gal-turned-bandit showed up her inexperience in a heavy-handed post-Civil War Western made by the company on the back of *Jesse James*' success. Also hindering the production was Alfred Newman's noisy score, complete with an abundance of Dixieland leitmotifs; played without a break throughout, this was a classic example of too much music spoiling the broth. Rich Technicolor compensated for the portrayal of stereotypical blacks toiling for their mistress in various plantations. Tobacco-chewing Chill Wills hogged the camera while Scott was slightly wooden as Confederate rebel Sam Starr, the man Tierney latches on to; in the acting stakes, it has to be said, he came off second best to Dana Andrews' Yankee major, Tierney's other love interest.

After Yankees burn her house to the ground for harboring rebel captain Scott, Southern belle Tierney joins the Confederate's band of renegades and becomes an outlaw on the run. Emoting like mad, the fiery lass ignores the fact that the Confederacy has lost ("It hasn't ended for me," she pouts, defiantly), joins Scott's guerrillas and becomes a rootin' shootin' wildcat, robbing trains, running off carpetbaggers, marrying her hero after a spot of tease ("Keep your filthy hands offa me!" the vixen shouts at Scott with a grin on her heavily made-up face) and finally getting shot down at the age of 41 while riding to warn Scott and his men of an ambush.

A stodgy, darkly lit movie, *Belle Starr* suffers terribly from Tierney's unconvincing turn and disjointed action sequences. It fails to involve and Randy doesn't look very happy as the rebel leader either. A case, for Scott at least, of two steps forward, one step back.

Scott returned to Universal in 1942 to film version number four of the old Rex Beach pulp novel *The Spoilers*, second billed to Marlene Dietrich but appearing in the credits above John Wayne, a point that Wayne didn't take too lightly. In the Klondike town of Nome, 1900, a saloon owner is wooed by two men, one a mine owner (Wayne), the other the brains behind a gang of claim-jumpers (Scott, a baddie for a change). The much vaunted five-minute punch-up between Wayne and Scott occurs in the movie's final stages; what leads up to it is a flimsy plot concerning the duo's battle for the affections of Marlene Dietrich and untrustworthy gold commissioner Scott's attempts to steamroll over the local miners by challenging the legality of their claims. He bites off more than he can chew when he questions the right for Wayne to work the Midas Mine; Wayne also has his hands full with sassy Margaret Lindsay, who wants the hunk for a husband. With Lindsay ready to dig her claws in, who will Dietrich choose—philandering Wayne or swindling Scott?

Wayne made 47 Westerns prior to this one (mostly B-programmers), Scott (playing Alexander McNamara) 22. Compared to Scott's forceful presence, exuding silky smooth menace, the Duke appeared too casual, still not quite the macho-man he would morph into. It's well documented that the two actors didn't hit it off and in some instances it showed on screen: Scott simply out-performed him, something which didn't often happen in a Wayne picture. The film successfully recreated the muddy streets and bustling atmosphere of an Alaskan gold mining town and, apart from the prolonged slugging match, contained a terrific slice of excitement in which Wayne and his followers use a locomotive to smash down barricades erected by Scott to prevent access to their property. In addition, composer Hans J. Salter, taking time off from his Universal horror pictures, contributed a fine score and silent star Richard Barthelmess, as Dietrich's second-in-command, put in one of his last screen appearances. But director Ray Enright spent an inordinate amount of time in the first half shooting Dietrich's legendary profile in soft focus (the actress virtually reprised her role from 1939's *Destry Rides Again*), while the frequent romantic interludes stalled the pace. *The Spoilers* isn't classic Scott, or even classic Wayne, and it's interesting to note that Dietrich, Scott and Wayne did it all over again in Universal's *Pittsburgh*, released a few months later. But you could denote a certain amount of gravity creeping into Scott's performances; he was shrugging off the light comedic roles, getting ready to prove that what Wayne, Cooper and Fonda could do, he could manage just as well, and quite often better.

Columbia Pictures and Harry Joe Brown feature heavily in Randolph Scott's '50s register of action pictures. *The Desperadoes* (1943) saw Columbia, Brown and Scott all working together on a movie that could have turned out slightly better than the finished product. We're in Utah, 1863. During a gold strike, the unscrupulous manager of the Clanton Bank in Red Valley arranges for cash to be stolen by outlaws, paying back 50% of the loot to satisfy customers but keeping the remainder for himself and his partners in crime, raking in a hefty $80,000 profit. The company's first Technicolor feature, adapted from a Max Brand novel, teamed Scott with a young Glenn Ford, old buddies pitted against one another; Scott is Sheriff Steve Upton, Ford a fugitive with a $10,000 bounty on his head. While one's eyes were treated to some gorgeous color photography, shot around California's Simi Valley region, the overall scheme was weighed down by a top-heavy plot that slowly, and not very expertly, unwound, with a multitude of characters nursing hidden motives tangling themselves up with their neighbors' comings and goings. Porter Hall played the devious bank manager, in league with outlaw leader Bernard Nedell and cantankerous Edgar Buchanan; Ford, after stealing Scott's horse, is framed for the murder of three men during a bank holdup and falls for stable girl Evelyn Keyes, deciding he wants to go straight; Claire Trevor is in on the act, a saloon/hotel owner known as "The Countess" whose right-hand man, Guinn "Big Boy" Williams, messes around with nitroglycerin; and veteran Raymond Walburn's judge can't make up his mind which side he's on. *The Desperadoes* turned out to be a plot-driven oater and a mighty confusing one at that, the only main action sequence coming in the final stages: A herd of stampeding horses causes bedlam in the town, followed by a gun battle in the saloon marred by the bartender acting like a clown, dodging the bullets and trying to save his glasses from damage. Nedell and his gang are blasted to bits by Williams' explosives and Buchanan shoots Hall, ending up behind bars. Scott, wrongly imprisoned, is released, and Ford marries Trevor.

For a supposedly uncomplicated cowboy picture, *The Desperadoes* was a little too slack and wordy in parts (John Leipold contributed a boisterous score), with Ford slightly juvenile in his role. Scott, though, was edging ever closer toward that Westerner persona that audiences would identify him with and he brought some semblance of seriousness to the overheated shenanigans. Scott, above all others, stood out.

Great things were about to happen in the Western sphere for Scott; he was forging ahead in the genre, almost, at this point in time, out there on his own, with Errol Flynn's rousing $2,000,000 *They Died With Their Boots On* (Warner Bros. 1941) the only picture of its type of any note when compared with what else was out on the circuits around 1941-1943: *Arizona Roundup* (Monogram), *Bad Men of Thunder Gap* (Alexander-Stern Productions), *The Ghost Rider* (Monogram) and *The Kansan* (Harry Sher-

Gypsy Rose Lee and Randolph Scott in *Belle of the Yukon* (1944)

man Productions), all B-fodder theater-fillers. And the welter of Western chapterplays continued unabated, passing Scott by: The *Billy the Kid* series, the *Range Busters* serials, the *Lone Rider* serials and *The Three Mesquiteers* serials. But before those great things got underway, he starred in the downright peculiar *Belle of the Yukon* (International Pictures Inc., 1944), his one Western that, by a hair's breadth, just about manages to escape falling into the category of "turkey."

During the Canadian gold rush, "Honest" John Calhoun runs the local emporium becoming owner of the Malemute Bank, even though, in reality, he's a con man known as Gentleman Jack, wanted by the Seattle police. In a gaudy, stage-bound musical burlesque containing no storyline to speak of, Scott belatedly enters the frame 15 minutes in with the look of a man who wishes he could turn on his well-polished boot heels and walk straight off set, pronto. A great cast including legendary stripper Gypsy Rose Lee, glowing Dinah Shore (Mrs. George Montgomery), Guinn "Big Boy" Williams and Robert *King Kong* Armstrong wade through turgid sketches based on misconceptions and the fact that Scott (romancing the statuesque Lee) and his oddball entourage are supposed to be incognito while running a riotous dance hall and defrauding the town's miners of their cash. William Marshall, mooning over love-struck Shore, is also on the run from the police; villainous Armstrong plays a gambler waiting for his chance to waltz off with the bank's stash of gold dust; Victor Kilian is a bogus nutty professor specializing in weather forecasts, and bumbling old-timer Charles Winninger sets his eyes on matronly Florence Bates in a vain attempt at injecting some romantic comedy. The other vain attempt by director/producer William A. Seiter is trying to convince us that screen heavy

Williams could play comedy, especially in his Marx Brothers–type skits with dullard Bob Burns; he couldn't, and the end result is a disaster. Even Johnny Burke and Jimmy Van Heusen's tunes, well below their normal high standards, are, in fact, virtually forgettable, as sung by Shore and Lee in four lengthy musical interludes. What salvages this plot-less mishmash, designed no doubt to cheer up wartime audiences, is the bold use of Technicolor and Mary Wills' flamboyant costume designs (apart from Scott's hideous baggy striped trousers), plus Don Loper's energetic dance numbers. The film ends with the chorus line doing the high-kicking cancan.

All hustle and bustle with nowhere to go, *Belle of the Yukon*, as mindless as popular entertainment can get, is quite possibly the '40s worst-ever conceived musical (alongside the '30s worst conceived, *The Road to Reno*—and Scott has the dubious honor of starring in both). Such productions brought to a temporary halt Scott's aspirations to become a fully-fledged cowboy star. It was a major dip in his prodigious output and marked the end of a particular phase in his career. The next chapter in the actor's cinematic life would prove to be the launch pad to a string of Scott classic Westerns, beginning with *Abilene Town* in 1946. He had paid his dues—his time had now come.

Scott had no Westerns released in 1945, his two productions from this year being RKO-Radio's *China Sky* and Miracle's *Captain Kidd*. Toward the end of the year, he began filming on United Artists' *Abilene Town*, his own landmark movie, the one that finally reinforced the public's conception of him as a tough Westerner, now able to sell the picture off his own name alone and receiving top billing for his efforts. *Abilene Town* was to Scott what *Stagecoach* had been to John Wayne, a pivotal turning point from which he would never look back. The Randolph Scott Western was born—25 had preceded this one, some great, others not so good, but all had guided the actor to this next highly productive stage in his career. Scott had at last found his métier; with the exception of Fox's *Home, Sweet Homicide* (1946) and Miracle's *Christmas Eve* (1947), Westerns were his mainstay, right up to his final celluloid appearance as a cowpoke, 1962's *Ride the High*

Randolph Scott, Ann Dvorak and Edgar Buchanan in *Abilene Town* (1946)

Country. At this particular juncture in Hollywood's long history, Randolph Scott was indisputably the Western's leading figurehead.

Abilene Town (United Artists, 1946), directed by the reliable and underrated Edwin L. Marin, is the decisive moment in Scott's movie career that finally cemented his persona as a Western man of action. Swaggering through the hard-edged activity with all the calm assurance of an actor who has finally found his main niche in life, this was the movie that made you say, "I'm off to see a Randolph Scott Western" instead of, "I'm off to see a Western with Randolph Scott in it." An uncompromisingly dark and violent study of frontier law for its time set in Kansas, 1870, Scott, playing tough marshal Dan Mitchell, shirked by the townsfolk and spineless sheriff Edgar Buchanan, exuded command and respect, a fearless town tamer not afraid to wade into a saloon full of ruffians and use his gun, as much a lowdown killing hombre as they were (as Rhonda Fleming points out to him). "Real meanness comes natural" he growls, ordering the saloons and gambling dens closed down to prevent chaos when Dick Curtis and his cow punchers ride into town, intent on wrecking the joint in drunken revelry. Similar in tone to *High Noon* (Scott even looks and dresses like Gary Cooper), the odds of keeping the peace are stacked up against Scott: Saloon owner Richard Hale puts business before everything else, siding with the cattlemen; the locals argue that the cowboys bring prosperity to the town, despite their roughhouse antics; dancer/singer Ann Dvorak, in love with Scott, is infuriated by his strict enforcement methods, not wanting him shot, but not willing to give up her act to cozy up with him; shopkeeper's daughter Fleming also pleads for the marshal to quit, afraid for his safety; Buchanan is a hard-drinking fraudster; and

gunslinger Jack Lambert is out for Scott's blood. To make matters worse, homesteaders, led by Lloyd Bridges, pitch camp on property that Curtis sees as his ("This is cattle country!"), so a range war develops between the two factions, Scott's sympathies lying with the newcomers in the dispute.

"We'll tear this town apart," storms Curtis, intent on allowing his rowdy cowhands to let off steam, no matter what Scott says or does. Meanwhile, after being kicked yet again in the shins by fiery Dvorak (the actress possessed a lovely pair of legs!), Scott's caveman approach to calm her down is to tell her, "What you need is a ride in the hills," and then he kisses her passionately. In an incident-packed finale, stampeding cattle flatten barbed wire barricades erected by Bridges and trample over the homesteaders' land and wagons, seven killed as a result. Curtis and his buckaroos rampage through Abilene, causing mayhem; the cattle boss is gunned down by Scott and, defeated, the rest of the crew are sent packing by the settlers in a face-off confrontation. Bridges gets Fleming, while the ravishing Dvorak decides to jettison her scanty dance costumes, don a kitchen apron and play house with Scott.

Gunfire heard during a church service at the beginning emphasized the good versus evil aspects of the dense plot; *Abilene Town*, the first of seven oaters Scott made with director Marin, was an adult-orientated Western with depth, centering on divided loyalties, Scott just as ruthless as the men he was after. "You took this job because it's fun," cries Fleming, horrified at the callous way her tarnished hero shoots Lambert in the back as he flees on horseback. The timid townsfolk can't make up their minds whether to back their elected marshal or give in to greed; Buchanan blunders his way through the violence, avoiding gunplay at all costs and takes credit where it isn't due; and, against

Ann Dvorok and Randolph Scott get into a romantic mood in *Abilene Town*.

type, Scott winds up with the town's bad dame, not goody two-shoes Fleming. Scott hit pay dirt with *Abilene Town*, the film setting the seal on everything he did from this moment on. It's amazing to see the authority he carries in all his scenes compared to his previous roles in Westerns when, in some instances, he was simply going through the motions, albeit in a professional manner. *Variety* enthused "Vigorous ... entertaining." Cinematically speaking, he had come of age. The Randolph Scott cycle of Westerns, as fans would later perceive them, started right here!

The question arises—could Wayne, Flynn, Cooper, Fonda or Stewart have carried off *Abilene Town* with the same *savoir faire* that Scott managed so adroitly? Flynn, no. He was far too showy, not one for understatement. Stewart was a might homespun and lacked, at the time, gravitas, as did Cooper. Fonda maybe—he brought a similar kind of quiet deadly charm to his Wyatt Earp in *My Darling Clementine*, released the same year as *Abilene Town*. Wayne was later to perfect this "lawman versus town" role, most notably in Howard Hawks' *Rio Bravo*, but didn't figure in a single Western during 1946, his next the romantic *The Angel and the Badman* in 1947; he only took off on the Western stage in 1948 in the first of John Ford's cavalry trilogy, RKO's *Fort Apache*. So it goes without saying that Randolph Scott was the Western's principal player at this time, with *Abilene Town* the archetypal '40s Western. Why the actor's output from the 1940s still remains hard to recall by many aficionados can be put down, to a certain extent, to Scott's shunning the Hollywood glamour scene. He tended to avoid the movie gossip/celebrity social network (unlike Flynn, Wayne or, at first, Montgomery), preferring the quiet life to the partying and roistering, staying out of the headlines. Perhaps this aversion to self-publicity

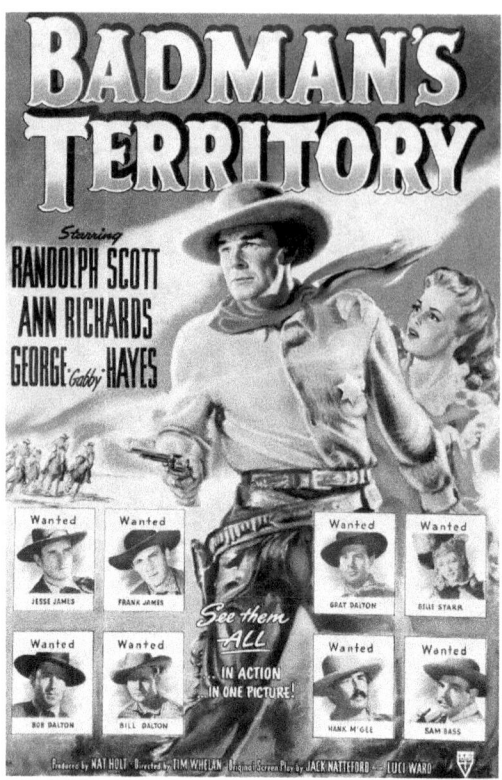

contributed to his not becoming so well known in the eyes of filmgoers. Scott was content to just get on with it without fuss or bother, leaving in his wake a far worthier, and more diverse, retinue of Westerns other, bigger names had not managed so far to do.

Scott moved over to RKO-Radio in 1946 for the first of three *noir*-type black-and-white movies made for them in the latter part of the decade, the first of which was Tim Whelan's *Badman's Territory*. In a strip of land not designated as a state, the town of Quinto, the self-proclaimed "Outlaw Capital," has become the haunt of outlaw gangs used to getting their own way with no interference from lawmen—until Marshal Mark Rowley appears on the scene. Well, if Universal-International, in 1944, could gather together the Frankenstein monster, the Wolf Man, Dracula and assorted mad doctors for one of their monster rallies (*House of Frankenstein*), RKO could rope in the James gang, Belle Starr, Sam Bass and the Daltons and house them under one roof, as it were. Scott played a marshal seeking out his wounded brother (James Warren), who is lying low with Frank and Jesse James in Quinto. Taking off his badge but not denying he's a peacemaker, Scott soon has the obligatory two women on his tail: Ann Richards, a newspaper editor, hell-bent on purging the town of its criminal element, and Isabel Jewell as tomboy Belle Starr. Aided and hindered in equal turns by grumpy old sidewinder George "Gabby" Hayes, Scott becomes embroiled in a convoluted storyline taking in a train and bank robbery, a tussle with Nestor Paiva's Sam Bass over stolen stake money bet on a horse race, unhappy Indians, the fight to get the territory legislated with Oklahoma and adversary Morgan Conway, a vicious sheriff employing heavy-handed methods, assigned to bring law and order to Quinto *and* arrest Scott for supposedly siding with the bandits. And, as in *Abilene Town*, the town's leaders, headed by Richard Hale and Ray Collins, are only too content to tolerate the bad guys' behavior if it brings in cash to replenish their coffers.

Westerns of the '40s differentiated from the '50s output in as much that they tended to concentrate their action more within the confines of a town occupied by a myriad of characters; dramas within a Western setting. From 1950 onwards, the cowboy movie moved outdoors, taking greater advantage of the West's magnificent natural rugged scenery, and, by and large, was shot in color. In addition, '50s Westerns pulled no punches and were a lot leaner and concise. *Badman's Territory* was no exception to the '40s rule; at 97 minutes, the film was a tad too lengthy, losing pace in the middle section and

becoming a little too light-hearted for its own good. Hayes overdid the comedy act to the point of annoyance—after all, he *was* supposed to be in a town where many of the West's most notorious killers roamed. Richards, complete with clipped English accent, paled beside Jewell's feisty Belle Starr but still managed to grab Scott in the end; it was left to Scott to bring some much-needed sobriety to a sometimes meandering narrative where townsfolk and villains drifted in and out of one scene after another, carrying the picture on his own back. This film becomes a decent old-time horse opera that just missed out on classic status.

The second of the RKO trio, *Trail Street* (1947), featured Scott as infamous lawman Bat Masterson, hired by the mayor of Liberal, Kansas to protect the town by getting rid of its rowdier elements, brought about by a continuing dispute between cattlemen and wheat farmers. A fast-moving, formulaic and talkative picture, *Trail Street* trotted out the old well-worn yarn of trail herders versus farmers. Scott's given the task of preventing the farming community from being railroaded out of the area by cattle chief Steve Brodie and his bullying gang; strangely, Scott doesn't appear until 18 minutes in, coming to the aid of Robert Ryan in a street brawl. Ryan (one of the very few times in his career that he played a good guy) is buying up land left by the disheartened farmers, but only in an attempt to prevent Brodie from doing the same and owning the entire territory so that he can drive his cattle through without hindrance. Scott's pragmatic stance quickly establishes law and order, laying down a "No Guns" policy and arresting two of Brodie's gun hawks on a charge of murder. Holding up the flow somewhat is a complicated romantic entanglement: Singer Anne Jeffreys loves Brodie; winsome Madge Meredith (who hates Kansas) has fallen for Ryan; Brodie wants Meredith for himself and Scott

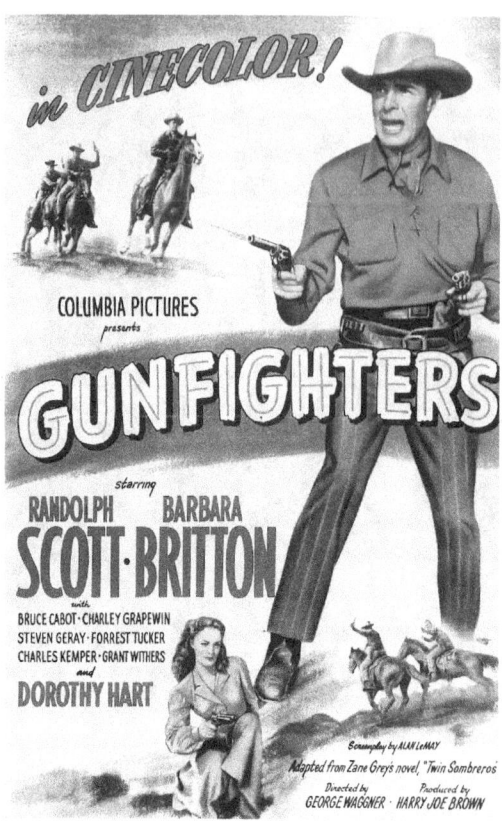

fancies Jeffreys. Add to this a semi-comic turn from George "Gabby" Hayes as Scott's reluctant deputy, a subplot involving the search for a strain of wheat that will adapt to the harsh Kansas summers, two musical turns and a slimy, overweight villain in Billy House's saloon owner—and we are left with a bit of a mixed Western bag that livens up in the second half, culminating in a fantastic nighttime shoot-out in which everyone gets his or her just deserts, including the unfortunate Jeffreys. The movie ends on an amusing note (it shouldn't have): Hayes' cousin, Brandyhead Jones (played by Hayes), who the whiskery chump has been gabbing on about for the entire film's length, arrives on the stage, much to the consternation of Hayes after Scott, mission accomplished, rides off to pastures new. This is a solidly crafted oater from Ray Enright (he directed five Scott Westerns), backed by Paul Sawtell's fine score, which could have done better featuring more prominently the man who, after all, received star billing.

Columbia's 1947 release, *Gunfighters* (aka *The Assassin*), was the picture that resulted in Harry Joe Brown and Scott getting their heads together and forming a production partnership, this the first Scott/Brown effort issued under the Producers-Actors banner. First meeting on the set of *Western Union* and again on Columbia's *Desperadoes*, the pair's successful collaboration, following *Gunfighters*, carried on through a further 16 Columbia cowboy movies, jointly produced by Scott and Brown via the auspices of Producers-Actors Productions and the Scott/Brown organization. A thoughtful, adult-oriented Western, more '50s in outlook than '40s (Alan Le May's screenplay was adapted from Zane Grey's novel *Twin Sombreros*), *Gunfighters* kicks off in fine fettle, a darkly shot sequence placed behind the credits in which Scott (as Brazos Kane, a renowned gunman) is called on to draw by a rival gunman. Scott wins the challenge, decides he's had enough of killing, hangs up his pistols and rides west, becoming framed in the murder of a best friend found shot near Charles Grapewin's ranch in a range dispute. The culprit is Bruce Cabot, the resident heavy at the nearby Banner Ranch and, very soon, Scott not only has to prove his innocence to avoid a hanging but fend off the attentions of sisters Dorothy Hart and Barbara Britton, daughters of Grift Barnett, the Banner Ranch's owner.

What *Gunfighters* lacks, until 60 minutes has gone by and Scott straps on Grapewin's pistols after Forrest Tucker blasts to death the kindly rancher, is full-blooded excitement. Scott actually soliloquizes over his frame of mind and what the future holds for him

Sisters match their wits and charms for the love of gunfighter Randolph Scott!

in a few voice-over narrated scenes not particularly handled well by director George Waggner, and the confusion over which sister is which, Scott mixing them up, really belongs in another picture. On the plus side, Cabot and Tucker make a terrific pair of gun-happy toughs, the vivid color photography lights up the screen (as does the rugged location shooting) and Rudy Schrager's music runs the gamut from rousing to romantic. The film also verges on the sadistic at times, reflecting changing censorial points of view over cinematic violence: Scott walks into an eerily quiet town waiting in readiness for him ("A wake for a man that ain't dead yet."), corners the shady town sheriff (in Barnett's pocket) and first shoots his right hand, then his left leg until, with a promise to shoot the sheriff's left elbow, his cowering victim spills the beans on the murder. And the final showdown between Cabot, Tucker and Scott is a humdinger, redeeming the slackness of narrative drive elsewhere—"Anytime you feel lucky," states Scott to smirking Forrest (who has a habit of stubbing out cigarettes on the palm of his left hand), before dropping him with a single bullet. Cabot arrives on the scene and Scott outguns him as well. Vengeance completed, Scott rides off to another soliloquy ("Try again. Some new place."), ditches his six-shooters and hitches up with Hart to start a new life.

Gunfighters, despite flaws (Scott and Harry Joe Brown didn't rate Waggner as the ideal man for the job), showed that the Western was beginning to shred its sometimes unsophisticated, rustic, character-led '40s skin by morphing into something tighter and meaner, as shown by the number of "A" ratings handed out by the strict British censor. As opposed to this rational change in outlook, cinematic showman Cecil B. DeMille's ponderous and patently unexciting $5,000,000 *Unconquered*, with Gary Cooper in the lead, was a throwback to the 1930s as far as Westerns went, even though it came out

Randolph Scott (holding pistol), Lon Chaney, Jr. (hovering in the back with a cigarette) and Barbara Britton, in *Albuquerque* (1948).

in the same year as *Gunfighters*. The adult Western, crammed with Freudian undertones and emotional hang-ups, was starting to emerge and grow up, with Scott as one of its figureheads.

Albuquerque (aka *Silver City*, Paramount, 1948), after the tough approach of *Gunfighters*, was a step backwards to '40s Western whimsy in many aspects. Scott returned to his former studio one last time to shoot this somewhat predictable actioner, predictable in as much that whereas *Gunfighters* drew attention to the raw edge that was to epitomize the '50s Western, *Albuquerque* was a throwback to the lightweight, folksy days of the early 1940s, complete with grizzled George "Gabby" Hayes going through his "darned varmint" shtick and the rascally cowpokes now looking slightly outdated. Once again, it was good gal (Catherine Craig) versus bad gal (Barbara Britton), Scott (as Cole Armin) coming to Craig's aid in the opening minutes: A stagecoach is robbed, Craig relieved of $10,000 and a passenger dies in the ensuing fracas. Scott's dishonest uncle, wheelchair-bound George Cleveland, is behind it all, in cahoots with iniquitous sheriff Bernard Nedell and his not-so-law-abiding men. Cleveland is trying to prevent Craig's brother, Russell Hayden, from setting up a rival business venture, transporting ore down hazardous mountain tracks in carts hauled by donkeys from two nearby prospects, Half-High Mine and Angel's Rest Mine, and offers his nephew a top job to stop the competition; Scott turns him down flat, returns the stolen money to Hayden and goes into partnership with him (Hayes is his "phantom" backer) under the aegis of the Wallace-Armin Freight Company, thus precipitating a series of confrontations between the two sides.

Filmed in bright, two-strip Cinecolor among Arizona's pink-striated canyons, Ray Enright's oater has a lot going for it: Lon Chaney, Jr., taking a break from horror roles, makes a great Western heavy, his lumbering *modus operandi* perfectly suited to his cigarette-smoking gang top dog; classy looking Britton plays a scheming two-timer to the hilt; child actress Karolyn Grimes is a cheeky delight as a little girl Scott rescues from a runaway stagecoach; Darrell Calker's lush score hits all the right notes and the picture climaxes in a fearsome shoot-out. But there's an abundance of too-obvious back-projected sequences which jar and the script (by Clarence Upson Young and Gene Lewis) fails to nail the narration as it should, leading to periods of *languor* and incorporating within its framework an intermittent sketch revolving around the shedding of Hayes' characteristic bushy whiskers. Scott doesn't get to wear a sidearm until the 40th minute and,

although shown to be a man of honor, could have been a bit tougher in his approach; hard case Chaney outshines him in this respect. Thought lost for many years, prints of this film have now become available, showing *Albuquerque* to be a colorful, reliable Western that, in some areas, vaguely disappoints ("Solid oater," said *Variety*).

Scott's second 1948 Western, Columbia's *Coroner Creek*, reached new and unexpected heights in excellence, a forerunner of things to come. Enright's revenge Western, the second Scott/Brown dalliance into Old West ethics, starts and ends in heartless fashion: George Macready and a bunch of Apaches bushwhack a stagecoach; Macready cold-bloodedly murders the drivers and passengers, steals the cash and abducts a woman on her way to marry Chris Danning, played by Scott. Three days later, she knifes herself to death. That very same knife causes the end of dead-eyed Macready. In the closing few minutes, Macready clambers up a ladder, Scott in pursuit; the rungs give way and he topples onto the blade, saving his nemesis the trouble of wasting bullets. Sandwiched between is the tale of how Scott locates his quarry and the confrontational methods he uses in running him into the ground.

Scott's a loner, remorselessly tracking down the man who, 18 months previously, held up a stagecoach, shot to death its occupants and caused his fiancée to kill herself. He's consumed by hatred, openly provoking Macready and his gunmen to draw on him. "His spirit is dead. You can see it in his eyes," states Russell Simpson to his daughter,

hotelier Marguerite Chapman. Chapman isn't the only woman in Scott's life—flighty ranch owner Sally Eilers, recently widowed, sets her sights on him, offering him the job of foreman, her land backing onto Macready's. Living off the stolen money, the oily rancher, when not physically abusing young wife Barbara Reed, orders Forrest Tucker and his boys to encroach upon Eilers' property, murder her hands and attempt to scare off Scott. A violent fistfight ensues, Tucker and Scott slugging it out; Tucker stamps on Scott's gun hand but he revives and reciprocates, crushing Tucker's hand after biting his arm and head-butting him, a savage five minutes summing up *Coroner Creek*'s underlying air of viciousness. Chapman is adamant to Scott that, "Your hatred may destroy Miles (Macready) but it can also destroy you," but the man is duty-bound to avenge his fiancée's suicide, relentless in his pursuit, and won't give way: "I've waited 18 months for this," he snarls. After shooting Tucker dead, Scott isn't averse to using one of Macready's accomplices as a human shield, Macready shooting his revolver into the hapless cowpoke before he falls onto the knife. Scott finally chooses Chapman to walk off with, man-hungry Eilers left to sort out her ranch and find a new feller to hitch up with.

Gruff Edgar Buchanan was hired to play yet another of his perfected next-to-useless sheriffs (he also perfected in his career the next-to-useless judge) in Macready's pocket because his daughter, Reed, is married to the reptilian thug; he pays with his life for seeing the error of his ways, shot by his employer for changing sides. The colorful scenery, filmed in the Red Rock Crossing region of Sedona, Arizona, was also given greater prominence, signifying the outdoor approach of the much-different 1950s Western—in fact, *Coroner Creek* embraces the '50s era of cowboy filmmaking more than the '40s, both in tone and adult subject matter. A slick, well-crafted cowboy movie blessed with a terse script by Kenneth Gamet (*Variety* thought his script "exceptional."), *Coroner Creek* was a change in the right direction over Scott's previous effort, *Albuquerque*; it's one of the top Westerns he made in the 1940s, proving to be a big financial hit for Columbia when first released.

1948 ended with Scott moving over to RKO-Radio for a third time, scoring a major hit with the magnificent *Return of the Bad Men*, an all-but-in-name follow-up to 1946's *Badman's Territory*, the second of the company's trio of *Bad Men* films (the third,

Best of the Bad Men, was released in 1951 with Robert Ryan in the lead). In Oklahoma 1889, former rancher, Texas Ranger and peace officer Vance Cordell is called upon by the military to be sworn in as Guthrie's new marshal when the town is threatened by some of the worst outlaw gangs in the West. More tightly structured than the first of the trio, Ray Enright's slam-bang oater, as historically inaccurate as they come (Billy the Kid, for instance, died in 1881), had the residents of Braxton, then Guthrie, up against the most fearsome bunch of desperadoes that ever rode together: Billy the Kid, the Daltons, the Younger Brothers, Wild Bill Doolin, the Sundance Kid, the Arkansas Kid and Wild Bill Yeager. This composite bunch of no-gooders robs banks, trains and stagecoaches with gay abandon, setting their sights on Guthrie's cash-rich bank presided over by none other than that troublesome old coyote, George "Gabby" Hayes, whose daughter, Jacqueline White, is due to marry Scott but has second thoughts when he's appointed town marshal—her first husband was a law officer killed in the line of duty. White then rapidly changes her mind when reformed outlaw Anne Jeffreys (Wild Bill Doolin's niece) declares her love for Scott, the lunkhead not cottoning on to the realization that both women (one saintly, one not so saintly) are fighting for his affections, as is the case in most of his Westerns.

Assisted by J. Roy Hunt's sharp black-and-white cinematography, Paul Sawtell's thundering score and first-rate production values, the director choreographs the helter-skelter engagements to perfection, ensuring that there isn't a single dull spot over the 90-minute running time. Of particular interest (and something of a revelation) is Robert Ryan's Sundance Kid, here portrayed as a bestial, black-clad psychopath. He shoots in the back, pumps Scott's unarmed Indian servant full of lead (a *noir*-ish moment if ever there was one, Ryan filmed from the rear, full frame), argues incessantly with boss Robert Armstrong (as Doolin) and brutally strangles Jeffreys before ending up in a bruising three-minute fistfight with Scott, after which he's shot dead. Ryan, snarling and spitting venom, is absolutely compelling in the part, one of the great Western villains of all time, the direct opposite to Robert Redford's roguish Sundance Kid in the 1969 *Butch Cassidy* picture. Apart from Ryan's hypnotic take on the Kid, the movie's other high spot is a daring nighttime raid on the outlaws' nest in the ghost town of Braxton, resulting in a prolonged gun battle in which Armstrong is captured. The rest of the gang split up, but Ryan and two men decide to take Scott on, leading to their eventual demise.

Enright is not afraid to use the oft-used '30s and '40s standby of soft focus in a couple of romantic interludes between Scott and White and, for once, Hayes tones down his "Old Windbag" act, presenting us with a less irritating characterization than normal, even though the movie finishes on an amusing note—Hayes ("Yes Siree Bob!") and his pal leave for California, the bank now in the hands of Scott and White, their unexpected wedding gift. The best of the Scott RKO Westerns, with the actor in commanding form, *Return of the Bad Men* has a frantic energy running through it plus a streak of meanness (mostly down to Ryan's star turn) uncommon in Westerns of this period. 1940s sagebrush sagas don't come any finer; judged against these standards, only Ford's *Fort Apache*, Howard Hawks' *Red River* and William A. Wellman's superb psychological Western, *Yellow Sky*, set in a desert ghost town, all issued in the same year, come close to Enright's feature in sheer visceral thrills and excitement.

It was a bit of a come down from Scott's two dazzling 1948 movies to the next Scott/Brown Columbia effort, *The Walking Hills* (1949), even though action director John Sturges was at the helm. Nine men and a woman search for a $5,000,000 fortune in gold bars, lost in 1852 when a wagon train became buried in an area of shifting sand dunes known locally as the Walking Hills. A modern-day Western running on similar lines to John Huston's *The Treasure of the Sierra Madre* (1948), Scott (as Jim Carey) received top billing but was content to share the acting kudos with a splendid ensemble cast which included cop John Ireland, prospector Edgar Buchanan, loose cannon Arthur Kennedy, fugitive William Bishop and one of Hollywood's most neglected actresses, the beautiful Ella Raines. Tautly scripted by Alan Le May, with the Death Valley and Lone Pine scenery benefiting greatly from Charles Lawton, Jr.'s crisp photography, Sturges' take on man's greed for gold was a talkative affair set in unusual locations, focusing on imploding relationships in addition to the tension generated by the treasure hunt itself. Ireland is tailing Bishop, who accidentally killed a man after a card game; Bishop was also romancing Raines at the time but ran out on her, as has on/off beau Scott, who seems more concerned over the state of his pregnant mare, about to give birth (this "looking after your horse" motif cropped up in many of Scott's features, illustrating his humane outlook toward man's four-legged friend). The drama is played out to the sound of Josh White singing a few blues songs, the glaring, forbidding landscape a stark

Randolph Scott gets rough in *The Walking Hills* (1949).

backdrop; fragmentary remains of the wagons are uncovered, but no gold is found, only empty boxes, Buchanan starting to doubt the gold's existence but resolved, like the rest, to carry on with the search. When Ireland shoots young Jerome Courtland by mistake in a tussle, Scott decides to show the twitchy agent who's head honcho: "If you've killed this boy, keep that gun handy," he warns him, later slapping headstrong Kennedy around the face because, "I ran out of words."

There's the nagging suspicion that *The Walking Hills* would have worked much better as a conventional Western rather than a contemporary one. A couple of flashbacks, detailing the Bishop-Raines affair, scupper the Spartan desert mood, and one can't help feeling that it would have been nice to see Scott wearing a gun and holster, dealing with troublesome duo Ireland and Kennedy in a more conventional manner rather than a fight with shovels. The ferocious sandstorm climax makes up for several lapses in dramatic vitality and, just when we thought there wasn't an ounce of gold in this godforsaken place (the storm uncovers the old wagons), wily Buchanan admits to finding one bag of the stuff. And Scott rides off, not with Raines (who follows after Bishop) but with his mare's newborn colt, an apt final salute to the one person among this disparate bunch to emerge with any integrity.

Many dismiss 20th Century Fox's *Canadian Pacific* (1949) as lightweight Scott, containing little of interest ("Vaudevillian and mediocre," said the *New York Times*). Yet this yarn concerning railroad surveyor Tom Andrews tasked with mapping out a route through British Columbia for the Canadian Pacific Railway in the 1870s, thwarted at every turn by Indians, a dishonest trading post owner and a rebellious crew, not to mention two

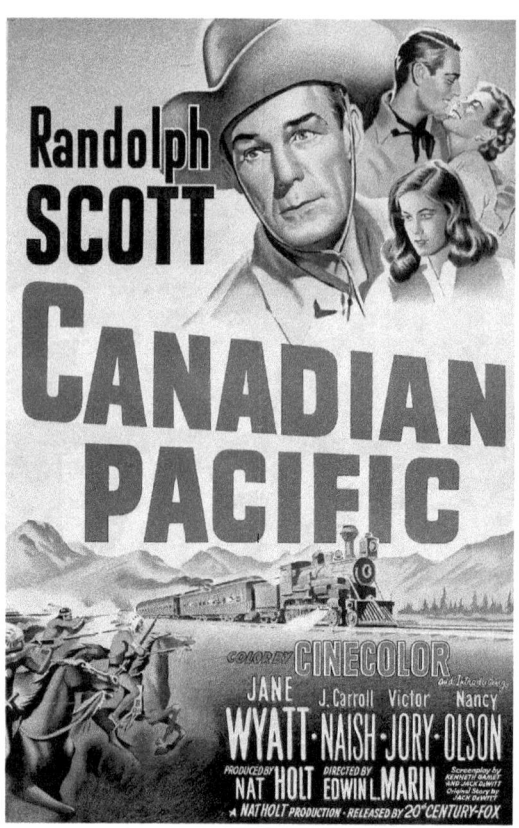

women vying for his favors, is something of a fun-packed thrill ride. Yes, Fox's noisy, frenetic remake of Cecil B. DeMille's 1939 production *Union Pacific* has had a bit of a bad press in recent film compendiums, but unfairly so. Not officially available on DVD, it admittedly contains two scenes that would have looked fine in a Bob Hope comedy Western, but not in a Randolph Scott Western: In one, Scott is handling boxes of dynamite that are detonated by a sniper, somehow escaping with only a head wound; in the other, J. Carrol Naish, Scott's sidekick, gives a group of Indians sticks of dynamite to smoke, the result total obliteration ("Danged fools smoked their heads off!"). But counteracting those rather silly episodes, we have Fred Jackman, Jr.'s sparkling photography bringing to vivid life the amazing topography of Alberta's Banff National Park, a lush Dimitri Tiomkin score, Scott in brown leathers (his rust-colored leather jacket would become a trademark of his up-and-coming Columbia Westerns) angrily rasping out a few choice one-liners, a great climactic Indian attack and villain Victor Jory at his mirthless best. *Canadian Pacific* has a lot to recommend to the Western fan; yes, it's different and not all that historically accurate, but it's nowhere near as dreadful as some critics suggest, and director Edwin L. Marin keeps the pace moving nicely. It's also one of only three major Westerns released during 1949, the others being John Ford's stirring tribute to the 7th Cavalry, *She Wore a Yellow Ribbon* and Scott's own *The Doolins of Oklahoma*.

Workmen on the line put their tools down in frustration; Scott, the man they all look up to, has been absent for too long, attempting to discover a suitable pass for the railway to progress beyond the Rockies. First seen strolling through brightly colored forests and wading across rapids, he arrives at the camp with the new route's details and promptly tells the owner, Robert Barrat, that he's quitting; he needs a break, some time off to continue his liaison with tomboy Nancy Olson. But when he finds out that Olson's father is in league with Jory, stirring up trouble with the Indians to prevent the railroad from forging ahead, determined that their string of trading posts should not suffer by the business the railway will bring in ("The iron monster will swallow up your lands!"), he decides to put his holiday on the back burner and prevent Jory from sabotaging the rail link. Complications in his love life arise with the arrival of prim and proper humanitarian doctor, Jane Wyatt, who abhors fighting and gunplay ("Violence breeds violence."), even more so when Scott informs her of his own way of handling troublemakers: "I break 'em apart. You put 'em back together." Uncaringly ditching Olson for Wyatt, Scott has to pacify the sullen crew (he demolishes the one and only saloon to prevent drunk and disorderly behavior), the action leading to a full-blown Indian uprising, the Redskins laying siege to the rail workers who have barricaded the Hospital carriage as a makeshift defense. Barrat and his men arrive in another locomotive, routing the attackers; Scott pursues Jory up to a ridge where the slimy one perishes under a burning tree branch. The final frame sees the Indians walking into camp and declaring peace, while Scott does the sensible thing in giving snooty Wyatt the heave-ho and taking up where he had left off with Olson, setting up house in those glorious woods.

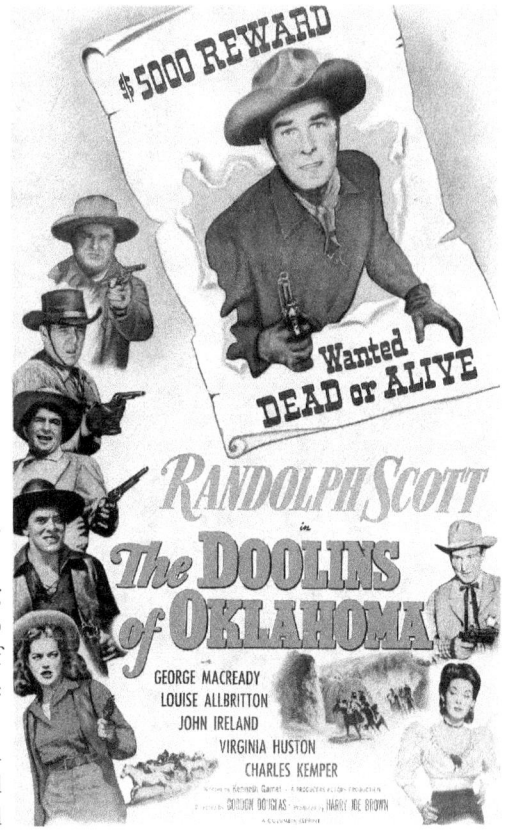

Scott underplays his heroics in this invigorating outdoor yarn but still remains the man in control, stoical and as hard as the spectacular rocky scenery. Offbeat and departing from the normal run of Scott Westerns from this late '40s period, *Canadian Pacific* is enjoyable, entertaining knockabout fodder for those fans who like their Western menu dished up straight without too much in the way of frills and deep, hidden meanings.

If *Canadian Pacific* is classed as lightweight, then Columbia's 1949 offering, *The Doolins of Oklahoma* (aka *The Great Manhunt*), is most definitely heavyweight. The fourth Producers-Actors production ranks as one of the '40s roughest, toughest "outlaws on the run" Westerns: Gordon Douglas' effectively-paced direction, showing flashes of *noir* in the more intimate interludes, moved the various incidents along at lightning speed, while the Scott/Brown ensemble of writer Kenneth Gamet, cinematographer Charles Lawton, Jr. and composer Paul Sawtell and George Duning ensured that what we had here was a future classic in the making. 1892: Gunman Bill Doolin, founding member of the Doolin gang, decides to settle down and go straight, but his former collaborators in crime trick him into taking up his old ways of bank and train robberies. Scott dominates as Doolin, head of the Doolins who sprung up in the aftermath of the James and Dalton Brothers' ill-famed exploits. Opening with an explosive ambush sequence outside the Coffeyville National Bank in which most of the Dalton mob are annihilated (replicating the climactic scene in *When the Daltons Rode* but more violently handled), Scott, a key member of the gang but not participating in the holdup, wanders into a

Randolph Scott engages in a grueling tug of war in *The Doolins of Oklahoma*.

saloon and is challenged by George Macready, playing (against type) a marshal. "I didn't get your name," asks Macready. "Didn't give it," snaps Scott, walking off. After gunning down the traitor who snitched on the Dalton bank raid, Scott forms his own band, superbly played by Noah Beery, Jr., John Ireland, Charles Kemper, Frank Fenton and Jock Mahoney. But after several successful robberies (mines, banks, safes, trains), Scott reckons it's time they split up and go to ground; meeting lovely Virginia Huston in Clayville's church has made the outlaw leader reconsider his life and all that it has to offer from the love of a good woman.

Douglas astutely draws the audience into Scott's short-lived domesticity without going all cutesy on us; Scott marries Huston under an assumed name (Bill Daley) but then has to admit to who he really is when Ireland and Fenton (posing as deputies) hand Huston a wanted poster on purpose to entice their leader back into a life of crime. Huston's father lays it on the line to Scott, pricking his conscience: "You're dead, Bill. I don't want my daughter married to a dead man. The only way to set her free is to ride out of her life," and when Scott does depart, Huston is told by her father, "He's gone. Forget Bill Daley. He was a man who never lived."

The action picks up, the outlaws always one step ahead of Macready and his posse. Escaping from Ingalls and other towns by the skin of their teeth and heading off into the Lone Pine wilds, Scott becomes increasingly disillusioned with his role ("He's as sour as vinegar," states Fenton) and misses the woman he left behind. The picture is

crammed full of altercations and characters (another lengthy shoot-out in a livery stable; Louise Allbritton as Ireland's fancy piece; feisty Dona Drake playing tomboy Cattle Annie), also allowing time to reflect on the passing of the Old West ("Men like you and I are becoming obsolete," mourns Beery, Jr. to Scott, the only two survivors of Scott's bunch). The inevitable tragic climax sees Scott sneaking into Clayville, screened from the lawmen by stampeding horses (a similar scene was used in *The Desperadoes*); after a brief reunion with his wife, he's riddled with bullets outside the church where he first met her, a noble death for a bad guy who was, at heart, on the side of the good. It's not too hard to guess where audiences' sympathies lay after Scott's demise—not with Macready and his deputies, that's for sure!

Scott bowed out of the 1940s on (for him) an inconsistent note with Fox's *Fighting Man of the Plains*, playing a wanted killer who once rode with Quantrill's guerrillas but, in 1872, takes up the post of town marshal in Lanyard, Kansas, under an assumed name, his dubious past soon catching up with him. Edwin L. Marin's energetic Western opens in breathless style, a five-minute montage of the Quantrill gang torching Lawrence in Kansas and rampaging across the countryside before calling it a day. Jim Dancer (Scott) mistakenly shoots the wrong man in a street battle; he was after the person who killed his brother but he guns down the father instead. Captured by James Millican from the Pleasanton Detective Agency, the pair are thrown into a raging torrent on a ferry crossing and the detective dies; gambler Victor Jory and girlfriend Jane Nigh appear on a stage, hack Millican's hand off to free Scott (he's handcuffed to the corpse and lost the key), leaving the outlaw free to adopt Millican's identity and push on to Lanyard where, after shooting dead an unruly cowpoke, he's given the job of marshal by the man he was supposed to have killed—the town's big white chief Barry Kelley.

EXHIBITOR'S CAMPAIGN BOOK

Fighting Man of the Plains is something of a ragbag, but diverting enough to please most Scott buffs. The two women featuring in Scott's troubled life are Nigh and Kelley's niece, Joan Taylor. Jory loves Nigh, but she's in love with Scott, who casts his beady eyes on Taylor. A fresh-faced Dale Robertson turns up as Jesse James, preventing his one-time associate from being lynched at the end by young neurotic gunslinger-cum-law officer Bill Williams, who steals every scene he's in. The old farmers versus railroad plot is thrown into the mix, with Kelley, setting up the Homestead Development Company, fanatical about owning so much property that he'll charge both cattlemen and railroad magnates exorbitant prices for herding cattle through his land, as well as demanding 25% of all gambling dues. Why Jory, who is aware of Scott's real name, should latch onto him and constantly tread in his footsteps like a lapdog isn't made clear: "Violence seems to follow you around," he remarks to the taciturn marshal, who later responds, "A man has to be good in a gunfight. He has to kill or be killed." Although Scott has tamed Lanyard, once the citizens are let in on the secret of who he is, all hell breaks loose and the town is in an uproar, but the killer-turned-lawman wins by the final reel: With help from Robertson and the Younger Brothers, Scott empties his revolver into Kelley and Williams after Jory has been brought down, and the curtain falls with Scott and Nigh wrapped in a loving embrace.

Backed by a noisy Paul Sawtell soundtrack, the play-it-by-numbers action in the movie is fast and furious (Scott breaking up a ruckus during a dance and jailing several troublemakers at once), the cowboy star looking suitably ill humored (and unshaven) throughout because of the effort in keeping up the pretence of his dual personality. It's not Scott's greatest piece of work, but good enough for aficionados. Unfortunately, as at the time of writing, all prints in Cinecolor appear to have vanished apart from an atrocious green-tinted issue of questionable quality. Monochrome DVD releases are more clearly defined, although far from perfect. Perhaps one day, fans will be treated to *Fighting Man of the Plains* in color, as it was supposed to be presented to the public.

Chapter 11
1950: Murphy Makes It Big

A new breed of Western motion picture mushroomed in the 1950s, far more muscular and violent in aspect than its predecessors, tending to base much of the narrative on the mental state of both hero and protagonist, the chief reason why, in the United Kingdom, many carried a restrictive (to cowboy-mad kids) "A" certificate. This gritty, psychological angle would culminate in Fox's 1958 release *The Fiend Who Walked the West*, a merging of Western and the then moneymaking psycho thriller that garnered an "X" rating in the United Kingdom, the film banned in some parts of Europe. Gordon Douglas' brooding, horror-*noir* oater showed just how radical the genre had become since the days of Roy Rogers, Hopalong Cassidy and Gene Autry entertaining the masses in their fancy outfits; now, these rather harmless-looking former heroes of the open range seemed to belong to another time and place, anachronisms at large in this fresher, sterner revisionist outlook. Without doubt, the 1950s saw the Hollywood Western flourishing as never before, in terms of superior product, public interest and box-office

A cute publicity photo of Audie Murphy and children on the set of *The Kid from Texas* (1950).

receipts—even a low-budget effort such as Lippert's *The Bandit Queen* (1950) had something in its creative body to recommend itself to the punter and made reasonable money. As was the case with horror, science fiction and fantasy, the 1950s gave birth to the Western boom. No other decade, before or since, has served the genre as well as this one. Adding several notches on the gun belt, the bar had been raised.

Scott was still (in Britain, at least) unaccountably classed as a B-movie Western star, but most of his prolific output during this hectic period, 26 Westerns, far outstripped those of the star names guaranteed to pull in the paying fans. Surprisingly, Wayne, looked upon as *the* big money-spinning cowboy star, only made five Westerns in the 1950s; Gary Cooper was in 11, Alan Ladd nine, Kirk Douglas seven, James Stewart seven, Burt Lancaster six, Richard Widmark six and Henry Fonda two. But whereas in the '30s and '40s Scott was one of Hollywood's main Western stars with little opposition, the explosion of cowboy pictures that took place in the '50s threw up plenty of rivalry as studios promoted a clutch of jobbing actors into the Western leading man role, albeit in low- to mid-budget oaters: Audie Murphy, Joel McCrea, George Montgomery, Rory Calhoun, Rod Cameron, Sterling Hayden, Stephen McNally, Dale Robertson, Jeff Chandler, John Payne, to name but a few. So in addition to Scott's 26 Westerns, George Montgomery made 24, Rory Calhoun 20, Joel McCrea 19, Audie Murphy 18, Rod Cameron 14, Sterling Hayden 14 and Stephen McNally 11. Scott, Montgomery, McCrea, Murphy, Calhoun, Cameron, Hayden and McNally, all lumped under the heading of "B-Western Movie Actor," therefore starred in, between them, nearly three times as many Westerns as the perceived eight giants of the genre (we can also add to these films the 15 Westerns Tim Holt made between 1950-1952, before he called a halt on his cowboy career). Yet today, people remember *Rio Bravo*, *High Noon*, *Shane*, *The Indian Fighter*, *The Man from Laramie*, *Vera Cruz*, *The Law and Jake Wade* and *Warlock* (and rightly so—all are superb examples of the genre). Scott's *Hangman's Knot*, Montgomery's *The Texas Rangers*, Calhoun's *Apache Territory*, McCrea's *The Tall Stranger*, Murphy's *Ride Clear of Diablo*, Cameron's *Wagons West*, Hayden's *Flaming Feather* and McNally's *Apache Drums* remain relatively unknown and tend to live in the shadow cast by big-bucks productions populated by actors of a much higher magnitude. Star quality, acting chops and those

Gale Storm and Audie Murphy (as Billy the Kid) as they appeared in *The Kid from Texas*.

hefty budgets had a lot to do with it, and who was or who wasn't under the glare of the celebrity flashlight also mattered, but there's no getting away from the fact that scores of medium-budget Westerns released in the 1950s by lower mortals such as the eight listed were every bit as good as those made and starring the eight higher Hollywood mortals. Scott, McCrea, Montgomery, Murphy et al. were just as vital to the Western during these glorious years as Wayne, Stewart and Cooper, and were just as good at acting within the Western setup—it's so easy to overlook the contributions made by these "lesser" actors when, collectively, they produced such a monumental body of work on much smaller budgets than the superstars were used to managing with.

The seven major studios latched onto the Western phenomenon with a vengeance, Columbia emerging top dog with a total of 86 cowboy flicks produced between 1950 and 1959. Second was Universal with 72, followed by United Artists (63), Warner Bros. (46), 20th Century Fox (44), Paramount (24) and MGM (22). Astonishingly, low-budget outfit Monogram knocked out 53 mostly hour-long Westerns from 1950 to 1952 before merging with Allied Artists, themselves responsible for a further 22. RKO-Radio, Republic Pictures and a plethora of independent studios (Howco International, Lippert, Astor, Empire, Wheeler, Commander Films) upped the figure to over 600, an indication of just how in-demand the Western was with postwar cinema audiences. This then was the hothouse climate into which Audie Murphy entered at the start of 1950 to commence his career as a cowboy star with Universal-International.

Audie Murphy's Billy the Kid becomes a precursor to the juvenile delinquent movies soon to storm Hollywood, with Murphy's moodiness and morality conflicts.

By the time Murphy hit box-office gold with *The Kid from Texas* in March 1950 (the movie blatantly cashed in on his fame as a wayward kid from Texas), Scott had starred in 74 movies including 36 Westerns; McCrea's total came in at 70 (11 Westerns if you include *Scarlet River* and *Barbary Coast*); and Montgomery's was 57, 30 of which were Westerns (the majority as a bit player). Yet despite this yawning gulf in acting pedigree, the baby-faced novice's Westerns for Universal in the 1950s (he made one for Columbia in 1957, *The Guns of Fort Petticoat*, and another for United Artists, *Cast a Long Shadow*, 1959) quickly became popular crowd-pleasers, up there with the Scotts, the McCreas and the Montgomerys, without the much younger main star having had the cinematic grounding that the others had toiled through. Like them, Murphy had no inflated illusions about Hollywood, the expected role of a movie star and the hedonistic way of life, preferring simple, outdoor pursuits to the partying, social scene (Montgomery's frenetic lifestyle had settled down a bit following his marriage to Dinah Shore). In his films, he tended, once in a while, to be acting out his own real-life situations, the determined youngster battling against obstructive authority that wins through in the end. Saddled with the "Kid" tag in most of his early pictures because of his youthful looks, Murphy at times appeared unsure of himself in the presence of his much stronger leading ladies; for instance, voluptuous Mari Blanchard looked as though she could eat him for breakfast in *Destry*. But his boyish charm usually got the gal, even though he sometimes appeared slightly dazed as to why he should!

Most fans are in agreement that Murphy's moody William H. Bonney far outstrips any other screen Billy the Kid, especially Robert Taylor's interpretation in MGM's 1941 whitewashed version, *Billy the Kid*; he seemed to fit the part like a glove. Kurt Neumann was retained as director following the critical praise heaped on 1949's *Bad Boy* and at just 78 minutes long, the pace in *The Kid from Texas* (aka *Texas Kid, Outlaw*) never dragged. The action was also enhanced by a decent score, cobbled together from the works of six composers: Paul Sawtell, Frank Skinner, Hans J. Salter, Miklos Rozsa, Daniele Amfitheatrof and Walter Scharf. Opening in 1879 during the Lincoln County wars, Murphy is first seen lounging nonchalantly at the back of lawyer Albert Dekker's office: Wearing black hat, black neckerchief, blue leather jacket and sporting a double holster, he looks the business. And he proves he can use those deadly

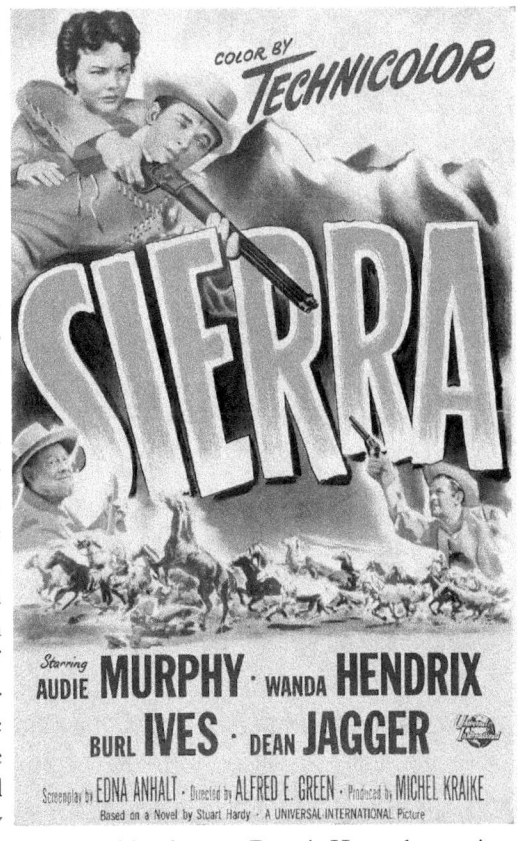

revolvers when a bunch of toughs sent by rival landowner Dennis Hoey charges into the office to arrest Dekker and partner Shepperd Strudwick on trumped-up charges, sending them packing in a burst of bullets ("Pretty heavy artillery for a banty rooster to be carrying around," sneers one gunslinger before regretting he said it). Murphy is taken under Strudwick's kindly wing and given a job on his cattle ranch, becoming a son to his father-figure and hanging up his lethal pistols ("A gun draws trouble," Strudwick states solemnly), longing for a spread of his own. But when the affable rancher is gunned down in a standoff, Murphy turns violent, straps on his holster and goes all-out for revenge, forming his own gang of sharpshooters and embarking on a trail of bloodshed, a $10,000 bounty placed on his head.

Neumann orchestrates a couple of blazing gun battles, such as inside a jail when Murphy breaks free and a fiery finale at Dekker's opulent house where burning torches flush out the outlaw and his bunch. The rather indifferent Gale Storm, Dekker's young wife, the piano-playing lass that Murphy yearns for from a discreet distance, provides romantic temptation. Shot in the end by Pat Garrett (played by Frank Wilcox), the outlaw notched up 21 killings in his short-lived 21 years; without resorting to overacting, Murphy, in his own quiet methodical way, reflected the troubled youth's inner turmoil to perfection and his capacity for remorseless shooting (partly based on the actor's wartime exploits). His sheer difference to the Western genre shone through; a storming start to Murphy's 19-year occupation in the saddle.

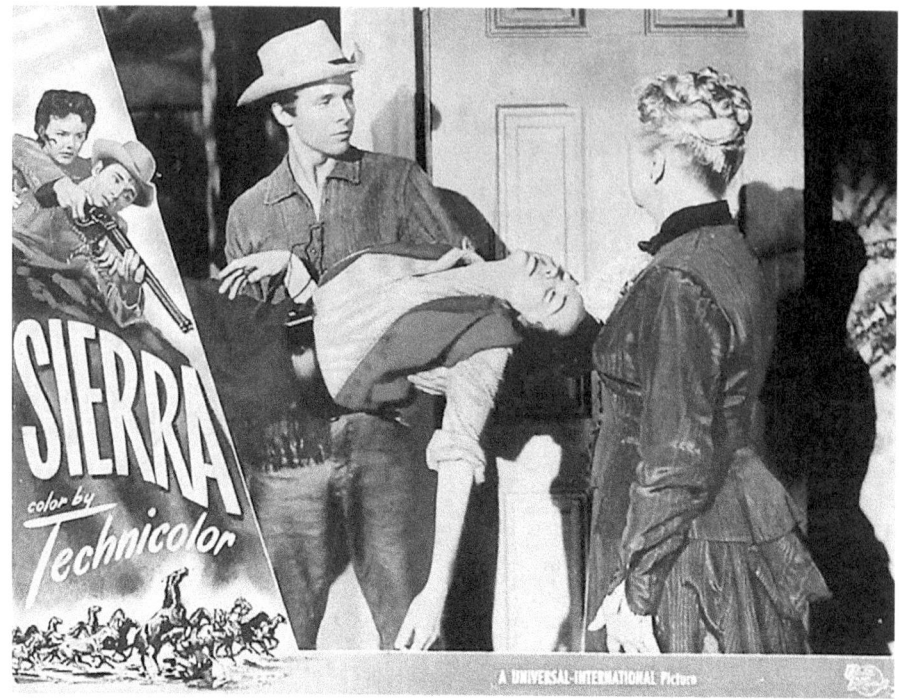

Audie Murphy and Wanda Hendrix (the victim of a snake bite), in *Sierra* (1950)

Universal's $700,000 investment in their new star had reaped dividends. The movie rang cash tills and was critically well received ("Commendable," said *Variety* of Murphy's performance); Murphy's unique war heroics obviously had a lot to do with its success, newspaper hacks not wishing to appear unkind to him. His next, *Sierra*, was a remake of a virtually unknown Universal Western made in 1938, *Forbidden Valley*, starring Noah Beery, Jr. *Sierra*, directed by Alfred E. Green, is a little-seen Murphy oater from this period that saw him billed above then-wife Wanda Hendrix (the two were divorced shortly before the film's release in June 1950; Murphy then got hitched to air stewardess Pamela Archer in April 1951). Beautifully photographed by Russell Metty among Utah's Cedar Breaks pink-walled canyons, and boasting a stirring Walter Scharf score, *Sierra* is heavenly fodder for horse lovers, but not perhaps for those preferring a more conventional Western. Murphy played Ring Hassard, holed up in a secret homestead in the mountains for 15 years because Dad Dean Jagger has been wrongly accused of murder. The two busy themselves by rounding up wild mustangs, taming them and selling the steeds to ranches. When lawyer Hendrix accidentally stumbles across their secluded retreat and Jagger suffers a serious back injury, the scene is set for romance between the two youngsters; Murphy escorts her into the nearest town in search of a doctor, saving her life en route after she is bitten by a rattlesnake. A confrontation then arises with burly horse thief Richard Rober and his boys who are also set on grabbing the mustangs, particularly the leader of the pack, a big black stallion (this stunner of a horse featured in McCrea's *Black Horse Canyon* and Montgomery's *King of the Wild Stallions*). Hendrix's fiancé, Elliott Reid, jealous of her friendship with Murphy, sides

Audie Murphy and his mature love interest, Marguerite Chapman, in *Kansas Raiders* (1950).

with Rober's mob and the law to get even and joins in the noisy action at the end when Murphy's group and Rober's confederates clash in the canyons over who gets to own the horses. Reid is trampled to death and Rober, dying, confesses to the sheriff that he committed the murder that Jagger has been framed for all these years. The final frame sees Murphy and Hendrix riding off into the distance but not, as one unkind scribe sarcastically suggested, to the divorce courts!

Murphy acquits himself well in his second Universal Western, demonstrating a genuine prowess on horseback, but overall it's pretty routine fare, the narrative switching from canyons to town to hideout and back again without generating a great deal of suspense (Murphy has to stand trial for rustling but escapes from jail with a little help from minstrel Burl Ives). Ives trots around the picturesque landscape on his mule, warbling a few tuneful ditties, Tony Curtis (billed as Anthony Curtis) makes his eighth screen appearance and keen-eyed buffs might spot James *The Thing* Arness among Rober's riders. But below par or not, that final shot of Murphy and Hendrix riding into Utah's vast wilderness to the sound of Ives singing the lilting "Hideaway" might well bring a lump to the throat when one thinks of all those actors and technicians, now long gone, who brought such features to the silver screen 60 years ago. A lament, if you like, for times gone by.

Audie Murphy as Jesse James; Richard Long as Frank James; James Best as Cole Younger; Dewey Martin as James Younger; and Tony Curtis as Kit Dalton: This has

to be the Western genre's best-looking, most dynamic bunch of young guns and young talent ever assembled under one roof. In the opening shots of them riding across California's Garner Valley region, these smartly attired dudes exude sex appeal mixed with cold hardware, a potent combination that has rarely been repeated. In modern-day vernacular, they look cool. Murphy and his go-getting desperadoes are off to join up with Quantrill's Raiders during the Civil War, hungering for some much-needed action after the quiet life on a Missouri farm. Murphy has a thirst for shooting Yankee Red Legs following the death of his parents by Union renegades, enlisting because he wants "to do some killing." Yes, Murphy's third Universal flick, *Kansas Raiders*, was a cracker; director Ray Enright brewed up a storm in this none-too-factual account of the last days of Colonel William Clark Quantrill after the bloodthirsty mass raid on Lawrence, Kansas (the Lawrence raid appeared in two Scott Westerns: *Fighting Man of the Plains* and *The Stranger Wore a Gun*), ensuring that Murphy's 1950 output ended with a bang.

Brian Donlevy played Quantrill as a stiff-necked, modern-day drill instructor, hitting the whiskey bottle when off duty, dishing out hangings left, right and center and planning his next bloody onslaught on the local populace in the name of the Confederacy, but, in fact, more for personal gain. Murphy and his friends ride into camp to volunteer and get sworn in after being harassed by the law in Lawrence, viewed as Quantrill spies. Earning respect straight-off by knifing second-in-command David Wolfe to death in a fight, Murphy and his gang take part in the first raid under the infamous Quantrill black flag but are appalled at the wanton, senseless violence; men, women and children mown down without mercy. Robert L. Richards' screenplay places stress on the gang's juvenile aspect (at Universal's insistence): "They're boys, mere boys," "Go home and take your kid friends with you," and "You have a winning way with children, Colonel," playing up to Murphy's "Kid" persona that was to haunt him throughout his '50s film career. Donlevy's erstwhile girlfriend, Marguerite Chapman, tries to get the young gunman to change his mind and leave the "butcher's brigade" and also takes a shine to his innocent demeanor (Chapman was probably a bit too mature in her role as Murphy's love interest, but she looks ravishing). Murphy, who hero-

worships Donlevy and is in tune with the man's code of violence, does have a change of heart after that unnecessarily ruthless massacre on a homestead, but reverts back when the Lawrence raid is announced; he and his pals are after the money from the bank, not wishing to share the loot ("The fortunes of war," Donlevy tells him). Putting four bullets into sadistic henchman Scott Brady who continually needles him, Murphy then decides to stick with it and remain loyal, but eventually Quantrill's guerrillas split due to unrelenting Union pressure. Donlvey, blinded in a gun battle at his burnt-out headquarters, goes into hiding with Murphy's bunch and Chapman, electing to die in a hail of Yankee lead in the climax as soldiers home in on their hideout. Murphy kisses Chapman goodbye after escaping the ambush and rides off with his pals to begin a life of notoriety, a $10,000 bounty on their heads.

Boosted by Milton Rosen's thundering musical soundtrack (as usual, Universal's musical director Joseph Gershenson claimed the credit) and sparkling cinematography from Irving Glassberg, *Kansas Raiders*, more so than the preceding two movies, set the formula for the flashy, fast and furious Universal Murphy Westerns that were to follow. He had taken the movie industry by surprise, rapidly establishing himself, in the course of a single year and in three contrasting motion pictures, as a newcomer to be reckoned with in the world of the medium-budget Western, gaining the necessary swagger to carry off a production. Murphy looked great on a horse, always well turned out and sporting throughout his Western career a hefty gun belt, worn waist-high for instant action, solid hardware any cowboy-mad youngster could identify with. Whether he was yet capable of handling something like Anthony Mann's *Winchester '73*, released by Universal that same year, is open to question. *Winchester '73* featured the same production values, the same cast of company regulars (James Best, Tony Curtis), a stock score of eight composers' works but a bigger star (James Stewart) in the lead. Transpose Stewart with Murphy and you wouldn't have all that much of a difference. But Murphy wasn't yet a "name," although he was fast becoming one. So now, as 1950 drew to a close, we had four cowboy stars running neck-and-neck in this most profitable medium-budget framework: Murphy, Scott, McCrea and Montgomery. Between them, they were to produce a body of work that, five to six decades on, still resonates with a vision of Western clarity no longer existing in modern-day cinema.

Chapter 12
Scott at Columbia and
Warner Bros., 1950-1957

Randolph Scott entered the '50s Western arena with his status at an all-time high, having signed, in late 1949, a lucrative 10-picture deal with Warner Bros. worth $100,000 a movie (he juggled his output from now on between Warner Bros. and Columbia with three exceptions—Fox's *The Cariboo Trail* (1950), RKO's *Rage at Dawn* (1955) and MGM's *Ride the High Country*). During the early '50s, he was never out of the *Motion Picture Herald* list of top-10 box-office stars, quite a feat for an actor still viewed by many as being cut out for the B-Western programmer only. His dour "I can handle myself" guise was in perfect harmony with how the genre presented itself during this decade, a decade in which hundreds of Westerns were churned out conveyor-belt style, from grade-Z theater fillers to grade-A epics. Scott hit a purple patch with the first Scott/Brown production of the 1950s, Columbia's *The Nevadan* (aka *The Man from Nevada*), a classy chase Western filmed among the rocky wilds of Lone Pine that could so easily have been directed by Budd Boetticher. As it was, Gordon Douglas brought flair and grit to a familiar tale of various factions searching for a fortune in stolen gold. Scott played Andrew Barclay, a federal marshal who forms an uneasy alliance with likeable bank robber Forrest Tucker, without the outlaw cottoning on to who he really is. Scott wants to bring Tucker to justice and retrieve a quarter of a million in stolen gold (only Tucker knows its whereabouts) but is harassed in his endeavors by creepy ranch owner George Macready and his three henchmen, squabbling brothers Frank Faylen, Jeff Corey and fist-happy Jock Mahoney. To complicate matters, Macready's strong-willed daughter (Dorothy Malone) takes a fancy to Scott and joins in on the hunt, peaking in a shoot-out near an abandoned mine where the bullion is stashed.

Plot-wise, one could level the accusation that *The Nevadan* is no different than countless other oaters concerning the search for missing gold and the different emotions that rise to the surface as all parties involved home in on the loot. However, Douglas' forceful camerawork, scriptwriters George W. George, Roland Brown and George F. Slavin's pithy dialogue laced with dry humor, Charles Lawton, Jr.'s pleasing color photography and Arthur Morton's tuneful score breathe new life into a well-worn layout, promoting the movie to that of a minor classic. A vicious fight between Scott and Tucker in the derelict mine, roof beams collapsing over their heads in clouds of rock and dust, brings to a satisfactory conclusion a taut little Western that rivets from start to finish; even the upbeat ending seems permissible, a repentant Tucker wishing he had met Scott five years earlier so that he wouldn't have strayed off the straight and narrow. Not seen for many years, this remains one of Scott's foremost, yet largely undiscovered, excursions out West during the 1950s.

The *New York Times* classed Scott as an "old cowhand," proof of his long association with the cowboy flick in the eyes of the public and critics. The old cowhand's first 1950s Warner Bros. Western, *Colt .45* (aka *Thundercloud*), was a fast-moving affair, taking place in 1852: Gun salesman Steve Farrell has his two Colt .45 six-shooters (the symbol of the Old West) stolen by a psychotic bandit and enlists the aid of local Indians to bring

Randolph Scott and George Macready in *The Nevadan* (1950)

the outlaw and his band of men to justice. An enjoyable standard cowboy flick, it lacks finesse in several departments, not least of all in Zachary Scott's serious bout of overacting as the loony outlaw. Hitting the bottle off set, director Edwin L. Marin should have reined the actor in and forced him to tone things down; it's a pantomime, almost one-dimensional, performance that jars instead of intrigues. Zach Scott, let out from behind bars, steals Randy's brand new shooters ("Law and order in six-finger doses.") and goes on a rampage, robbing and murdering *en masse* anyone standing in his way with a twitchy smirk on his face. Randy, imprisoned for four months on suspicion of being in with the killer, is released through lack of evidence and pursues the outlaw to retrieve his guns and clear his name. Using miner Lloyd Bridges' homestead as a base, and lusting after Bridges' wife (Ruth Roman), Zach soon has the town of Bonanza Creek in his pocket, including crafty sheriff Alan Hale.

Colt .45 is all about treachery: Bridges falls in with Zach because of financial gain and even shoots his own wife in the back when she rides into town to warn Randy that he's about to be ambushed; Hale deputizes Randy, but he plots feverishly behind his back, and mistrustful Zach double-crosses everyone, even members of his gang. At every fresh turn of events, Chief Thundercloud and his braves come to Randy's rescue (Randy saved him from Zach's lethal guns at the beginning), stealthily eliminating the schizo's

Randolph Scott strikes a dashing pose, in *Colt .45* (1950).

gunslingers and leaving Randy, smartly turned out in dark black shirt, trousers and hat, with a white neckerchief, to shoot Zach with one of the selfsame pistols that brought him notoriety. With Bridges out of the way, dead from a gunshot wound in the back himself, Roman wastes no time in falling into Randy's arms in the final few seconds.

Hoping to cash in on the huge commercial success of James Stewart's *Winchester '73* (Universal 1950), *Colt .45* is too frantic and disjointed by half, evincing marked signs of the sadism that was to creep into the Western genre throughout this decade. An interesting touch is that the movie spotlights gun belts with no cartridge holders; these would appear after the advent of the six-gun. The picture was a hit, mainly on Randolph Scott's box-office clout alone, and the actor strutted his way through the action, looking weather-beaten and charismatic; but the fact that Thomas W. Blackburn's script underwent several revisions tells it all. It's one of Scott's less-worthy titles from this period.

Set in the period of the Canadian gold rush, *The Cariboo Trail* tells of Jim Redfern and his companion, who drive a small herd of 36 cattle from Montana along the Cariboo Trail to the Chilcotin area of British Columbia in search of pastures anew, coming up against the two-timing head of the Walsh Trading Company opposing their every move. The best of the three Nat Holt–produced Fox Westerns, the movie is awash with Cinecolor's striking two-strip color tinting; rustic browns, shiny greens and pastel blues abound, giving it the look of an old Klondike print come to life. Shot among Colorado's mountain peaks and California's Bronson Canyon, and retaining virtually the identical production team behind *Canadian Pacific*, this energetic outdoor adventure marked the

Randolph Scott, George "Gabby" Hayes and Dale Robertson in *The Cariboo Trail* (1950)

final film appearance of that bewhiskered old critter George "Gabby" Hayes, playing a prospector who teams up with Scott and argumentative, gold-hungry Bill Williams. Refusing to pay a toll charge by driving their steers across a narrow bridge, they fall foul of Carson Creek's oily town tyrant, Victor Jory, resembling, with his thick glasses, slicked-back hair and servile delivery, an insane serial killer. As in *Fighting Man of the Plains*, Jory is in love with the leading lady (saloon owner Karin Booth), but Scott soon becomes a rival when the sassy dame sets her big beautiful eyes on him. Densely plotted, the movie sees Williams, embittered at losing an arm in a cattle stampede, savagely turning against Scott (he didn't want to herd cattle anyway), who disappears with Hayes and Chinese cook Lee Tung Foo up into the mountains to find suitable grazing land. Captured by Redskins, the trio escapes (Hayes' mule, on instructions, kicks out at the Indians, scattering them like leaves in the wind); by chance, Scott then finds a few gold nuggets worth over $900, joins forces with another outfit herding 300 head of cattle (a young Dale Robertson is one of their number) and eventually, with the help of a reformed Williams, puts paid to Jory and his crew. With Booth at his side, Scott, Robertson, Hayes and the rest of their entourage discover a fertile valley appropriate for setting up a cattle ranch, and Hayes' lost mule Hannibal appears on a mountain ridge, reunited with its owner.

Blessed with a terrific Paul Sawtell score and atmospherically directed by Edwin L. Marin, *The Cariboo Trail* showcased Scott at his '50s finest, attired in black and handling

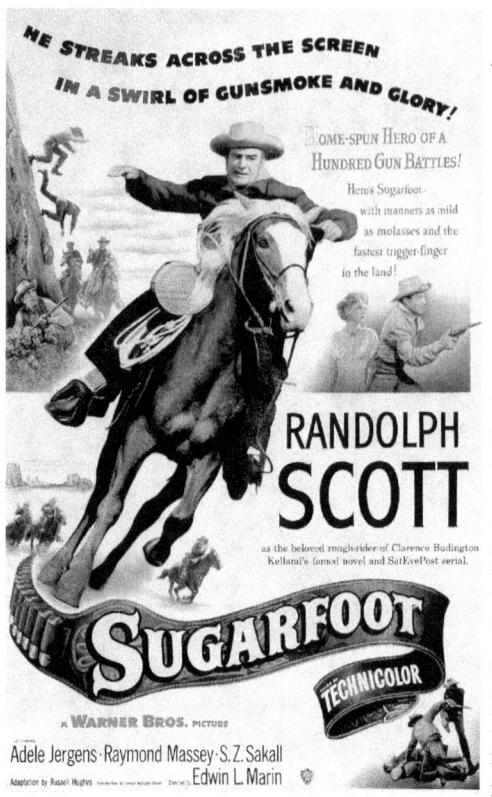

courage, determination, enthusiasm, jocularity, derring-do and pathos with consummate ease, one of his most pleasing performances from those far-off days. Decent color prints of the film are hard to come by; some DVD issues are still stuck with a black-and-white version that fails to do justice to an underrated actioner of the type that, regretfully, the studios gave up making many moons ago.

Marin was on shakier ground in the next Scott Warner Bros. oater, and his first in 1951, *Sugarfoot* (aka *Swirl of Glory*), the actor starring as ex-Confederate Captain Jackson "Sugarfoot" Redan, bringing his small wagon train into Prescott, Arizona, unable to decide where his future fortunes lie. Against type, he played a greenhorn Southern gentleman (typical of countless cowboy epics, Arthur Hunnicutt has to show him how to use a gun) who wanders into the frontier town of Prescott. Turning down gambling hall owner Robert Warwick's guarantee of a job as a card sharp, Scott throws his hand in with trader S.Z. Sakall, taking his wagon to La Paz, bidding for goods at auction and ferrying the freight back to town, with grizzled Hunnicutt acting as guard. Scott has two adversaries—detestable Raymond Massey and underhanded dealer Hugh Sanders, both bent on causing trouble. Buxom singer Adele Jergens supplies the love angle while Gene Evans stars as Massey's trigger-happy sidekick.

That's it in a nutshell. *Sugarfoot* is an undistinguished Scott effort that canters instead of gallops, the only lively thing being Max Steiner's catchy title music, used as a leitmotif throughout the movie. The storyline is minimal to say the least: There's a "who's quicker on the draw" square-off between mild-mannered Scott and Massey and a shoot-out at the La Paz trading depot; Massey and Scott (too polite by far) have a couple of arguments ("I knew this town wasn't big enough to hold the two of us," snaps Massey), Scott has a couple of clinches with Jergens, Hunnicutt speaks some drily humorous lines and Apaches make a brief appearance to the sound of Steiner's score pinched from *They Died With Their Boots On*. The film has a rushed, incomplete feel, accentuated in the far-from-absorbing romantic interludes and an abrupt climax when Scott guns down Massey, Sanders and Evans, the gunfight over in a flash, quickly followed by the end credits. Later turned into a TV series with Will Hutchins in the lead, *Sugarfoot* is, to be honest, a bit of a damp squib, one of the very few Westerns Scott made that could justifiably be termed "forgettable." The actor looked uncomfortable in some scenes, perhaps aware that playing a not-so-tough character wouldn't go down too well with the fans. He did a lot better in his next Scott/Brown production for Columbia, *Santa Fe*, playing yet again an ex-Confederate officer (Britt Canfield) taking on the tough job of assistant foreman on the trailblazing Santa Fe railroad. Trouble rears its head in the shape of his three brothers who insist on earning their money by falling in with a gang of crooks intent on preventing the railway reaching its destination.

Scott wants to let bygones be bygones after the end of the Civil War. ("You gotta stop fighting a war that doesn't exist.") The snag is that his three siblings (Jerome Courtland, John Archer and Peter Thompson) bear an almighty grudge against the Yankees and mean to put a stop to the new railroad reaching the Kansas-Colorado state line, joining up with sneering Roy Roberts and his lieutenants, led by surly Jock Mahoney. *Santa Fe*, a distinct improvement on the lackluster *Sugarfoot*, opens in splendid style. The four brothers walk into a saloon and are immediately branded as spineless cowards by the clientele; the provocation goes too far, one Union soldier is shot dead and the four take to their heels, making off on a train. Unfortunately, the tension built up in this scene isn't sustained for the remainder of the picture; the action is strictly by-the-book, with little depth to the characters or story, and it's left to Scott, and Scott alone, to carry the jumpy narrative to the end.

Clothed in his by-now usual black shirt and trousers with a fetching canary yellow neckerchief, topped off by his customary brown leather jacket, Scott not only has to grapple with his wayward brothers but hostile Indians (Chief Thundercloud gets to drive one of the Iron Horses, giving it the thumbs-up) and a pretty dull love interest in the form of a colorless Janis Carter, one of the least fetching of Scott's many leading ladies. There's a few hard-boiled highlights to shake up the leaden plot (a saloon burnt to the ground, two payroll robberies, a fight on a moving train and a couple of shoot-outs) and an intermittent comedy turn by rail drivers Billy House and Olin Howland, while the huge steam locomotives look magnificent in rich '50s Technicolor. After competing with the Rio Grande Railway Company to lay tracks through Raton Pass, the new rail network is finally established, leaving Scott to take up a position with a rail organization in Nevada, his three brothers dead. Needless to say, Carter intends to join him, even

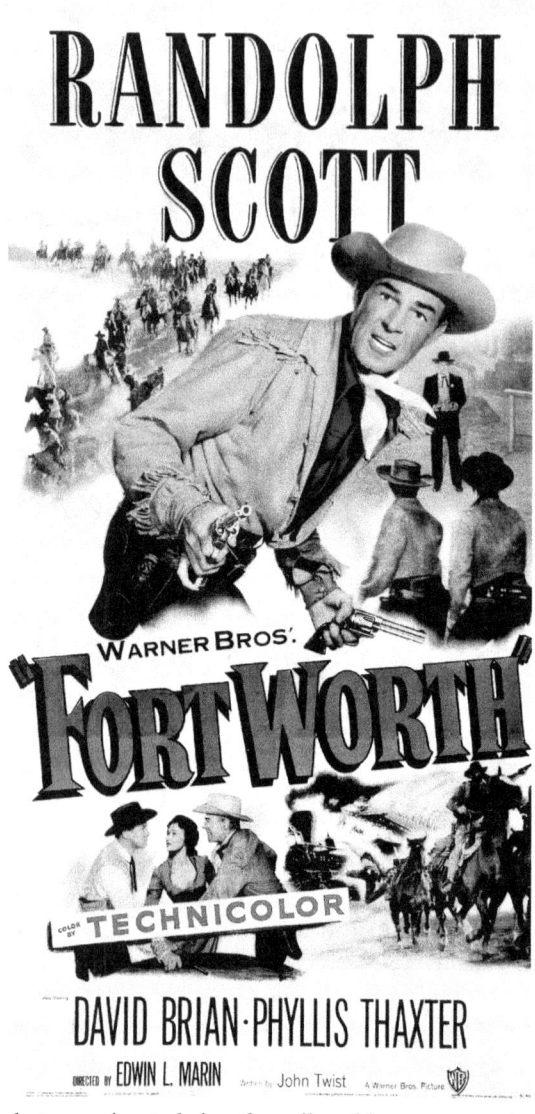

though she previously blamed Scott for the death of her husband in a skirmish during the war.

Santa Fe is an all right Western; it's not one of Scott's best, but the color photography (Charles Lawton, Jr.), score (Paul Sawtell) and director Irving Pichel's use of the colorful scenery, plus those imposing locomotives, help it to steam along at a fair pace without the viewer pondering too much on the motives behind many of the duplicitous conducts carried out by members of the cast.

Marin's seventh and final Scott Western, *Fort Worth*, (and the director's last film—he tragically died at the age of 52 after completion of the picture) trod the same trail as most of the actor's Warner Bros.' features from this early '50s period—undemanding fare, lacking a certain amount of substance but well performed by the cast and shot in delightful Technicolor. Ex-Confederate gunman Ned Britt (Scott) turns newspaperman, promising the Texas town of Fort Worth that he will expose his one-time friend as a crooked opportunist. Screen heavy David Brian, playing Scott's former buddy, almost steals the acting honors as Fort Worth's big shot, wanting to bring the railroad into town so that cattlemen can utilize the line for conveying freight and, by doing so, feather his own nest in the bargain. Scott has two women to contend with in his life: Phyllis Thaxter, his ex who is now hitched to Brian; and another ex, Helena Carter, who flits in and out of the action without contributing too much to what is going on.

Scott rides into town minus his shooting irons (despite his repute as a "one man arsenal") and starts printing provocative material, much to the chagrin of Brian, backed up by gunfighter Ray Teal and his bunch of ruffians. Bent on payback time for the death of a young boy in a cattle stampede caused by the gunman, Scott's aim is to "destroy by press" people like Teal, falling out with Brian over Thaxter's feminine wiles ("You better get yourself some guns," he warns his friend). But when Emerson Treacy, the

RANDOLPH SCOTT

Randolph Scott (right) works up a sweat in a rousing fight from *Fort Worth* (1951).

elderly newspaper boss, is stabbed in the back, Scott has had a bellyful of pacifism. In the 38th minute, he deputizes himself, straps on the sheriff's double-holstered gun belt and shoots three of Teal's thugs without batting an eyelid. On this macho display of one-upmanship, Thaxter quickly rejects Brian and looks at Scott in a different light; it's amazing what a piece of violence can do to a girl's libido! "I'll print you out of Texas," Scott again notifies Brian before the two, on the face of it, make up, posing as train guards to lure Teal out of hiding. Double-crossed by Brian and wounded in a gun battle, Scott has a final confrontation with his old foe in town; Teal shoots the maverick in the back, Scott cuts down Teal and, naturally, winds up marrying Thaxter who announces, just before the curtain falls, that she's pregnant, the colorful railroad backdrop a scene filched from 1939's *Dodge City*.

Fort Worth, like Scott's other Westerns before it, was a huge hit and is still entertaining today without taxing the brain, Scott's performance considered "consistently good" by *Variety*. But its limitations as a serious cowboy flick were exposed in Scott's fourth 1951 Western, Columbia's *Man in the Saddle* (aka *The Outcast*); André De Toth took over the reins as Scott's principal director, the Scott/Brown production team hoisting the horse opera into new levels of dynamism and longevity which reached hitherto untold heights in the seven Budd Boetticher oaters Scott made between 1956 and 1960. The first of six Scott Westerns directed by De Toth, *Man in the Saddle* showed the genre growing up, proving that the director with the eye patch had a genuine grasp of Western ethics: This was for adults only, with its accent on betrayal and collapsing relationships. It's

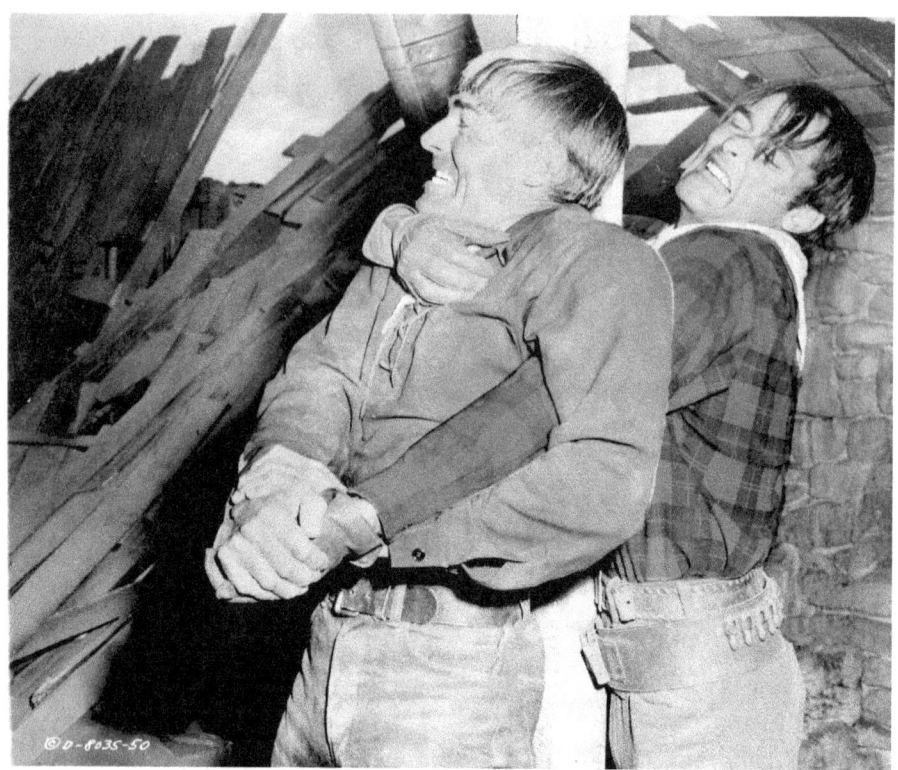

Randolph Scott and Richard Rober fight it out in *Man in the Saddle* (1951).

also unusual in featuring an unfamiliar, non-American actor as the main protagonist; although Alexander Knox was born in Canada, he made his name in scores of British movies throughout the 1940s and 1950s and his clipped English enunciation sounds nothing if not novel in an Old West framework. With its stunning backdrop of the snow-covered Alabama Hills at Lone Pine and an incisive script from Kenneth Gamet, plus George Duning's melodious score, De Toth's oater, strong on human drama, doesn't put a foot wrong over its 87-minute running length; it's a movie to savor time and time again, to reinforce the belief that during the 1950s, the Western reached an all-time peak of excellence.

Scott's a good-natured rootless drifter (Owen Merritt), unable to settle down anywhere and with anyone (as sidekick Guinn "Big Boy" Williams continually tells him). Gold digger Joan Leslie jilts Scott to marry the boss of Skull Ranch, played by dictatorial Knox with large helpings of smarmy relish. Ellen Drew, owner of a nearby spread, longs for Scott's manly arms to caress her; she's stalked by half-crazy suitor John Russell, while Knox's chief honcho, Richard Rober, is out to score notches on his gun belt by beating Scott to the draw in a gunfight. A heady concoction to set the pulses racing: Scott still hankers after Leslie, and she for him; Knox, seething with jealousy, wants Scott off his ranch and resorts to bullying tactics as he'll share with no one, killing and stampeding his cattle to ram home his point; Drew fancies Scott, and mad Russell is determined to have his wicked way with Drew. When Richard Crane, one of Scott's young wran-

Randolph Scott takes on the tough job of railroad foreman in *Carson City* (1952).

glers, is shot in the back of the head, Scott discards any pretence of being the nice guy and turns nasty ("A man can't run all the time. Has to fight sooner or later."). A range war busts wide open, a kind of David versus Goliath scenario where we know that our leather-clad hero will win out in the end; it's how he does it that makes this Western such a beauty to watch.

De Toth orchestrates his violent shoot-outs in darkened rooms to heighten suspense and includes a tremendous fistfight between Scott (or the actor's obvious stunt double) and Russell on a snow-laden mountain cascade. There are some wonderful exchanges to be had for connoisseurs of good dialogue. Scott to Knox: "I've been havin' trouble with you. But from now on, you're going to have trouble with me." Knox: "Is that an offer, Owen?" Scott: "Yeah, it's an offer," and when Scott and Rober meet for the inevitable showdown on a windswept street, Rober, losing his gun, sarcastically asks, "You wouldn't shoot a man in the back, would you?" to which Scott tersely replies, "I could you." In an about-face conclusion, Knox agrees to sell up and move on if Leslie honors her contract with him and treats him more like a husband, thus freeing himself from the curse of Scott's presence. Unfortunately, having won back his errant wife, Knox's accidentally shot dead by Rober, croaking to Leslie with his dying breath, "Skull's yours. Never sell it." But Scott had it in mind to romance the much more down-to-earth Drew anyway.

Tennessee Ernie Ford sang the title song (and had a small role), while Mexican Alfonso Bedoya provided snatches of scatterbrained quipping, but not enough to mar the film's serious mood. *Man in the Saddle* also demonstrated conclusively that Scott's '50s Columbia Westerns had the edge on those he made for Warner Bros., which tended to

Randolph Scott and Lucille Norman in *Carson City*

verge on run-of-the-mill. The Scott/Brown partnership, using virtually the same team for each production, were sharpening their skills by turning out brilliant, mature horse operas which, like this one, still remain amazingly fresh after 60 years.

1952 saw our rangy hero moving over to Warner Bros. for the lively *Carson City*, directed with rattling pace by André De Toth. Railroad engineer Jeff Kincaid is hired for the job of laying a rail track between Carson City and Virginia City, despite opposition from the townsfolk and a criminal mine owner, the mastermind behind the the Champagne Bandits. Although only gifted with sight in his right eye, De Toth proved he had a good eye for a Western, as *Carson City* showed (the director was the man behind Warner Bros.' *House of Wax*, one of the biggest box-office smashes of the 1950s). In a role originally earmarked for Errol Flynn, Scott played the railroad engineer reluctantly taking on the tough job of foreman, constructing a proposed rail link via the shortest possible route, which meant blasting his way through inaccessible mountain ranges. Scott's hindered at each and every turn. Half-brother Richard Webb, working for the Carson City Clarion newspaper, doesn't agree with the railroad bulldozing its way through the territory, mainly because of personal reasons. He's in love with the boss' daughter, Lucille Norman, who takes a sudden shine to Scott when he rides into town. And Raymond Massey, organizer of a string of stagecoach holdups under the name of The Champagne Bandits, and using the derelict Golden Elephant Mine as cover for his activities, sees his source of income drying up if the stage line becomes redundant (Massey's deluding himself that he's perceived as some kind of Robin Hood figure.)

A rollicking barnstormer enlivened by David Buttolph's thumping soundtrack, *Carson City* doesn't let up for a second, becoming one of the better of the Scott Warner Bros. oaters. Opening with a stage robbery in which the passengers are treated to a banquet by the thieves, the action moves swiftly on to saloon face-offs (Scott and Massey's thug, James Millican), Scott rescuing Norman when she strays into a blasting area, a cart loaded with drills sabotaged by Massey's lot, a barroom brawl and a tremendous lengthy sequence in which Scott (stripped to the waist for the benefit of his female disciples) and his crew are trapped in a tunnel caused by a landslide (filmed in Bronson Canyon). Scott spits out a few menacing one-liners to perpetually sneering Massey and his cohorts: "I'm trying to keep the lid on but don't force your luck," and, direct to Massey, "I'll keep out of your way and you keep out of mine." Even jealous-as-hell Webb gets a scathing rejoinder when he calls Scott a liar. "If you weren't my brother, I'd call you on that," the square-jawed one snaps, Webb backing off sharply. The climax is a rousing winner, a real rollercoaster ride, Massey and his men boarding the new locomotive to relieve it of its gold bullion and then having to fight it out with Scott's gang of railroaders in a blazing gun battle. Fetchingly dressed in dark blue, with white/yellow neckerchief, Scott gives chase to his number-one quarry that has retreated to the rock-strewn hills. A repentant Webb joins the manhunt and is shot, dying in Scott's arms; after a tense stalking through clefts and boulders, the engineer puts a bullet in Massey, ending up marrying Norman and going on honeymoon by (what else) taking a train.

Scott is a rock-hard man of action in this movie, in total mastery of all that is thrown at him, not burdening himself with anyone else's motives, content to get the job done because that's what he's been paid to do. Beside his monolithic presence, the rest of the cast are either dishonest or weasels, lacking backbone. It's a great piece of acting, one of his most telling in a Warner Bros. oater. Shot in early Warnercolor, *Carson City*, among all the "railroad construction" class of flicks dating from the '30s, '40s and '50s, remains one of the finest, as enjoyable now as it was way back then.

Columbia's *Hangman's Knot* is a forgotten Scott classic, as relevant to the genre as anything Stewart or Wayne were making at the time. Roy Huggins' one and only motion picture predates Scott's Budd Boetticher Westerns by four years but, like *The Nevadan*, could have been directed by Boetticher himself, as it contains elements that were to push the seven Boetticher oaters into almost mythical status: a terse script (written by Huggins); spare direction; tight editing; mean performances from a predominately small cast; a

A publicity photo of Randolph Scott from *Hangman's Knot* (1952)

moralistic slant to the narrative; and colorful rocky Lone Pine location work. Mischa Bakaleinikoff's music is also used prudently and intelligently. Boetticher's outings aside, *Hangman's Knot* is the best Western Scott made in the 1950s and one of the greatest he ever starred in. Forget the big-name stars and their big-name directors—with minimal finances and an unknown name at the helm, Scott and producer Harry Joe Brown came up with an incident-packed Western of such high standards that it's a mystery why it hasn't received more acclaim over the years.

Confederate guerrillas waylay a wagon containing over $1,000,000 in Union gold; learning that the war is over, they decide whether or not to share the spoils while having to fight for survival, cornered inside a stage line relay station by others greedy for the gold themselves. That's the basic plot, but all involved flesh it out to riveting proportions. Scott (Major Matt Stewart), disrespectful "pardner" Lee Marvin and their men rob a

Inside their stone-built prison, Randolph Scott serves as the moral centerpiece as one compromised morality faces another, in *Hangman's Knot*.

wagon of a fortune in gold bullion, slaughtering the entire squad of Union soldiers sent to guard it. The money is earmarked for the Confederacy cause but, when they learn from a dying soldier that the war ended a month back, they ride on to confront Glenn Langan and confirm it; he's the person charged with ferrying the gold to the Confederate forces. Langan knows darn well that hostilities have ceased and wants the gold for himself; Scott and Marvin are aware of this, confronting Langan in stony silence before dismounting to thrash it out with him, a marvelous set piece dripping with latent tension. "There's no Confederacy," Scott says evenly, and just as his words come out, Marvin shoots Langan dead, one bullet in the back. This brilliantly handled, edgy scene pinpoints the antagonism between the two men, zeroing in on Marvin's continual attempts to challenge Scott's authority. He's sick of taking orders and doesn't like being pushed around. "Is it that easy to kill a man?" Scott asks Marvin after Langan has been shot. "Well, isn't it?" Marvin callously retorts. "What else have we been doing for the past five years?" But he backs down quick enough when Scott tells him in no uncertain terms that he's the man in charge of the outfit and won't stand for any nonsense, from anyone ("If I'm gonna have trouble with you, let's have it now.")

Hangman's Knot is a film of two parts: the outdoor location and the confined setting. Sheriff Ray Teal, sidekick Guinn "Big Boy" Williams and their posse are in hot pursuit, Scott having purloined a stage containing Richard Denning and Donna Reed. Twenty-five minutes into the story, Scott and his small force plus captives are holed up in the Sierra Stage Line caboose, Teal and his ragtag posse surrounding them. Conflicts arise on both sides. Teal's posse isn't all that law-abiding, hatching plans to grab the

Randolph Scott embraces Donna Reed

gold for themselves; meanwhile, cooped up in their stone-built prison, Scott has more than enough on his plate, coping with rebellious Marvin, weak-willed Denning and Reed (more downbeat than other Scott movie heroines), a nurse who is doing her best to patch up a wounded man. Marvin makes a play for Reed, slobbering her with kisses, culminating in a brutal fistfight with Scott, after which Marvin is blasted by young Claude Jarman, Jr. as he goes to shoot his leader in the back. Following a gunfight in the middle of a blazing fire on the building's roof, a chaotic finale filmed during a violent storm sees Teal, Williams and Denning all dead: Scott and Jarman, Jr. ride off, promising to return, Scott to commence a new life with Reed (with some of the gold) and Jarman, Jr. to live with the kindly residents of the stage line (Jeanette Nolan and Clem Bevans), who want to adopt him as their son.

Scott, on a roll during 1951/1952, was the moral centerpiece of *Hangman's Knot*, Marvin the harbinger of doom, and the two actors played off each other superbly. For many reasons, *Hangman's Knot* can be seen as the definitive Randolph Scott Western, the actor bringing all of his skills to the fore with that ease that so characterized his performances. It was also one of his most financially successful, unanimously praised by the critics; however, Huggins, in spite of the acclaim, refused a new Columbia contract at the end of it, making the picture something of a "one-off." Apart from Reed, who remained nervous on set, overawed by such a male ensemble of beefcake, the rest of the cast tried for one-take shoots, adding spontaneity to the finished product. A tremendous Western from the genre's golden age, completing a trio of classics from Scott—if only it had been just a few minutes longer!

Just how good was Scott in his early '50s Westerns, and how high was his standing with the fans and critics? Scott's pictures made a decent profit for Columbia and Warner Bros., and he usually received praise from the film reviewers, however clichéd his role could be—they seemed to like him as a person, always hoping for better things to come his way. Budd Boetticher once commented that he considered Scott a better actor than Wayne. He could be right: Both were naturals, at one with the elements, eschewing the need for over-dramatization. It might be argued that Scott, Wayne, Gary Cooper, Audie Murphy, Joel McCrea, George Montgomery, Rory Calhoun and Sterling Hayden approached the Western in a similar manner, not displaying the flashiness (or even egotism) evident in, say, Burt Lancaster's performances (it is fascinating to compare Lancaster's all-grinning, flamboyant black-clad gunslinger in United Artists' *Vera Cruz* to Cooper's taciturn gunman, his reluctant partner). Kirk Douglas could also resort to histrionics every so often, while the hugely underrated Richard Widmark was the one actor that seemed, in all of his films, to get the balance just right (as did James Stewart). So you could quite easily substitute Scott into a Wayne Western, and vice versa, and not notice that much of a difference, as their character interpretations were practically the same. But Wayne, of course, had the audience pulling power that Scott didn't possess, a reason why Wayne's Western output was minimal in this decade, confined to limited but highly regarded big-budget productions. However, Scott *was* employed by two of Hollywood's more prestigious movie companies (Murphy, McCrea and Montgomery were also with the big guns), his budgets coming in at an average of $800,000 per Scott picture, large money in those days. His Westerns really fall into the category of medium-budget; *Vera Cruz* and *The Searchers* cost a whopping $3,000,000 each, while Murphy and McCrea's oaters cost between $500,000 to $750,000; Montgomery's were lower down the scale, around $200,000 to $400,000. Most grade B- and Z-Westerns were produced on peanuts. Scott never reached the stratospheric heights commanded by Wayne, Douglas, Stewart, Cooper and Lancaster, and was never directed by a big name, but his '50s features don't lack bite and entertainment value, standing head and shoulders above most Western fodder of the period.

In 1953, Scott seesawed back to Warner Bros., starring in the unsatisfactory *The Man Behind the Gun*, flatly directed by Felix E. Feist. Do politics and the Western milieu mix and, in particular, do they work in what should really be a straightforward Randolph Scott crowd-pleaser? Not in this setup they don't. "A maze of intrigue" intones Scott (as Major Ransome Callicut) over the opening credits, followed by a double shooting in the second minute. Supposedly wanted for desertion and murder, Scott goes undercover and investigates a political administration in Los Angeles that is planning an insurrection by taking over Southern California's water supplies from the Union.

It looks and sounds promising, but unfortunately the premise isn't. *The Man Behind the Gun* is one of the very few Scott Westerns that audiences would have difficulty watching more than once. Apart from the final 10 minutes, the action is firmly anchored to the world of sound stages and painted backdrops, lending the movie a cramped air, while John Twist's wordy screenplay is so tangled that non-American audiences would, during the time of the film's release, have been scratching their heads in puzzlement, wondering who was who, what allegiance they served and what they were up to—it's a little *too* intricate for its own good. Further irritations come in the form of Dick Wesson's near-comic turn, starring as one of Scott's two partners (in that final 10 minutes, he's

Randolph Scott poses as a schoolteacher in *The Man Behind the Gun* (1953).

fitted out as a woman), Philip Carey's arrogant cavalry officer (Carey was an expert in playing pain-in-the-butt characters; he more or less repeated this role in Columbia's *They Rode West* [1954]) and Lina Romay, overacting like mad in her portrayal of a fiery Hispanic singer-cum-bandit queen. Scott is his usual confident, solid self (he thought highly of the picture), but for the most part, Feist's semi-oater makes for turgid viewing.

Scott (posing as a harmless schoolteacher), Wesson and Alan Hale, Jr. turn up in the City of Angels just prior to the outbreak of the Civil War (Hale plays Olaf Swenson, as did his father in *Virginia City*). Senators Roy Roberts and Morris Ankrum are at loggerheads over California's water rights, and mistrustful Carey is under the impression that Scott is an escaped killer while Errol Flynn's third wife, radiant Patrice Wymore, going out with Carey, soon realizes that Scott is the better bet and gives her aloof cavalry officer beau the cold shoulder. Most of the first-half encounters take place in the Palacio dance hall, a colorful setting where Romay struts her stuff, young Mexican gunrunner Robert Cabal causes trouble as does flashy gunman Anthony Caruso, and Roberts is assassinated—or is he? After Scott has revealed to Carey who he really is (and cut him down a peg or two), he takes command in an effort to flush out the vigilantes, re-enlisting his two buddies into the army ("He wasn't born. He was issued," complains Hale). By flushing out the baddies, it's revealed that Roberts wasn't bumped off after all: It was a put-up job to enable the corrupt politician to gain control of the valuable water supply, while Ankrum, his rival, has been murdered in his place. A lively shoot-'em-up finale sees Roberts dispatching Romay before Scott drowns the politician in a river ("You wanted

George Macready separates Randolph Scott (left) and Lee Marvin (right) in *The Stranger Wore a Gun* **(1953).**

water, you got it. Here's some more."). Scott also ends up kissing Wymore, Carey too ambitious to give a hoot about his ex-love.

Although not quite the dud that many think it is, *The Man Behind the Gun* is not your standard Randolph Scott actioner. It's more a thinly disguised attack on McCarthyism, rife in Hollywood at the time. The color photography and costumes are a treat, the acting above average, but the whole package is something of a bore. Scott belonged to the wide-open spaces; an enclosed setting wasn't really his forte, as this slight dropping off in his otherwise excellent '50s output proved.

Things didn't really get a lot better with the next Scott/Brown Columbia offering, 1953's *The Stranger Wore a Gun*. Disillusioned with the nonstop looting, pillaging and killing carried out by Quantrill's guerrillas, a one-time spy for the band (Scott, as Jeff Travis) tries to go straight but his past catches up with him in the form of the unprincipled bigwig of Prescott, Arizona. Fox's *Fighting Man of the Plains* commenced with the Quantrill gang rampaging through Lawrence, Kansas. So does *The Stranger Wore a Gun*. In the opening five minutes, we're left in no doubt whatsoever that the movie was originally issued in 3-D format: Burning torches are thrust at the camera, furniture is hurled straight-on and guns are pointed toward the audience to fabricate the impression (at the time) that we were in the thick of the action. Sick of the violence (150 were slaughtered in this one raid alone), Scott quits Quantrill's mob ("Tell Quantrill to get himself another spy."), meets a saloon girl with a heart (Claire Trevor on a riverboat), foils a murder attempt

Randolph Scott does not appear to be getting too friendly with the Conroy Stage Line, in *The Stranger Wore a Gun*.

on his life and rides into Prescott, intending to go straight. Hiss-boo villain George Macready has other ideas—fully aware of Scott's former activities and taking advantage of this knowledge, he badgers him into getting friendly with the Conroy Stage Line, gain employment as a shotgun guard and pass on information regarding gold shipments so that his outfit, led by smirking polecats Lee Marvin and Ernest Borgnine, can rob at leisure. Macready has a rival, grinning Mexican bandit Alfonso Bedoya, so Scott finds himself playing devil's advocate, manipulating both gangs to his own advantage (all this years before Clint Eastwood got up to the same tricks in *A Fistful of Dollars*). A second romantic distraction comes in the shapely form of Joan Weldon, the boss' daughter, but she's no match for Trevor; the dame, in full regalia, enters the Prescott arena to claim her man, regardless of Macready's sudden interest in her.

A Columbia generic Western made in the days when dozens were being knocked out assembly line-style by studios both major and minor, this Scott/Brown effort is, for want of a better word, slightly messy, and it's a chore to sit through. Kenneth Gamet's screenplay steadfastly refuses to establish Scott's motivations and just who is playing off who, particularly in the central section's prolonged (and confusing) holdup sequence in which Macready's boys and Bedoya's confederates both converge on the stagecoach, with Scott changing sides with alarming alacrity. Perhaps key scenes were left on the cutting room floor, because this glaring lack of cohesiveness runs throughout the entire length of the picture. The best dialogue is reserved for Scott's well-aimed barbs at Marvin: "Don't ever do that to me again," he barks when Marvin spits a wad of tobacco at his feet. "You better take a good look next time you pull that trigger. You shot my hat off,"

Randolph Scott and Phyllis Kirk in *Thunder Over the Plains* (1953)

states Marvin to Scott, who tersely responds with, "If I'd known it was you, I would have done better." "Soon, real soon, I'll give you your chance," he warns Marvin, and when Marvin does take his chance, he loses out to Scott's faster trigger finger. The rest of the script is strictly ABC stuff, stating the obvious at every step of the way. Two more black marks against the film: Mischa Bakaleinikoff's dull, rumbling score, and several murky segments featuring rear-projected backdrops to generate the illusion of depth for the 3-D screen, creating, in the process, fuzzy, indistinct images (the Lone Pine scenery is completely ruined.)

Before riding off with Trevor in the end, Scott announces, rather ironically, "Guns never settle anything the right way. I'm through with them," a comment that none of his legion of fans would ever swallow. Climaxing with a tremendous gunfight in a burning casino, flaming roof beams putting paid to Macready in the conflagration, *The Stranger Wore a Gun* doesn't make a great deal of sense and is loose around the seams as far as narrative drive is concerned (director André De Toth hated the picture), a cockeyed, illogical contribution to Scott's repertoire that, when you consider that it came from the Scott/Brown team, is a thumping disappointment.

Thunder Over the Plains (Warner Bros., 1953) was a thankful return to form for both Scott and director De Toth. In 1869, following the end of the Civil War, the citizens of Texas, at the mercy of exploitive carpetbaggers, rebel against authority, so an army of occupation is introduced, even though many of its officers sympathize with those breaking the law. Another fizzing Western from workaholic De Toth in which the director demonstrated his canny skill in putting together two cat-and-mouse scenes

Randolph Scott and Charles McGraw in *Thunder Over the Plains*

of quiet malevolence: In the movie's middle section, where Scott (playing Captain David Porter) tracks rebel leader Charles McGraw among a series of gullies; and the climactic five-minute spell in which Scott and cheating tax commissioner Hugh Sanders stalk one another through back alleys in half-shadow. Real tension and suspense is generated in these sequences, helped considerably by David Buttolph's ominous score (director and composer performed a similar feat in *House of Wax*, where Vincent Price pursues Phyllis Kirk down foggy streets). Kirk crops up here as Scott's wife, bemoaning her lonely, dreary life in a frontier town and yearning for the bright lights and gossip of the big city. So when smooth-talking and highly ambitious Captain Lex Barker arrives (fresh from a run of five *Tarzan* potboilers), she flirts and fawns all over him, leading to a sexually explicit (for 1953) moment where he tries to rape her—Scott breaks in on the pair, leading to a particularly bloody fistfight (hence the "A" rating in Britain). Sadistic Barker is also a little too fond of his guns for Scott's liking, shooting a rebel in the back, which prompts Scott to acidly remark, "Finally used that shiny new gun, didn't you." Accountable for bringing McGraw to justice, moralist Scott has to balance his hatred for the carpetbaggers (led by Sanders and timorous Elisha Cook, Jr.) with the need to quell the rebellion and his concern for the farmers' plight in relinquishing their cotton supplies in order to pay for trumped-up tax bills; in addition, loose cannon Barker makes matters awkward by disobeying every order that Scott issues.

Shot amid the picturesque rolling hills of Calabasas, California, *Thunder Over the Plains* is a rigorous, well thought-out Western containing an incisive script by Russell S. Hughes and fine color photography from veteran cameraman Bert Glennon. Old

Randolph Scott and Joan Weldon in *Riding Shotgun* (1954)

stager Henry Hull puts in an appearance as Scott's irascible commanding officer and there's an early role for Fess *Davy Crockett* Parker. Comparable themes relating to Texas joining the Union (which it did in 1870) were explored in 1938's *The Texans*, but made with far less panache than was on offer here. De Toth's fourth Scott vehicle hits all the right Western buttons; it's fast moving and snappy, another outstanding representation of a true '50s saddle-buster with the leading man in full control of every situation.

The goodies continued with *Riding Shotgun*, Scott staying at Warner Bros. for the start of 1954 and playing a shotgun guard fixed on clearing his name in the town of Deepwater by bringing to ground the gang of miscreants who framed him for robbery and murder three years back. *High Noon*-ish in concept (the action takes place over a single day in a town setting), De Toth's expertly paced "an eye for an eye, a tooth for a tooth" Western is a solidly constructed oater with a certain dose of profundity, Scott (as Larry Delong) narrating the events from the start. "I didn't want to capture Marady. He's the only man I've ever known that I've wanted to kill," sums up the man's mindset as he's tricked into being waylaid by the outlaws ("That's what hate does to you. It makes a man careless."), trussed up and left for dead. The stagecoach holdup the outlaws then carry out is a ruse; James Millican and his crew (including a young Charles Bronson) plan to lure the sheriff and his posse out of Deepwater, leaving the field wide open for them to raid the local casino. Scott frees himself, gallops hell for leather into town and tries to convince the hostile citizens that the robbery is about to take place. None of them believe him; taking cover in Fritz Feld's decrepit cantina, Scott finds himself cornered

Randolph Scott strikes a very *High Noon*-ish vibe as the proud loner hero in *Riding Shotgun*.

by the hypocritical, spineless townsfolk ("Even the kids had me marked as a monster."), although deputy Wayne Morris, more concerned with the state of his food-depleted stomach than anything else, is half-inclined to go along with Scott's story that he is innocent of any wrongdoing and that Millican will shortly be entering town to grab the takings from William Johnstone's gambling joint. Dark-haired Joan Weldon, Johnstone's daughter, reckons Scott is up to scratch; besides, he's the only real man in a town full of bigots, so a gal will certainly feel safe in his arms.

Scott acquits himself with merit in *Riding Shotgun*, a man alone, the odds stacked up against him but triumphing in the end (Millican is shot with his own derringer, while Bronson is floored by a slingshot from an unruly kid before Scott guns him down). Warner regular David Buttolph contributes a fine score, complementing Bert Glennon's pristine cinematography and Thomas Blackburn's incisive script, which errs on the side of gravitas for a change. De Toth shoots predominately in close-up, bestowing an air of immediacy to the proceedings and, by doing so, ups the level of tension. Although not in the same class as *High Noon*, within the realm of the isolated hero matching his wits against a town full of narrow-minded disbelievers, *Riding Shotgun* a good enough example of that sub-genre and one of Scott's worthier '50s Warner Bros.' Westerns.

The Bounty Hunter (Warner Bros., 1954) is more word-bound than action, Scott starring as bounty hunter Jim Kipp, asked by the Pinkerton Detective Agency to find the whereabouts of three outlaws who robbed a train of $100,000 and disappeared without a trace. The opening six minutes of André De Toth's final Scott Western are gripping stuff: Against Red Rock Canyon's rugged backdrop and boosted by David Buttolph's bombastic score, Scott, attired in a dust-smeared navy blue getup, tracks a killer through bluffs and ridges, shooting his quarry and riding into town to collect the

Randolph Scott and Dolores Dorn in *The Bounty Hunter* (1954)

$500 reward. When asked by the sheriff why he does it for a living, Scott answers, "I'm counting the reasons—and they're 10 short," the lawman under the mistaken belief that Scott will contribute 10 bucks toward the coffin (he doesn't!). A detective from Pinkerton's approaches Scott, taking on the lucrative job of hunting down three outlaws and recovering the loot they stole, with minimal information to go on. After a fracas inside a cantina in the desert relay station of Crows Nest, he rides into Twin Forks, convinced the killers are hiding out there by masquerading as righteous, upstanding townsfolk. Once Scott's identity becomes known, his very presence acts as a catalyst; a whole host of skeletons in the closet are revealed, the citizens, all nursing guilt feelings, not quite sure who grim-faced Scott is gunning after (a comparable theme, exploring small-town paranoia brought on by one person, was refined to perfection in Audie Murphy's *No Name on the Bullet*, directed by Jack Arnold for Universal in 1959).

Originally to have been issued in 3-D (the "throwing items at the camera" scenes are thankfully dropped after the first 10 minutes), *The Bounty Hunter* showed signs of tiredness, in plot, direction and scope. It's also a little short on excitement, failing to deliver exciting set pieces, despite Scott's "driving, hard-boiled performance" (*Variety*). De Toth was later to say that he felt that the Scott Westerns had nowhere to go and nothing new to say. Nevertheless, the picture has its moments as we are left guessing who among this unwholesome bunch is behind the train robbery. Is it limping hotel proprietor Ernest Borgnine? Could it be the town sheriff, Howard Petrie? What about young gun-shooter Tyler MacDuff, who harbors a grudge against Scott? Kindly doctor Harry Antrim knows more than he's letting on. Postmaster Dub Taylor acts suspiciously, as does gambler Robert Keys and his "tart with a heart of gold" wife Marie Windsor. Dolores Dorn, Antrim's daughter, plays the love interest, and a pretty wishy-washy one

Howard Petrie (playing the sheriff) and Randolph Scott in *The Bounty Hunter*

at that (Scott marries her in the end), but it's not all bad news. When Scott is shadowed by Keys at night, De Toth conjures up one of his nervy cat-and-mouse sequences; a couple of shoot-outs liven matters up and Scott, as *Variety* noted, is as hard-boiled as ever. When approached by the town committee to leave Twin Forks on a payment of $1,000, he declines the offer. Why, they enquire? "I like my work," grins Scott, fixing them with a cold stare. The three fugitives are eventually exposed, and shot, and bounty hunter Scott becomes the town's new sheriff; his name alone is enough to strike fear into anyone, as witnessed when three toughs ride into town bent on mischief. Informed that Jim Kipp is the new lawman, they quickly hightail it straight back outta town.

It may have had its ups and downs, but *The Bounty Hunter*, like Scott's numerous horse operas from this period, made money for Warner Bros. Although lacking in shoot-'em-up thrills, the movie is yet another durable reminder of the power of the Western at the box-office in the '50s and of Scott's monumental bearing that made these oaters so watchable; other stars may not have carried the sometime hackneyed storyline so convincingly with the deftness that he does here.

Columbia's 1955 offering, *Ten Wanted Men*, directed in cartoon-like fashion by H. Bruce Humberstone, is certainly no deep-thinking Western, relating the tale of former partners John Stewart (Scott) and Wick Campbell (Richard Boone), who become deadly rivals when Scott provides sanctuary to Donna Martell. The girl, brought up as an orphan by Boone, is terrified of the bully's sexual depredations, and Scott offers to make her his ward, thus setting in motion a vindictive range war. Scott is a self-made man who has it all: With his own bare hands, he's fought off Injuns, rustlers and outlaws to create the perfect haven in the Arizona badlands, and he's holding a welcome party for his lawyer brother (Lester Matthews) and nephew (Skip Homeier). Matthews is setting up a practice in the nearby town, a lawless backwater populated by saddle tramps and assorted rabble. Boone arrives at the shindig with Mexican gal Martell on his arm; she immediately takes a liking to Homeier and waltzes off with the young dude, leaving Boone fuming. Back in town, Martell storms out of Boone's room after a heated argument, sets up house with Homeier on Scott's ranch and all hell breaks loose. Boone, envious of Scott's success and his perceived "empire," calls in 10 desperadoes (headed by Leo Gordon and Lee Van Cleef) to terrorize his enemy, arranges for old-timer Clem Bevans to be murdered (Boone wickedly claims he shot the old man down in self-defense), inherits Bevans' ranch, rustles 200 head of cattle from Scott, kills Matthews in cold blood (three shots—one in the wrist, one in the arm, one in the heart) and turns the town into a war zone, all for the love of a woman. Yes, *Ten Wanted Men* is centered on sexual obsession and the havoc one man's warped feelings can create if pushed to the edge. Wrapped up in standard goodies-versus-baddies comic book cowboy format, it's a fast-paced, highly gratifying yet somewhat brainless oater, a real blast that's a lot jollier than some critics might otherwise suggest.

Wilfrid M. Cline's sunny photography, utilizing the Tucson, Arizona scenery with its forests of giant saguaro cacti to grand effect, sets the tone (as does Paul Sawtell's fine score) for this tough-as-old-boots saga containing some great acting: Boone is truly venomous as the lying, double-dealing hotel owner-turned-lunatic rancher; Scott is his normal, sturdy self, although slightly sanctimonious in his role as the resident land baron and do-gooder; Homeier shines as a reluctant hero thrust against his will into the thick of the gunplay; Alfonso Bedoya goes through his grinning Mexican drill; and broad-shouldered Gordon is in brutish form, staring icily at his opponents and throwing his considerable bulk around, forever needling Boone about his lack of success with women (Don Siegel, who worked with Gordon on Allied Artists' 1954 prison drama *Riot in Cell Block 11*, claimed that the actor was the scariest man he had ever met). Dennis Weaver is on hand as a rather green-around-the-gills sheriff, and the only downside is

Randolph Scott confronts Richard Boone in *Ten Wanted Men* (1955).

Jocelyn Brando (Marlon's older sister), rather nondescript in her role of Scott's fiancée (as she would like to see herself). Humberstone piles on the conflict and saloon standoffs with gusto, creating a *Rio Bravo*–type climax involving an explosive shoot-out and much throwing of dynamite bringing to an end Boone and Gordon's reign of terror ("Fill that hotel with lead," barks Scott at one point). Fair enough, Scott's black attire changes to dark blue and black again several times over and those 10 men become at least 14 at one point, and remain at 10 even when several are mown down. However, Humberstone's one and only Randolph Scott Western hits the bullseye more often than not, making for boisterous entertainment of an unsubtle kind. And for all the ladies, the movie ends with a double wedding—Scott and Homeier to Brando and Martell.

Made at a time when RKO-Radio's position as a leading film studio was in sharp decline (the company folded in 1957), Tim Whelan's 1955 biopic, *Rage at Dawn*, told of a federal marshal teaming up with an agent from Peterson's Detective Agency in 1866 and going undercover, infiltrating the notorious Reno Brothers gang in an endeavor to terminate their unending succession of bank and train robberies. Set in Southern Indiana, *Rage at Dawn* boasted a sterling cast: Scott (as James Barlow); Forrest Tucker, J. Carrol Naish, Myron Healey and Richard Garland (the four bad Reno siblings); Denver Pyle (the only law-abiding Reno brother); Kenneth Tobey (Scott's assistant); Mala Powers (the Renos' sister); Edgar Buchanan (once more, a corrupt judge); and strong support in the shape of Ray Teal and Howard Petrie. The Reno Brothers are accredited with being the first bunch of outlaws to stage train robberies; Whelan stop/

starts the narrative drift by interspersing personal vignettes with action-packed sequences. The curtain raiser packs a powerful punch: The Renos enter North Vernon in a horse-drawn buckboard to rob the bank, only to find themselves ambushed—someone has squealed to the authorities. In a gun-blazing fracas, Garland is shot dead, leaving his three brothers to cross the border into safe territory and argue the rights and wrongs of their way of life with "mealy-mouthed psalm singer" (Naish's words) Pyle. The so-called upright leading figures of Seymour, Indiana, including the sheriff, judge and lawyer, headed by Buchanan, are in the outlaws' pockets, creaming off a percentage from their robberies and even giving the bunch shelter from the law. When the barman responsible for the ambush is caught, tied up and left for dead in a burning stable ("Cremated Alive!" scream the news headlines), Scott (at 26 minutes in) enters the fray, posing as a train robber in order to become a Reno gang member and show them a few tricks of the trade. But he doesn't count on sexy blonde Powers falling in love with him, being afraid of exposing his true identity to her and his reciprocated feelings. (Tobey is fully aware of his partner's reputation as a womanizer.)

Rage at Dawn is a schizophrenic kind of production, lacking that vital spark to really bring it to life, compulsive in some areas, vaguely unsatisfactory in others; it just misses out on being a great Western, although the main man himself, now 57, was in tip-top form, both physically and mentally, showing no signs of flagging whatsoever in spite of his unremitting motion picture schedule. The final shooting spree, for example, is a humdinger—lured by the bait of $100,000 on board a train, the Reno mob holds up the locomotive; Scott pretends

Randolph Scott forces another hombre to eat some dust in *Tall Man Riding* (1955).

to participate in the robbery and then turns volte-face, blasting away at Tucker and his cohorts. Genial Tobey is unfortunately killed in the crossfire and the three brothers, all wounded, give themselves up. Offset against this exciting sequence are some of the slower interludes portraying the Reno family in turmoil, Pyle and Powers at the end of their tethers in trying to force their errant brothers to go straight by calling it quits on their nefarious activities. The movie ends on a disturbingly violent note: Tucker, Naish and Healey are strung up by a lynch mob and hanged inside a jail, Scott looking on in disbelief and horror, the camera zooming in on his shocked expression. It was never like this in the RKO Westerns of the 1940s!

Tall Man Riding (Warner Bros., 1955) is what many would term a traditional Randolph Scott 1950s Western. Sitting astride his handsome palomino horse Stardust, Scott (playing Larry Madden) looks every inch the "tall man riding" as, from a ridge, he watches William Ching being chased by three gunmen. Coming to Ching's aid, he shoots one pursuer dead and then declares his hatred of the man he's just saved from a bullet. It's personal payback time for Scott; eaten up by five years of bitterness, he returns to confront the cattle baron, Robert Barrat, who once bullwhipped him for daring to court his daughter. Ching then married Scott's ex-love, Dorothy Malone, and resides on the Warbonnet Ranch. Scott has ridden to the town of Little River to exact retribution ("I wanna look at Tuck Ordway through gun smoke.") but also gets caught up in a land-grab. It transpires that Barrat doesn't legally own his ranch, so oily dance palace proprietor John Baragrey ("That cheap smellin' chunk of cow grease," Scott calls him) wants to lay his hands on the land, sending out black-clad gunslinger Paul Richards—The Peso Kid—to murder anyone who stands in the way of his ambitions.

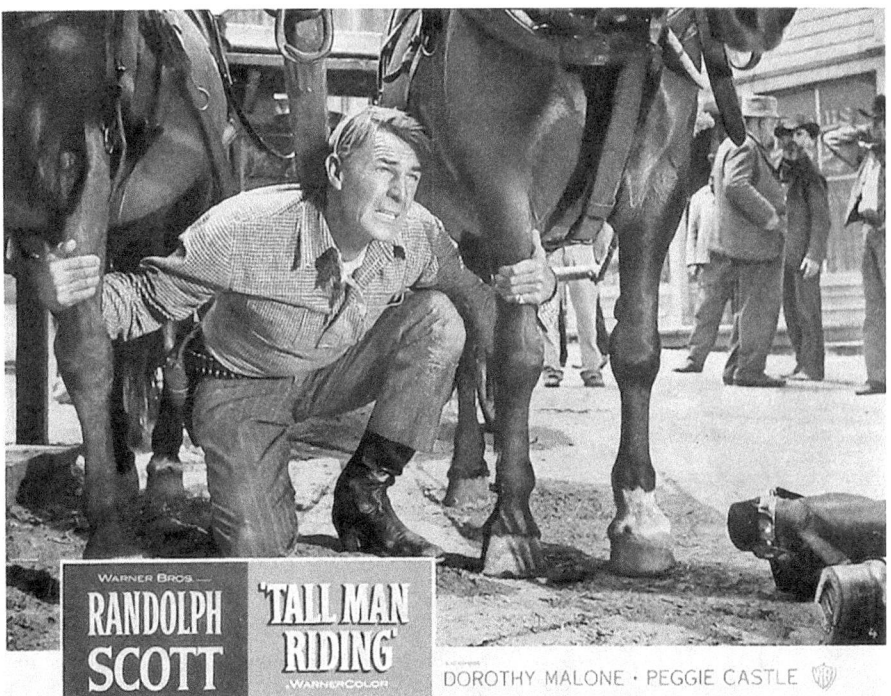

Tall Man Riding **becomes a traditional Randolph Scott 1950s Western.**

Like many of Scott's pictures for Warner Bros. and Columbia in the 1950s, *Tall Man Riding* has a mass of twists and turns guaranteed to keep an adult audience on its toes (the plot's too tricky for the kids, hence the British "A" rating). Malone still loves Scott but won't admit to it, telling him in no uncertain terms, "Your hate has brought you back." Saloon singer Peggie Castle is Baragrey's gal, although deep down she despises his underhanded methods at getting what he wants; John Dehner, a solicitor working for Scott, changes sides at the last moment for monetary gain; Scott has a showdown in a darkened room with Barrat ("I came back to kill you."), not realizing his old nemesis is half-blind and we know that somewhere along the line, Scott is itching to have a clash with smarty-pants Richards, which he does—and wins. Throw in a grueling, vicious fistfight between Scott and thuggish deputy Mickey Simpson, the pair spilling out of the sheriff's office into the dusty street, a thunderous rush for land, a final shoot-out between Scott, Dehner and Baragrey and several lines of sardonic dialogue courtesy of Joseph Hoffman, and audiences are left with one of Scott's more substantially satisfying Warner Bros.' oaters, competently directed by B-movie stalwart Lesley Selander. Scott, having staked his claim for the Warbonnet property, returns it to its rightful owners, an act guaranteed to have Malone fall straight back into his arms, which, of course, she does.

Mention must be made of Paul Sawtell's music for this film, both the first-class title theme and incidental soundtrack. Sawtell, David Buttolph, Mischa Bakaleinikoff, Hans J. Salter and a host of other creative composers contributed so much to the Western genre in the 1950s, and the power of their work shouldn't be underestimated. The unsung heroes of movie production, their symphonic scores had a resonance that could elevate a mundane outing to an acceptable one just by musical presence alone. Take time out to listen to Sawtell's multitude of cadences, leitmotifs, signatures, codas and overall notation in *Tall Man Riding*; they form a complex aural backdrop that complements the action throughout, rising and falling with the tempo and underscoring nuances. Western soundtracks, and the men who composed them, should never be taken for granted!

The second Scott/Brown 1955 Columbia outing, *A Lawless Street*, had B-movie hack-of-all-trades Joseph H. Lewis seated in the director's chair, hopefully to bring a much-needed sense of urgency to a movie in which Scott looked ever-so-slightly worn around the edges and dispirited, but not surprisingly

At the conclusion of *A Lawless Street* (1955), Randolph Scott turns in his badge and leaves town to start a new life.

so. Randy was thinking of calling time on his Western film career, acknowledging the fact that plots had now become so commonplace, with storylines repeated time and time again, that audience apathy was setting in; he himself was becoming less than enthusiastic about the end product. First, two nice touches—Paul Sawtell's haunting title theme played over the opening shot of a lone cowpoke riding into town, a man hired by Medicine Bend's two lowdown leading citizens to shoot Scott who, as Marshal Calem Ware, is tired of dealing in lead and longs for a quieter life; and when Scott tears off a page from his calendar, the logo on the calendar reads "GAMET'S VEGETABLE COMPOUND," a nod in the direction of scriptwriter Kenneth Gamet whose screenplay crams everything in to keep us alert. Scott blasts the cowboy (while seated in a barber shop) and then has to face the wrath of the dead man's simpleton brother, man-mountain Don Megowan, and leading to a spectacular fistfight between the two. Scott's estranged wife of nine years, delectable singer Angela Lansbury, dressed resplendently in red (her glittering mauve stage costume that she later dons is a wow in any language), arrives in Medicine Bend to put on a show in Warner Anderson's gambling den; Anderson wants to marry Lansbury, unaware she's already married; Jean Parker, wife of a local bigwig, is having a clandestine affair with Anderson; hotel owner John Emery is in collusion with Anderson, both wanting the town "wide open" to entice the miners and rake in the profits from their spending; and snake-eyed, leering Michael Pate is the hired gun, assigned to kill Scott and anyone else he takes a dislike to which, in this setup, is practically everybody.

The first hour of Columbia's colorful, intricately plotted oater engages the attention: Scott has to deal with his raging emotions over seeing Lansbury after so many years (she abhors violence and couldn't live with her husband in Apache Wells because of it), while tackling Anderson, Emery and Pate's dirty lowdown machinations. Fortunately for Scott, the mighty Megowan goes over to his side, ensuring that Anderson and company steer well clear when Scott is shot by Pate and presumed dead, Medicine Bend plummeting into lawlessness. But the final 20 minutes falls disappointingly flat and has a "let's get it all over" feel: Like Clint Eastwood's "Man With No Name" in *A Fistful of Dollars*, Scott seemingly returns from the dead, eliminating the loathsome Pate in a saloon shootout; Anderson guns down Emery by

mistake and is arrested; and Scott, after giving in his badge, heads off in a buggy to a new life with Lansbury.

Lewis, schooled in the "knock 'em out quick and cheap" department of schlock thrillers, directed with proficiency but was not fully able to overcome the predictability of it all; nevertheless, Scott and Brown were sufficiently impressed by his efforts to take him on for their next venture, *7th Cavalry*. However, it was at this juncture in his profession, in 1955, that Scott was offered Burt Kennedy's script for *Seven Men from Now* after John Wayne, Joel McCrea and Robert Preston turned it down. Directed by Budd Boetticher, this movie, and the six Boetticher' that would follow in its successful wake, would prove to be a new lease on life for Scott and producer Harry Joe Brown. So significant are the seven precision-made Boetticher Westerns in the annals of cinematic Western lore that they are dealt with more fully in chapter 16.

Accused of dereliction of duty by his commanding officer, an army captain volunteers to take a detail of misfits out to the site of the Little Bighorn massacre to retrieve General Custer's body. No, *7th Cavalry* (Columbia, 1956) is not *They Died With Their Boots On* revisited; there's hardly a shot to be heard, little in the way of bloodshed and only two fights. Moreover, Scott, playing Captain Tom Benson, is branded a coward right up to the final reel; he's far from being the gun-toting hero we are all used to seeing. *7th Cavalry* goes against the grain; it's slow and thoughtful, Peter Packer's insightful script examining one man's need to regain both his tarnished reputation and self-esteem in

Jay C. Flippen, Randolph Scott and Frank Faylen in *7th Cavalry* (1956)

the face of open hostility. Here, motives speak louder than action. Rubbished in many quarters, this latter-day Scott opus, produced in the same time frame that the Budd Boetticher classics were getting underway, is offbeat, talkative but rewarding, proving that we don't need to have a succession of gunfights every few minutes to come up with a worthwhile analytical Western that is different from the rest of the pack.

And that difference begins with the scenery—not Lone Pine or Red Rock Canyon but Durango, Mexico, substituted for the actual location of the Custer battle in eastern Montana, a snow-capped dormant volcano forming a breathtaking panoramic backdrop to Fort Lincoln. Scott, leaving fiancée Barbara Hale outside, approaches the fort to find it apparently deserted (*Beau Geste* anyone?). But this isn't the case; a woman appears and straight off, the accusations fly thick and fast. "Dead. All dead," she wails, having lost her husband, pointedly glaring at Scott and sniping at him "You were Custer's favorite." The battle-weary, bedraggled remnants of the cavalry ride in from the Little Bighorn massacre and Scott is soon tarnished with the tag of "The man who wasn't there." But was that his fault? At the court of inquiry into "this shocking defeat," led by prospective father-in-law Russell Hicks, Scott's fellow officers claim that he used his close friendship with Custer in order to quit his post and bring Hale back to the fort to get wed. In addition, Scott isn't from West Point; he's an ex-gambler and drifter who has worked his way up through the ranks the hard way, another reason why Hicks and his antagonistic colleagues look down on him. Custer comes under attack for perceived tactical blunders; Scott leaps to his defense ("A whitewash!" he shouts) and is confined to barracks, an outcast among his own men ("My place was with them," he tells Hale, stricken with guilt and grief). However, when a presidential order is received stating that

Custer and his soldiers' bodies must be retrieved from Little Bighorn for proper military burial, Scott grabs at the chance to redeem himself by volunteering for the command of what could well turn out to be a suicide mission. Putting together a ragtag outfit comprised of the garrison's lowlifes (Leo Gordon, Jay C. Flippen, Frank Faylen and Denver Pyle included), he sets off for Little Bighorn with his very own "Dirty Dozen," knowing that the Sioux regard the site as big medicine ground, a holy place, and will in all probability prevent the soldiers from reclaiming Yellow Hair's body.

After quelling a mutiny, Faylen unexpectedly coming to Scott's assistance, Pyle and beefy bruiser Gordon cause further trouble for him: Pyle is shot dead by Flippen after attempting to stick a knife into Scott's back, while Gordon (he loses out to Scott in a savage free-for-all) gets an arrow between the shoulders when the Sioux encircle the patrol at the burial site, intent on starving them to death. But help of a supernatural kind is on the way from Harry Carey, Jr. Knowing that Scott is innocent of cowardice (he overheard Custer giving him permission to go on leave), he rides out to join up with the detail on Custer's second horse, Dandy, but is brought down by an Indian brave. Dandy gallops ahead and appears on a ridge above Little Bighorn; when they see him, the superstitious Sioux turn tail and vamoose, convinced that Custer's spirit has returned on his ghostly mount. "They go in peace," intones Sioux warrior Pat Hogan in perfect English. "The spirit of Yellow Hair has spoken." The onerous task of collecting the dead completed, Scott is vindicated of charges of desertion, marries Hale (her father now approves of the match) and becomes Fort Lincoln's new commanding officer.

Director Joseph H. Lewis treats the audience to two tremendous 360-degree pans in this movie: the first, when Scott enters the silent fort and looks around him; the second, a ground-level shot of the troopers lying flat on their stomachs, mud-caked boots toward camera, the circling Indians spotted by the legs of their cantering horses. There's also an atmospheric scene filmed at dusk, a bugler outlined against the soaring bulk of the volcano and fort ramparts, the screen awash in violet-blue tones. It's attention to detail like this that can make or break a production; here, Lewis, Scott and Harry Joe Brown (aided by Mischa Bakaleinikoff's jaunty, military-type score) hatched an intelligent, psychological horse opera short on thrills and spills but high on emotional content. Considering that Scott, around this date, was seriously considering packing up moviemaking altogether, *7th Cavalry*, in its own modest, quiet way, is quite an achievement.

The last of Scott's 10-picture deal with Warner Bros., *Shoot-Out at Medicine Bend* (1957) was shot quickly and cheaply in black-and-white, the company viewing the actor as a star on the wane, reasoning that his adjudged lessening in popularity didn't warrant the cost of a color movie. As it stands, *Shoot-Out at Medicine Bend* has to qualify as the most bizarre Western Scott ever made in his long tour of duty in the saddle, deadly serious one minute, just plain silly the next, with comedy director Richard L. Bare in the driving seat (between 1942-1956, Bare directed 63 10-minute comedy shorts, the little-known *So You Think* series, plus a handful of Z-Westerns. That's how much Warner Bros. thought of Scott's status at the time!). *Shoot-Out at Medicine Bend* would have been the perfect vehicle for the Marx Brothers to lampoon in the '30s, Bob Hope and Bing Crosby to satirize in the '40s and The Three Stooges to fool around with in the '50s. But not as a Randolph Scott spoof. More or less wrapped up in 1955 but released two years later because Warner Bros. didn't know how to market it, the film begins in vintage knockout mode: Scott (as Buck Devlin), James Garner and Gordon Jones wade into a murderous

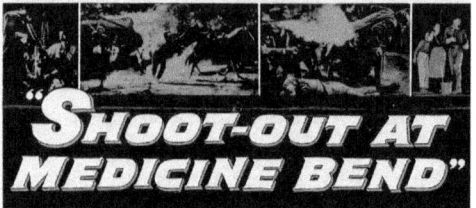

Indian attack on settlers, women and children, screaming for their lives and horses bolting, the Redskins going berserk, Roy Webb's high-powered score adding to the excitement as the warriors are driven off. Scott is then alarmed to discover that the settlers' rifles and ammunition are unusable (coal dust for gunpowder); as his brother died in the raid, he decides to visit Medicine Bend and ferret out those miscreants who sold the defective hardware to the homesteaders, classing them by default as murderers. Stopping off to cool down by a spot of skinny-dipping in a lake, the three soldiers find to their consternation that their clothes, horses and money have been stolen and the movie, from a barnstorming beginning that promised so much, goes wildly off-balance, descending into vaudeville farce or, if you prefer, embarrassing self-parody.

Skimpily clothed and looking hilariously ridiculous (Jones wears a grass skirt!), the trio chance upon a Quaker's camp, dress up in brethren garb and wander into town masquerading as religious fanatics, speaking in "thees" and "thous," drinking buttermilk and attracting the attention of the two local beauties, singer Dani Crayne and storekeeper's daughter Angie Dickinson. James Craig and Myron Healey play the resident bad guys, running the town between them and trying to put Dickinson's father, Harry Harvey, out of business. Scott sneaks into Healey's emporium during the night, dons black shirt, trousers and guns and creeps around town like an Old West version of Robin Hood, giving back to the poor what he steals from the rich, in this case Healey. After several almost comical situations (Jones spiking his buttermilk with bourbon; villain John Alderson falling headfirst into a well, a trap set for Scott; a 30-second trial by jury in a jail cell; Trevor Bardette the liquor-swilling, ineffective sheriff), Garner and Jones sidestep a hanging, the brethren coming to their rescue; Healey is shot dead; and Craig impales himself on a scythe after a tussle with Scott. Back in uniform, Scott waltzes off with Dickinson, Garner takes up with Crayne and Jones decides to become a full-time Quaker, *if* he can beat his habit of lacing buttermilk with whiskey!

"Thee has to talk like them," states Scott to Garner and Jones, his tongue most firmly in his cheek, while Webb's thunderous score carries on nonstop, seemingly belonging to another, more meaningful, production, not the empty-headed hokum on offer here. Yes, it does bring a smile to the face at times and Scott actually looks as though he's enjoying himself (perhaps glad to be free of his contractual commitments to Warner Bros.), but will *you* be smiling after sitting through this oddball finale to his Warner Bros. repertoire? A Randolph Scott vengeance-driven Western with a difference, that's for sure!

Chapter 13
McCrea in the 1950s

1950, the year it all took off, over 120 Westerns issued in this one year alone. On the starting line were Hollywood's big-hitters: James Stewart in Fox's *Broken Arrow*; Gregory Peck in Fox's *The Gunfighter*; John Wayne in Republic's *Rio Grande*; Alan Ladd in Paramount's *Branded*; Robert Taylor in MGM's *Devil's Doorway*; Errol Flynn in Warner Bros.' *Montana* and Gary Cooper in Warner Bros.' *Dallas*. All classed as A-productions. But giving the big boys a run for their money were the medium-budgeters: John Payne in Paramount's *The Eagle and the Hawk*; Tim Holt in RKO's *Dynamite Pass*; Jock Mahoney in Allied Artists' *The Kangaroo Kid*; Stephen McNally in Universal's *Wyoming Mail*; Rod Cameron in Columbia's *Stage to Tucson* and the four subjects of this book who were to reign over all others in this less-than-expensive setup: Scott in *The Nevadan*, Murphy in *The Kid from Texas*, Montgomery in *Indian Scout* and McCrea in *The Outriders*.

Has there ever been a more gorgeous female lead in a Western than Arlene Dahl? Her flawless beauty radiates from the screen, one of the real reasons to watch MGM's *The Outriders*, a predictable programmer treading very familiar territory. During the last days of the Civil War, three escaped Confederate convicts (McCrea, Barry Sullivan and James Whitemoor) enlist in one of Quantrill's splinter groups, led by Jeff Corey, whose aim is to waylay a million in gold from trader Ramon Novarro's wagon train (widow Dahl is one of the passengers) and present it to the Confederacy to aid the war effort. When the war ends halfway through their mission, Sullivan reveals that the gold is meant for Corey's gang only and that the wagoners (or mule skinners) will still have to be massacred, whether hostilities have ended or not ("You want to take over, it will have to be with a gun," McCrea warns his partner). McCrea, who with Sullivan has

Joel McCrea and Arlene Dahl in *The Outriders* (1950)

fallen for Dahl's smoldering charms (and who wouldn't), turns about-face, not wanting unnecessary blood on his hands. Organizing Novarro's men into a fighting force, they put paid to Corey's gunmen in a blazing shoot-out finale at Cow Creek and, for good measure, McCrea empties the entire contents of his revolver into treacherous Sullivan.

Unlike Universal, Warner Bros. and Columbia, MGM didn't invest heavily in Westerns during the '50s and, although the Technicolor photography is as stunning as Dahl's red locks, plus André Previn provides a resounding score, the picture falls flat after a 10-minute sequence coming in on the hour involving a hazardous river crossing. McCrea (as Will Owen) also seems to go off the boil at this stage, his character switching from bearded tough guy to saintly savior: At one point, he gives the train's entire stock of ponies to a bunch of harmless-looking Pawnee and moons a bit too much over Dahl, who emotes like mad ("Because you want me most," she breathes to McCrea, who wonders what she sees in him), particularly in the scene where McCrea fits new green dancing shoes on her feet, the male ensemble looking on, drooling with lust. The dazzling Utah location work, a rousing finale and MGM's overall high production costs save *The Outriders* from middle-of-the-road status, a picture whose plot themes were explored to better effect in Scott's *Virginia City* and *Hangman's Knot*. And why Hollywood failed to cash in on Dahl's talent remains a mystery: The girl could act (she was outstanding in Fox's *Journey to the Center of the Earth*) and she certainly had the looks, although it has been quoted (notably by James Mason) that she could be difficult and unpunctual on set. The actress positively glows in this movie, floating across set in her widow's dress, a treasure not to be missed. The picture also marked the debut of McCrea's horse Dollar, with his distinctive white blaze and circular white spot on his left hindquarters. Fed up with the unreliability of the "Hollywood horses" that had one master after another and could be temperamental as a result, McCrea bought his own steed (Scott did the same, buying his palomino mount, Stardust) and never let anyone else ride him except on one occasion, allowing Doris Day to use Dollar in *Calamity Jane*.

The second of only two MGM Westerns McCrea made in the '50s, *Stars in My Crown* featured the actor as tough preacher Josiah Doziah Gray, and a role he claimed to be one of his favorites. Directed by that master of the suspenseful horror movie, Jacques Tourneur, this nostalgic vision of small-town America in the 1870s strayed into Mark Twain/Huckleberry

Joel McCrea and Ellen Drew in *Stars in My Crown* (1950)

Finn domain and was a might twee for some tastes. McCrea arrives in town with two six-shooters, takes young orphan Dean Stockwell under his wing, gets in a tangle with Doc James Mitchell over an outbreak of fever, comes to the rescue of black farmer Juano Hernandez who's being terrorized by the Ku Klux Klan (The Nightriders or "Yellowbacks in fancy dress," as McCrea terms them) because of a mica lode crossing his land and saves Arthur Hunnicutt (as Chloroform Wiggins) from a whip-lashing. Folksy humor and much homespun philosophizing abounds, along with plenty of fishing, the only real tension coming when McCrea prevents the Klan from lynching Hernandez by reading out to the mob a fictitious will in which the farmer has left everything to them, thereby pricking their consciences. Maybe McCrea was presenting a classic Western hero as a man of the cloth, but the end result was a pleasant-enough family-oriented picture that had little to do with the Old West. Horror fans will note James Arness (*The Thing from Another World*) in a minor role, while another horror stalwart, Marshall Thompson, narrated the plot. Lovely Ellen Drew supplied the romantic interest.

In 1950, McCrea struck a three-picture deal with Universal-International at around the same time the company was busy promoting Audie Murphy as their exciting new Western star, following his success as Billy the Kid in *The Kid from Texas*. Universal Westerns of this period were punchy and gritty with loads of razzle-dazzle, and it was hoped that this harder approach would rub off onto McCrea's more phlegmatic method of acting. Judging by *Saddle Tramp*, it didn't. Roaming the wide open spaces, unshackled by having no responsibilities whatsoever and as free as a bird ("Just passin' through,"

is his mantra), rootless Chuck Connor's (McCrea) easy world is turned upside down when he takes on four young boys (Jimmy Hunt, Orley Lindgren, Gordon Gebert and Gregory Moffett) after his best pal falls off a horse and breaks his neck during a storm. The ex-bronco buster has to now knuckle down and get a job, which he does, on child-hating John McIntire's ranch. Leaving the kids in the woods and ferrying food to them at night, he comes under the suspicion of surly John Russell, involved in rustling cattle from his boss' ranch and placing the blame on fellow rancher Antonio Moreno. Then along comes Mrs. Audie Murphy, Wanda Hendrix, playing a 19-year-old waif on the run who stays to look after the boys while McCrea is having to contend with accusations of siding with the rival ranch, Russell throwing his weight around and needling the cowhand at every given opportunity.

Avuncular McCrea doesn't even wear a gun and holster in *Saddle Tramp*, indicative of the film's light-hearted touch, the storyline moving from comedy to farce to a couple of brawls to dampen the sweetness of it all. Jeanette Nolan (McIntire's real-life wife) reckons the children are leprechauns, or "the little people," nobody gets shot and perky Hendrix, although half McCrea's age (she was 22 and he was 45 during filming), wants romance with the good-natured drifter. It's a happy, colorful enjoyable mix from director Hugo Fregonese (more famous for his 1954 X-rated Edward G. Robinson gangster thriller, *Black Tuesday*), a catchy leitmotif, "The Cry of the Wild," running through it (Frankie Lane had a hit single with the tune in the same year). Russell is eventually unearthed as the traitor in the camp in a lively climax and McIntire gets to bond with the orphans. As McCrea and Hendrix, now wed, prepare the unhappy lads for school, one of them moans, "Creepin' Creepers, we wanna be saddle tramps like you." "Man's got responsibilities," grins McCrea, summing up a picture that's far more suitable to a younger audience than those wanting gunfights, killings and warring Redskins on their platter. And despite the shortage of gunplay, the leading man is in highly watchable form.

While Scott, Murphy and Montgomery were pushing onwards and upwards with their own tough action epics (*Colt .45*, *Kansas Raiders* and *The Iroquois Trail*), McCrea's fourth 1950 picture was another soft-pedaler, *Frenchie*, an unofficial, loose revamp of *Destry Rides Again*; Murphy would revive the original in 1954's highly successful *Destry*, so Universal toned down *Frenchie*'s publicity to give Murphy's penciled-in production the prominence it needed. Once more, McCrea, playing Sheriff Tom Banning, eschewed a gun and holster, adopting the verbal approach in dealing with villains and giving up most of his screen time to brassy Shelley Winters. She's Frenchie Fontaine, new

owner of Bottleneck's Scarlet Angel saloon, pal Elsa Lanchester, a Countess, at her right-hand side, and the lass has a hidden agenda: She wants to kill the duo who murdered her father when she was a small girl. Rival saloon owner Paul Kelly, top dog in nearby Chuckaluck, is one of them, but who's the other? It turns out to be John Emery; his wife (Marie Windsor) once had the hots for McCrea and still hankers after him. Throw in a barroom brawl between Winters and Windsor, lots of drunken horseplay, a jealous rival (John Russell) scowling continuously at McCrea, Winters hustling and bustling, all heaving bosom and flamboyant costumes, and an ending where Windsor shoots her husband and McCrea shoots Kelly, and we have a lukewarm Universal Western that doesn't amount to much. "I'm looking for a man," states Winters, to which McCrea replies, "Lucky man!" This becomes an example of some of the witty banter taking place between the two. Needless to say, they end up hugging and kissing in the final reel, Windsor's criminal act shrugged off as justifiable homicide!

Hans J. Salter provided a decent score to an indifferent Western that, compared to others of the day, patently failed to promote McCrea as a forceful man of action. The picture was neither involving nor exciting and one was left with the feeling as to whether or not McCrea was able to cut it as a hard-headed cowpoke. Scott, Murphy, Montgomery and the rest of the bunch—Rod Cameron, Jeff Chandler, Dale Robertson, Sterling Hayden, Rory Calhoun, Tim Holt, Stephen McNally—were starring in some rousing stuff, and McCrea was somehow being left in their dusty wake. Although not classed as high-budget productions, his films, like Murphy's at Universal, were costing

Joel McCrea (right) and Dean Stockwell in *Cattle Drive* (1951)

up to $700,000, a tidy-enough sum in the early '50s. Universal obviously felt they were getting their money's worth—the McCrea oaters, although nowhere near as lively as Murphy's, were successful on his name alone and still look good today. *Cattle Drive*, his only 1951 Western, contained no bad guys, no gunplay, no fistfights and no women (McCrea shows a picture of Frances Dee to Dean Stockwell and that's it) but benefits from superb color location work in California's Death Valley (photography by Maury Gertsman), a great score written principally by Frank Skinner and Milton Rosen and assured direction from Kurt Neumann. In its rite of passage tale of a spoiled rich kid (Stockwell) transforming from obnoxious brat to level-headed youth on a cattle drive, this Universal Western, though lacking in full-blooded incident, represents Old West traditions in realistic fashion, with McCrea redeeming himself after his less-than-riveting show in *Frenchie*.

Stepping off a locomotive when it stops to take on water, child star of the time Stockwell wanders into the scrub to hunt for lizards and gets left behind when the train resumes its journey. Picked up by cowhand McCrea (Dan Matthews), he's taken into camp protesting his rough treatment and ordered to assist cook Chill Wills in his chores. With beans on the menu morning, noon and night, saddle sores and Henry Brandon labeling him a jinx, Stockwell's holier-than-thou attitude ("Dirty, smelly cow country," is his view of the great outdoors) crumbles; he begins to learn how to be civil and starts to embrace the humble, honest life of a cowboy, keeping watch on the herd, appreciating the arduous job it entails and even helping Joel bring in a magnificent wild black stallion to tame (footage from Universal's 1949 *Red Canyon* was used in some sequences). There's a thrilling stampede and grumpy Brandon (he was Chief Scar in John Ford's *The Searchers*) eventually softens his hostile way of thinking toward the lad, appreciating his horse-riding skills. Credit must go to Neumann for filming outside in the night scenes, giving the production an added authenticity; usually, these movies were shot in a studio in '50s Westerns. Reunited with his father (Leon Ames) in Santa Fe, Stockwell, now a fully-fledged cowpoke and sensible with it, takes off with McCrea to try to rope that big black stallion with Ames, decked out in cowboy gear, coming along for the ride. The action ends with a marvelous view of the three riding into the sunset.

Captains Courageous out West sums up *Cattle Drive*, a movie that's difficult not to like. McCrea plays the hard-working regular guy with charismatic ease ("a winning performance," said the *New York Times*), demonstrating that he could pull it off if he set his mind to it and had the right material to work on (he even sings a lullaby at one point). All right, the picture wasn't as rambunctious as Murphy's *The Cimarron Kid*, Scott's *Santa Fe* or Montgomery's *The Texas Rangers*, all released the same year; McCrea's sagebrush sagas from this period tend to be understated examples of the genre, the man's role-playing understated also. That was the McCrea way and he wasn't about to change it, not one iota, for the rest of his career on horseback.

Following *Cattle Drive*, McCrea renegotiated his contract with Universal, allowing for a percentage deal on his next three features with the company instead of a straight salary; but he still got paid a basic $50,000 per picture. He then returned to Warner Bros. for one final time in 1952 to make *The San Francisco Story*, a political espionage-type thriller that was to him what *The Man Behind the Gun* would be to Randolph Scott in 1953 (the movie was one of McCrea's favorites). Set on 'Frisco's Barbary Coast in 1856, McCrea played mine boss Rick Nelson, visiting the city with partner Richard Erdman to replenish supplies and become embroiled in Sidney Blackmer's plans to control the state; the corrupt big shot has the Committee of Vigilance on his case (led by newspaper chief Onslow Stevens) who hang anyone breaking the law. Blackmer wants to recruit McCrea for his own devious purposes, even though he worked for Stevens five years back. Luscious Yvonne De Carlo is Blackmer's girl but she soon sets her sights on McCrea, who has to undergo a couple of beatings, a bushwhacking, a shooting in a planned ambush and a duel on horseback with Blackmer, both sporting shotguns, before he lays claim to her charms.

Shot in black-and-white, *The San Francisco Story* veers all over the place thanks to Robert Parrish's uneven hand, moderately exciting one minute, tedious and talkative the next. D.D. Beauchamp's script is quite witty at times, as when McCrea escapes from the

Joel McCrea rises above forgettable fare in *The San Francisco Story* (1952).

hold of a ship bound for Hong Kong and staggers over to De Carlo's house, dirty and disheveled. "Does everyone who tips his hat to you end up in a boat?" he asks. "No," she replies. "I save that for you." And when McCrea and Blackmer agree to shotguns at dawn, McCrea growls, "I always figured they were good for shooting buzzards and rats." Horror buffs will spot hulking Tor Johnson as a barman in a waterfront saloon while atmospheric camerawork depicting the fog-shrouded muddy streets makes the picture appear like a '40s horror flick. McCrea performs to the best of his abilities, De Carlo lights up the screen, but the end result is as far removed from his Universal Westerns as you could possibly get; it didn't do all that well at the cash registers and, to most diehard cowboy fans, is instantly forgettable fare.

Before he resumed his Universal career in 1953, McCrea traveled to England to appear as Lt. Colonel Robert Taine in Raymond Stross Productions' *Rough Shoot* (aka *Shoot First*). This low-budget thriller sank without trace, probably convincing McCrea and his backers that the Western milieu was where the actor should now really concentrate his future career. Returning to the States, he shot *The Lone Hand* in the picturesque mountains of Durango, Colorado, directed by George Sherman, the first of his new three-picture deal with Universal. Like *Cattle Drive*, *The Lone Hand* was geared more toward a family audience, with young Jimmy Hunt narrating and starring as McCrea's son, worried that his father, who has just purchased a rundown ranch near the town of Timberline, is resorting to banditry to clear his debts. In fact, widower McCrea (as Zachary Halleck) happens to be a Pinkerton detective, going undercover by teaming up with robbers Alex Nicol and James Arness in the hope that they will lead him to the outfit's boss. There have been a spate of violent holdups in the area, and the local regulators want whoever's responsible brought to heel.

We are not aware that McCrea is on the side of the law until over an hour has passed. Up until then, we might be left wondering if this is the first Western in which he really is a bad 'un, such is the change his character undergoes, from caring father to quick-tempered hard case. He's surly to his son, telling him to keep his mouth shut when Hunt sees him rob a stagecoach, claims he's sick and tired of farming and only appears to marry Barbara Hale to gain a substitute mother for Hunt. Suspicious of his repeated disappearances, all followed by news of another holdup, she tells him, "You only married me to provide a mother for your boy" and leaves. On his planned final job, 10 mules hauling $16,000 in gold bullion from a mine, he instructs Hunt to send a telegram to Pinkerton's giving details of the robbery, but the youngster is caught by nearby horse rancher Charles Drake, the brains behind the robberies. Sherman ups the pace in the final reel; McCrea confesses all to Hale ("I had to play it safe and slow") and tells her that he really loves her, while Drake is arrested after a fight in a river.

A thoughtful script by Joseph Hoffman includes an amusing interlude where all and sundry try to explain to Hunt why McCrea and Hale would want to be left alone for a couple of days on their honeymoon, and McCrea's amusingly worded attempts at being a family man with his new bride and son. But we are still left with the feeling that, this being McCrea's seventh Western of the 1950s, things would start to heat up for him. There's very little action in *The Lone Hand*—it's a soft-centered round-'em-up-cowboy offering that can't hold a candle to Murphy's magnificent *Tumbleweed*, Montgomery's tough *Gun Belt* and Scott's rousing *Thunder Over the Plains*, all released the same year ("A wholesome family-type Western," summed up the *New York Times*). McCrea is solid in the part but doesn't betray much emotion, even coming across as wooden in some scenes. His Westerns were admittedly good to look at and, all credit to his standing, audiences could enjoy pictures like *Saddle Tramp*, *Cattle Drive* and *The Lone Hand*, even though they weren't rough and rowdy shoot-'em-ups, because of McCrea's languid individuality. His line to Hale, quoted above, summed up his standpoint on filmmaking—"Safe and slow." Perhaps it was now time for him to cut loose a bit.

Border River, his 1954 outing, was marginally more exciting than *The Lone Hand*, again directed by George Sherman. It's 1865: Major Clete Mattson (McCrea) crosses

Pedro Armendariz, Yvonne De Carlo and Joel McCrea in *Border River* (1954)

the U.S./Mexico border river pursued by eight gun-blazing Union cavalry soldiers with the intention of striking a deal with General Pedro Armendariz; he's stolen $2,000,000 in gold bullion from the North and wishes to trade it for arms, gunpowder and supplies urgently required by the Southern army. Set around the rugged Colorado River area of Moab, Utah, Irving Glassberg's striking Technicolor photography and a fine score from Milton Rosen and Frank Skinner enlivens this "we've seen it all before" tale of stolen Union booty heading for the Confederates in one last effort to prevent the North from winning the war.

Armendariz, a renegade, is head honcho of Zona Libre, a haven for those above the law; deserters, killers and mercenaries roam the streets, Armendariz's men shooting anyone accused of spying without a proper trial ever taking place. Armendariz's mistress, Yvonne De Carlo, catches McCrea's eye and he refuses to take Howard Petrie's advice—"Send her a letter. It's safer,"—about pursuing her. There's plenty of double-dealing, intrigue and talk in the first part of Sherman's 80-minute "down Mexico way" feature: Each time McCrea enters his hotel room, someone is lurking in the shadows to cause him harm; Petrie turns out to be an agent on McCrea's tail, but can't pull a gun on him ("You're no killer, but I am," growls McCrea, snatching Petrie's revolver); Armendariz grows suspicious of McCrea's real agenda and his overt attentiveness in De Carlo; a shady baron (Ivan Triesault), in charge of the supplies McCrea so desperately wants, decides to line his own pockets; Alfonso Bedoya overacts like crazy in his standard grinning Mexican bandit routine and McCrea takes a savage beating from two dudes after the gold, returning the favor with a vengeance a few moments later. Forty-odd minutes go by before the action moves away from the confines of the town into Utah's splendid rocky outback. McCrea, after an alarming scene when his horse flounders in a quicksand (it wasn't Dollar—he vetoed the idea), arranges a meeting with two of his men to stash the gold bars near the bog but is followed by De Carlo, who loses her expensive necklace on the trail. Armendariz's troops, searching for the gold, find the necklace and the Mexican leader puts two and two together ("So. You prefer the gringo," he snarls at the lass). Triesault is shot in the back for his two-timing ("The price of treason!") and that quicksand proves to be the downfall of Armendariz; McCrea drowns him in it during a muddy fistfight, the supplies eventually bought from General Salvador Baguez, the new boss of Zona Libre.

Border River would have been an ideal vehicle for Randolph Scott, a cowboy veteran adept at playing the happy-go-lucky soldier of fortune-type character. McCrea ambles through the proceedings with a spring in his step and conducts himself with honors, seeming to put more muscular energy into his role than before. De Carlo, it has to be said, is a real beauty, *and* she could act. Perhaps *Border River* was overshadowed by United Artists' *Vera Cruz*, released the same year, a big-budgeter featuring Gary Cooper and Burt Lancaster, the undisputed king of all those Confederate gold/Mexican army/soldiers of fortune sagas that the studios had relied on since the 1940s. As it is, McCrea's more moderate offering is a good example of a solid, middle-of-the-decade Universal Western that might have been that little bit classier in some departments where it vaguely disappoints.

McCrea rounded off his Universal contract with his second release of 1954, Jesse Hibbs' *Black Horse Canyon*, which was to him what *Sierra* had been to Audie Murphy. Hardly any gunfire, a couple of punch-ups and a plot revolving around the capture of a rampaging wild horse—not your average Universal action-packed Western, that's for certain, but in its less-than-showy way, this proved to be one of the best of McCrea's six outings for the company. The simplified storyline had drifter McCrea (as Del Rockwell) and rival ranchers Mari Blanchard and Murvyn Vye all attempting to tame a magnificent wild black stallion called Outlaw ("A convict on the run."); the horse is charging around the canyons and mesas, breaking down fences to release captive steeds and refusing to be caught. McCrea wants to corral the horse to win the affection of Blanchard, while troublemaker Vye views Outlaw as a breeding machine for his bloodstock. Race Gentry,

McCrea's young sidekick, naively falls in love with Blanchard, but she's far too mature for him; rough and ready McCrea is more her type of guy, and they eventually end up with wedding nuptials on their minds, Outlaw having been tamed and Vye given a well-deserved thumping for being such a thorough nuisance throughout.

Daniel Mainwaring's sharp script allows McCrea to demonstrate his light comedic skills, as when he pinions Blanchard to the ground and kisses her. "It's a nice view from up here," he grins. "Why did you kiss me?" she asks, coyly. "I wanted to see if I could," he replies, "and I can." And when Blanchard tries to rope Outlaw, backing away from his rear hoofs, she states, "The last time he kicked me he wasn't trying to shake hands." Attractively filmed near Bloomquist Ranch, in Douglas, Arizona, George Robinson's bright photography perfectly captures the sun-baked arid locations and Outlaw (an entry in 1955's Patsy Award of Excellence for animal actors) is a horse lover's dream come true. *Black Horse Canyon* must have looked grand in a packed theater; it's 81 minutes of pure family entertainment and McCrea's laconic delivery fits the horsey action like a glove.

McCrea parted company with Universal in 1954, lending his talents almost exclusively to United Artists and Allied Artists from 1955 onwards (as did Montgomery), Fox's 1958 *Cattle Empire* being the one exception. He hadn't really made the impact that Universal's *numero uno* cowboy star, Audie Murphy had achieved; there is more lead expended in *Kansas Raiders* than there is in all six of McCrea's Universal Westerns, and moreover, Murphy had scored a box-office smash with *Destry* in 1954, while *Black Horse Canyon* was only moderately successful. Looked at 60 years on, McCrea's Universal features may lack the helter-skelter action set pieces that Murphy's pictures possessed in wagonloads, and in many instances he's too self-controlled for his own good. This is a criticism often leveled at McCrea, that, as an actor of some considerable experience and with a broader public appeal, he could have put much more effort into his characterizations. Scott, although never a huge Hollywood star, fell more easily into the Western role from as far back as 1932. His rugged looks were at one with the parts he portrayed, almost, if you like, born into the saddle; one could imagine him as a cowboy riding the open range in a former existence. Boyish-looking Murphy had to work darned hard to prove his worth as an actor, and *did* put in the required effort. George Montgomery, as we shall see, was almost the stereotypical low-budget Western tough guy but didn't pretend to be otherwise, fully aware of his acting limitations. Because of McCrea's undeniable reputation forged during his productive pre-1950 period, it's easy to write off his Westerns from 1950 to 1954 as lightweight family fodder, but scratch the surface and they become a shade more meaningful than that. Collectively, they represent a time when the Western motion picture hit the heights of perfection, standing up six decades later as colorful additions to the genre. McCrea's star qualities undoubtedly shine through but in a different light than Scott's, Murphy's and Montgomery's. Keep that in mind and audiences might enjoy his easygoing oaters just that little bit more.

Into the town of Bannerman rides circuit judge Rick Thorne (McCrea), firmly resolved in bringing Tom Bannerman (Kevin McCarthy) to trial for murder; McCarthy's father (John McIntire) rules the town and its inhabitants like a feudal state and will not stand for any stranger poking his nose into his affairs. Constructed on similar plot lines to *High Noon* and *Rio Bravo*, *Stranger on Horseback* (adapted from a story by Louis L'Amour), McCrea's first United Artists film of the '50s, may well lay claim to being his best from this decade. Over a short running time of 66 minutes, he brings a quiet authority to the part of a gun-toting judge who won't take "no" for an answer. Recently restored by the British Film Institute, fans can now see for themselves the short-lived Ansco Color process in all of its garish glory and appreciate McCrea's finely-tuned performance as the black-clad judge who rides roughshod over McIntire's clan with a disarming, but steely, smile on his face.

Joel McCrea and John Carradine in *Stranger on Horseback*

Paul Dunlap's majestic title theme gets us off to a great start. "A circuit judge needs three things," narrates McCrea. "A law book, a horse and a gun." In town, he meets crooked jack-of-all trades Colonel John Carradine and spineless Marshal Emile Meyer, both under McIntire's omnipresent thumb. Arresting McCarthy in a saloon and marching him to jail, McCrea and Meyer have to face up to McIntire's gunmen, who move in but find their match in the harder-than-nails judge. Strolling down the street, a tough throws water in his face. "Thanks. It's a hot day," says McCrea and, minutes later, gives the man a taste of his own medicine, ducking him in a horse trough. "This is my land and I'll run it my way," barks McIntire, perturbed at some of the townsfolk gaining a little too much self-respect under McCrea's forceful disposition, including Meyer. McCarthy's cousin, fiery dark-haired Miroslava, spots McCrea swimming in the nude and makes a play for him, while Nancy Gates and her father (Walter Baldwin) see the shooting and agree to be witnesses at McCarthy's trial, if he ever gets one. The last third of the movie has McCrea, Meyer, Miroslava, Gates and Baldwin escorting McCarthy to Cottonwood over dangerous terrain (shot in Arizona's rugged Sedona region), ever-grinning McCarthy revealing his vicious nature by pushing Baldwin off a cliff to his death. Surrounded by McIntire's men on the open prairie, a stalemate situation occurs, Miroslava informing everyone that McCarthy is indeed a killer and deserves all that's coming to him. "You're licked," McIntire tells the judge, then stares at his wayward son, halfheartedly impressed by McCrea's dogged determination in bringing the hothead to justice. "Shoot him or let him go," he adds. McCrea rides away on his own, to all intents and purposes defeated, but that's not the end of the matter. In an explosive few seconds, he quickly jumps off his horse, letting loose with a rifle, Meyer joining in the furious shoot-out. Miroslava grabs McCarthy's horse and rushes off with him, McIntire finally calling off the gunplay. "He'll have a fair trial," he concedes with resignation. The picture ends with McCarthy's trial in full swing, "The People versus Thomas Bannerman."

Jacques Tourneur directed *Stranger on Horseback* in a series of quick edits, refusing to let the audience be bored for a single second. McCarthy, although a killer, is a strangely likeable one, on the cusp of his greatest movie success as Doctor Miles Bennell in Don Siegel's seminal sci-fi thriller *Invasion of the Body Snatchers*. It is sad to relate that two weeks prior to *Stranger on Horseback*'s release, on March 23, 1955, Czech-born actress Miroslava committed suicide, reputedly over an unrequited love affair with a Mexican bullfighter. As for McCrea, he virtually came of Western age in this superb little picture, carrying the action from start to finish with the calm assurance of a seasoned professional. It was his standout 1950s moment and he would never better it.

From 1955 to 1959, McCrea's output has been described as fitful: brilliant one minute, average the next. Perhaps by taking on the part of Ben Stride in Budd Boetticher's *Seven Men from Now*, things might have worked out differently, but he turned down Burt Kennedy's script, leaving the door open for Randolph Scott to make his comeback. But it's difficult to subscribe to the oft-held view that McCrea was on a downhill slope; in re-evaluating his work from this latter stage of his career, he in fact starred in some very respectable Westerns, growing ever more rugged in looks and putting in some telling and tougher performances. When we consider the six main constituents of any motion picture—acting, direction, plot, script, cinematography and soundtrack—McCrea rarely had a misfire, and two of his films, *Stranger on Horseback* and 1958's *Fort Massacre*, can be classed as overlooked classics; not bad going for someone who, many feel, was played out. And seven were made in CinemaScope—how many Western stars could boast about that on their résumé? Of the nine remaining pictures he would star in up to the end of the decade, six were produced by Walter M. Mirisch, two for United Artists and four for Allied Artists. All were made in CinemaScope and color to boost audience appeal alongside McCrea's box-office muscle, and all offered pretty good value when compared to the big-budget oaters of the period. Allied Artists' *Wichita*, the first of the Mirisch-produced Westerns, was released in July 1955, two months before Hugh O'Brian's acclaimed TV series *Wyatt Earp* took off, a credible, fast-paced but heavily laundered interpretation of the Wyatt Earp legend pre-Tombstone days, expertly directed by Jacques Tourneur. Daniel B. Ullman's insightful screenplay painted Earp as a troubled lawman determined to do things his own way, regardless of outside interference. Now aged 50, McCrea's weathered features and hard demeanor perfectly matched the uproarious trail town of Wichita, Kansas where, following the death of a five-year-old boy in a drunken shoot-up, he pins on the marshal's badge, promising to bring law and order to those untamed streets.

McCrea is first introduced as a wandering cowpoke, coming across Walter Sande's camp, introducing himself ("The name's Earp. Wyatt Earp.") and partaking of a plate of beans with the cowhands. During the night, Lloyd Bridges and Rayford Barnes steal his money. McCrea wakes, beats up Bridges, draws on Barnes, retrieves his cash and rides off in a black mood, setting the scene for a final showdown later on in the movie. Wichita, when McCrea rides in, is destined to be a new railhead, a thriving town on the

Vera Miles and Joel McCrea in *Wichita* (1955)

rise, living up to its reputation as an "anything goes" destination for cowboys to let off steam after months herding cattle: "Wine. Women. Wichita." Foiling a bank robbery by shooting two of the three participants, McCrea befriends newspaper proprietor Wallace Ford and young reporter Keith Larson (as Bat Masterson), reluctantly agreeing to become marshal after a woman is wounded and a boy killed. But town bigwigs Edgar Buchanan, Walter Coy and Carl Benton Reid soon rue the day they decided to swear in McCrea: The stern-faced lawman is a little *too* good at his job, jailing a whole bunch of Sande's out of control drovers ("You're all under arrest for disturbing the peace," he barks) and enforcing a "No Guns" policy on anyone entering town limits; if word gets out that Wichita is a law-abiding town, the trail herders won't come near the place, and lack of trail herders, however troublesome they may be, means lack of money ("Wichita depends on these men for its livelihood."). It's the old "profit versus sense of duty" scenario but presented here to maximum effect. Coy objects to McCrea romancing his daughter (Vera Miles), Buchanan lives up to his rascally image by hiring Jack Elam and Barnes to put paid to McCrea and Reid refuses to get rid of the marshal on the grounds that he's just what the town needs. At a social gathering, McCrea spells it out to them: "I won't change my methods and I won't quit. You'll have to fire me."

There's an amusing sequence where two gunslingers (Peter Graves and John Smith) appear in town, taken on by Buchanan to shoot McCrea for a reward of $1,000. Word gets out that they're packing shooting irons; McCrea strolls over to the saloon where Graves, dressed in black, is lolling nonchalantly against the bar sporting some pretty hefty hardware, Smith lurking behind a door, gun at the ready. There's a face-off. Then

Joel McCrea is sturdiness personalified as Wyatt Earp in *Wichita* (1955).

Graves, Smith and McCrea break into grins. Turns out these tough-looking dudes are his brothers, brought in as deputies. Buchanan, red-faced at being caught in a trap, is railroaded out of town.

It takes another death to bring Wichita to its senses; Cory's wife is accidentally killed when Elam and Barnes open fire outside Cory's house. With newly deputized Larson in tow, Barnes and Elam are hunted down and shot, Buchanan turning up at the end with Sande's mob, the cattle boss seeking retribution for the loss of two of his men. However, when he learns of Cory's own loss, he turns tail and rides off, but not before McCrea and Buchanan drop hothead Bridges, who then receives a fatal (but well-deserved) shotgun blast from Cory. McCrea, wed to Miles in the final moments, heads off to Dodge City and everlasting fame in Western folklore.

Very popular with the public, *Wichita* is the kind of 80-minute, solidly crafted Western that ceased to grace our screens many, many sunsets ago. Medium-budget specialists Allied Artists really pushed the boat out on this rigorous production; there's a great cast of heavies (Bridges, Elam, Buchanan and prolific screen villain Robert J. Wilke), Wichita Town hustles and bustles with hundreds of extras, a hotbed of drink and vice, Hans J. Salter provides a vibrant soundtrack and McCrea is sturdiness personified as Earp, a mean-shootin' gun enthusiast striking fear into his opponents. And if that tense, final confrontation between Sande's boys and McCrea's squad is reminiscent of Sam Peckinpah's *The Wild Bunch*, you could be right: The future director had a bit part as a bank teller and contributed a few minor entries in Ullman's script.

1832: Clad in buckskins, Sam Houston (McCrea), recently resigned as governor of Tennessee, his wife having left him after a few days into their marriage, crosses the

Red River into Texas and becomes embroiled in a plot to enforce a coup and make the state independent of Mexican rule. Allied Artists' *The First Texan* (1956) related key events in the life of Houston, from his first meeting with Jim Bowie (Jeff Morrow) in San Antonio to the barnstorming defeat of General Santa Anna's crack regiments at the Battle of San Jacinto on April 21, 1836, leading to a Mexican surrender. A well-intentioned stab at an important moment in time in American history, *The First Texan* was too verbose and earnest by far, particularly coming hot on the heels of the energetic *Wichita*. The picture only livened up in the 70th minute, Byron Haskin directing the seven-minute demolition job of the 1,500-strong Mexican army by Houston's motley selection of units with panache. Morrow played Bowie, William Hopper was Colonel William Travis and James Griffith's skinny Davy Crockett was the complete opposite of John Wayne's bulkier Crockett in *The Alamo*—all three perished in that famous siege, but you never get to see it here; it's mentioned in dispatches only. Daniel B. Ullman's script concentrated for the most part on political intrigue and the mawkish romance between McCrea and Felicia Farr, an on/off courtship that falls flat on its face. Farr was 24, McCrea 51, and the difference in ages shows; he looks awkward, mouthing clichéd lines of endearment to a woman who's made it perfectly clear where she stands in the relationship: Either it's the revolutionary crusade, or her; he can't have both. McCrea brings a certain measure of sincerity to the part of Houston, but his passionless performance verges on the wooden at times, a McCrea Western where the co-stars—Morrow, Hopper, Myron Healey, Wallace Ford, Chubby Johnson, Roy Roberts and Nelson Leigh—put a touch more application into what they're about than the lead star appears to do. It's not one of the man's better efforts from the '50s;

Wilfrid Cline's colorful photography and the final skirmish contribute to a sluggish actioner that fails to ignite, as it should have done.

1957's *The Oklahoman*, released by Allied Artists, is strictly second division McCrea fare once again, no more, no less. The attractive widescreen color photography just about manages to drag out of the realms of mediocrity a tale that could have been written in under a minute. McCrea stars as Doctor John Brighton, whose wife dies in childbirth out on the trail. Seven years later, he's Cherokee Wells' kindly physician, who hires an attractive Indian girl (Gloria Talbott) to attend to his young daughter's needs. Bad guys Brad Dexter and Douglas Dick are trying to bully Talbott's father, Michael Pate, off his land because of oil on the property, while Barbara Hale is a might worried that her marriage plans to McCrea might be threatened by Talbott's interest in her man. In his play-it-by-the-book screenplay, Daniel B. Ullman touches briefly on pro-Indian sympathies (McCrea commands that Dexter apologize to Talbott after he calls her a "tame little Indian girl.") but not too deeply, while the only slice of action to keep aficionados awake is at the end, when McCrea and Dexter go head-to-head in the street, the whole town, including the sheriff, watching ("I'm gonna kill you, Doc," shouts Dexter); after blasting away at each other, Dexter hits the dust and McCrea, although wounded, recovers. No prizes for guessing which of the ladies he chooses to settle down with, either.

Relaxed and conventional, *The Oklahoman* is a pleasant-enough but unexciting time-passer that McCrea must have drifted through in his sleep. Francis D. Lyon's direction verges on static, the supporting cast act with efficiency if not passion and Hans J. Salter's flowery score fails

Joel McCrea and Barbara Stanwyck in *Trooper Hook* (1957)

to ignite the production. Take McCrea out of the picture, and this would have disappeared without a trace years ago. Even by his own laid-back standards, *The Oklahoman* is a very mundane, uninspiring McCrea Western, suitable only for a late-night showing after a few beers.

A group of soldiers is herded together by Apaches and forced toward a cliff edge overlooking an Indian camp (one trooper has an arrow sticking out of his left leg). The bucks open fire, killing the whole bunch. Then a bugle is heard; cavalry storm into the encampment, shooting, burning and taking prisoners. Chief Nanchez is captured, along with a white woman and Nanchez's young son, and taken to the fort. Charles Marquis Warren's violent opening to *Trooper Hook* (United Artists, 1957) promised much in the way of cavalry versus Indians thrills and spills but it's a promise that doesn't materialize. Instead, Warren, David Victor and Herbert Little, Jr.'s wordy screenplay is all about human conflict and interracial intolerance toward the Redskin, with the catalyst being Barbara Stanwyck, playing the white woman who bore Nanchez's son. Only stalwart Sergeant Clovis Hook (McCrea, paunchy and mustached) has the guts to stand up to rampant small-town prejudice as he escorts Stanwyck and her son (Terry Lawrence) by stagecoach to reunite with her husband (John Dehner) at their ranch.

If John Ford had made *Trooper Hook* with Wayne in the lead, the critics might have classed it as a minor classic, embodying as it does themes found in many of Ford's Westerns (*The Searchers* and *Stagecoach* spring to mind here). But he didn't, and the picture has more or less sunk into obscurity. The bulk of the narrative concerns the trio's trek across the Utah wilderness (beautifully photographed in black-and-white by Ellsworth Fredericks), stopping off at towns where the pious citizens don't take lightly to Stan-

wyck's previous ties with an Apache chief. It's an adult treatment, not for the kids, and works well thanks to McCrea and Stanwyck's professional empathy honed by years of experience (this was their sixth and final movie together). McCrea sympathizes with Stanwyck and prevents any bullying by fist and a hard stare. She asks him what he thinks about an Indian running his hands all over her body. It doesn't bother him. Passengers are picked up en route: Earl Holliman, a likeable young cowpoke, a contessa and her daughter and cowardly Edward Andrews, who loses his life after offering the escaped Nanchez (Rudolfo Acosta) $15,000 to let them alone. In another suspenseful incident, Holliman holds a gun to the boy's head while McCrea parleys with the chief, who rates the soldier as a man of honor. "My people have long called you face of stone. They are wrong. It should be heart of stone," he intones. "I will let you go—today," and he does, riding off with his braves.

Needless to say, Stanwyck's reunion with Dehner turns out to be a disaster. "You expect me to live with him?" growls the rancher, staring at the boy, followed by dinner, undertaken in a frosty silence. A face-off with McCrea ("You can take the boy. But not the woman.") ends with Dehner joining them on a wagon; the Indians attack, the chief shoots Dehner who, dying, kills the chief; the warriors call off the fight. McCrea finally proposes to Stanwyck. "I'm 47," he tells her (he was actually 52), but she reckons he's still a good catch, particularly as he's taken a real shine to her impish little boy.

If there's one intrusion in this otherwise excellent, underrated slow-burner, it's the constant insertion of Tex Ritter's title song into various scenes, which becomes tiresome after the third hearing. Gerald Fried's thump-thump jaunty score seems more at home in the horror genre (he scored *The Vampire* and *I Bury the Living*, among others) but is at least offbeat. The real pleasure to be had is in watching two screen veterans effortlessly

playing out their roles to perfection ("A pair of easy, natural performances," wrote the *New York Times*). Although not a great success, the critics liked the film and it's one that definitely grows on audiences after two or three viewings.

A few of McCrea's Westerns occasionally appeared very up and down from this busy period, United Artists' *Gunsight Ridge* a case in point, partly captivating, partly dull, but managing to hold it together better than *The Oklahoman* and more or less on a level with *Trooper Hook*. In the third of his four 1957 releases, he played a Wells Fargo undercover agent (Mike Ryan), who goes to the aid of Sheriff Addison Richards in the town of Bancroft; the area is being terrorized by a thief who kills without scruples, and Richards, under threat of being booted out of his job for incompetence, can't figure out who the robber is. It's Mark Stevens, known as Velvet, a piano-playing mine owner plagued by insecurities who, so we are led to believe in Talbot and Elisabeth Jenning's convoluted script, turned to a life of crime so that he could learn how to play the piano properly. To muddy the waters further, four rowdy cowhands from George Chandler's Lazy Heart Ranch are carrying out their own string of robberies, so McCrea has two separate incidents to sort out, as well as Joan Weldon (Richards' daughter) making eyes at him.

The action begins with a stage holdup in which Stevens callously shoots his partner dead because his mask slipped, enabling driver Slim Pickens to recognize him. Pickens then gets drunk, losing control of the stage; McCrea takes over the reins, we arrive in Bancroft and director Francis D. Lyon switches to *noir* mode, concentrating on angst-ridden Stevens' relationship with Darlene Fields and McCrea's investigations into the crimes. McCrea goes through the paces but looks tired and, for a large part of the picture's middle section, is strangely absent as Stevens, after robbing the town's bank, stores the cash in two boxes of dynamite, while the four cowpokes, led by L.Q. Jones, hold up a train. In the type of brutal act that was a part and parcel of Westerns during that time, Stevens puts two bullets into Richards, one to bring him off his horse and the coup de grace to the head. It's in the final third that Oscar-winner (*Ship of Fools*, 1965) Ernest Laszlo's superb, deep-focused monochrome photography comes into its own, the Old Tucson wasteland filmed with an expert eye for the area's stark natural beauty, David Raskin's melodious score used sparingly. There's an effective interlude where Stevens encounters a young girl (Carolyn Craig) in a remote ranch. All on her own but not nervous, she suffers an immediate attack of hero-worship for the introverted outlaw, especially when he sits at a dusty old piano and conjures up a tune, a touch of softness belying his tough image. Quietly handled, this moment perfectly sets the scene for the final showdown, McCrea firing at the boxes of dynamite that explode, destroying the money and the unfortunate horse carrying it. A tense chase over the rocky ridge of the title ends with Stevens receiving a bullet and McCrea more or less promising himself to Weldon. "You gave him back his pride," she tells McCrea after Stevens' funeral. "I want you to stay."

McCrea's son Jody crops up as a man about to be married but deciding, at the last moment, to join in the hunt for the four train holdup bandits, spurred on by the $1,000 reward. Dan Blocker, of *Bonanza* fame, appears briefly as a bartender. *Gunsight Ridge*, although mainstream in design, contains more depth than most but tends to sag in the middle due to the uneven script and direction. McCrea's rock-steady turn plus Laszlo's amazing cinematography save the day, promoting the movie to one of the worthier of the star's efforts from the second half of the 1950s; *Variety* called it "routine" and it's no classic (Scott was making those with Budd Boetticher in 1957), but it's not all that bad, either.

Allied Artists' *The Tall Stranger*, another contender for top McCrea Western of the decade (and the final screen appearance of his fine horse Dollar), followed the same year. Unfairly dismissed by a lot of film writers, Thomas Carr's CinemaScope range feud oater is packed to the rafters with roughhouse incident and undeniable violence, featuring a livelier-than-normal performance from the taciturn star, now on an upswing as far as his remaining '50s Westerns were concerned. Scrumptious Virginia Mayo is in it, rekindling the partnership she had with McCrea in *Colorado Territory*, as is Leo Gordon, playing, against type, a good guy (well, more or less!). Randolph Scott made his own brainless Western in 1955 with *Ten Wanted Men*; it was McCrea's turn with this one—and charismatic Gordon starred in both.

The picture opens with a hard-hearted scene and refuses to compromise on this angle. McCrea (Ned Bannon), spotting a herd of cattle that is in the process of being rustled, is shot off his horse and left for dead, the animal also barbarically shot. Before the loner passes out, he notices a fancy rifle and silver spurs as the perpetrator empties his water bottle for good measure. Recovering in Mayo's wagon (as befits a frontier woman, she's slightly frayed around the edges, but still looks sexy), he finds himself among ex-Confederate settlers (Ray Teal is their leader), who plan to cross Bishops Valley and proceed on to California. The problem is, McCrea's hostile half-brother, Barry Kelley, owns the land and won't, under any circumstances, allow the newcomers, or "squatters" as he terms them, access. What's more, he hates McCrea, holding him responsible for the death of his son, who was executed for being a member of Quantrill's Raiders—McCrea

was one of the Yankee officers who apprehended the lad, so by default, reasons Kelley, he must shoulder the blame. Further trouble comes in the form of bogus guide George Neise, who's joined the wagon train to supposedly escort them over the trail to the promised land. In reality, the gunman is in connivance with Michael Ansara, a Mexican assassin, the psycho who put a bullet in McCrea. With their combined forces, the pair is preparing to murder the pesky colonizers *en masse* and help themselves to the spoils. McCrea quickly latches on to Neise's motives, but can he bury the hatchet with obstinate Kelley in time to prevent a wholesale slaughter taking place, not only of the settlers but Kelley's ranch hands, bossed by burly, black-clad Gordon.

There are three extreme, no-holds-barred fistfights in Carr's movie, mirroring changing, more adult, trends in the sagebrush saga as a whole: The first is between McCrea and Kelley (Kelley refuses to quit and is literally battered into submission); the second between McCrea and the venomous Ansara, caught in the act of trying to knife Mayo after he spots her bathing in a river; and the third between Kelley and Ansara, the beefy ranch owner strangling the killer to death. Add to this a lengthy, high-octane closing gun battle, which turns into a veritable massacre, plenty of blood spilled, and audiences are left with a sprightly Western that is mean, rough and tough, commendably lacking in any form of sentimentality. A fine supporting cast (Whit Bissell and Michael Pate, again playing an Indian called Charley, as he did in *The Oklahoman*) and Hans J. Salter's grandiose score enliven a great McCrea actioner; you feel like rooting for the man as he rides off down the dusty trail after Mayo and her illegitimate son in the end, despite the lady's shady past when an escort girl in St. Louis during the

Civil War. Although suffering from insipid color photography, *The Tall Stranger*, tautly scripted by Christopher Knopf from Louis L'Amour's novel *Showdown Trail*, is definite proof that when McCrea put his mind to it, he could come up with a horse opera as good as those Scott, Murphy and Montgomery were making during this period. Ignore the critical put-downs—this is one hell of a '50s Western that deserves an official widescreen digital release. *The Hollywood Reporter* said: "Fair Star Western."

Fox's *Cattle Empire* (1958) is a further example of a McCrea Western receiving bad press in some quarters. But let's examine the facts. Adapted from a Daniel B. Ullman story, Endre Bohem and Eric Norden's pithy script is short and to the point; Brydon Baker's widescreen color photography (Lone Pine's Alabama Hills was the location) sparkles in the sunlight; Paul Sawtell and Bert Shefter provide an outstanding score; and McCrea is tougher than usual, putting in a solid performance as a trail boss convicted of a crime he didn't carry out. So, as an end-of-the-decade oater, made at a time when McCrea, like Scott, was thinking of calling it a day, *Cattle Empire* scores highly, a cattle drive opus that maybe isn't up there with the likes of *Red River* but is just as entertaining. The movie must have looked stunning on the big screen in a darkened auditorium on a Saturday night.

Fresh out of prison after a five-year term, McCrea (as John Cord) is dragged through the streets of Hamilton by horse in front of an angry crowd for daring to show his face; his drovers once wrecked the place, leading to a spate of injuries, town boss Don Haggerty blinded in the affray. However, that doesn't prevent Haggerty from coming to McCrea's rescue and offering him the job of trail boss, herding 5,000 head of cattle to Fort Clemens. McCrea, puzzled by the offer, agrees, but also agrees to act as trail boss to Richard Shannon's rival outfit who are driving cattle to the same destination; first one there gets to sell their beef to the army and reap a healthy profit. However, McCrea has a score to settle, planning to scupper both parties' plans for his own personal satisfaction.

Phyllis Coates, Joel McCrea and Don Haggerty in *Cattle Empire* (1958)

Seems that five years back, Haggerty and then-partner Shannon, jealous of McCrea's success on the range, knocked him out and supplied liquor to his cowpunchers who went on a rampage and caused all that trouble. McCrea was jailed when it wasn't his fault, and he has returned a bitter man.

To complicate matters, McCrea's ex-girlfriend, Phyllis Coates, has married Haggerty while Haggerty's brother, Bing Russell, is burning up with a need to beat McCrea to the draw. McCrea hires a group of the resentful townsfolk as wranglers ("On the trail, my men call me Mister Cord," he tells them), plus Paul Brinegar and Hal K. Dawson to be in charge of the chuck wagon and tomboy Gloria Talbott to ride point; the gal develops an almighty crush on McCrea (apparently, while filming, she did!) and can't keep her eyes off him. Haggerty, Coates and Russell are also dragged into the trek, a stipulation made by McCrea. A short way into the drive, McCrea decides to throw in his lot with Haggerty, giving Shannon false information concerning a river crossing, thus setting the stage for a final showdown between the two outfits.

Mutiny in the ranks (McCrea refuses to allow the men to ride into Tumbleweed for a break, supplying them from his own keg of hooch), Coates still lusting after McCrea (the scene where she throws herself on him during the night and the screen swiftly fades out is a hoot), Talbott dropping hints about a possible relationship (even though she's young enough to be his daughter) and a deciding shoot-out among the Alabama Hills rocks; *Cattle Empire* has it all, an enjoyable star action picture directed with real flourish by Charles Marquis Warren, who achieved worthier results with Westerns than he did with horror (*Back from the Dead*; *The Unknown Terror*). McCrea, a bad guy that at heart was a good guy, looked trim, fit and mean, more Randolph Scott than Joel McCrea, and that's a compliment to the actor's ongoing love affair with the Western genre and all that it stood for. After wounding Shannon, he rides off into the Lone Pine wilderness, leaving both outfits to settle their differences and promising love-struck Talbott that he'll be back to play house—or so she hopes!

McCrea's penultimate 1950s outing, *Fort Massacre* (1958), is a gem of a psychological Western, featuring the actor in one of his most unsympathetic parts, Sergeant Vinson, an embittered, Indian-hating soldier leading the tattered remnants of the Sixth Cavalry's C Troop across the wilds of New Mexico to supposed safety at Fort Crane. Scriptwriter Martin Goldsmith's influences must have included John Ford's 1934 *The Lost Patrol* and Lewis Milestone's 1945 *A Walk in the Sun*, and even *The Searchers*; here we had McCrea's battle-weary troopers arguing, bickering, giving vent to their innermost thoughts and despising their leader, all the while faced with an implacable, hostile enemy.

Shorn of all sentimentality and humor (some humor is present, but it's dark to tie in with the film's grim feel), Goldsmith's delicious, sarcasm-laced dialogue presents us with a starkly violent image of a cavalry battalion at the end of its tether, mistrustful of both themselves and McCrea. Along with *Stranger on Horseback*, this counts as McCrea's defining '50s Western hour.

Director Joseph M. Newman places the action amid the rocky splendor of New Mexico's Gallup area and Red Rock State in 1879, the mighty sandstone walls, cliffs and deep canyons lovingly caught in all their glory by photographer Carl E. Guthrie. After suffering 50% casualties in a clash with Apaches, reluctant troop leader McCrea heads for a waterhole commandeered by 50 braves, mouthy Irishman Forrest Tucker a critical thorn in his side. "You want these stripes? You can have them. They weigh a ton," McCrea barks at the constantly needling soldier. The sergeant, unbeknown to his men, is on a one-man vendetta; they're hallmarked as sacrificial lambs being led to the

Forrest Tucker and Joel McCrea in *Fort Massacre* (1958)

slaughter in order to satisfy his craving for retaliation. Reaching the waterhole, everyone remarks to McCrea on how to get at the precious water, seeing that it's swarming with Indians. "Tap a rock with your wand like Moses?" is the acid suggestion. What follows is a blazing, six-minute shoot-out; one trooper gets an arrow in the neck, others are wounded, Tucker glibly states, "If I could remember a prayer, I'd say it," and McCrea's fragile standing plummets even further when he shoots down the chief like a mad dog after he has stood up and surrendered. "I wonder if it's treason to hate a butcher," mumbles Tucker mutinously under his breath while John Russell, one of the more intelligent members of the squad, sums up the perceived valueless life he leads: "I'm just something that comes with a horse." In an intimate talk with McCrea, it transpires that the sergeant's wife was raped and murdered by Indians and, before dying, shot their two children dead to save them from torture. McCrea carries her photograph in a watch, along with the watches taken off all of his fallen detachment. "The only way for that hate to come out is through a neat round bullet hole," he tells Russell, and from his statement, it's quite clear that this unrelieved hatred will only end in one way—tragedy.

With 15 men remaining, including Pawnee tracker Anthony Caruso, the squad encounters a trader and his wife before holing up in an abandoned Indian cliff dwelling inhabited by two Paiutes, Susan Cabot and her grandfather, Francis McDonald; Denver Pyle is seriously injured and needs rest. When questioned about his decision not to proceed south to the fort, McCrea spits out, "They're insane with hate, burstin' with it. You gotta feed them bullets." In other words, he wants to stay put and slay more Apaches; he has no intention of running south. The final bloody confrontation sees the troop open fire on an Apache scouting party who have wandered into the ruins; his bloodlust up, McCrea goes to shoot McDonald in the back (he's promised to "tell the truth" when he reaches Fort Crane, appalled at the sergeant's ruthless passion for killing his red brothers) but Russell puts a bullet in him. "For a lot of Indians and a lot of soldiers," is his justification to Tucker for shooting McCrea, emptying his tunic of all those watches.

Fort Massacre saw McCrea, for about the one and only time, shedding his upright image to play the closest he ever got to a bad guy nursing deep-seated mental issues. It's his and director Newman's "Budd Boetticher" moment and a memorable one at that, a minimalistic oater featuring a smaller-than-average cast, every sharp line of Goldsmith's screenplay matching the obdurately aggressive tone and the craggy scenery;

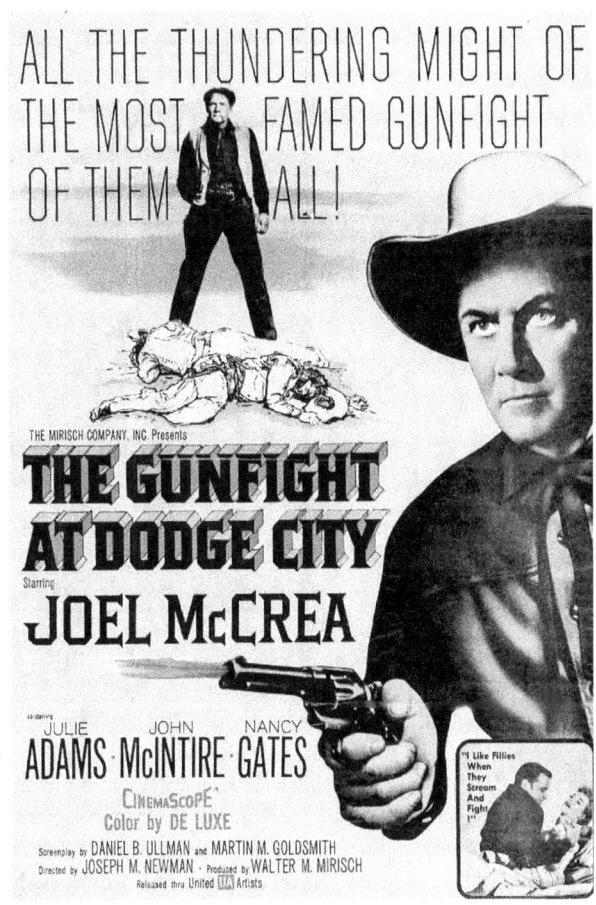

like Boetticher's work, an adult morality play set in waterless, unforgiving surroundings, where life isn't worth a dime and hard-bitten characters nurse hidden grievances. A Hans J. Salter or Paul Sawtell score would have been the icing on this particular Western cake, but that's a minor quibble; Marlin Skiles' musical arrangement is more than adequate and in many sequences is absent, allowing the action to speak for itself. The last sunset almost beckoned for Joel McCrea, with a final shout before the '50s Western folded for good. *Fort Massacre* is a great high in any actor's book, a marvelous, seldom-seen movie from the genre's golden era that enthralls from beginning to end.

McCrea's last Western of the 1950s, United Artists' *The Gunfight at Dodge City* (1959), has, like *Cattle Empire* and *The Tall Stranger*, come in for its fair share of critical flack but unduly so (*Variety* labeled it a "program picture."). Daniel B. Ullman and Martin Goldsmith's succinct script is unusually multi-layered for a standard actioner of this type, giving much more emphasis on character development than normal. Densely plotted, Joseph M. Newman's version of the Bat Masterson legend kicks off with the notorious lawman (McCrea) describing to Wright King, a developmentally challenged youth with an unhealthy fascination for guns, the rights and wrongs of killing a man in a gunfight, and the effect it has on one's state of mind (King's character, Billy, was clearly mod-

eled on Billy the Kid). "What's it like to shoot a man?" asks the boy. "It's not so good," replies McCrea. In Hays City, where McCrea sells his buffalo hides, we have the first slice of gunplay; he shoots one of his enemies, charging in through a saloon doorway, jealous of McCrea's past association with his woman. McCrea is wounded, the woman and the gunman both killed. Ex-associate Richard Anderson turns up, now a no-good grinning rat, and warns McCrea to stay out of Dodge City (his next port of call) where an election for new town sheriff is underway. But McCrea's brother (Harry Lauter) is the marshal, so he heads for Dodge where a saddle-full of complications await him: Lauter is engaged to prim and proper minister's daughter Julie Adams, but she doesn't really love him; Nancy Gates, owner of the failing Lady Gay saloon, accepts McCrea's offer of $6,000 for part-ownership of the joint; would-be sheriff Don Haggerty and his paid guns advocate lawlessness and resent McCrea's presence *and* reputation; McCrea decides to put himself forward as sheriff; and Lauter has his work cut out keeping the peace on the weekly Saturday night drunken shoot-out.

"What is it that makes a man wear a badge?" is the question put to Lauter, who gets a bullet in the back from cowardly Anderson during one of those rowdy Saturday night free-for-alls. Before that, McCrea lays it on the line to Haggerty when they discuss matters in his room. "If he breaks that door down (referring to one of Haggerty's henchman), you get the first bullet," followed by, "If I see one of your men make a move, or even cough, you'll get it first." When his brother is murdered, Adams blames McCrea who admits, "Everywhere I go I make trouble." There's a second confrontation with Haggerty, busy making a thorough nuisance of himself by bursting unannounced into

McCrea's room: "If you'd come in here five minutes ago, I would have killed you. Now I'm gonna half kill you," and McCrea does just that in the resultant bruising fistfight.

Elected as sheriff after Haggerty admits defeat, McCrea imposes a strict "No Guns" policy on Saturday night, imposing a $100 fine for anyone carrying a firearm and takes Adams for a picnic, playing house. The storyline then goes a stage further when old friend Walter Coy enlists McCrea and Doc John McIntire's aid in snatching King, his brother, from the arms of the law. The simpleton has inadvertently shot a deputy after playing around with a gun and is due to be hanged. King is saved, but by participating in this act, McCrea loses his badge, leaving the field wide open for Haggerty to become sheriff. Back in Dodge City, reptilian Anderson forces his unwelcome attentions on Gates, is shot dead by McCrea, who then decides that prissy Adams isn't the gal for him. "We're not the same kinda people," he tells her, meaning that Gates, who has worshiped the lawman ever since she set eyes on him, is free to plant a big juicy smacker on his lips.

The inevitable showdown between McCrea and Haggerty is a cracker. Gates doesn't want her new man to go through with it, but McCrea delivers the movie's one great line to her: "I don't want to, Lily. But the difference between here and the street is the distance between a rabbit and a man." Newman orchestrates the final street face-off like a Spaghetti Western, years before there *were* Spaghetti Westerns, the two protagonists slowly walking toward each other. Haggerty gives the call and is brought down with a single shot. "Well, as far as I'm concerned, that takes care of Tuesday's election," is the cry as McCrea renews his role as town sheriff.

The Gunfight at Dodge City spelled out the virtual end of Joel McCrea's career as a Westerner in the cinema apart from three more outings. The movie was relegated to second-feature status in America and the actor, probably realizing that the genre was past its best, concentrated on playing Marshal Mike "Duke" Dunbar in the TV series *Wichita Town*, 26 episodes running from September 1959 to April 1960; son Jody was his deputy. Attired in black duds, McCrea cuts an imposing figure in his last '50s Western and puts a great deal of thought into his portrayal of Bat Masterson, more so than he's given credit for. The whole cast acts with conviction, there's bags of incident and Carl E. Guthrie's cinematography really stands out in the night sequences. Plus of course, we must never forget composer Hans J. Salter's weighty soundtrack. Produced on a $5000,000 budget, the picture looks more expensive. No, McCrea didn't bow out of the '50s with a damp squib. He left with a rousing, traditional widescreen 1950s Western, the type of which would cease to exist in a few short years. Universal star Audie Murphy alone carried the torch for all those actors and technicians who had helped make the '50s the must-see (to quote a modern-day expression) decade for the once-mighty cowboy flick.

Chapter 14
Montgomery at Columbia and United Artists 1950-1955

George Montgomery's '50s Western career got off to a shaky start with *Davy Crockett Indian Scout*, or just plain *Indian Scout*, an Edward Small production for United Artists set in 1848 that relied almost exclusively on stock footage taken from Small's 1940 opus *Kit Carson*, starring Jon Hall, for its action set pieces. Minus Crockett's trademark coonskin cap, Montgomery played Crockett's nephew (but still Davy Crockett!), investigating a spy who is relaying information to the Kiowa Indians on wagon train movements, leading to a string of attacks. Montgomery's sure it isn't his friend, Cherokee tracker Red Hawk (Philip Reed), even though racist Erik Rolf reckons he is; the gruff bully's turned into an Indian hater ever since his wife was wounded in an ambush. Half-Indian schoolteacher Ellen Drew and deaf-mute Paul Guilfoyle appear out of the blue in a wagon; are they as innocent of all this as they appear, or is the pair in collusion with Chief Thundercloud, Robert Barrat and their warriors? Montgomery attempts a powwow with Thundercloud to stave off any more massacres, but the old chief isn't interested, breaking the peace treaty and setting up a war council with neighboring tribes to wipe out the cavalry outpost at Great Plains Fort.

The first half of this cobbled-together actioner is told in flashback, Montgomery relating incidents to a court which he believes will show Reed in a favorable light and

clear his name, proving him to be an Indian worthy of trust, not a treacherous savage as charged. The second half concentrates on a prolonged skirmish at Manitou Pass, the warring tribes eventually defeated when the man from Tennessee steers a wagonload of explosives into the canyon's entrance, blowing the braves to kingdom come. Guilfoyle turns out to be the spy, not deaf-mute at all, and Montgomery, in this instance, doesn't get the girl; she rides off into the sunset with Reed (both cleared of any crimes), Montgomery none too pleased at this outcome, continuing his adventures with partner Noah Beery, Jr. who *does* wear a coonskin cap.

Montgomery's first Western of the decade unexpectedly brought in good reviews, *The Hollywood Reporter* stating that George was "a virile and convincing scout." United Artists reissued the movie in 1955 on the back of these reviews to cash in on the enormous commercial success of Walt Disney's *Davy Crockett: King of the Wild Frontier*, a massive hit with school kids of all ages in the mid-1950s (as was the memorably catchy theme song); Montgomery, in fact, was considered for the lead role in the Disney flick but little-known Fess Parker grabbed it instead. Montgomery's own Davy Crockett outing remains an obscure item that, truth be told, should stay that way, Paul Sawtell's music about the only point of merit. Speaking in a thick Tennessee drawl and poker-faced throughout, he spends most of his time acting in front of a back-projected screen featuring that *Kit Carson* footage, not the best way to impress an audience. Things would slowly perk up, though, with the second of his 1950 Westerns, Edward L. Alperson Productions' *Dakota Lil*, distributed through Montgomery's old studio, 20th Century Fox.

In 1897, the notorious Hole-in-the-Wall gang (Butch Cassidy is a member) is making life hell for lawmen in Matamoras on the Mexican border. Following the theft of $100,000 in unsigned treasury notes from a train, in which a guard is brutally strangled, federal agent Tom Horn is assigned to travel to Matamoras, go undercover and apprehend counterfeiter Dakota Lil; the dame's in collusion with the outlaws, forging the banknotes to make them usable. Fox's sturdy Western has one big thing going for it—a Dimitri Tiomkin soundtrack. A true Hollywood composing giant and a legend in his chosen field, the Russian-born maestro's imaginative scores were guaranteed to hoist any motion picture, however humble, a few rungs higher up the ladder, and his music does so here, in spades. Filmed in Cinecolor on a budget of $250,000 (a lot less than the Scotts, Murphys and McCreas of the time), existing

Marie Windsor and George Montgomery (right) in *Dakota Lil* (1950)

DVD issues (as of 2014) come in monochrome, which hardly matters to Montgomery fans, as he's attired from head to toe in black throughout the movie.

"What's a smart girl like you doing in a broken-down cantina like this?" Agent Montgomery (who carries Geronimo's war knife strapped to his back) introduces himself to singer Marie Windsor (as Lil), while her pianist, John Emery, belts out Chopin's Prelude, Opus 28, no. 4 (somewhat out of place in a room full of rowdy toughs), casting lovelorn eyes on Windsor as she sizes up the black-clad hunk in front of her. Posing as Steve Garrett, Montgomery's job is to infiltrate the gang, gain their confidence, retrieve the stolen money and bring everyone to justice, a tough task. He falls for Windsor and she for him, thus clouding his actions; Emery, suffering from a severe case of rejection, hovers in the background, suspicious of Montgomery's motives; and Rod Cameron, leader of the gang, is a psycho nursing a short fuse, strangling those who get on his wrong side. Another lunatic is Jack Lambert, firing off dumdum bullets with a smirk on his face. A third of the way into the picture, Windsor and Emery turn the tables on Montgomery and hightail it to Red River, Wyoming, where she sets herself up in Cameron's saloon as his new singer and card dealer, letting it be known that she alone can forge signatures on those notes, demanding a 50/50 cut of the proceeds. Montgomery tracks her down, and they resume their tit-for-tat relationship. Scriptwriter Maurice Geraghty comes up with a great piece of dialogue in the saloon scenes: After singing "Ecstasy," Windsor manages the card table and Montgomery makes a disparaging remark concerning Emery. "Vincent is a real artist," she reprimands him. Quick as a flash, he replies "So am I—with a Colt .45."

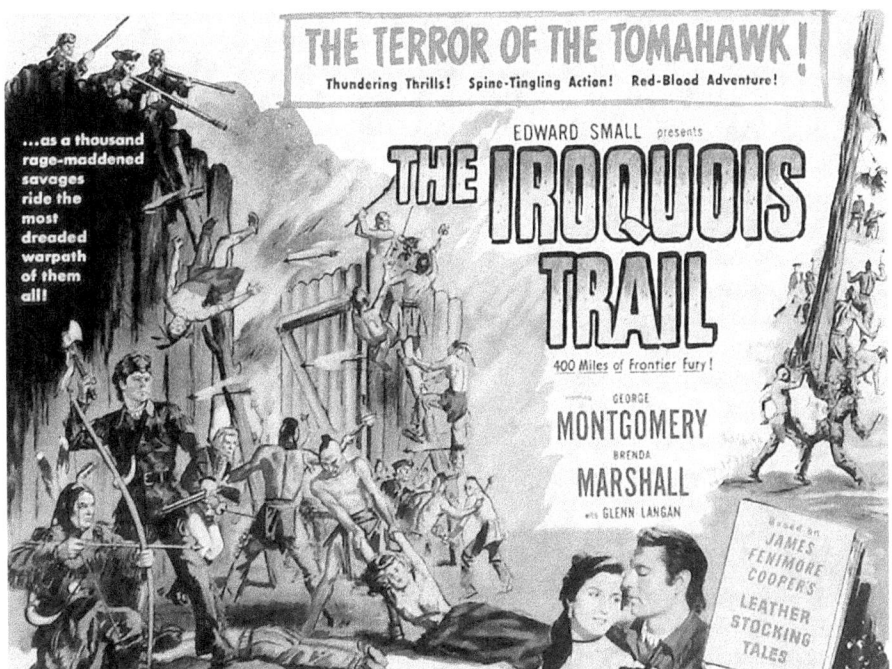

Totally inept Larry Johns, the town sheriff, is convinced that Montgomery is an outlaw, especially after the Secret Service man is taken to the Hole-in-the-Wall's camp and, during shooting practice ("A school for outlaws."), introduced to Butch Cassidy, played by B-movie regular Walter Sande. Eventually, Montgomery confesses all to Windsor, promising her leniency if she gives herself in. Vicious Cameron strangles Wallace Ford, Montgomery's contact, and, in the climax, timid Emery, also throttling Windsor semi-conscious after she's set up her forging equipment, enraged at discovering that the girl he lusts after is in cahoots with a federal agent. A frantic horse chase ensues, Cameron getting Geronimo's knife in the back, his body dragged away by his steed; Johns and his posse commence a hunt for the rest of the gang, leaving Montgomery and Windsor to ride off. An outright pardon is hers for the taking *if* she sets up house with him.

A highly entertaining Western directed with purpose by Lesley Selander, *Dakota Lil* saw Montgomery beginning to make a name for himself in the realm of the cowboy flick, exhibiting a brusque technique in his characterizations that one could identify with. From this point up to 1955, he divided his time between Columbia and United Artists, working on six films apiece for producers Sam Katzman and Edward and Bernard Small. For his final 1950 offering, he donned coonskin cap and buckskins to play Hawkeye (aka Nat Cutler) in United Artists' *The Iroquois Trail*, also issued under the title of *The Tomahawk Trail*. How executive producer Edward Small loved those period Westerns; his was the name behind Randolph Scott's 1936 excursion into James Fenimore Cooper country, *The Last of the Mohicans*; Montgomery's effort differed only slightly from Scott's version, the man himself putting in a weighty performance as the woodsman up against the French and Huron Indians during the colonial wars of 1756/1757, easily the equal of Scott and all those others who had taken on the part in the past (and those who would do so in the future).

Monte Blue and George Montgomery in *The Iroquois Trail* (1950)

The tale was by now well known to all Western fans except in one aspect: Montgomery's relentless thirst for vengeance is triggered when his young infantryman brother, Don Garner, is shot in the back by evil Huron Chief Ogane (Sheldon Leonard in a truly vitriolic performance) and accused of being a spy on his deathbed, even though it's a frame-up, John Doucette the real betrayer-of-secrets. With faithful Mohican Chief Sagamore (Monte Blue) by his side, Montgomery kills Doucette and goes on the run ("Whole English army look—you," intones Blue to his worried buddy), then enlists with the Redcoats as a scout. Arrested for being a traitor after a nighttime massacre engineered by Leonard (Blue warns the English, to no avail: "Ogane like fox. Make trail safe for chickens. Soon nothing left—feathers!"), he escapes after fighting warring Indians in the siege of Fort Williams and hunts down Leonard, who's busy stirring up trouble with local tribes; although he's allied to the enemy while working for the English as a tracker, the Huron, dismayed at a French flag of truce in the aftermath of the Fort Williams battle, decides to fight his own private war against the "Yangees" and take plenty of paleface scalps, plus he's singled out colonel's daughter Brenda Marshall as his new squaw-in-waiting. Captain Glenn Langan, Marshall's fiancé, gets all hot and bothered when his beloved shows an unhealthy preference for Montgomery over himself; Captain Reginald Denny is unearthed as the spy in the camp, sending dispatch papers to the French army via Leonard; and Langan has to concede that Montgomery isn't treacherous after all when Blue sacrifices his life to save the priggish British officer from a Huron blade.

The incidents which took place in the natural passage between the St. Lawrence and Hudson River valleys, the famed "Iroquois Trail," were filmed in the Big Bear Lake region of California's San Bernardino National Forest, adding pictorial magnificence to Phil Karlson's in-your-face style, showcased in a tense struggle between Montgomery and Leonard during the final stages, the two engaged in a knife-to-knife struggle in front of a tribe of neutral Odawa Indians. As Langan rides off to war, an exonerated Montgomery states, "Folks like a happy ending," and they get one, the frontiersman kissing Marshall right in front of her *ex*-fiancé. Like many of Montgomery's other earlier Western features, *The Iroquois Trail* (it should have been shot in color) remains out of reach to the vast majority—ragged issues of questionable quality are all that's available at present. But these are enough to confirm George Montgomery's status as a Western leading man in the making—Davy Crockett and Hawkeye in a one-year spell isn't bad going for any actor, even one perceived to be a B-lister by the major Hollywood studios.

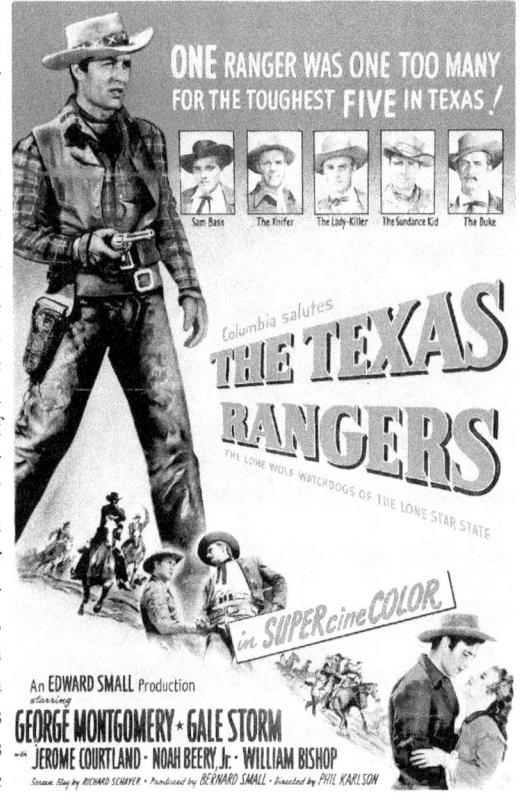

Taking time off from cowboy flicks, Montgomery starred in Edward L. Alperson Productions' period romp, *The Sword of Monte Cristo* (1951), before returning in what many consider to be his best Western, Columbia's *The Texas Rangers*, the first of nine pictures for the company. Phil Karlson was the main driving force behind this superlative sagebrush saga, demonstrating his penchant for framing fistfights, acts of bloodshed and shoot-outs in close-up, bringing a new kind of realism to a genre now up to its ears in unheard-of brutality and excessive violence. Shot by Ellis W. Carter in bright SuperCinecolor (California's wooded Simi Valley was the location), Karlson's 74-minute taut-as-a-bowstring offering ranks as Montgomery's significant Western hour; he looks the part, sporting substantial hardware, throwing his weight around, spitting out blunt one-liners, appearing menacing to his opponents and sexy to the women (well, one to be exact—Gale Storm), *and* performing his own stunts, including a bruising climactic train fight, all achieved without the use of back-projection. It's a picture in which Montgomery stamps his authority over every single frame. Far more active than Joel McCrea ever purported to be, his energy level is on a par with that of Audie Murphy's from this early '50s period. He's tremendous in a decisive Western that doesn't pause for a second; it's a real golden cowboy oldie if ever there was one.

The exciting climax to *The Texas Rangers* (1951), where George Montgomery gets the upper hand of the outlaw band aboard a speeding train.

Richard Schayer's screenplay rehashes the familiar "outlaw cycle" setting, bringing together, among others, Butch Cassidy (John Doucette), Sam Bass (William Bishop), the Sundance Kid (Ian MacDonald) and John Wesley Hardin (John Dehner). Bass' Long Riders are terrorizing Texas in 1874, leading to the formation of the Texas Rangers, whose aim is to bring peace to the territory by scourging Texas of banditry ("The man's become a legend. They're even singing ballads about him," states Major John Litel about Bass). Outlaw members Montgomery (as Johnny Carver) and Noah Beery, Jr. are incarcerated in the pitiless state penitentiary when the Sundance Kid opens fire on them in a double-cross, and they're arrested. Released on a directive from Texas Rangers' founder Litel, the duo find themselves sworn in as Rangers with the task of infiltrating Bass' mob in the Lampasas area and curtailing their activities on promise of a full pardon. Montgomery's kid brother, Ranger Jerome Courtland, wants to tag along, but big brother says no; he wants to put paid to the Sundance Kid and then call it a day. In the meantime, Gale Storm, proprietor of the Waco Star, is incensed that the authorities are allowing ex-criminals to become Rangers ("Fight fire with fire," is Litel's excuse) and lets her feelings be known, both verbally and in her newspaper. But that doesn't stop her fancying Montgomery from afar.

The Texas Rangers brims with incident, action and tantalizing plot twists. Karlson orchestrates a blazing gun battle when MacDonald ambushes Montgomery, firing off round after round from his repeating rifle, filmed from the back to give added punch. Montgomery sneaks up behind him and tells the outlaw to drop his gun belt; he goes

An autographed photo of George Montgomery from the climax of *The Texas Rangers*

for his gun and Montgomery drops him with two bullets. "Buzzard meat," he sneers, looking down at his adversary's body, and decides to quit. Beery pulls a gun on him, now firmly on the side of the law. Courtland rides up to join them and is killed in a second ambush (in which Butch Cassidy gets it), dying in Montgomery's arms (a moving, well-acted scene). Montgomery, enraged at his loss, then has an about-face turn and heads for Belton to join Bass' men undercover, rob the bank of $50,000 to convince the suspicious gang leader that he's no longer a Ranger and arrange for the whole bunch to be captured during a proposed $1,000,000 train heist of Union cash. Amiable Beery is beaten up and shot dead, lying to Bass about Montgomery's allegiances to save his friend from a bullet, but revenge is sweet; during the exciting finale, Montgomery boards the locomotive, shoots Jock Mahoney and engages in a terrific tussle with Douglas Kennedy, firing a slug into his back and pushing his corpse off the train. Bass' Long Riders surrender to a posse of Rangers after a noisy gunfight, the train arrives in one piece with its money intact and haughty Miss Storm thaws enough to plant a sloppy kiss on Montgomery's grinning face.

Remade less successfully by Columbia in 1965 as *Arizona Raiders*, with Audie Murphy in the lead, *The Texas Rangers* is a tremendous '50s oater where, after watching it, one will agree with that oft-used phrase: "They just don't make 'em like that anymore." They certainly don't; the movie is an out-and-out example of just how good the Western once was and that directors like Karlson brought so much to the Western genre while remaining unrecognized for their sterling work, living as they did under the shadows of men

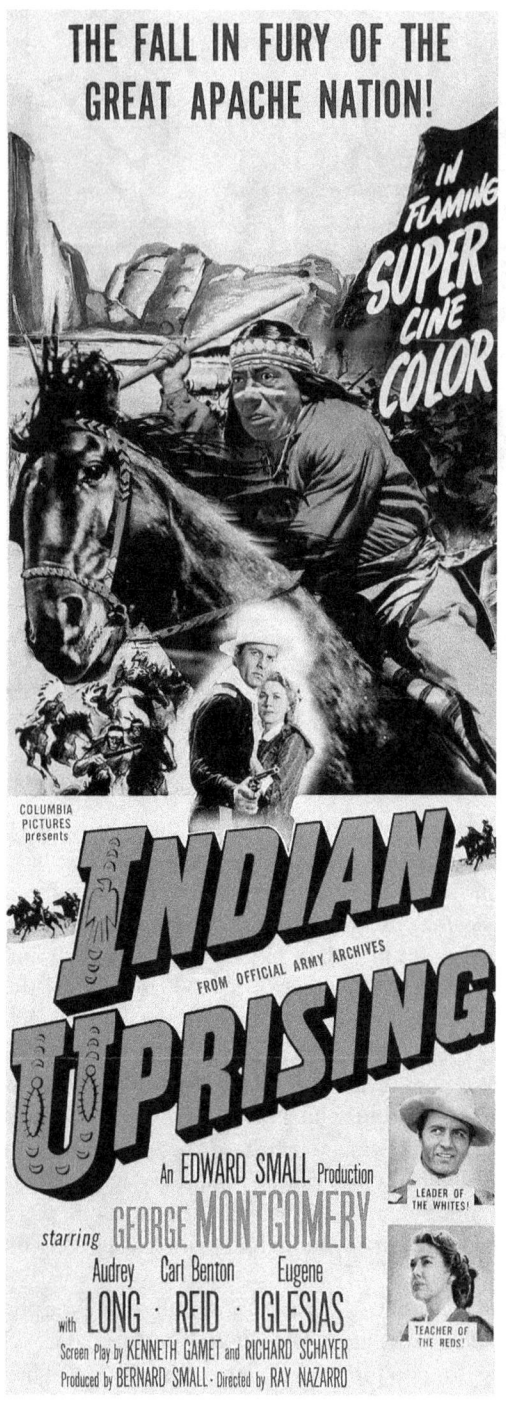

like John Ford and Anthony Mann. Karlson didn't have the big budgets or the big stars at his disposal, but his features were every bit as dynamic as Mann's or Ford's. Yes, Westerns *used* to be guaranteed money-spinners, an integral ingredient on any cinemagoer's list of "What's on next week." Montgomery's first-rate oater is a rock solid reminder of that fact. *The Hollywood Reporter* called it "a gripping, stirring motion picture," while *Variety* stated that: "George Montgomery definitely establishes himself as a Western star to contend with."

Like Scott, Murphy and McCrea, Montgomery had a production team operating around him at this period in time to ensure that he shone in the right material: scriptwriter Richard Schayer (he wrote seven Montgomery Westerns), producers Edward and Bernard Small, virtually the same support cast of journeymen B-Western extras and a relatively unknown, bullish director at the helm. Ray Nazarro was one such director, a man who, like Phil Karlson, could put together a rattling good actioner on low finances, eschewing superfluous padding in favor of exciting, bloodthirsty incident. Columbia's 1952 *Indian Uprising*, the first of four Montgomerys directed by Nazarro, introduced the actor to a cavalry officer's uniform, playing Captain Case McCloud, an Indian sympathizer attempting to keep the peace between Geronimo (Miguel Inclan) and the dastardly whites who want to trespass on Apache land in the hunt for gold. The film is hardly original in design: Sergeant Joe Sawyer does a passable impersonation of Victor McLaglen's Sgt. Major Quincannon in John Ford's *Rio Grande*; Inclan appeared as Cochise in Ford's *Fort Apache*; the scene where Montgomery pours whiskey into Robert Griffin at gunpoint to render him

George Montgomery and Miguel Inclan (as Geronimo) in *Indian Uprising* (1952)

so drunk that he'll confess as to who stuck that Arapahoe arrow in prospector Eddy Waller's back to trigger an Indian war was filched from *They Died With Their Boots On* (Errol Flynn's General Custer does it to coward Arthur Kennedy days before the Little Bighorn battle) and the well-worn "Indians breaking away from the reservation in defiance of the white man" situation had been committed to celluloid many times before. Notwithstanding these familiarities, *Indian Uprising* is a real mover, Montgomery filling those cavalry breeches swell, even though he's a tad wooden in his delivery at times.

Nazarro's picture (set in 1885) kicks off with a stirring fight between the Apaches and Montgomery's troops, taking place among the red-walled canyons of Sedona, Arizona, stunningly realized in glowing SuperCinecolor by photographer Ellis Carter. The plot is based on treachery: Montgomery desires peace with the Apache, saving Inclan's son twice from certain death; crooked trio Douglas Kennedy, Hugh Sanders and Robert Griffin scheme behind Montgomery's back, plotting to have him labeled an Indian lover and cashiered out of the army so that the miners can move in for gold; Kennedy offers Montgomery a $2,500 bribe to turn his back on the peace treaty and is pitched into the dust for his affront; starch-dry Major Robert Shayne takes command of Fort Steel, arresting Montgomery for insubordination and reducing his rank; and sorely aggrieved Inclan doesn't know which way to turn, trusting only the honorable Montgomery, who's confined to barracks. When Shayne's squad becomes trapped in Snake Canyon by Inclan's warriors and reinforcements are called for, Montgomery, against orders, leaves the fort and comes to his commanding officer's aid; under a flag of truce, he tries one more time to make a pact with the Apache chief, but Shayne's having none of it. Ignoring the flag, he tells the reinforcements to attack the Indians, Montgomery receiving a spear wound in the affray.

George Montgomery and Karin Booth in *Cripple Creek* (1952)

Indian Uprising is a movie that will have audiences rooting for the persecuted Redskins, reflecting a more positive attitude toward the American native Indians than attempted in 1930s and 1940s Westerns. They're slaughtered by Kennedy's gunslingers at an agency and bullied off their land at every given opportunity. All the whites, except for Montgomery, Sawyer and young officer John Baer, are disagreeable scoundrels out only for themselves, portrayed in a bad light, but at least they get their comeuppances. Indian agent Griffin winds up a drunken loser without an ally in the world; Kennedy shoots Sanders in the back and, after a fistfight with Montgomery, reveals the truth behind the planted arrow to Shayne and his officers; and Shayne, after his ineffectual showing against the Apaches, leading to an unacceptable loss of men, is carted off to another posting on instructions from Washington. Geronimo, tired of war, is imprisoned, stating solemnly that Montgomery (reinstated as Fort Steel's commanding officer) and he will part in friendship, and the cavalry hero proposes to Audrey Long, decorative but not really contributing much to this rousing outdoors cavalry versus Indians oater that looks glorious in color even to this day. The Audie Murphy 1964 remake, Fox's *Apache Rifles*, was a poor imitation of this lively caper.

Ray Nazarro also directed Columbia's *Cripple Creek* (1952), the action taking place in the final gold rush fever days of 1893. Huge quantities of gold are disappearing from the ore-rich fields of Cripple Creek, enough for the government to be concerned about national reserves drying up. Three Secret Service agents are dispatched to the town to act as decoys and unearth those responsible: Montgomery (playing Bret Ivers), Jerome

George Montgomery gets the drop on John Dehner in *Cripple Creek*.

Courtland and Richard Egan. Saloon boss William Bishop, assassin sidekick Don Porter, cordwood trader John Dehner and corrupt marshal Roy Roberts are combining their disreputable talents to waylay ore dug from the rock by honest miners, smelting the gold in an underground furnace hidden away in a ghost town and shipping the lead-plated bars to China for a handsome profit. Egan works as a card dealer in Bishop's joint while gun-slinging dudes Montgomery and Courtland are taken on as security guards to protect Dehner's wagons as they carry the stolen ore to the secret smelting works. The pair have proved themselves handy with a six-shooter by gunning down four villains caught lifting the contents of Bishop's safe; the saloon owner's impressed enough by these two "Texas tornado gun artists" to offer them jobs with Dehner's outfit, although remaining suspicious of their true identities.

Richard Schayer's sharp screenplay carries a plethora of twists and turns over a 78-minute running time; plenty of night riding, a lot of shooting and the audience constantly left wondering whether oily Bishop will figure out that he has three stool pigeons in his camp. In a tense scene, Egan is uncovered as an agent after he shoots Roberts dead; forced to play Russian roulette with Bishop (one cartridge in six chambers), he wins by force of nerve, goes to leave the room and is callously shot in the back by Porter. Saloon gal Karin Booth's father, mine owner George Cleveland, is secreted in a

cabin to prevent him coming to harm by voicing his concern over Bishop's activities and the movie finishes in a lengthy fistfight, Montgomery, Courtland, Porter and Dehner going at it hammer and tongs in the saloon, the two crooks handed over to the new town marshal. Schayer's final bombshell is yet to come; Bishop walks over to a Chinese laundry to collect half a million dollars for selling the gold. Booth turns up, Montgomery and Courtland inform Bishop that the gold never made it to China and Bishop is cut down after drawing his gun. Booth, along with the laundry proprietor, turns out to be the real brains behind the operation *and* Bishop's wife. So in this instance, Montgomery *doesn't* get the girl! "Born to die poor but honest," he grins at his partner as they leave town to deliver the money to those in authority.

Cripple Creek is another Montgomery triumph, the star, dressed in trademark brown leather chaps and wearing heavy artillery, going about his assignments with a disarming swagger. William V. Skall's Technicolor photography shimmers as it did in all of these early '50s Westerns, while Columbia's composer-in-residence, Mischa Bakaleinikoff, provides a decent stock soundtrack to underscore the action; it's also acted with total conviction by all concerned. An official DVD release is urgently required.

The Pathfinder (Columbia, 1952) saw George back in coonskin cap and buckskins, playing the eponymous hero of James Fenimore Cooper's 1840 novel, based on the colonial wars of 1754. Jay Silverheels took the part of Chingachgook, the duo plus Helena Carter infiltrating the French fortress of St. Vincente to uncover details of the enemy's forces and armaments; Carter is along for the ride because she's fluent in French and can act as an interpreter. Cooked up on a budget of $200,000 by quickie specialist Sam Katzman, Sidney Salkow's period romp (the first of this director's four Montgomerys) is curiously dated for the year it was made, resembling an early Technicolored '40s action adventure. It commences well, with a ferocious battle between Mohicans and Mingos, and ends with a bang, the English storming the French port, but what falls in between is routine to the point of lethargy, with a "seen it all before" air about it. Montgomery does what's required of him, but we're a long way from those dusty frontier towns and the actor seems to be missing his cowboy garb. Carter is pretty but wooden, spending an inordinate amount of screen time kissing her handsome leading man, while villain of the piece Bruce Lester's idea of marital bliss is to slap his young Indian wife (Elena Verdugo)

A romantic publicity shot from *Jack McCall Desperado* (1953) showing George Montgomery and Angela Stevens

across the face and call her a "red pig." Some wry lines of dialogue show Montgomery to be a bit of a male chauvinist as well as Lester: "Why aren't you having a flock of kids like other women?" he says to Carter, annoyed at her being in on the spying deal, adding: "Bring along a cookbook, Ma'am." There's a couple of skirmishes involving the blowing up of a supply train, the Pathfinder fights Mingo chief Arrowhead to the death but spares him a knife in the throat. Silverheels has the last word: "Yes—much better than a horse," he observes dryly when Montgomery and Carter engage, for the umpteenth time, in some lip action.

This was the first of three Sam Katzman–produced Columbia Westerns produced in succession that Montgomery would become involved with, and it didn't bode well for the other two. However, 1953's *Jack McCall Desperado* was heaps better all round, even though John O'Dea's screenplay rewrote the facts surrounding the assassination of Wild Bill Hickok on August 2, 1876 by ex-buffalo hunter Jack "Crooked Nose" McCall. Hickok was shot in the back by McCall during a poker game in Deadwood, South Dakota, a grudge killing, it has been claimed; pronounced "not guilty" at his first trial, McCall was tried for a second time, found guilty and hanged. Hickok was no saint, but in Katzman's effort, directed by Sidney Salkow, he's painted blacker than black, a back-stabbing, lying swine responsible for not only killing McCall's father but whipping up trouble with the Sioux to allow prospectors to poach on their land for gold. McCall (Montgomery), on the other hand, is portrayed as being perfectly justified in his actions, not a goody-goody by any stretch of the imagination but a darned sight more honest than Hickok (played by Douglas Kennedy) and his acolyte, Montgomery's sniveling cousin James Seay.

James Seay and George Montgomery in *Jack McCall Desperado* (1953)

The killing of Hickok bookends the movie; Montgomery relates to a court what led up to the shooting ("That's the whole story. Now the debt's paid.") and it's a serpentine tale that makes the 76-minute running time appear twice the length. Union buddies during the Civil War, Kennedy, his feathers constantly ruffled by Montgomery's well-to-do Southern background, frames him for the annihilation of a Yankee camp and its personnel, ransacks his country mansion, murders his father (cowardly Seay shoots Montgomery's mother dead) and, wearing a marshal's badge, double-crosses Sioux chief Jay Silverheels, feigning friendship by passing himself off as his ally when, in fact, he's plotting to have the nomadic tribes driven out of Painted Valley to allow the miners to take over. Montgomery certainly goes through the mill in this movie: He's wounded twice in the first 10 minutes, chased across country, branded a traitor, sees his beloved home vandalized, breaks out of jail, becomes a fugitive on the run and is deceived by William Tannen, the one man who can verify his innocence; Tannen turns him into the law, bribed by Kennedy. Thank goodness then for good-time gal Angela Stevens, picked up on the trail when her buggy loses a wheel. The plucky lass takes on the role of Montgomery's partner, the Bonnie to his Clyde, extricating him out of one sticky situation after another. Also on the fugitive's side is Silverheels' son, Eugene Iglesias, saved in a gun battle by Montgomery and assisted by him in the end when Kennedy's mob set a trap, massacring the Indians to a man. At the climax to the fray, Iglesias plugs Seay and beggars the question: How to stop Kennedy? "I have the answer in one bullet," states Montgomery with intent. It's no wonder that the scowling Montanan crashes through those saloon doors, flings Iglesias' beaded necklace on the card table and fires a well-deserved slug into the amoral marshal; if any man had had to put up with what Montgomery had to go through in this picture, they would do the same.

Inaccuracies apart, *Jack McCall Desperado* is a fast-paced oater directed with zeal by Salkow, Montgomery top-notch in the saddle when dishing out rough justice with fist and gun, his sparkly scenes with blonde Stevens producing an unusual Western screen pairing. After the court hearing, Tannen is dragged away by Iglesias' braves to a fate worse than death, and Montgomery carries new bride Stevens over the threshold of the newly furbished family pile, watched by two pleased-as-punch servants. Not the way it happened way back in 1876, maybe, but a fitting end to a lively George Montgomery Western, one of his most enjoyable. "Montgomery does a good job," stated *Daily Variety*.

As an interesting side note, Wheeler's *I Killed Wild Bill Hickok* (1956) was even more wildly inaccurate, showing Hickok to be a claim-jumping, murdering varmint open to bribery, shot to death in the street by one Johnny Rebel (who?), aggrieved at the lawman's interference in horse trading. A 63-minute low-budget black-and-white disaster of epic proportions, Richard Talmadge's '30s-style Western plumbed new depths in production, acting, cinematography and music and is best avoided at all costs, even by diehard fans of the genre.

Produced in three-dimension, *Fort Ti* was Montgomery's third, and worst, colonial Western in as many years, Robert E. Kent's screenplay failing to breathe life into a stale format. A return to the English/French/Indian wars of 1759 featuring Montgomery as Captain Jed Horn, a member of Rogers' Rangers, Montgomery flushes out a spy who is trading secrets with the enemy. Producer Katzman and director William Castle (king of the horror gimmick film, starting in 1958 with *Macabre*; this was number one of his three Montgomery Westerns) left all artistic pretensions on the cutting room floor, concentrating on a barrage of objects hurled at the camera to ensure the audience ducking in their seats: cannon balls, flaming embers, firing rifles, bodies, tomahawks, arrows, torches, advancing Indians and fists, even a terrified woman having her blouse ripped by a lecherous brave—all were guaranteed to give Columbia a bumper return

at the cash registers, whether the overall product was good or below par. And let it be said, Montgomery's pictures, average or not, were still raking in good reviews, the *Los Angeles Daily News* observing: "Montgomery makes a properly dashing hero."

French spy Louis Merrill blackmails Montgomery's brother-in-law (James Seay) into giving vital information to the French; Seay's wife and children are being held hostage to ensure that he plays ball. Confessing his misconduct to Montgomery and General Lester Matthews, it's decided that Seay will go on feeding intelligence reports to the French, but *false* intelligence, to enable the Redcoats to attack Fort Ticonderoga properly forearmed. On the march to the fort, with the added objective of rescuing Seay's family, Montgomery's old friend, Frenchman Ben Astar, turns up, his frisky young wife (Phyllis Fowler) passionately in love with the Ranger. Joan Vohs also appears after an Indian attack, labeled a spy (is she in cahoots with Seay?), wasting no time in getting into a clinch with her leading man and clinging to him like a leech. There are a couple of skirmishes in which more items are thrown at Castle's camera; Montgomery's sidekick, whiskery old coot Irving Bacon, does a passable impersonation of Walter Brennan; Fowler is the spy, knifing herself to death in remorse because Montgomery spurns her advances; Seay's wife and kids are saved; and the English take Fort Ti after a disappointingly bloodless battle. Vohs is cleared of treachery and kisses the hero of the hour as the end credits roll.

Montgomery, thank goodness, never returned to this by now tired-looking historical costume period drama format, leaving Sam Katzman behind and getting straight back in the saddle, holster and gun for United Artists' excellent 1953 offering *Gun Belt*, directed with panache by Ray Nazarro. Let down by muddy color and an unconvincing performance from moody teen heartthrob of the day Tab Hunter (his third film), Nazarro's Western nevertheless pressed the excitement button full-on, a tale of cross, double-cross and multiple frame-ups in which George (as Billy Ringo) doesn't strap on his iron until the 27th minute. Up until then, he's a reformed gunman-turned-rancher, looking after nephew Hunter whose father, John Dehner, is in prison for murder. Montgomery's engaged to millinery shop owner Helen Westcott and owes $3,000 to the bank; Dehner goes over the wall, assisted by desperadoes Douglas Kennedy, Jack Elam and Joe Haworth, and heads for his brother's spread to coerce him into joining them on a half

(Standing) Jack Elam, George Montgomery and Tab Hunter in *Gun Belt* (1953)

million dollar Wells Fargo raid masterminded by corrupt businessman Hugh Sanders. Montgomery doesn't want to know ("I want no part of the deal."), visits the bank to present a check and becomes embroiled in a holdup orchestrated by Dehner, who has the crafty idea of framing Montgomery to bring him in on the Wells Fargo job. Now branded a criminal through no fault of his own, Montgomery, seething with fury, slugs it out with his wayward brother, shooting him dead by accident during the struggle. The rancher returns to Tombstone to explain the situation and is almost hanged before Marshal Wyatt Earp (played by James Millican) rides up, saves his neck and parleys with him; it's agreed that he'll take on the role of boss with Dehner's boys and deliver them to the law, thereby clearing his name. Back at the ranch, Hunter dons a gun on learning of his father's death, vowing to shoot his uncle when he gets the chance. He also wants to hit the outlaw trail, sick of farming.

Into writers Jack DeWitt and Richard Schayer's fictitious (Earp was never involved with a Billy Ringo) but intelligent mix comes William Bishop, a gun-toting rat in cahoots with Sanders and also in on the Wells Fargo hijack. Sanders wants the troublemaker out of the way, so in a meeting with Montgomery, he gives him an incentive to kill Bishop during the robbery—Montgomery relays the information to Millican with a promise that he will turn *both* gangs into the marshal's hands and prove his innocence. Bishop, learning of Montgomery's involvement from Sanders, dissolves their partnership with a bullet but craftily agrees to join forces with his rival's bunch, planning to get rid of them after the robbery. The combined group rides off toward a Wells Fargo staging post where two wagons loaded with coin are taken after a terrific gunfight. The showdown occurs in Red Canyon where Earp's posse is due to rendezvous with Montgomery; when it does, everyone is dead (most shot by the double-dealing Bishop) except for a victorious Montgomery, holding wounded Bishop at gunpoint ("Looks like Custer's Last Stand," comments the marshal wryly, staring at the corpse-littered ground). As expected, Montgomery and Westcott are married, returning to his ranch, and Hunter is back on the straight and narrow.

Remade by United Artists in 1960 under the title of *Five Guns to Tombstone* (Edward L. Cahn directed), *Gun Belt* was another tough, satisfying Montgomery vehicle, edging him out in front of a plethora of actors starring in Westerns around this bounteous period in the genre's history, Rory Calhoun, Rod Cameron, Stephen McNally, John Payne and Sterling Hayden among them. He possessed a smidgen more allure than they did, plus the good looks women went for (it's noticeable that many of Montgomery's leading ladies appeared to throw a lot more into their passionate embraces with him than the director probably called for). His acting performances didn't really alter from one production to the next, but did that really matter within your standard, medium-budget Western framework? Anyway, he received consistently first-rate reviews and the films themselves were successful; he couldn't have been doing that much wrong. *The Hollywood Reporter* praised the movie to the hilt: "A fast-moving Technicolor Western crammed with action."

Montgomery's strapping frame also suited a cavalry uniform better than most, as Columbia's 1954 *Battle of Rogue River* proved. Back with Sam Katzman and William Castle, he starred as Major Frank Archer, a stern-faced disciplinarian taking command of an unruly outpost where the main occupation appeared to be drinking rum and carousing with the ladies, Martha Hyer among them. Militia leader Richard Denning, although busy recruiting civilians to bolster the cavalry ranks, plays a shifty no-gooder, in collusion with associate Charles Evans to start an Indian war so that (yes, you've guessed it) settlers can move into the Rogue River area and commence hunting and mining. Evans and Denning, for their own selfish reasons, don't want Oregon to become a state; they're much better off without government interference, and troublesome Redskins on the warpath will suit their nefarious purposes just fine. Hyer, although romanced by Denning, is bowled over by Montgomery's unapproachable manner, even if his men aren't. "Easy, Major. One campaign at a time," she coos at him when he gets up close and personal. Montgomery rides out to meet Michael Granger (as Chief Mike) and proposes a 30-day peace pact: Indians to stay on the north side of the river, whites on the south. Denning's having none of it; he arranges for Hyer's father (Emory Parnell) to wipe out a band of six bucks and places the blame on Montgomery when Parnell is presumed dead (he isn't, staggering back to the fort and spilling the beans on Denning). Granger, incensed at this wanton killing, holds a council of war with his chiefs, plasters on the war paint and takes up arms, his warriors clashing with Montgomery's outfit on both banks of the river.

Despite its B-movie leanings, writer Douglas Heyes presents us with a thoughtful script highlighting the quandary that Indian tribes found themselves in during the 1850s. Montgomery is in a long line of white men during the 1950s to feel sorry for the Indians, even saving the tribe at the end from destructive cannon fire. As for Denning, he has a hand-to-hand fight with Montgomery in Granger's camp after being exposed as a lying cheat; about to hurl a spear at the officer, Granger shoots him dead. "He is guilty by your law. He is dead by mine," intones the chief to his cavalry friend. The Indians finally agree to peace, Montgomery gets to grips with Hyer and Oregon is admitted into the union of the United States of America.

Nice Technicolor photography from Henry Freulich and Castle's careful pacing made *Battle of Rogue River* one of the worthier of the countless cavalry versus Indians features dished up to the paying public throughout this decade. George, in his early to mid-'50s period, was on a high, and his next in 1954, United Artists' *The Lone Gun*, was another slimline good guys versus bad guys opus directed with a commendable lack of fluff by Ray Nazarro. Montgomery was Cruze, teaming up with tinhorn gambler Frank Faylen and bringing peace to the town of Marlpine, a pairing that

mirrored the Wyatt Earp/Doc Holliday relationship in all but name only. Three of the Westerns' roughest hombres—Neville Brand, Douglas Kennedy and Robert J. Wilke—played brothers, up to their necks in cattle rustling, using Skip Homeier and Dorothy Malone's ranch to graze the stolen herds. During a game of poker, Homeier, who owes money to the deadly trio, is shot in the back by Wilke using Faylen's derringer, and the card sharp is arrested for murder. It's then up to Montgomery, now town marshal, to exonerate Faylen, bring the three brothers to justice and play house with Malone.

A simple plot, maybe, and one that a 100 or so Westerns made in the 1950s must have based their foundation on. But it's all in the telling: From the first sight of Montgomery, unshaven and looking as mean as hell, audiences know they're in for a thrilling ride. Richard Schayer and Don Martin's script sizzles with acerbic exchanges, notably in the first meeting between Montgomery, loquacious Faylen and the brothers ("Who are these apes?" says Montgomery), a standoff that Sergio Leone would have watched and thought "Yes. One day …" The lily-livered townsfolk refuse to back their new marshal when he asks for volunteers to form an eight-man posse, and bartender Douglas Fowley, supplying information to Brand regarding fresh cattle to steal, does his level best to discredit the lawman. Wilke and two henchmen attempt to ambush Montgomery on the edge of town but fail to kill him; the marshal, wounded, drops the two

Dorothy Malone, George Montgomery and Frank Faylen in *The Lone Gun* (1954)

heavies, and snarling Wilke slinks off to lick his wounds. There's an exciting shoot-out on horseback among rocks and Nazarro fashions a taut climax, Montgomery, Faylen (now deputized) and the brothers facing each other in a clearing. Wilke kills Kennedy by mistake; Montgomery guns down Wilke and has a lengthy, bone-crunching fistfight with Brand before the fallen rustler is cuffed, along with Fowley. Faylen escorts the villains into town, while his boss gallops off with Malone to get better acquainted with her charms. United Artists remade the movie in 1961 as *The Gambler Wore a Gun*, Edward L. Cahn directing Jim Davis in the lead role.

Fine color photography and a standard Western score from Irving Gertz highlighted the last of the Montgomery/Ray Nazarro oaters, and a great one at that. Like so many filmmakers of B-movie fodder during the decade, Nazarro rolled up his sleeves on restricted finances and got on with it. No padding, no verbalizing, not one second of screen time given over to wastage—Budd Boetticher wasn't the only one around at the time to come up with a Western forged on solid hard graft that came in at under 80 minutes. Nazarro, Phil Karlson, Sidney Salkow and even William Castle could also manage it and produce acceptable results. *The Lone Gun* is a supreme example of how great Hollywood Westerns used to be, and how underrated Montgomery was in appearing in them. Long may they continue to be revered by true genre fans.

Lawman Bat Masterson and Doc Holliday form an uneasy alliance to save an innocent man from the rope; his death could precipitate a full-scale Indian war. None of it's true, of course, but *Masterson of Kansas* (Columbia, 1954) showed that Montgomery's Western career was refusing to let up for a single second. In William Castle's taut actioner, the leading man was almost upstaged by character actor James Griffith's sharp portrayal of the legendary Doc, a cynical gambler with a hair-trigger temper, living under the cloud of tuberculosis; Griffith emerges with honors, as good as the many others who have taken on the role of the doctor torn apart by his inner demons. The old standby chestnut of greedy cattlemen requiring Indian land was trotted out, Montgomery preventing William Henry and his drovers from lynching John Maxwell, framed for the murder of an army officer. If Indian sympathizer Maxwell dies, Chief Jay Silverheels, a friend of his, will ignore the peace treaty and go on the warpath; the cavalry will take action, wipe out the Redskins and the land will be left open for Henry to move in. Rancher David Bruce knows that Henry was responsible for the murder, but has a yellow streak running down his back the size of Texas and lied under oath; it's up to Montgomery to track him down so that he can testify against the smarmy cattle boss, and Griffith is needed as an extra gun hand even if the two have promised each other a "who's quickest on the draw" contest when it's all over.

Dodge City is where the two meet, a face-off in the street, both sporting double holsters. In steps Wyatt Earp (an ineffectual Bruce Cowling), also wearing two pistols, breaking up the fight. "He's a cold-blooded killer," Cowling admits to Montgomery, warning him not to go gunning for the Doc (his "blind spot" in Dodge) through personal animosity. Maxwell, tried and convicted of murder in front of lying witnesses, is put on a stage for Hayes City, Montgomery making sure that he gets there in one piece. "A man out here is one of three things," he tells Maxwell's anxious daughter, Nancy Gates. "Hard, fast or dead." Bruce, meanwhile, has gone into hiding, scared of reprisals from Henry's gang if he tells the truth; he also owes $3,000 in gambling debts to Griffith. In Quolari, Bruce's death is faked and there's a gun battle at the livery stables where he's been spirited away—he's smuggled out of town by the lawman while Griffith elects to stay behind for a bit of card dealing. Finally, in Hayes City, Maxwell is about to be strung up by Henry's gorillas when Montgomery, Griffith and Cowling approach menacingly. With six guns at their disposal, the trio pick off the mob like flies, a tremendous sequence put together with skill by director Castle; Maxwell is cleared, Griffith gives old foe Montgomery a begrudging half-smile, there's no Indian war in

George Montgomery as Bat Masterson and Bruce Cowling as Wyatt Earp in *Masterson of Kansas* **(1954)**

Kansas and Gates throws in her lot with Montgomery after having turned down the Doc's proposals earlier on.

According to Douglas Heyes' script, William Barclay Masterson earned the sobriquet "Bat" through his skill in shooting down bats on the wing when he was a youngster. Montgomery played him with the customary severe, gruff approach that fans now expected to see of him, the equal to Scott (*Trail Street*) and McCrea (*The Gunfight at Dodge City*) in the part. He had found his niche and stuck to it; he very rarely deviated from his interpretation of how a cowboy hero should come across to a 1950s public crammed in a pitch-black auditorium, waiting breathlessly for the next slice of gunplay. His performances could, on occasions, be regarded as one-dimensional, the dialogue spat out in short, sharp sentences, but at least he meant what he said without preamble and, in this context, George Montgomery scored very highly on the "what excites a Western-mad audience" pleasure-meter.

That sense of wild abandon was in little evidence in Columbia's *Seminole Uprising*, Montgomery's first for 1955, a movie fully qualifying itself for the title of a Sam Katzman "quickie." Apparently, the Florida-dwelling Seminoles have migrated to Texas and half-Indian/half-white Montgomery (as Lieutenant Cam Elliott) has his hands full keeping the peace with one-time blood brother Chief Black Cat (Steven Ritch);

like most Indians, Black Cat is sick and tired of white men tramping all over his property and refuses to settle down to a boring life on a reservation. Robert E. Kent's clichéd script concentrates on Montgomery's relationship with man-hungry Karin Booth; he once had a torrid affair with her (sex outside of Fort Clark's walls?), but she's now engaged to inflexible Ed Hinton, a rank above Montgomery—yet she still loves her former beau. Colonel Howard Wright, Booth's father, sends out both men on a mission to bring Ritch to heel at Devil Pass after the chief's bucks abduct Roy Mallinson's wife and son. What with Montgomery and Hinton glowering at each other, Mallinson and his men on the hunt for the woman, Booth taken hostage by Ritch and Ritch's braves on the attack, you would have thought that a splendid time was guaranteed by all. This isn't the case: Too much footage from *Fort Ti*, *Indian Uprising* and *Battle of Rogue River* is included to bolster the 74-minute running time, giving the production a patched-up look; Montgomery appears stiff and wooden, only managing to smile once; and the battle scenes don't work because of that mismatched stock footage. Once again, it's revealed in the end that Montgomery isn't a half-breed as he was led to believe; the Seminoles brought him up following a massacre, so it's now perfectly acceptable for him to marry Booth. Hinton has copped it from one of his own troopers for allowing Montgomery's outfit to run out of water on a forced desert march. There are a couple of nods to new age violence—Mallinson's wife and child are knifed and scalped, so he does the same to Ritch's squaw and young son—William Fawcett is a joy as Montgomery's grizzled scout (he also narrates the action) and there's one thrilling sequence in which tons of boulders and flaming brushwood are dropped onto the warriors' heads, resulting in Ritch asking for new Terms of Surrender. But, all in all, it's a dispiriting affair that Montgomery aficionados will want to forget in a hurry.

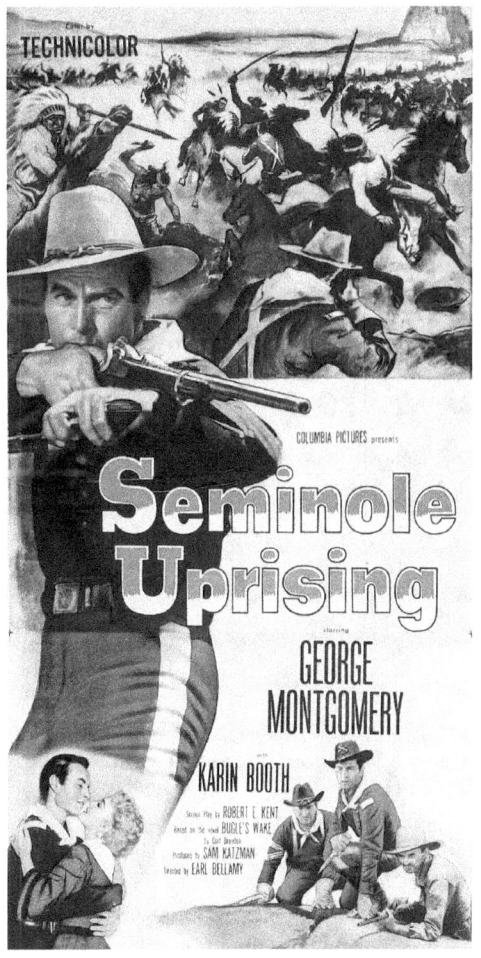

Zane Grey's *Robbers' Roost* (United Artists, 1955) was next up, and Fox had filmed it previously in 1932 with George O'Brien in the lead. A fine cast headed this revenge Western: Richard Boone and Peter Graves playing warring gang chiefs; heavies Leo Gordon and Warren Stevens; Bruce Bennett as a wheelchair-bound ranch owner; and William Hopper, hoping to take over Bennett's ranch *and* his daughter, actress Sylvia

George Montgomery, Sylvia Findley, Peter Graves and Richard Boone in *Robbers' Roost* **(1955)**

Findley, making the second of her only two screen appearances (the first was in UA's violent *Black Tuesday* in 1954). Paul Dunlap provided a noisy score while Jack Draper's muted Eastmancolor photography was a tad too dark in the night shots, coming into its own during the later scenes, filmed in Durango, Mexico.

Montgomery is Jim "Tex" Wall, a man with a price on his head, quick on the draw with both guns and tight-lipped with it, a "woman-hating gunman," as someone later describes him. Bennett has decided that to safeguard his 1,000 head of cattle, he'll employ two out-and-out rustlers and their gangs to watch over them: "Set a thief to catch a thief," he tells sister Findley. Montgomery joins up with Boone's boys, who meet with Graves' gang on the Herrick Ranch and grudgingly put aside their mutual differences, agreeing on one thing: Play ball for a spell, then sell off the herd a few hundred at a time, cleaning Bennett out. Bennett assigns the duty of chaperoning Findley to Montgomery; she's suspicious of Graves and Boone and has little time for Hopper, whose attempts at romancing her fall on stony ground. Five hundred head of cattle are sold to a dealer and greed takes over: Boone and Graves decide to rustle the remaining cattle in one fell swoop, kidnapping Findley as a possible bonus. Boone then double-crosses Graves, ties him and his men up, sells the herd, collects the money, abducts Findley and heads for the canyons. Soon, both Graves and a sheriff's posse are on Boone's tail, but so is Montgomery. Why is he so fixated with that livid scar running down Boone's chest, and why does the law want him? Is there a connection? As Graves and the posse close in on a derelict hacienda situated deep within a canyon, we learn the real reason why Montgomery chose to ride along with Boone and his mob in the first place.

Sidney Salkow directs with pace, although he has an over-fondness for panning across the admittedly striking wilderness before getting on with the job, while Montgomery's taciturn gunman is in nice contrast to Boone's grinning villain—he gives Gordon a good hiding and outdraws Stevens, clipping his left ear with a well-aimed slug. Graves tries too hard to be unlikeable, not really his forte (he was equally unconvincing as a bad guy in 1956's *Canyon River*) and regrettably, hard-man Gordon fades from the action early on. The denouement is satisfyingly tied up in the exciting climax, fought out amid Durango's rugged canyon scenery: That scar on Boone's chest was made by Montgomery's wife during a raid on his ranch; she clawed at Boone before dying (did he rape her?), so he's out to kill the rustler. Findley does it for him, causing an avalanche of rocks to crush Boone and his men (Graves has already been dispatched with a bullet); fatally injured, Boone confesses to the sheriff that he was responsible for the death of Montgomery's wife and expires. Montgomery, cleared of any crime, is a free man, able to take up with Findley (judging by her near-nude bathing scene, he's one lucky fella!).

By the end of 1955, Montgomery's tally of 15 '50s Westerns compared favorably to those of Scott's 18, Murphy's 11 and McCrea's 11; he was, artistically speaking, on the same level with them as one of the linchpins of the new generation of medium-grade Westerns, and it's worth examining their '50s output, and role-playing, at this midway stage of the decade.

Scott was the authoritarian figure, older and wiser, the vastly experienced Westerner, bringing more gravity to his parts than his compatriots, mirroring the Old West in those rugged features; boyish Murphy could be classed as the young upstart, bulldozing his way from one situation to another; laconic McCrea's unflustered style could be infuriatingly *too* relaxed at times, his Westerns improving noticeably in the latter half of the decade; while virile Montgomery, the best looking of the bunch, was your archetypal '50s cowpoke, stern of countenance, a no-nonsense attitude, quick with his guns and fists. Yes, he could be viewed, and accused, by some as being slightly cardboard in his approach, but in many ways, Montgomery's feature films had more of an enjoyment factor built within their framework. If Scott had an off day with *The Man Behind the Gun*, or McCrea with *The San Francisco Story*, the end result could be a bit of a bore. Murphy, to his credit, never featured in a single mediocre Western up to the end of 1955. But if Montgomery starred in a bummer (*Davy Crockett Indian Scout*; *Fort Ti*), the movie, stuck in the standard B-Western bracket, was still watchable because audiences didn't expect greater things from him, as they did with Scott and McCrea. Their diverse pedigree could work against them—Montgomery didn't possess quite the same legacy, his briskly blunt play-it-by-numbers method more acceptable, and more suitable, to both the masses *and* to your average '50s oater. Looking back, Montgomery's *The Texas Rangers* and *The Lone Gun* are every bit as good as Scott's *Hangman's Knot* and *Ten Wanted Men*, Murphy's *Kansas Raiders* and *Ride Clear of Diablo* and McCrea's *Black Horse Canyon* and *Stranger on Horseback*. Maybe his work did fluctuate between classic and uneventful but, in this respect, his fellow stars' pictures did so as well. George Montgomery, in the sphere of Westerns made during this generative span, comes across as an underrated talent whose Westerns were typical of the age in which they were conceived. Let's recall them with pleasure, not derision.

Chapter 15
Murphy: The Universal Years, 1951-1959

Audie Murphy's one major release in 1951 was playing "The Youth" in John Huston's ill-fated $1,600,000 American Civil War epic, *The Red Badge of Courage*. Virtually disowned by MGM, shorn of 30 minutes, critically mauled and a financial flop, Murphy at least emerged with flying colors from the expensive debacle, his performance one of the best things in the movie. "The Kid," as he was still being referred to in his movies, was catching on fast. But could his experience on *The Red Badge of Courage*, with its corrosive fallout, have affected his self-belief? Judging by Murphy's stuttering turn as outlaw Bill Doolin, his third bad guy in his fourth Universal picture, *The Cimarron Kid*, it did. Completed in December 1951 and released a month later, Murphy appeared slightly nervy and unsure, some measure of self-doubt creeping into the role. Not helped by Louis Stevens' leaden script, a below-average composite score strung together by Joseph Gershenson and Budd Boetticher's erratic direction (Boetticher was to cultivate his unique style in the psychological-themed Randolph Scott Ranown Westerns from 1956), Stevens' screenplay recycled the Coffeyville raids carried out by the Dalton gang previously filmed in two Scott outings, *When the Daltons Rode* and *The Doolins of Oklahoma*.

Audie Murphy as "The Youth" in *The Red Badge of Courage* (1951)

First seen getting paroled on condition that he steers clear of trouble, Murphy is soon a key member in the Daltons' criminal activities after being wrongly accused of being in on a train robbery they carry out. The infamous Coffeyville bank jobs appear a third of the way into the picture, and Boetticher handles the crackerjack action sequences with flair, the Daltons shot to pieces; it's when the remnants of the gang reform and discuss their future that the director applies the brakes and things go off the boil.

Holed up at Roy Roberts' ranch (his daughter, Beverly Tyler, falls for Murphy), redhaired troublemaker Hugh O'Brian cherishes the role of leader but Murphy, the more astute, takes over, allowing Boetticher to stage one more violent shoot-out in a train yard, O'Brian gunned down by Murphy. The rest of the bunch are undone by agent

John Hubbard and Palmer Lee's treachery; in the end, surrounded by a gun-toting posse in a barn, Murphy gives himself up to lawman Leif Erickson, promising to go straight and hitch up with Tyler when he's released from prison. (Universal executives wanted him shot in the back, but Boetticher persuaded them to change their minds.)

The Cimarron Kid boasts pleasing color photography and a good support cast: Noah Beery, Jr., James Best, William Reynolds and lovely dark-haired Yvette Duguay (billed as Dugay), playing Best's girl. As Westerns go, it's no better or worse than dozens of others produced around this time. But Murphy looked as though he was still learning the ropes instead of cementing his reputation, as he should have been doing. He needed a director to coax that extra mileage out of him, to instill some much-needed confidence. Luckily for him, Don Siegel was waiting in the wings to do just that.

Claim jumpers are terrorizing the Silver City area, forcing mine owners to hand over their deeds for a dollar before being gunned down without a second's thought. The opening few minutes to Don Siegel's *The Duel at Silver Creek* (1952) are grim and brutal, a foretaste of the director's future trademark X-rated cinematic exploits. Luke Cromwell (Murphy) discovers the blood-soaked corpse of his father after Gerald Mohr's apes have shot him to death; he dispatches three of the crooks and then disappears from the proceedings until the 26th minute, when he turns up in Silver City as "The Silver Kid," toting a double holster and a revengeful chip on his shoulder. Looking dapper in black hat, black neckerchief and gray shirt, Murphy has an assertive poise that he didn't possess in *The Cimarron Kid* and that's all down to Siegel, who took him under his wing and nurtured his talents. "He wasn't that good an actor," Siegel went on to say, "but he had star quality, and that's what counts."

A bizarre list of character names inhabits Siegel's intelligent Western: Marshal Lightning Tyrone (Stephen McNally), Opal Lacey (Faith Domergue), Dusty Fargo (Susan Cabot), Johnny Sombrero (Eugene Iglesias), Tinhorn Burgess (Lee Marvin) and Ratface Blake (James Anderson). In fact, for a good part of the film, audiences could almost be forgiven for thinking that this was a Stephen McNally cowboy flick, such is the extent of his screen time. The solid McNally starred in 11 very fine Westerns throughout the

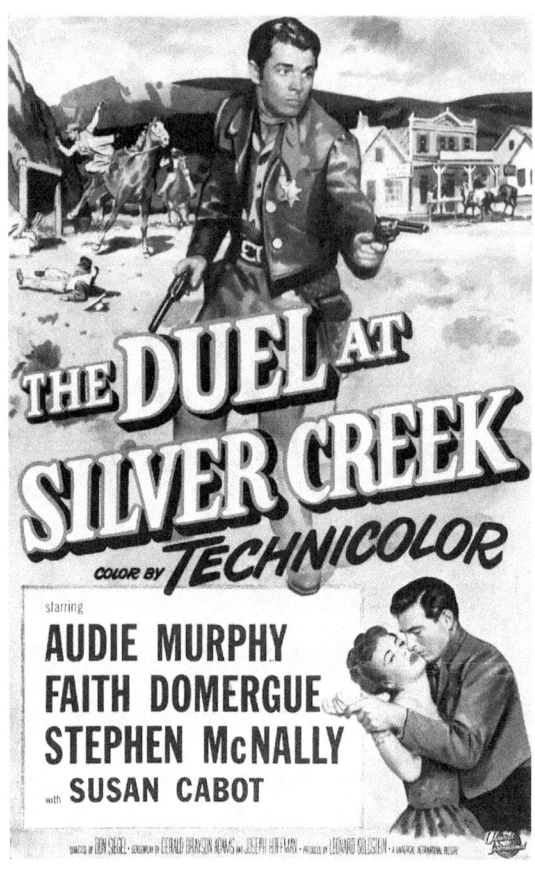

1950s, a more accomplished actor than Murphy but lacking the requisite charisma to promote him to star status. He's the town marshal trying to track down the criminals, deputizing Murphy after he sees some fancy gunplay between him and Marvin in a saloon ("When you gonna start shavin' kid," sneers Marvin before Murphy shoots the gun out of his hand). McNally can clear a holster quicker than most but is unable to pull the trigger following a bullet wound in the shoulder; Murphy is just the kind of sharpshooting young dude to have at your side in case of trouble ("He didn't have a face of a killer, but he had the cold-steel look of one," narrates McNally). In an involved storyline, flirtatious dame Domergue, a partner in the bogus Acme Mining Company, makes a play for McNally (he calls her "Brown Eyes") but the seductress is in with Mohr's claim jumping scam and is trying to put the marshal off the scent. In one scene, she callously strangles a bedridden witness who could identify the claim jumpers, strong stuff for 1952. Lurking in the background is the swaggering Iglesias, determined to beat McNally to the draw at all costs, while tomboy Cabot, hero-worshipping McNally, casts her big lovely eyes on Murphy, scanning him from head to toe and stating, "Kinda young to be a deputy, isn't he."

After Murphy plugs Iglesias in a street standoff and obtains proof that Domergue isn't all that she appears to be, McNally, incensed at being made a fool of, forces the femme fatale to lead him and his posse to Mohr's hideout, resulting in a five-minute, full-blooded finishing gun battle. Watch out for Murphy's fabulous piece of stunt work, hurling himself through a cabin window, glass cascading everywhere, his two guns blazing hot lead. Mohr kills Domergue and is then finished off by McNally among the rocks; Murphy, as expected, wins Cabot in the final frame.

Universal's Western scores were always a cut above the rest, perhaps because most of their roster of composers worked on the company's renowned horror and sci-fi movies. Here, Herman Stein produced a rousing soundtrack whose various themes can be discerned in his score for *This Island Earth* (1954). Photographer Irving Glassberg brought a gloss to location shooting around California's Simi Valley area, while Gerald Drayson Adams and Joseph Hoffman's taut script was a joy to the ears. At 77 minutes,

The Duel at Silver Creek didn't hang about: It was a big step up for Murphy after the lackluster *The Cimarron Kid*; he seemed galvanized, ready to take on his next project, the even-better *Gunsmoke* in 1953.

Murphy's Westerns from this early '50s period were livelier than those of Scott's, McCrea's and Montgomery's, not as deep as Scott's or McCrea's, maybe, but more often than not possessed with a manic energy due in no small part to the star himself. They appealed to those kids who loved to play cowboys and Indians in their backyards. *Gunsmoke* saw Murphy attaining the same kind of authority that Scott, McCrea and Montgomery carried in their pictures, even though he was still being called "Kid" most of the time and was considerably younger than two of his three Western compatriots ("A Dead End Kid on horseback," wrote *Time*'s film critic after viewing the picture). He looked sweaty, dusty and unshaven in this one, playing another bad boy, Reb Kittredge, a hired gun. First seen galloping at speed from the cavalry with cohort Charles Drake, the two split, Murphy hitching a ride on a stage (his horse is shot from under him) and meeting delectable Susan Cabot. In town crook Donald Randolph hires Murphy ("A two-bit gunslinger") to kill Cabot's father (Paul Kelly). Changing his mind after shooting the amiable ranch owner in the hand, Murphy wins the deed to Kelly's spread, the Square S, in a poker game and drives a herd of Longhorn steers across country to the sound of Herman Stein's raucous score (the wooded San Bernardino National Forest was used for location filming),

tailed by ex-pal Drake, who has been hired by Randolph to bump *him* off and prevent the herd from reaching its destination. After several skirmishes with Drake, henchman Jack Kelly and his mob (Murphy is beaten up by them) and a cattle stampede, the beef

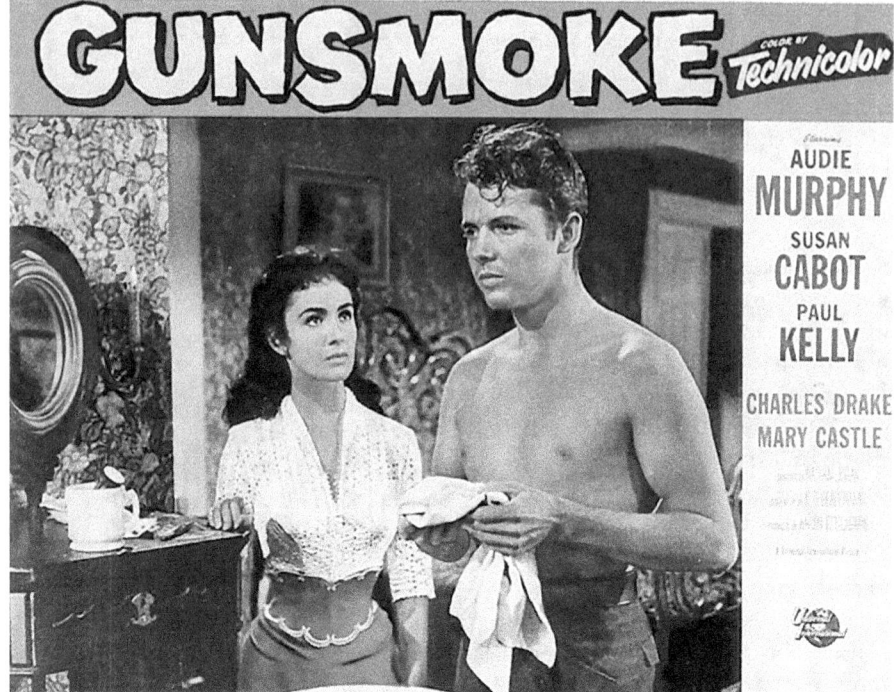

Susan Cabot and Audie Murphy in *Gunsmoke* (1953)

is safely delivered to the railhead. Back in town, Murphy is a reformed character, handing back the land deeds to Kelly; the rancher now appears to be Murphy's prospective father-in-law, judging by the way the "Kid" and Cabot are gazing into each other's eyes. Drake, after gunning down Randolph, who was on the point of shooting his old partner Murphy in the back, winds up with decorative singer Mary Castle on his arm.

Nathan Juran directed with real style (as he would do on a few Universal and Columbia monster movies), while scriptwriter D.D. Beauchamp brought a touch of humor to the dialogue, Murphy beginning to relax and handle his lines with deadpan assurance: Hotel clerk: "We got mice." Murphy: "I won't bother them." *Gunsmoke* turned out to be Murphy's first real gritty adult Western, rougher and tougher than before, and Universal was now ready to ditch that "Kid" tag by promoting him to hero status. And it's poignant now to see sexy young lovers Murphy and Cabot in each other's arms when you consider the tragic ends to both stars: Murphy in a plane crash on May 28, 1971 and Cabot beaten to death by her mentally unstable son on December 10, 1986.

Frederick de Cordova appeared to be an odd choice to direct Murphy's next feature, *Column South*, in 1953. The man behind Ronald Reagan's classic brainless chimp comedy, *Bedtime for Bonzo* (1951), and the producer/director of over 100 episodes of TV's *George Burns and Gracie Allen Show*, 1953-1958 (he also produced/directed *The Jack Benny Program* from 1955 to 1964), one would have thought that he would have been the last person on the Universal block to handle an Audie Murphy Western. Set amid the desolate splendor of California's Apple Valley and photographed in bleached-out color by Charles P. Boyle, the comedy director, notwithstanding a dearth of Western movie credibility, managed to do a decent-enough job on a rather complex tale of cavalry versus Indians on the warpath (and the cavalry versus themselves), the movie set in 1861 as the Civil War threatens to burst into flames.

What with divided loyalties among the troops, a new greenhorn commanding officer (Robert Sterling) intent on a glory campaign and Sterling's flouncy sister (Joan Evans) going all hot and cold over him, Lieutenant Murphy (as Jed Sayre) has his work cut out keeping peace between the friendly Navajos (led by Dennis Weaver) and the army. Sterling is convinced the Redskins are up to no good and wants them moved to a new locale; Murphy disagrees, anxious not to upset the delicate relationship he has with the Indian chief (as a nine-year-old, he was dragged along by his father to witness an Indian massacre and sympathizes with their plight). Then along comes scheming General Ray Collins (sporting one of Westerns' worst fake beards) to throw a wrench into the works. Up to his neck in political intrigue and siding with the Confederacy, Collins first cooks up a plan to blame the shooting of a prospector on the Navajos (the real guilty party, a fellow prospector, later confesses to the murder). Second, he further provokes the Indians into moving camp to Yellow Springs when a huge quantity of rifles is stolen, part of his strategy into forcing Murphy and Sterling to head south with a detachment to fight a fictitious offensive against the Apaches, thus enabling the Confederates to take over the area when war is declared. Sterling is in on the duplicity and it's not until the column is several days out that Murphy uncovers the truth, returning to Fort Union helter-skelter to prevent an Indian uprising.

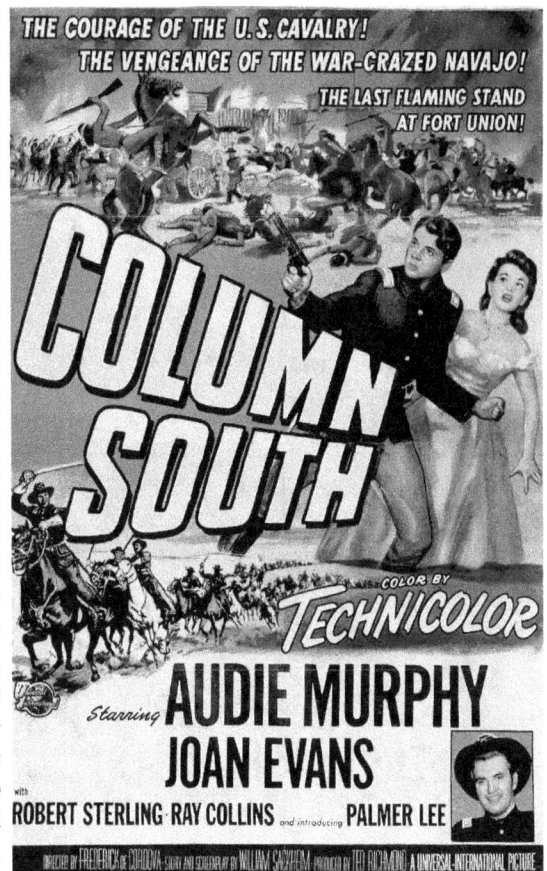

There's a considerable amount of perilous danger and cavalry action in *Column South* (Henry Mancini and Herman Stein's stock score pounds away incessantly in the background) but Murphy, like Scott and McCrea, looked out of his comfort zone in a Yankee officer's uniform (Montgomery, on the other hand, filled out a uniform just fine). His playing is a little on the stiff side, while his love/hate affair with Evans isn't as charming as Universal would have hoped for. It's standard rather than excellent fare, even though de Cordova staged the final dramatic battle between cavalry and Weaver's braves at Fort Union in a most exciting manner. The climax sees the patrol winning the

day and splitting: The Unionists stay with Murphy, the Southerners take off with Sterling; Evans has sufficiently thawed in her haughty indifference toward Murphy to engage in a prolonged kiss with her hero as the end credits roll.

Nathan Juran's *Tumbleweed* is the best of Murphy's trio of Westerns he made for Universal in 1953, a seldom-seen gem that kicks off with a mesmerizing tracking shot of Audie on horseback, a second horse tethered to his, riding slowly through the sun-blasted wilderness of Death Valley, an evocative few minutes that reminds us just what Westerns were all about during this productive period and how great Murphy looked in the saddle. Scenery plays a big part in *Tumbleweed*—not only Death Valley but also Red Rock Canyon and the striking formations at Vasquez Rocks Park. Murphy's a drifter (Jim Harvey), coming to the aid of wounded Indian Eugene Iglesias before taking on the job of wagon train scout, leads Ross Elliott's contingent of three covered wagons across Yaqui Indian territory to the next town. On board are Elliott's wife, Madge Meredith, and his sister-in-law, Universal blonde pinup girl Lori Nelson, who quickly takes in their young, handsome trail guide and likes what she sees, even though she's engaged to smartass Russell Johnson, Meredith's brother. The odd reference to Murphy's boyish looks works its way into John Meredyth Lucas' lucid screenplay (Elliott: "Say, you're kinda young, aren't you?" and "You reckon this kid knows what he's doing?" when he forms a protective wagon circle at night) and Russell Metty's cinematography adds a harsh gloss to the savage landscapes. Finding themselves boxed up in a canyon, the wagoners have to fend off a Yaqui war party who launch an all-out assault; Murphy hides the two women in a rock cleft and rides off to meet the chief (Ralph Moody), banking on the fact that as he saved his son, they'll be allowed to carry on their way. Wrong! Murphy is tethered to stakes and left to die in the sun and the wagon train is wiped out, although the two women survive. Back in town after Iglesias' mother has cut him loose, Murphy is accused of desertion by the townsfolk, who want to put his head in a noose and is jailed for his own safety by Sheriff Chill Wills. Escaping with the aid of Iglesias, who gets shot (with his dying breath, he tells Murph, "White man told my father about wagons."), Murphy, wounded, hightails it into the desert to meet up with the Yaqui chief and clear his name.

Audie Murphy and Chill Wills in *Tumbleweed* (1953)

Where, you might ask, does Tumbleweed fit into all of this? At the 35-minute mark, Murphy, his horse lame, chances upon Roy Roberts' horse corral and spots a mangy white Cayuse, Roberts' "best horse" Tumbleweed. The ranch owner takes pity on Murphy, asks wife K.T. Stevens to patch his wound and lends him the horse, fending off Wills, second-in-command Lee Van Cleef and his posse and leaving Murphy to gallop off and head for the nearest waterhole, Coyote Springs. What Juran treats us to for the remaining 40 minutes is a chase movie of sorts combined with one man's relationship with his horse. Wills and his bad-tempered, very thirsty, bunch of hombres pursue Murphy across a poisonous paradise of arid salt flats and through dry gulches, Tumbleweed cantering on regardless of the heat and hostile conditions. Murphy was an ardent horse lover and his amusing exchanges with Tumbleweed are a delight; he comes to admire his scraggy companion, especially when it can climb up near-vertical ridges that others can't manage (Van Cleef attempts one ridge and falls off his mount) and discovers water at Coyote Springs' dried-out beds, saving his master from possible death. Murphy shows his good side by giving water to a parched Wills, who then turns the tables and trusses him up; released to combat an Indian attack, Murphy tells the others to play possum and fool the Redskins into thinking that they have died of thirst. In the ensuing gun battle, Moody is killed, but not before spilling the beans on Nelson's would-be fiancé Johnson, who has also turned up at the scene. He's the white man who told the Indians about the wagon train; gold nuggets have been found in the area, and he doesn't want anyone else nosing in on a possible strike. By default, he's a murderer and pays for his

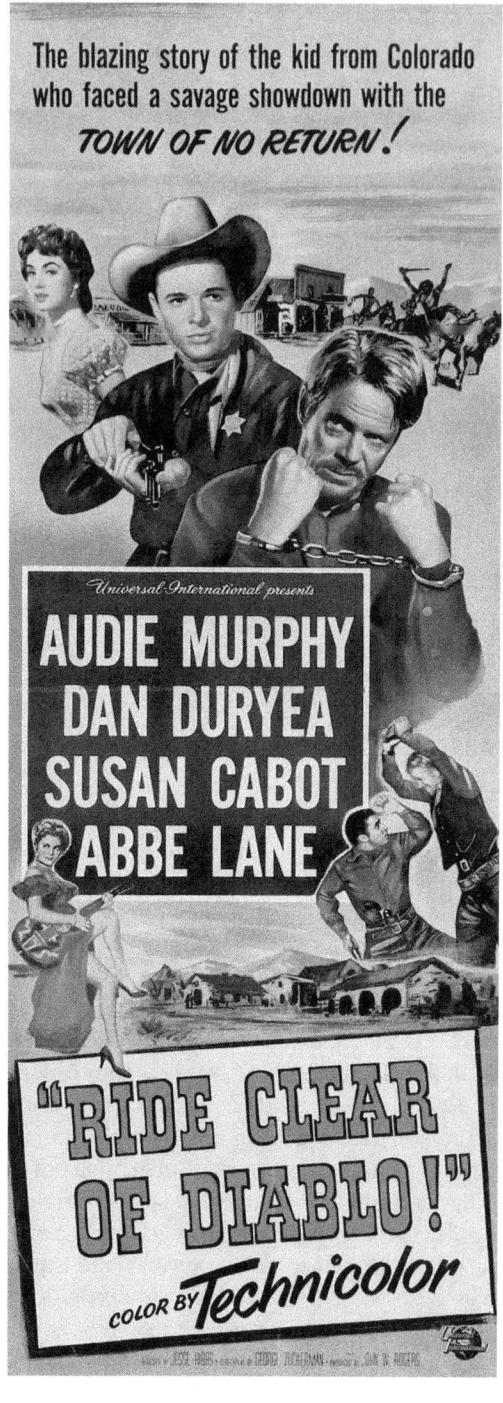

misdeed by tumbling off rocks after a tussle with Murphy, leaving our hero to fall into Nelson's arms. Roberts also gives him trusty (or should that be quirky!) steed Tumbleweed, his "best horse," as a parting gift.

Backed by an invigorating Henry Mancini/Herman Stein/Milton Rosen combined score, *Tumbleweed* is a thoroughly sublime and ultimately satisfying sagebrush saga expertly put together by director Juran. It's a firm favorite with Murphy fans, taking on the mantle of the archetypal Audie Murphy Universal-International '50s Western; the man himself reckoned it was one of his personal favorites also. As at the time of writing, this spiffy little Western has never officially been released on DVD, and that applies to many other Murphy pictures as well. A retrospective box set from Universal is long overdue.

There's no two ways about it—in the very early '50s, Murphy's cowboy pictures were fresher in substance than some of Scott's, McCrea's and Montgomery's outings, and he was outgunning all the rest of the opposition, literally! He had spent far fewer years in the saddle than the other three, a young upstart who possessed a kind of appealing naivety about him that won audiences over. Wisely surrounding himself with Universal's stock company of actors, most of whom were B-movie professionals, he was, with very little experience, knocking out one humdinger after another and his first for 1954, *Ride Clear of Diablo*, was no exception. Railroad surveyor Clay O'Mara (Murphy) comes to the town of Santiago with a score to settle, determined to exact retribution on the cattle rustlers responsible for the murder of his father and brother. Directed by Jesse Hibbs, who would go on to participate in many TV Westerns includ-

Audie Murphy beats Dan Duryea to the draw in a saloon standoff, in *Ride Clear of Diablo* (1954).

ing *Laramie* and *Rawhide*, *Ride Clear of Diablo* features a scene-stealing performance from Dan Duryea as psychotic but likeable outlaw Whitey Kincade, perpetually breaking into a maniacal laugh when something amuses him. The fun-to-watch Murphy/Duryea relationship mirrors that of the Randolph Scott relationships with his outlaw adversaries in the Budd Boetticher Westerns to come; in both, the bad guy becomes the focus of attention, almost at the expense of the leading man, but *only* almost; Murphy carries this engaging oater with effortless charm—*Ride Clear of Diablo* is 80 minutes of pure Western gold.

Sheriff Paul Birch, lawyer William Pullen and bar bum Russell Johnson are behind the killing of Murphy's family, trying to put the rap on Duryea, a notorious gunman wanted for another murder. He could be the man Murphy is looking for, they tell the fresh-faced surveyor, hoping that Duryea will finish Murphy off. He doesn't. Beating Duryea to the draw in Diablo after a saloon standoff (Hibbs plays up to all of Murphy's strengths in this brilliant sequence, the actor's youthful looks, reserved persona and sheer *silence* belying a hard streak his opponents aren't expecting). Murphy, deputized by Birch ("So young and so inexperienced," sighs Susan Cabot to Birch), escorts the grinning bandit back to Santiago, the two building up an unlikely rapport en route. Hibbs and screenwriter George Zuckerman throw everything into the plot to keep us on our toes: Pullen is engaged to Birch's niece, Cabot, who in turn takes an almighty shine to Murphy; Johnson lies on oath to enable Duryea to walk free from court, worried that if found guilty, he'll tell the judge about Birch and Pullen's activities; Duryea, forming a bond

Audie Murphy is framed for a stagecoach robbery in *Drums Across the River* (1954).

of sorts with Murphy (or "the Kid" as he continually calls him), decides to help him bring the killers of his family to justice, needing a bit of excitement in his life; following a silver bullion robbery planned by Birch and Pullen, Johnson (he gets a tremendous two-fisted battering from Murphy in one scene) double-crosses them and dies after a shoot-out with Murphy in an abandoned mine; and saloon girl Abbe Lane, resplendent in scarlet to match her red locks, sings a couple of old-time ditties. It all builds to a satisfactory conclusion, but in many ways a sad one: Cornered in Diablo's cantina by Birch, Pullen and gunslinger Jack Elam, wounded Duryea ("Feel like a human being at last.") goes out in a blaze of glory, lurching through the swing doors into the street and shooting Birch before expiring in a hail of gunshot. In a furious gunfight, Murphy puts paid to Elam and punches Pullen senseless, ending up on a train newly wed to Cabot.

Cinematographer Irving Glassberg shot the action amid Lone Pine's Alabama Hills, a favored locale for Scott, while Herman Stein and Milton Rosen's combined score exuded menace, as did most Universal Western soundtracks of the time. *Ride Clear of Diablo*, like *Tumbleweed* before it, was a critical and commercial success and is almost a blueprint of how to make a great Western on medium finances. Not one second drags, the playing by all is exemplary and Hibbs directs with pace, moving from one scene to another seamlessly. It's a solid form of roll-up-your-sleeves craftsmanship long since vanished from cinema screens, one valid reason why so many fans admire the Audie Murphy Westerns even to this day.

Among the many pro-Indian movies of the '50s, Nathan Juran's *Drums Across the River* (1954) has gone unnoticed, perhaps because of its lack of a bank-busting budget, no big-name Hollywood star and a refusal to preach. It presents the familiar plight of the downtrodden Redskin in a more down-to-earth way, straightforward cowboys versus Indians fodder. 1880: Jay Silverheels is the son of a Ute chieftain, refusing to let the citizens of Crown City in Colorado search for gold on his land. Lyle Bettger (he made a career out of playing Western slimeballs) and his mean bunch of no-goods, acting on behalf of corrupt mining officials in Denver, are trying to stir up enough trouble to start an Indian war, thus leaving the San Juan Mountains wide open for the prospectors to move in. Opposition to his plans comes in the form of Murphy (as Gary Brannon) and his father, Walter Brennan, who run a freight company.

Although the Utes killed Murphy's mother, Murphy shows a degree of compassion with the tribe and wants peace, but that doesn't stop him from leading an expedition, which includes Bettger and his men, to Indian territory in search of gold. Under ambush from Silverheels' warriors, Murphy rides out to the Indian encampment with the chief, is shown their sacred burial ground (a stupendous amphitheater backed by hundreds of fluted rock columns) and is told that if the townsfolk can keep to the peace treaty, there will be no uprising. Naturally, Bettger has other ideas and goes all out to kick-start a war by holding Brennan hostage, robbing a stage and blaming it on Murphy and the Utes and employing black-clad killer Hugh O'Brian (a marvelous, sneering performance) to finish the interfering youngster off.

A typical Universal/Audie Murphy oater of its time, *Drums Across the River* has all the essential ingredients in place to ensure 78 minutes of Western joy: a tremendous main theme from Henry Mancini and Herman Stein; eye-catching location filming at Red Rock Canyon; sharp-as-a-pin Technicolor photography (Harold Lipstein); incisive script (John K. Butler and Lawrence Roman); a myriad of plot twists; some ferocious Murphy fistfights (poor Bob Steele receives a real hammering); and a worthy support cast. Where it falls down is in the female lead role. Lisa Gaye plays Murphy's gal, a part that should have gone to Bettger's dame, Mara Corday. Stunning, raven-haired Corday, filling her low-cut green costume nicely, is shamefully wasted in her few scenes and would have made a great pairing with Murphy; Gaye leaves no mark on the film whatsoever. As with a lot of these Westerns, the hero lands up in jail falsely accused of

"Destry's comin' after you," with Audie Murphy's guns blazing, from *Destry* (1954).

a crime but escapes a hanging at the last moment. Murphy mouths a few choice one-liners (facing Bettger, hand hovering over gun butt, he snarls, "If you wanna stop me, now's the time.") and puts paid to Bettger's underhand tactics by leading him to the secret burial site. Bettger's confederates are terminated and Murphy puts a bullet in their leader during a fracas at the crook's hideout. Finally, he settles the dispute between Utes and cavalry; the Indians get the rights to hunt on white man's land in exchange for mining rights on their land. It's just a pity he didn't have the lovely arms of villainess Corday to fall into at the end of the action!

1954's *Destry* was an impressive, scene-for-scene remake of Universal's 1939 *Destry Rides Again*, both directed by George Marshall. Murphy proved he was more than capable of filling James Stewart's boots while Mari Blanchard, playing the tart with a heart of gold, outshone Marlene Dietrich's performance in many of her scenes. The familiar tale of the milksop deputy sheriff becoming town tamer was given a dusting off and presented to a new audience, four writers (Max Brand, D.D. Beauchamp, Felix Jackson and Edmund H. North) contributing to the witty screenplay. What a shame that musical director Joseph Gershenson took the credit for Frank Skinner's jaunty title music, which stuck in the mind long after the film had finished. Murphy (Tom Destry) doesn't appear until the 22nd minute, exiting a stagecoach in the town of Restful carrying Lori Nelson's pink parasol and birdcage, an inauspicious entrance guaranteed not to impress. He also isn't wearing a gun, great news for devious saloon owner Lyle Bettger and his team of crooks, including disreputable judge Edgar Buchanan; they've murdered the sheriff and bullied rancher Walter Baldwin (Nelson's uncle) off his land in a fixed poker game, charging cattlemen exorbitant fees for crossing the property. What's more, newly appointed sheriff, Thomas Mitchell, was once the town drunk. A cause for celebration, thinks Bettger, with the whole town under his crooked thumb. In this he's wrong, totally unaware that the boyish upstart is very handy with a gun indeed. Murphy gets to work immediately, sniffing out the real reasons behind the previous sheriff's death from a supposed heart attack (he was shot in the back) and demonstrating his superlative skills with firearms to Bettger and his unsavory pals after 50-odd minutes have gone by, leaving them distinctly worried. Wry humor is Murphy's weapon, used to defuse potentially inflammable situations. Song and dance dame Blanchard also has a soft spot for Murphy, wracked with guilt over boyfriend Bettger's wrongdoings, so when she's not flashing her legs to a rowdy cowpoke audience during one of several dance  numbers, the gal is lending the shy deputy her lucky rabbit's foot charm and mooning all over him, falling under his self-effacing spell.

When Murphy finally buckles on his father's gun belt after the kindly Mitchell has been shot down in the street on Bettger's orders, we know he means business, gunslinger George Wallace scuttling into Bettger's saloon, informing the boss: "Destry's comin' after you." Bettger: "That's something I should be worried about?" Wallace: "This time you should. He's packing a gun." A splendid saloon shoot-out sees Bettger and his toughs cut down by Murphy with a little help from hulking cattle boss Alan Hale, Jr. and Doc Wallace Ford, Blanchard taking a bullet while trying to save Murphy. Our town hero is last seen walking down the street with Nelson's cheeky son, both twiddling on pieces of rope, Restful at last living up to its name.

Released in December 1954 just before Christmas, *Destry* was another Murphy smash and consolidated his reputation as an all-round performer, honed by starring in 11 truly great Westerns, fantastic examples of the genre ("Murphy does exceptionally well ... is a big asset," crowed *Variety*). But, in a lot of ways, *Destry* also marked the end of Murphy's classic Universal Western period. Those 11 Westerns, from *The Kid from Texas* right through to *Destry*, showed the actor growing in stature from nervous youth to accomplished leading man, tightly knit productions constructed with professionalism, all designed to herald a new star and push him along the road to public acceptance. What came after was very good, but lacked in the intense urgency that was a highlight

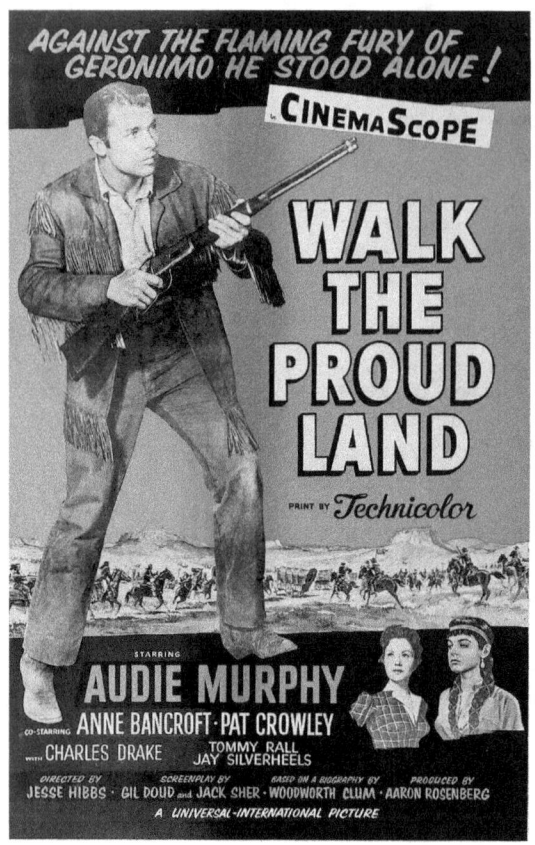

of Murphy's formative '50s period. If any fan were to choose their favorite Audie Murphy Western, it would be one that was made between 1950 and 1954.

Following *Destry*, Murphy took on the role of himself (which he was expert at doing!), charting his Second World War military exploits in *To Hell and Back*, directed by Jesse Hibbs, his only release of 1955. Initially against the idea because he didn't want the public to think he was cashing in on his wartime bravery (Tony Curtis was suggested for the part), Universal convinced him that as he didn't look all that different from when the action took place in 1943, so what would be the point of anyone else playing him? The film made an absolute fortune for Universal and remained their biggest-ever box-office success until Steven Spielberg's *Jaws* knocked it off the top spot in 1975.

The Murphy juggernaut that had steamrollered merrily on since 1950's *The Kid from Texas* threatened to come off the rails with the release of the 1956 biopic *Walk the Proud Land*, a plodding, uninvolving "pro-Indian" effort concerning government Indian agent John Philip Clum's attempts in gaining the Apaches' trust to the extent of turning the braves into "useful citizens" during 1874. Budgeted at $1,000,000, director Jesse Hibbs made hard work of the narrative (based on Woodworth Clum's book about his father, *Apache Agent*), limiting the action sequences to a couple and focusing on Murphy's relationship both with the Indians and chocolate-faced Anne Bancroft, miscast as a widowed squaw yearning for Murphy's manly arms ("I want to make you happy," she declares, staring hungrily at Murphy's bare torso). Like a cut-price version of Fox's *Broken Arrow* (1950), the intention was honorable: Murphy, dressed in a gray suit and minus a six-gun strapped to his waist, is first seen in Tucson, arresting a pair of Indian killers who have a collection of Apache scalps, including two from women. "You call *them* savages," he sneers contemptuously; he then elbows his way over General Morris Ankrum's objections and forces the army to quit the San Carlos reservation, enabling him, without military interference, to pow-wow with Chief Robert Warwick about the benefits of peace and eventually becoming a blood brother to Tommy Rall. Clum was famous for bringing in Geronimo (played by Jay Silverheels) to the authorities after a spot of bother ("It's better to be dead than tame," growls Silverheels), ultimately earning the high opinion of the tribe. "Who will take care of us," laments Warwick before Murphy changes his mind about quitting the post and elects to stay on. In the long run, however, Murphy's domestic problems override the white eyes versus misunderstood Indian conflict, nullifying the drama it should have been. New wife Patricia Crowley takes an instant dislike to Bancroft; the glamorous squaw, forever hovering in the background, wants nothing better than to be Murphy's second wife and can't understand why the agent doesn't adopt the Indian custom of marrying several women instead of just one.

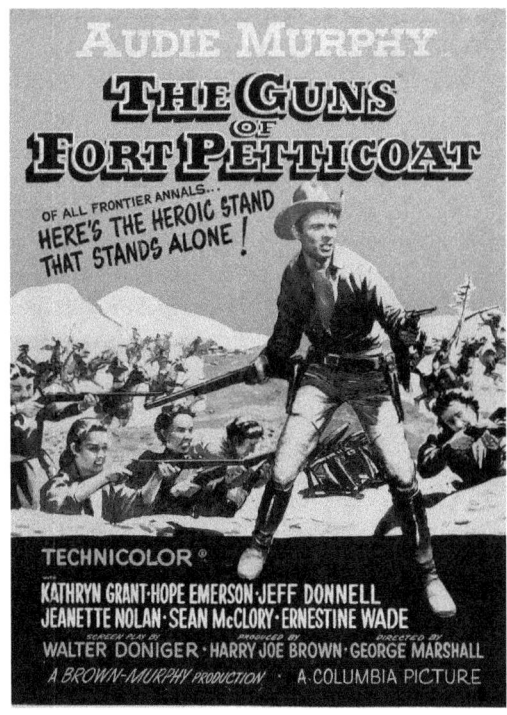

Charles Drake turns in a likeable performance as an ex-soldier who tags along with Murphy's ideas, such as training the Indians to become a police force, and Bancroft's young son (Eugene Mazzola) scampers around the set playing, well, cowboys and Indians! Murphy is excellent, the cactus-dominated Arizona wilderness is fetching in CinemaScope, but there's virtually nothing in the way of thrills to stop the fidgets. *Walk the Proud Land* is about the only Audie Murphy Western from this fruitful period in his career that audiences probably wouldn't want to catch more than once. The likes of *Kansas Raiders* and *Tumbleweed* seem a very long way off indeed. Even *Variety* claimed it "lacked excitement and action."

Murphy moved over to Columbia in 1957 to team up with producer Harry Joe Brown, forming the short-lived Brown/Murphy production company with the initial idea of making two movies together. The association ended after one picture, *The Guns of Fort Petticoat*; Brown couldn't build up the same working rapport with the sometimes difficult ex-war hero as he was enjoying with Randolph Scott, and Murphy returned to Universal on completion of the film. *The Guns of Fort Petticoat*, a kind of early feminist camp Western, isn't classic Murphy by any stretch of the imagination, but it's back to what fans expected of him. The script (Walter Doniger) is cliché-ridden, sailing dangerously close to comedy at times, and during the Indian attacks, some members of the female cast are guilty of serious bouts of overacting. Audie's also in cavalry uniform, and that look never quite suited him. Yet despite this, audiences are in for 82 minutes of corny fun, quite bloody at times, set amid the sun-baked Tucson scenery. And it's a darned sight more exhilarating than *Walk the Proud Land*.

Audie plays Yankee Lieutenant Frank Hewitt, trying to keep peace with the Redskin tribes traipsing from one reservation to the next during the latter stages of the Civil War. When his commanding officer, Indian-hating Ainslie Pryor, orders a massacre on the Sand Creek Cheyenne encampment (the actual events took place in November 1864),

Murphy refuses to join in on the attack, is accused of insubordination and leaves his post, heading into Confederate-held Texas to warn homesteaders of a possible Indian reprisal. Dressed as a Union soldier, this isn't such a good idea. Eventually, Murphy rounds up a bunch of disparate women (their husbands are away in the war) from the town of Jonesville, leads them to an old fortified mission, trains them into a combat unit, gives them all various commands and repels wave after wave of Indian raids in the manner of the Alamo battles before coming up with an ingenious solution to save their lives before they're overrun and scalped. He kills the chief medicine man, hangs his body up outside the mission and the Indians flee in superstitious terror.

If audiences think they've heard Mischa Bakaleinikoff's breezy opening theme before, they have; it's the identical score used in Scott's *7th Cavalry* a year earlier. And like the Scott Westerns, Audie has two women vying for his affections: ex-love Patricia Tiernan and tomboy/future Mrs. Bing Crosby Kathryn Grant. Rootin' tootin' Hope Emerson stands out as a matron who's a mean shot among a motley crew, including a saloon singer (Peggy Maley), a madam (Isobel Elsom) and her black maid, Tiernan's headstrong young son (Kim Charney) and a religious harridan (Jeanette Nolan). There's also a pointed reference to Murphy's own father, Emmett, who deserted him as a kid. Sean McClory is cowardly Emmett Kettle, who quits the mission and falls foul of Nestor Paiva's trio of bandit: He's robbed, strung up and shot dead. Director George Marshall stages the fight scenes with zest and Murphy, labeled a deserter and a coward from both sides, is reprieved in the end, Pryor facing a court martial for his role in organizing the Indian slaughter. Grant wins her own war with Tiernan, getting Murphy for keeps in the quick fade-out.

A big step up in production values heralded Murphy's next 1957 Western, Universal's critically mauled *Night Passage*: budgeted at $1,500,000; the first motion picture to be shot in Technirama had Borden Chase's intelligent, if wordy, screenplay; a tremendous score from composing giant Dimitri Tiomkin, containing his memorable theme title (with Ned Washington) "Follow the River"; breathtaking location work around Durango, Colorado and California's Inyo National Forest, and was beautifully photographed by William H. Daniels, with James Stewart in the lead (Murphy was billed second). On paper, *Night Passage* had a heck of a lot going in its favor. Yet this picturesque oater has gone down in history as the James Stewart Western that Anthony Mann, his collaborator on many classic cowboy movies, didn't make. Various reasons are given: Mann thought little of Chase's script and reckoned that five-foot-eight Murphy wasn't suitably cast as the sibling next to the much taller six-foot-three Stewart, his screen brother. Stewart, apparently, wasn't too enamored with the project himself, only wanting to display his skills on the accordion (ironically, his musical interludes were later dubbed). Stewart brought in James Neilson to direct (his first feature) after Mann turned the project down and the result was a movie that overall failed to deliver the goods. The feeling is that it should have been tighter and brisker, with a touch more meanness. But one thing is certain: Murphy puts everyone else in the shade, even the main star, in his portrayal of the charismatic Utica Kid (a return to the Universal "Kid" persona). When he appears after 35 minutes like a breath of fresh air, riding through the pine-clad hills dressed in black hat and dark blue leather jacket (stressing the good versus evil tone), what up until then has been a slow, talky exercise detailing Stewart's motives in arriving in a mining camp, with a proliferation of secondary actors flitting in and out of the scenario, suddenly livens up; Murphy then takes over much of the lead role and does a spanking good job of it. From this point on, he ignites a movie that was getting stagnant by the minute, turning it into something a bit more compelling. *Night Passage* therefore becomes a film of two halves—the James Stewart half and the Audie Murphy half, the former outshone by the latter (as an 11-year-old in March 1958, I vividly remember this defining moment in the picture, when Murphy first rides into view, and thinking: "Crikey. He looks amazing").

Gunman turned troubleshooter Stewart travels to Junction City and is hired by railroad boss Jay C. Flippen to put a stop to outlaw Dan Duryea's repeated train holdups. Murphy happens to be a member of Duryea's gang, so their memorable partnership from *Ride Clear of Diablo* is given a second airing, Duryea even called, not Whitey Kincade this outing, but Whitey Harbin, hamming it up to the hilt, complete with maniacal cackle. That first half hour or so drags, with very little of consequence to get one's teeth into: There's a seven-minute accordion song and dance opener; Stewart ambles about, meeting with Murphy's intended, Dianne Foster; Chase throws into the potpourri Brandon De Wilde as Joey, a homage (or rip-off) of his Joey character in *Shane*; and the magnificent mountain scenery seems to take precedence over the slightly stodgy events. But as stated, when Audie comes into the frame, matters take a turn for the better. On board a train, carrying a $10,000 mine payroll in a shoebox, rather than place it in the safe, Stewart and De Wilde get caught up in Duryea's latest robbery in which Flippen's wife, the decorative Elaine Stewart, is taken hostage, to be released on payment of the supposedly

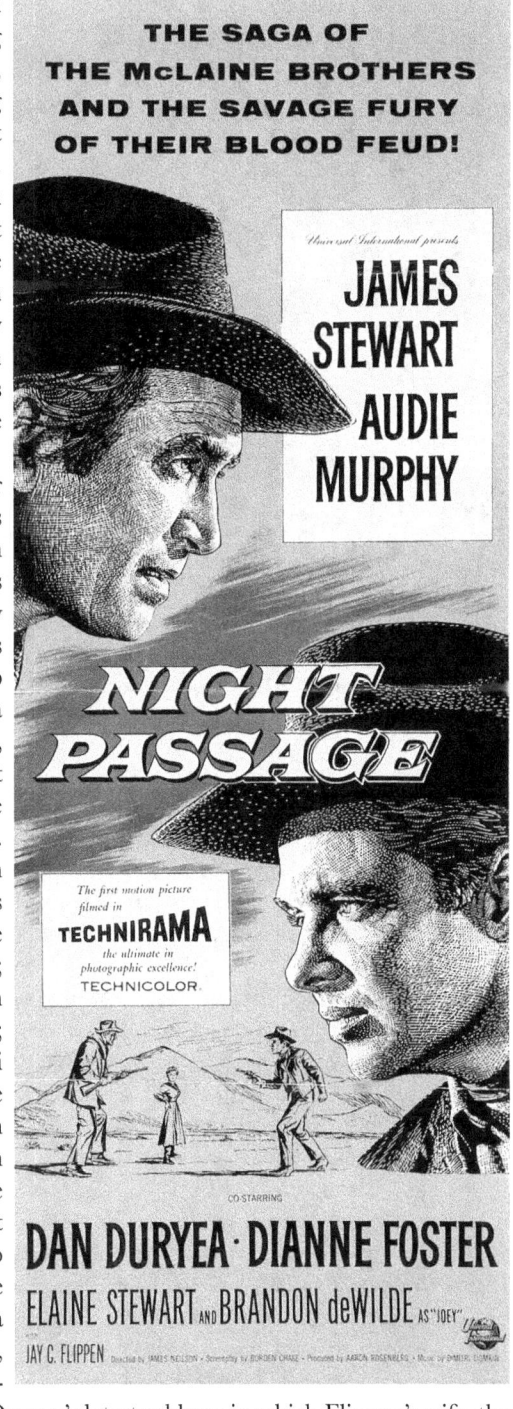

Dan Duryea, Elaine Stewart and Audie Murphy in *Night Passage* (1957)

missing cash. At Duryea's hideout (a bar and a barn), Stewart makes his play, pretending to want to join the outlaw's bunch and having a heart-to-heart with his younger brother. These scenes are weighed down somewhat by their obvious studio settings, but the standoffs between Duryea, Murphy, Jack Elam and Robert J. Wilke hold the attention. The thrilling finale rescues *Night Passage* from the doldrums: Following a fracas, Stewart and Flippen's wife ride off toward a mill, with Murphy, De Wilde and Duryea's boys in pursuit, leading to a prolonged gun battle amid the mining machinery (Ms. Stewart is sent to safety in an ore bucket). Seeing his brother outnumbered, Murphy has a change of heart and comes to Stewart's aid ("Would you mind if *I* played big brother just this one time?"), collecting a bullet from Duryea, who in turn is shot by Stewart. Back in town, Foster hitches up with Stewart, who decides to stay with Flippen's rail company.

Murphy has some of the best lines in the film, explaining to Foster why he is like he is, living in his older brother's shadow. "You don't know what it's like to be the kid brother. Everything you do is wrong. Everything you try. 'Til one day, I tried a gun. It fit my hand real good. And I wasn't a kid brother anymore." And asked why he lives a criminal life, his acid response is, "Because I like to steal." In answer to Duryea's repeated taunts as to who can clear leather quicker, Murphy faces him with a scowl and spits, "Don't push it. In a little while, you're gonna need me and I'm gonna need you." Yes, Murphy's terrific in a Western that's not-so-terrific. Without him, this would have been very ordinary fare indeed, a tribute to his screen personality and unassuming, but effective, acting style. Although given a critical pasting on both sides of the Atlantic (most found the film "empty"), *Night Passage* made money and that's mostly down to Murphy's commanding star presence and riveting performance. It's as much his film as Stewart's.

Audie Murphy looks menacing on horseback, in *Ride a Crooked Trail* (1958).

Not content to let the grass grow under his feet, Murphy flexed his acting muscles away from Westerns during 1957/1958, starring in a comedy (*Joe Butterfly*), a crime thriller (*Gunrunners*) and a political thriller (*The Quiet American*). All three proved that his underplaying style slotted perfectly well into other spheres of moviemaking, although the Western remained his favored setup. And it was back to the slam-bang oaters of the early '50s for Murphy's one and only 1958 Western, *Ride a Crooked Trail*, directed by Jesse Hibbs and co-starring Walter Matthau as a shotgun-toting judge who shoots first (mostly in the back) and asks questions later. But there was less accent on the slam-bang in Borden Chase's script: After an exciting start (Stanley Wilson's title music is a thunderous delight), when Murphy (as bank robber Joe Maybe) is pursued up a ravine by a marshal, only for the lawman to fall to his death into the river below, the picture settles down and exhibits comedic touches here and there. Murphy arrives in Matthau's riverfront town of Webb City, takes on the identity of the dead marshal, pretends he's married to old flame Gia Scala and becomes surrogate father to wayward kid Eddie Little and his pet pooch. Not a great deal happens during the first 35 minutes of Hibbs' light-on-the-feet actioner; Murphy attempts to play house with haughty Scala and Matthau, one eye on his new marshal, begins to smell a rat. It's only when Henry Silva, who could appear evil simply by staring at the camera, rides in with his gang to hit the local bank that Hibbs injects some grit and the picture ups a gear. Silva is an old buddy of Murphy's and both want to be in on the bank job, but Murphy tells him to wait for much richer pickings. The cattle herds are due to arrive, and with them the

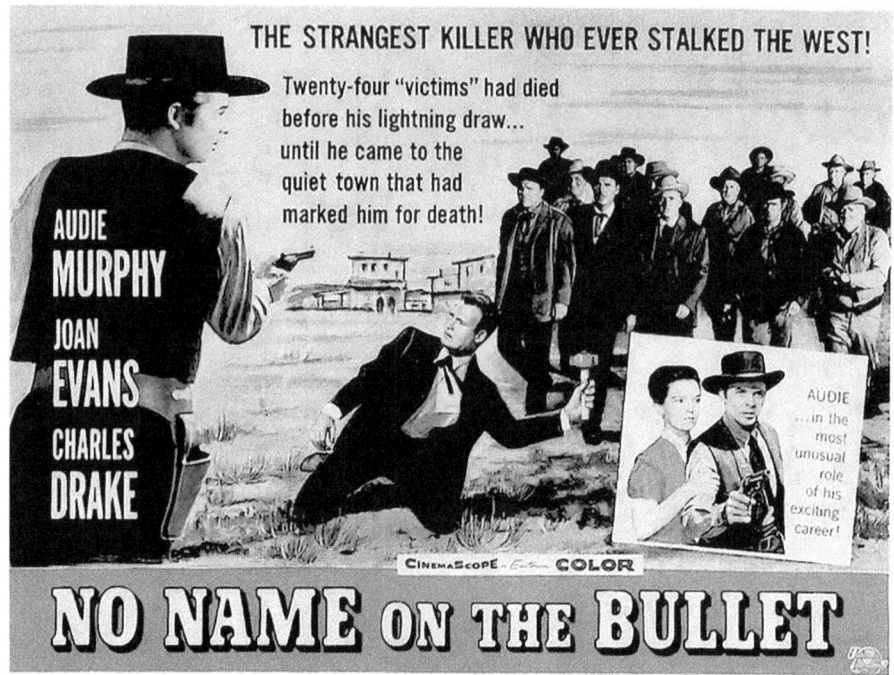

promise of a huge payroll. Silva's group disagree and split. The impatient breakaway bunch carry out the robbery as planned but are defeated in a gun battle; their leader returns to lay claim on Scala and relieve the bank of its riches. Out on the range, Silva is subjected to a typical Murphy two-fisted assault and is hauled back to town with the stolen cash. Matthau, who was suspicious about Murphy's true identity from reel two, decides he likes him well enough to pin a badge on his shirt, and the last humorous line is left to Little, who asks the judge, "Ever sleep in a bathtub?" (This is a reference to Murphy and Scala's bedroom arrangements, which the kid has sneakily observed.) "What?" responds Matthau. "You better marry them," the freckled-face youngster responds with a cheeky grin.

Ride a Crooked Trail, shot in widescreen, is easy on the eye, Murphy displaying a lightness of touch in his verbal exchanges with Scala and wily Matthau, showing real progression as an actor. However, a dearth of action sequences (the two bank holdups are lamely handled), a flat, oddly hurried ending and the overall cutesy mood relegate it to the level of an okay Audie Murphy Western, not one that can compete with others in his repertoire of "essentials." That was all set to change with Jack Arnold's 1959 offering, *No Name on the Bullet*, described by a leading critic as one of the 15 greatest Westerns ever made, up there alongside other '50s classics such as *High Noon*, *Shane* and *Rio Bravo*.

"The name is Gant. John Gant." The town of Lordsburg gets a visit from someone they'd rather not have on their doorsteps. Murphy, a smartly dressed professional killer, rides in with a job to carry out, and no one's going to stand in his way. But just *who* is it he's gunning after? Fresh from a run of terrific Universal monster/sci-fi movies (*Creature from the Black Lagoon*, *Tarantula*, *The Incredible Shrinking Man* among them), Jack Arnold brought his trademark economical style to *No Name on the Bullet*, a spare, psychological

Warren Stevens (left) is prepared to draw his gun on the coffee-drinking Audie Murphy in *No Name on the Bullet* (1959).

Western that mirrored what Randolph Scott was up to with Budd Boetticher at the same period. Projecting himself as a silent executioner, prowling the streets like a cat after its next victim and toying with the townsfolk's emotions, Murphy brought a new kind of villainy to Arnold's underrated masterpiece of Western minimalism. It could be, as many aficionados claim, Murphy's finest cinematic hour, the one film above all others that places him alongside Wayne and Stewart; if anything else, it equals the impressive work Scott and Boetticher were achieving over at Columbia.

Although filmed in CinemaScope, Arnold compresses his scenes into a series of tightly knit, claustrophobic vignettes to impart sweaty tension, as though the movie was in standard format (he successfully employed this method of filmmaking in his horror outings), apart from a tremendous iconic opening shot, right after Herman Stein's full-blooded title score: Murphy, clad in blue and black, is seen as a speck on the wide-open, parched prairie horizon, resolving into the figure Lordsburg will come to know and hate; a dog barks, sensing the horseman's dark side, as he asks a farmer for directions to town. Astride his ebony brown steed, Murphy epitomizes cool, just as Clint Eastwood would do five years later in his *Dollar* movies. In town, Gene L. Coon's biting script comes into its own, Murphy delivering his terse one-liners with icy menace. Booking a hotel, he's asked to pay. "I'll pay you when I leave," is the cold rejoinder, and very soon everybody in town is aware of his presence: physician Charles Drake, girlfriend Joan Evans, Evans' father, Judge Edgar Stehli, Sheriff Willis Bouchey, bank officials Whit Bissell and Karl Swenson, saloon boss Simon Scott, warring husband and wife Warren

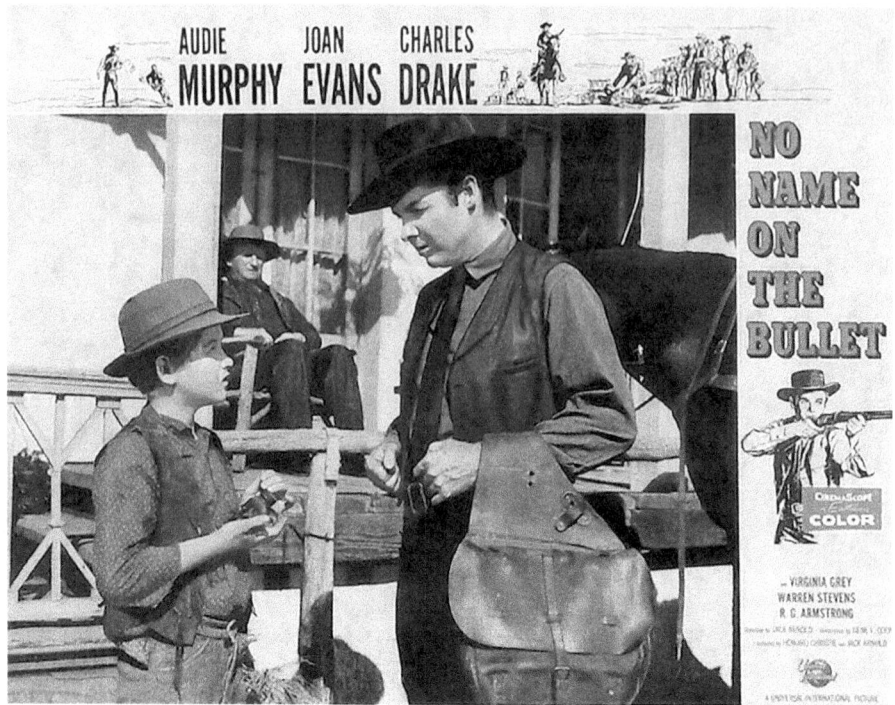

Audie Murphy brings a new type of villainy to the Western and delivers what may be his finest cinematic hour, in *No Name on the Bullet*.

Stevens and Virginia Grey and miner John Alderson. All nurse problems and all think Murphy has targeted them. "A gunman's one thing. Gant's another," "If Gant stays here, someone's gonna die," "Gant's like a disease they haven't found a cure for yet," and "Could be after anyone" are the remarks bandied about; skeletons in the closet tumble out, the not-so-honest citizens become jittery and bank manager Bissell is the first to crack, shooting himself, convinced that the local miners, led by Alderson, have hired Murphy to prevent him and Swenson from swindling them out of their land. The sheriff tells Murphy, "You're a public nuisance. Go away," and is shot in the hand after losing out on the draw. "Why didn't you kill me?" he asks Murphy. "I wasn't paid to," replies the unsmiling assassin. Meanwhile, Stevens, as yellow as a skunk, reckons his wife's ex-husband has brought in Murphy to finish him off; getting drunk, he foolishly challenges the tight-lipped stranger to a gunfight and then turns tail, running for his life.

The only person to get remotely close to this coffee-drinking harbinger of doom is Drake. Despite Murphy's fearsome reputation, the affable doctor "kinda likes him," trying to fathom what makes the man tick and the reasons why he enjoys killing as a trade (which Murphy admits to). This feeling of high regard is reciprocated; Murphy thinks Drake is the only honest person in a town full of hypocrites. But what to do about a hired gun that Drake himself labels "One big public health problem." A mob is formed but, like the cowardly Stevens, backs off after a confrontation with Murphy. Suddenly without notice, the stranger ups and leaves after assaulting Evans in her room, but for a purpose. Her father is the man on Murphy's hit list. His old associates want

Joanne Dru and a dapper Audie Murphy in *The Wild and the Innocent* (1959)

him dead and out of the way; he holds too many secrets into their shady dealings. But Stehli is sick and slowly dying anyway, given six months to live. Murphy knows this and, by waving a torn segment of Evans' dress in front of the old man's face, provokes him into picking up a shotgun. Outside the judge's house, Stehli saves Murphy the expense of a bullet by dropping dead from a heart attack. Drake turns up, Murphy shooting the doc in the hand, who then hurls a hammer at the killer, breaking his gun arm. With blood seeping from his shirtsleeve, Murphy thanks Drake for putting him out of action without the need for gunplay and rides off.

Is this a thinly disguised exposé of small-town narrow-mindedness? Certainly, *No Name on the Bullet* trod this much-favored '50s route, showing the mass paranoia that can result from one man upsetting a community's well-ordered structure; in this respect, it's almost a distant cousin to *High Noon*. Arnold tended to set his horror movies in small, isolated townships, producing instant classics, and he does so here. Why, then, has this spellbinding Audie Murphy Western not garnered the reputation it deserves? 1958/1959 were vintage years for cowboy pictures: *The Big Country*, *The Law and Jake Wade*, *Man of the West*, *The Hanging Tree*, *Rio Bravo*, *Warlock* and *The Wonderful Country*. Big budget productions with big stars to match. Universal's offering was a modestly produced assembly line oater with no major stars; it never received the attention the others were getting and was criminally overlooked at the time. Fifty years later, it can be recognized for its outstanding contribution to the genre, a pivotal Audie Murphy Western, perhaps his key piece of work, due in no small way to Arnold's expert, no-nonsense approach behind the camera. That critic who placed the picture in his all-time top 15 Westerns didn't get

Peter Breck, Audie Murphy, Sandra Dee and Gilbert Roland in *The Wild and the Innocent*

it wrong: *No Name on the Bullet* is a memorable Murphy classic, the actor playing Gant with, in the words of New York's *Daily News*, "calculated stolidity."

From disarming killer to naïve mountain boy—Murphy was branching out into the acting line as his next venture showed, the little-seen *The Wild and the Innocent*, directed by Jack Sher. For once, he looked too old for the part in a movie that resembled something cooked up in the late '40s instead of 1959. Virtually devoid of gunplay and fistfights, this "innocent rural lad abroad in the big city" offering had trapper Murphy (as Yancy) riding down from the forests to trade pelts in Casper during the Fourth of July celebrations. In tow is love-struck Sandra Dee; backwoodsman Strother Martin has offloaded her onto Murphy in exchange for a couple of furs and the gal is seriously smitten. Murphy, however, sets his sights on the far more glamorous, and worldly-wise, Joanne Dru, not realizing that she's a prostitute working in Sheriff Gilbert Roland's dance hall-cum-brothel. Roland lusts after wide-eyed Dee, brothel manageress Wesley Marie Tackitt wants to enroll the blonde lassie in her roster of good-time girls, Murphy escorts Dru to a dance, much to the disgust of the locals, and gunman Peter Breck unwisely picks a fight with the youngster, who breaks his gun hand after giving the cowpoke a good thrashing.

The Wild and the Innocent (it has never been afforded an official DVD release) is out of the ordinary fare, nothing like a standard Audie Murphy Western, but, in a strange way, fairly agreeable. A champion supporting cast includes George Mitchell, Murphy's Uncle Lije; Jim Backus, playing a storekeeper; Roland as the flashy sheriff, Dru the hard-bitten dame who melts under Murphy's awkward innocence and politeness; and

Audie Murphy and Joanne Dru dance the night away in *The Wild and the Innocent*.

virginal Dee, as cute as apple pie. Also a tad cute is Sy Gomberg and Jack Sher's script. When Murphy remarks on Dee's unkempt appearance, her response is, "We had soap but the baby ate it." "He doesn't know the kind of world he's in," observes Roland, watching Murphy cross a busy street, and when Murphy dresses up for the carnival, Dee ogles him and sighs. "Oh Yancy, you look beautiful." "You look pretty," he replies. "I wanna go with you," she coos back. After Murphy discovers what Dru really is and disapproves, she spits out, "Why don't you go back to the hills and grow up," which he does, deciding that Dee is the girl for him, but only after rescuing her from Roland's clutches and shooting him dead in the movie's one and only gunfight ("I can't kill no human being," Murphy moans as Roland dies in his arms).

Attractively filmed in the San Bernardino National Forest and featuring a decent score from Universal composer Hans J. Salter, *The Wild and the Innocent* is light-hearted froth containing a hard center, fairly forgettable but ably demonstrating just how far Murphy had progressed since playing Billy the Kid and Jesse James nine years earlier. It was a departure from his all-action sagebrush sagas that had lit up the screen and thrilled audiences between 1950 and 1954, as his next two movies would be, and in consequence met with a lukewarm reception from both fans and critics. In fact, Murphy and the traditional, medium-budget Western, as the public most wanted to see him appear in, wouldn't get together again until 1960, in George Sherman's *Hell Bent for Leather*.

Until then, we had Murphy's final '50s offering, the cheap looking *Cast a Long Shadow*. The star had a predilection for choosing the role of a bad guy, but never so

Audie Murphy in *Cast a Long Shadow* (1959)

much as here; *Cast a Long Shadow*, directed by Thomas Carr for United Artists in black-and-white, represents the nadir of Murphy's '50s Western curriculum, a dull, leaden feature in which he plays a totally unsympathetic character, saddle tramp Matt Brown, nursing a Texas-sized chip on his shoulder over his true identity. Is he, or is he not, illegitimate ("It's like being the extra joker in a deck of cards," he grumbles, adding later, "I'm a freak of nature."). When John Dehner tells the alcoholic gambling loser that he's inherited his father's ranch, he turns down an offer from the workforce of $20,000 for the spread and decides to make a go of it. Trouble raises its ugly head in two forms: The ranch owes money to the bank and is in danger of foreclosure, and Murphy's on/off gal Terry Moore has taken the fancy of gunman James Best, playing, for the umpteenth time in his career, an unhinged cowpoke. Murphy coerces his reluctant workforce into driving 3,000 head of cattle to Santa Fe in record time to pay off the bank loans and is forced to contend with jealous Best on the trip. Surly, snappy and laying down a no-drink policy ("One drink and you're fired.") isn't a popular way of getting the best out of your drovers, but he slowly wins their trust through sheer hard work. In the end, it's revealed that Dehner is actually Murphy's real father; the herd arrives in Santa Fe on time and Murphy, the curse of illegitimacy lifted, is a changed man, planning a new life with Moore. "You cast a mighty long shadow of your own," Dehner tells his son as they survey the cattle from a ridge, and Murphy, for about the first and only time in 82 minutes, allows a smile to crease those boyish features.

A word about Gerald Fried's highly melodramatic music must be said. Never has a composer worked so hard to inject some life and soul into a lifeless, soulless production. Fried, known for his stirring United Artists horror scores (*Curse of the Faceless Man*, *The Flame Barrier* and *The Return of Dracula*, among others), throws everything into the mix, including a banjo, all to no avail. At times, his busy soundtrack, underscoring every scene in a form of musical desperation, sounds as though it was meant for a far more prestigious picture than this one. You can't help but wonder why Murphy, after a string of ebullient, colorful Westerns, should lend his name to material so negative in approach that at times it's downright depressing (he co-produced but didn't receive a credit). And director Carr, doyen of dozens of Westerns, including quite a few Sunset Carson and Johnny Mack Brown oaters of the 1940s, should have had the experience to include at least one decent action sequence (there's a stampede and that's about it). Murphy had notched up 18 Westerns by the time the '50s came to a close; *Cast a Long Shadow* is the least captivating of the lot, not quite the film he would have wished to bow out from this golden period in the Western's long history.

Chapter 16
Scott: The Budd Boetticher Westerns, 1956-1960

Oscar "Budd" Boetticher wasn't a director of any great repute when he met up with Randolph Scott in 1955. A fanatic on bullfighting (he directed Republic's *The Bullfighter and the Lady* in 1951), he was no stranger to the Western platform, having directed four serviceable actioners for Universal-International: Audie Murphy's *The Cimarron Kid* (1951), Rock Hudson's *Horizons West* (1952) and *Seminole* (1953); and Glenn Ford's *The Man from the Alamo* (1953). By 1955, Randolph Scott's career with Warner Bros. was in an artistic slump and the man himself was becoming dissatisfied with appearing in Westerns, pondering whether or not to call it a day. Plotlines were becoming mechanical in design and he was getting bored with the whole business of making movies. He needed fresh impetus and it came in the unlikely form of the temperamental Boetticher. Screenwriter Burt Kennedy (who would direct a string of decent Westerns, starting with Fox's *The Canadians* in 1961), employed by John Wayne's production company Batjac, had manufactured a working script under the title of *7 Men from Now*, a classic tale of Western revenge. Robert Mitchum was one of the first to see the script before Wayne got his hands on it, Boetticher hired as director for the project. But Wayne pulled out as lead star because of filming duties on John Ford's own revenge Western, *The Searchers*. Joel

Randolph Scott is ready to blow away two of the seven outlaws who killed his wife, in *7 Men from Now* (1956).

Randolph Scott, Gail Russell and (in back) Lee Marvin in *7 Men from Now*

McCrea surprisingly turned the part down, as did unexpected choice Robert Preston, so Scott was offered the role grudgingly by Wayne; the two actors had, for reasons unknown, fallen out on the set of *The Spoilers* and the Duke held Scott in low esteem, seeing him as strictly B-movie class material. Much to Wayne's surprise and annoyance, *7 Men from Now* not only scored a hit at the box-office *and* with the critics but also revived Scott's fortunes ("I shouda been in that picture," Wayne later grouched to all concerned). In fact, Scott's most acclaimed period as a film actor stems from the Boetticher 1956-1960 output; the two got on like a house on fire and it showed in their teamwork. Scott, for his part, with 56 Westerns tucked underneath his gun belt, had seen and done it all; from the gauche young hero of the Zane Grey oaters to the fearless peace officer cleaning up lawless streets, he had morphed into an imperturbable figure of almost mythical proportions, at one with the cruel yet beautiful landscape that was to feature in Boetticher's highly distinctive Western compositions.

The combination of Boetticher, Kennedy and Scott was a meeting of like minds, a working chemistry that produced 100% Western gold in *7 Men from Now*, a movie that the public responded to in droves. The director and his leading man went on to make a further six distinguished movies that depicted the Old West in a harsher, stripped-down format than before, although Anthony Mann ran Boetticher a close second with his James Stewart oaters. Six come under the banner of the Ranown Films cycle; *Westbound*, in which Scott was forced to return to Warner Bros. to fulfill contract obligations, is not usually classed as a Ranown picture, although it is in all but name only. With Boetticher at the helm, Scott continued his business partnership with producer Harry Joe Brown: Scott/Brown backed five of Boetticher's Westerns, four of which were filmed in and around the spectacular Lone Pine/Alabama Hills region which forms part of the California Sierras; the director made the area his own, much like John Ford's famed affinity with Monument Valley, framing his protagonists amid the rocky outcrops, caves, deserts, ravines, winding rivers and majestic mountain scenery. Lone Pine had figured in many of Scott's early Zane Grey Westerns and Columbia outings (and a hell of a lot of Universal and Warner Bros. Westerns as well), and justifiably so; this was the kind of rugged, yet strangely hostile, habitat in which to enact these frontier dramas.

Boetticher's forays into Old West mythos have been termed the Sergio Leone Westerns of their day by more than one critic. He dismantled the format down to its bare essentials and reassembled it in a different guise—all coming in at under 80 minutes, they have various salient points in common: Scott, like Clint Eastwood's Man With No Name, is a monosyllabic antihero, on the selfsame level as that of the villain with whom he forms an uneasy alliance; his wife has been murdered or is missing; dialogue is as terse as the action; the strong, capable leading lady is hitched to a nice but ineffectual partner who invariably gets killed, leaving the field wide open for Scott, or his foe, to make their move; Scott is forced to shoot the bad guy in the end, even though he has formed a bond of sorts with him; and the gunplay is uncompromisingly violent. These were morality plays enacted in a bleak Western setting, each individual playing off, and preying on, the other's personality flaws; mean and hard, with a laudable deficit of superfluous padding. In other words, Boetticher designed the pitch-perfect Western.

Undoubtedly, the Ranown Westerns were Budd Boetticher's "breakthrough moment." His talents rose to the fore in these movies, crystallizing into the director's finest hour (and, in the latter part of his career, Scott's also). It didn't last: What came after never matched up to them, including his, and Audie Murphy's, final cowboy picture, Fipco's disappointing, and rarely seen, *A Time for Dying* (1969). Everyone has his day—the Ranowns were Boetticher's, however brief that moment was. Let's all be thankful that he was around at the right place and time to forge seven masterpieces that have well and truly stood the test of time when many others have fallen by the wayside over the years.

7 Men from Now, produced on a $750,000 budget, was the first of the Boettichers and an absolute cracker, released by Warner Bros. in 1956. Following the armed robbery of a Wells Fargo cashbox containing $20,000, an embittered ex-sheriff seeks retribution, track-

Randolph Scott, looking iconic, with Gail Russell from *7 Men from Now*

ing the seven men answerable for his wife's death during the holdup. Scott, taking up with Warner Bros. at their request, not his, played Ben Stride, first seen gunning down two of the robbers in their rain-swept hideout in a bout of largely unseen violence and then coming to the aid of settlers Walter Reed and Gail Russell, whose wagon is held fast in a muddy quagmire. Pulling them free, he reluctantly agrees to accompany the couple south to Flora Vista, Chirichua Indians making themselves a nuisance. For the next 10 minutes or so, Boetticher's approach remains unhurried, acclimatizing the audience to the distinctive Lone Pine landscapes which he will make full use of in later excursions, photographed in high-definition color by William Clothier and backed by Henry Vars' lovely score.

Things turn darker when gunslinger Lee Marvin and pal Donald Barry show up, creating tensions within the group; Boetticher pulls the plug on the leisure ride and directs with purpose in punchy, condensed vignettes. Marvin, an old opponent of Scott's, makes it clear—he wants a cut of that stolen cash, informing Scott that he's the one person standing in his way; he's not interested in the man's revenge operation, only that loot. Following a desert Indian attack, when Marvin puts a bullet into the third of Scott's intended targets, the ex-sheriff makes his feeling known to Russell, taunting her over her husband's non-existent fighting spirit. "A man oughta be able to take care of his woman." They then make camp; in a beautifully choreographed sequence leaking veiled menace, taking place inside Reed's cramped wagon during a storm, Marvin gives vent to his arousal brought on by Russell's charms ("Love. That's a mighty hard word."), virtually accusing Reed of being "half a man," while Scott, brimming with rage and watching Marvin like a coiled rattlesnake, warns him to back off.

Unbeknown to them all, Reed has the strongbox on board the wagon and has to deliver it to crook John Larch on payment of $500; he desperately needs the money. Scott retrieves the box in time, Reed trundles into Flora Vista without the goods and is shot in the back by Larch, who rides out to the desert with an accomplice to put Scott out of the picture and collect the $20,000; Scott, wounded in the leg after shooting two more of the gang, is holed up in the rocks. After Marvin (forever practicing the quick draw) has dealt with Larch, his partner *and* Barry for his own ends, blazing away with two guns, riddling them with bullets, it's the final score to be settled with Scott over the Wells Fargo cashbox. A marvelous couple of throwaway lines occur here between the two adversaries, summing up Burt Kennedy's spare script to a tee: Marvin: "Pete Bodene. I killed him." Scott: "Why?" Marvin: "Why not?" Needless to say, Scott finishes off Marvin with a single shot but slumps against a boulder in remorse as Marvin grabs the box's lock in his death throes, a scene edited for maximum impact. And it

looks as though the lawmaker will get Russell all to himself in the final reel when she decides to follow him to his next destination, taking up the job of full-time sheriff. After all, those huge blue eyes of hers are very hard to resist!

Sergio Leone admitted to Boetticher in 1971 that part of the inspiration behind his Spaghetti horse operas were the streamlined actioners that Boetticher had made, starting with this one. Scott, a man of few words and lightning-quick with a pistol, carries a quiet dignity, one that harmonizes with that rocky environment to perfection, his stone-set features noble yet infused with hidden passions and a steely determination to follow the job through. Mention must also go to Marvin's cocksure gunman, evil and likeable in equal measures, one of the best-ever turns in his numerous cowboy heavy roles (Scott fully appreciated Marvin's skills as a screen tough-guy). *7 Men from Now* was Scott's finest picture in years, and, along with *The Tall T*, *Ride Lonesome* and *Comanche Station*, represents the art of the Western in its purest form. Newspaper hacks commented on Scott's "unsmiling, straight-shooting avenger," *The Motion Picture Herald* announcing the film as a "money-spinner."

Columbia's *The Tall T* (1957), the second Boetticher/Ranown production, had "classic" stamped all over it, proving that *7 Men from Now* was no one-off fluke (some prints were expanded and screened as "MegaScope," but generally the movie comes in normal aspect format). The first talkative 15 minutes is relatively lightweight: Smiling Scott (playing ramrod Pat Brennan) stops off at a staging post, promises to buy candy for the stationmaster's young son, rides into town and then over to a ranch, betting his horse on whether or not he can tame a wild bull (he fails). We even see Scott wrenching off his boots and checking for holes in his socks! Boetticher, with cinematographer Charles Lawton, Jr., again concentrates his camera on the vivid Lone Pine vistas while Heinz Roemheld's jaunty music lulls us into a false sense of security; what follows is another Boetticher morality showpiece, even grimmer than *7 Men from Now*.

Randolph Scott smiles at Richard Boone's gun, in *The Tall T* (1957).

Hitching a lift on a stagecoach back to the station with newly married couple John Hubbard and Maureen O'Sullivan, the smile is soon wiped off Scott's face, reverting to a look of cold severity. The stationmaster and his boy have been murdered, their bodies callously dumped down a well. Who are the culprits behind this despicable act? They happen to be charismatic outlaw Richard Boone (from TV's *Have Gun—Will Travel*) and his two sidekicks, slack-jawed Henry Silva and lanky Skip Homeier (Homeier co-starred in many '50s Westerns, receiving top billing in Republic's *Thunder over Arizona*, released in 1956). After Silva has cold-bloodedly shot dead stage driver Arthur Hunnicutt, Boone decides to go along with cowardly Hubbard's plan to save his own neck—hold his wife captive and ransom her for $50,000; her father is a mine owner and local tycoon (he only married O'Sullivan for her money anyway and wants a cut of the payment). Boone hides out near a shack built over an abandoned mine tunnel set in a barren rocky wasteland, in which he incarcerates Scott and O'Sullivan. Hubbard and Homeier set off to arrange the ransom money, leaving Scott and the woman to play the survival game. Psychopath Silva is hell-bent on killing the pair once the cash has been collected; they have to find a way to outwit him and make their dash to freedom.

Interestingly, at this point in the film, Burt Kennedy's taut script focuses on Boone's unhappy frame of mind, his troubled character, to a certain extent, taking over from Scott's silent cowpoke, who patiently waits in the background for the opportune moment to make his break. "I like you, Brennan," he says to Scott, revealing that his trigger-happy acolytes leave much to be desired; both, in his view, inexperienced and hotheaded. In his ideal world, Boone would much prefer Scott as a partner anytime.

Maureen O'Sullivan, Randolph Scott and Richard Boone in *The Tall T*

Scott, in the end, even shows some regard for Boone in their payoff scene. "I'm gonna start walking," the outlaw tells Scott who responds with, "Don't do it, Frank," not wishing to shoot him in the back. Boone comes across as a highly intelligent individual, a victim of circumstance, unsure of what he *really* wants; he's unable to break from his way of life, however distasteful he finds it sometimes. In a blood-spattered finale, we almost feel sorry for him when he receives a shotgun blast in the face, as does Homeier; Silva is shot to pieces, Scott firing five bullets into his writhing body. As for O'Sullivan: After her husband has been killed by Silva, the hussy wastes no time in finding solace in Scott's manly arms. "Sometimes you (pause), you gotta walk up and take what you want," he grunts hoarsely, seizing her roughly by her hair and kissing her passionately. And his final reassuring words to her as they leave the scene of carnage are: "Come on now. It's gonna be a nice day."

The movie's odd title is derived from the Tenvoorde Ranch that Scott visits at the beginning; the original name, *The Captives*, having already been registered. *The Tall T* is a terrific pared-to-the-bone Western, as desolate in execution as the surroundings in which the drama takes place. With a small cast at his disposal, Boetticher produced a highly rated work of some distinction, recognized as such by the U.S. National Film Registry for being "culturally, historically and aesthetically significant." What greater accolade can a Western receive!

That made two classics in a row from the volatile director; unfortunately, the third offering, *Decision at Sundown* (Columbia, 1957), failed to reach the same giddy heights

Fred A. Roff, Jr. and Randolph Scott participate in a Colt pistol promo tied in with *Decision at Sundown* (1957).

set by his first two Westerns, Burt Kennedy stepping aside for Charles Lang, Jr., who supplied the script to a project that Boetticher didn't have much faith in, even though Scott wanted to film it. The sweeping vistas of Lone Pine were nowhere in evidence, the action solely taking place within the confines of a town. Scott plays Bart Allison, who rides into Sundown with jovial partner Noah Beery, Jr. and proceeds to stir up a hornet's nest. He holds smooth-talking John Carroll to account for seducing his wife and causing her death and is bent on revenge; barging in on Carroll's wedding ceremony, he makes his intentions clear, objecting to the union taking place: "If you marry this man, you'll be a widow by sundown," he flings at bride-to-be Karen Steele. Holed up in a livery stable and pinned down by Carroll's mob, Scott and Beery are unaware that the rest of the town are sick and tired of Carroll's scheming ways, as is even, it now appears, Steele, and are none too keen to back his case. But Beery knows full well that Scott's wife was a tramp, "wild and beautiful, but no good," who committed suicide when Scott was in the war, telling his buddy the bald truth: "She wasn't the girl you thought she was." When his comrade gets a bullet in the back, Scott shoots cowardly sheriff Andrew Duggan, injures his hand and is prevented from gunning down Carroll; the scoundrel is wounded in the arm by doting mistress Valerie French, who screams at Scott, "You were married but you never had a wife." Carroll and French then leave a town that has regained some self-respect after taking a long hard look at itself. As for Scott, after drunkenly propping up the bar, he also leaves, a morose and broken man, Doc John Archer reflecting on his going: "He changed things for everybody in town. Unfortunately, there's nothing we can do for him."

John Archer (the town doctor) and Randolph Scott, in *Decision at Sundown*

Scott and Carroll both turned in solid performances in a downbeat oater based on moral misconduct and sinfulness, backed by Heinz Roemheld's equally melancholy score. It's not exactly a fun-packed experience; everybody is fairly unlikeable, each with a best-kept-hidden secret, and Scott is just plain miserable throughout. What the picture presents to the fan is a tense, unusual mood piece, with Lang's script more verbose than potentially one that Kennedy would have conjured up. Set against the other six Ranown pictures, it's the least riveting, but as an exercise in character conflict within an enclosed Western town habitat, *Decision at Sundown* is an underrated winner, albeit a pretty depressing one.

Scott returned to Warner Bros., his old studio, to make another movie for them, *Westbound*, in 1958; having completed his 10-picture deal with the company in 1955 with *Shoot-Out at Medicine Bend*, they scrutinized the small print in his contract and claimed that he owed them one more outing. Scott's renewed success with *7 Men from Now* had a lot to do with Warner Bros. shrewdly undertaking an about-face turn, particularly when we consider their dismissive attitude toward the actor during the production of *Shoot-Out at Medicine Bend*. Written by Berne Giler and Albert S. LeVino, *Westbound* (not released until 1959), although classed as one of the Ranown cycle, somehow doesn't seem a part of the series. The movie is like a standard Warner Bros. cowboy film, competently directed by Boetticher but lacking the bite and toughness that a Burt Kennedy script would give it; David Buttolph's *Calamity Jane*-type score is also something of a distraction. The movie kicks off in fine style, the credits rolling over a shot of Scott riding into the sunset, a favorite scene usually reserved for the end of a Western! Scott is Union cavalry officer John Hayes, charged (initially against his wishes) to ferry gold bullion to the Union forces from the town of Julesberg, setting up station posts en route and re-establishing the Overland Stage Company. Aiding him are one-armed soldier Michael Dante and his wife, busty Karen Steele; attempting to thwart him are town slimeball Andrew Duggan and gun-tough Michael Pate, on the side of the Rebels. Duggan just happens to be married to Scott's ex-lady, the ravishing Virginia Mayo, so when Pate's gang,

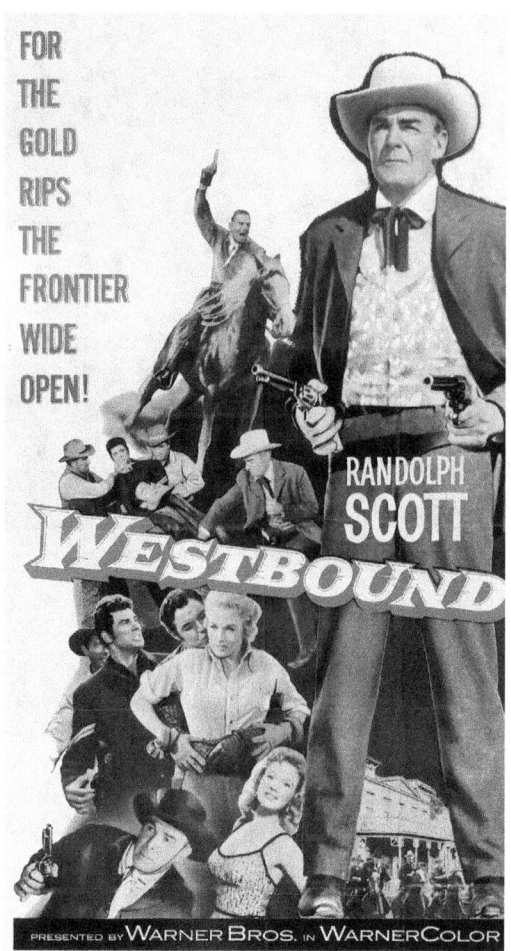

under orders from Duggan ("Make sure the Overland doesn't operate."), starts burning down stage stations, running off horses and causing the deaths of passengers, Scott takes up his personal vendetta with Duggan while trying to handle the villainous Pate, on the prowl and itching for a showdown.

As in *Decision at Sundown*, the townsfolk rise up against Duggan in the end (why is never made clear), as does Mayo, but she doesn't get to hook her scarlet fingernails into her previous beau: Dante is gunned down and, in a rip-roaring concluding shoot-out between the gunmen and the town's residents, Duggan and Pate meet their maker; Steele, casting aside her widow's robes with indecent haste, sets her sights on Scott, who says goodbye to Mayo and promises to return to Steele's ranch once his next job is over and done with.

With *Decision at Sundown* and *Westbound*, the Boetticher/Scott alliance suffered a minor glitch. Both were decent-enough Westerns in their own way but were crying out for a tight Kennedy screenplay and those high, wide and handsome Lone Pine settings. These would come, but not before the next Scott/Brown production, the more carefree *Buchanan Rides Alone*, released by Columbia in 1958. In this, Scott played West Texan loner Tom Buchanan who rides into the town of Agry and becomes embroiled in a plot to trade a young Mexican, jailed for murder, for $50,000 in release money. Photographed in a bleached-out color wash by Lucien Ballard, Tucson's arid, cactus-strewn landscape, allied with the lone figure of Scott riding into the shanty town outskirts of Agry with its huddle of adobe dwellings, smacks of the Spaghetti horse operas that were to proliferate six years later. Kennedy, Boetticher and Scott himself (their joint input went uncredited) augmented Charles Lang, Jr.'s loose script, producing an engaging Western whose convoluted framework was enlivened by sudden bouts of violence. Ever-smiling Scott is easygoing to begin with ("I don't linger no place until I get back to where I belong," he informs Sheriff Barry Kelley when questioned as to why he's arrived in town), but when the humorless lawman, one of the three Agry brothers, jails him for supposedly being in cahoots with Manuel Rojas, who has just shot the judge's son, he gets angry. A strong cast of characters includes a second Agry sibling, shifty judge Tol Avry, Avry's dour-looking henchman (Craig Stevens), deputy L.Q. Jones as an affable fellow Texan who sides with Scott and the third Agry brother, Peter Whitney, a bumbling, irritating oaf who scuttles here, there and everywhere, sweating profusely and listening in on the myriad plot machinations. No female leads as such—the director dispenses with romantic trifles; they would only hinder the skullduggery taking place as Scott is freed but misses being shot from behind by the intervention of Jones. Rojas is smuggled out of jail by Kelley because he wants to wrest the $50,000 ransom from Avry; Jones is shot dead while helping Rojas to cross the border; Scott and Rojas wind up back in jail but are set free by Stevens and the gunfight

A Belgian poster for *Buchanan Rides Alone* (1958)

finale sees Avry and Kelley both sprawled in the dust after trying to grab that $50,000 contained in a saddlebag, the "10-dollar town," as Scott disparagingly calls it, now in the capable hands of smart-as-a-button dude Stevens. The Texan rides out of Agry on Rojas' prize steed, a present for helping him avoid a lynching. As *Variety* stated, "a thoroughly satisfactory picture."

The one downside to *Buchanan Rides Alone* is the soundtrack. A stock score (composers Mischa Bakaleinikoff, George Duning, Paul Sawtell and Heinz Roemheld) was used and it tells; a specially commissioned score would have enhanced the action to greater effect. As it stands, the movie is a joy to watch and far lighter in tone compared to the other Ranowns, an antidote to the much more somber mood that was to prevail in the next two classics from the Boetticher/Scott stable.

A bounty hunter whose wife was abominably murdered by an outlaw uses his captured, deranged brother as bait to lure him out of hiding so that he can exact reprisal. Yes, for classic simplicity, revenge Westerns don't come any bleaker, or much sweeter, than 1959's *Ride Lonesome*, shot in CinemaScope. From the opening panoramic view of Scott (as Ben Brigade) worming his way through a rocky ravine to the final scene of the bounty hunter standing alone by a burning hanging tree, this is the Western stripped down to basics, almost Western *film noir* in color. And basic describes both the plot and Burt Kennedy's screenplay. Guilt-ridden Scott, whose wife was pitilessly hung by Lee

Randolph Scott and Karen Steele in *Ride Lonesome* (1959)

Van Cleef on that very tree when he was absent on a job, waylays giggling outlaw James Best, Van Cleef's younger sibling, but not for the bounty; Best is to be used to flush out Van Cleef in order for Scott to even the score with the killer. Boetticher treats us to a tremendous widescreen subjective shot in the opening minutes—Scott's back and holster, hand poised for the quick draw as he faces Best, half-fills the foreground frame, an iconic image that heavily influenced many foreign filmmakers trying their hands at the so-named "European Western" in the oncoming decade.

En route to Santa Cruz, Scott and Best are joined by just-widowed Karen Steele and amiable villains Pernell Roberts and (in his screen debut) loose-limbed James Coburn. As in the other Scott/Brown/Boetticher productions, Scott stands in the way of the bad guys' ambitions. Roberts wants Best; his capture can afford him and his buddy an amnesty from the law and a new way of life as ranch owners. Roberts also harbors ideas of playing house with Steele, as does, to a certain extent, Scott, admiring her for her strength, thus forming a familiar Boetticher *ménage à trois*. In a tete-a-tete with Steele, Scott curtly lets his feelings be known. "He left you alone," (referring to her stationmaster husband). Steele: "I can take care of myself." Scott: "If you were mine, you wouldn't have to." Steele: "Meaning?" Scott: "Meaning I'd never've brought you here in the first place." He also reveals a softer side to his hard nature, tending his sick horse throughout the night, much to Steele's undisguised approval.

The five cross sun-blasted gulches and deserts, shadowed by Mescalero Indians and pursued by Van Cleef's gang, Charles Lawton, Jr.'s diamond-hard photography throwing into sharp relief the mountain backdrops and sandy wilderness shimmering under

James Best (on horseback) and Randolph Scott in *Ride Lonesome*

a limitless blue sky, the journey underlined by Heinz Roemheld's lyrical music. After 20 minutes, an Indian chief barters for Steele, offering a horse in exchange, a scene that was reproduced in its entirety in the Audie Murphy Western *Six Black Horses* (Universal 1962), Kennedy (who scripted) even including snatches of identical dialogue. There's a *Searchers*-type Indian attack seven minutes later and, at 45 minutes, Scott finally allows the ghost of a smile to crack that craggy, unshaven countenance, but not for long. The anticipated showdown takes place in a clearing, in the center of which stands the skeletal remains of the tree where Van Cleef murdered Scott's wife. The sneering killer is gunned down by Scott, who then unexpectedly hands Best over to Roberts and Coburn, wishing them luck in their future endeavors, an uplifting ending that went against studio wishes that the two be shot dead ("Take him. I've got no more use for him," he says to a startled Roberts, who was all set for a gunfight). And Scott doesn't even get Steele—she rides off with Roberts and Coburn, leaving the bounty hunter a lone figure, like a statue against the flaming tree and Van Cleef's broken body, cleansed of his inner demons.

Scott ruefully admitted that the bad guys got all the best parts in Boetticher Westerns and *Ride Lonesome* is no exception. Roberts, like Lee Marvin, Richard Boone and Claude Akins in *Comanche Station*, almost steals the show, but *only* almost; Scott's don't-mess-me-around presence, spitting out short words of wisdom between clenched teeth,

Flanked by the Comanche, Randolph Scott stands stoically at peace in *Comanche Station* (1960).

is the driving force, as much a part of the scenario as the rocks and boulders. The pace never falters in this superbly structured little Western that rivets from start to finish, one of the best of the Ranowns and a brilliant exercise in economic filmmaking in anyone's book ("Another good Western from the Ranown team," noted *Variety*).

1960s *Comanche Station*, again filmed in CinemaScope, is rated by some as the finest Western Boetticher ever directed. Certainly, it's on a par with *Ride Lonesome*, almost, in many ways, a companion piece to it. A man searching for his wife who was captured by Comanche Indians years ago rescues another woman from their clutches, unaware that there is a bounty on her head and that three desperadoes are after her … and the bounty as well. Boetticher's final Ranown picture and Scott's penultimate movie is a contemplative, gritty tale of aging and changing attitudes patterned very much on John Ford's *The Searchers*. But while Ford's masterful two-hour fable of one man's venomous journey of revenge and atonement came in at $3,000,000 (and is now rightly regarded as the finest Western ever made), Boetticher's 74-minute similar-themed essay was produced for less than a quarter of that sum but in some instances manages to be almost as hypnotic. Scott's Jefferson Cody is Wayne's Ethan Edwards in another guise, a loner on an interminable mission, searching for his wife abducted by the Comanche 10 years back. For the first 12 minutes, there's little dialogue, Mischa Bakaleinikoff's melodious soundtrack complementing the stark volcanic rock formations (stunningly photographed by Charles Lawton, Jr.) as Scott is escorted into an Indian encampment and trades wares

Randolph Scott, in obvious pain, is having his wound attended to by Nancy Gates in *Comanche Station*.

and a rifle not, as expected, for his wife but for Nancy Gates, only to find out that a trio of bounty hunters led by Claude Akins are on her trail for $5,000 reward money. The scene is set for Boetticher's signature motifs to come into play: Scott, grown weary of his search, and Akins, looking to settle down, both fall for Gates and become rivals for her attention; Akins knows and likes Scott, even though he realizes that he may have to kill him for the bounty as Scott is simply going to return the woman to her husband, deemed a coward by both men; and partners Richard Rust and Skip Homeier discuss what they want out of life, ready to rebel against Akin's amoral pledge that he will kill Gates as the bounty holds good whether she's dead or alive. Rust and Homeier are, in fact, the counterparts to Harry Carey, Jr. and Jeffrey Hunter in *The Searchers*. As the latter recoiled at the idea of Wayne, their leader, killing kidnapped Natalie Wood because she had become (in the eyes of Wayne) "tainted," so do Rust and Homeier react at the thought of Akins doing away with Gates, for mercenary reasons.

Comanche Station's austere, pessimistic mood reflects the passing of the Old West and its hard-nosed traditions succinctly, without an ounce of flab; the five protagonists are caught in a time warp of sorts, playing out their individualized dramas amid those exposed boulder-strewn wastes. The inevitable gun duel is a beauty: After Homeier dies from an arrow wound and Rust is shot in the back by Akins due to his defection to Scott, the stone-faced one bushwhacks Akins' planned ambush, sneaking up behind him in a gully, his nemesis holding a rifle. Burt Kennedy's well-chosen few lines sum up the duo's tension-fueled final moments:

Scott: "Drop the gun."
Akins: "If I spin and do you, I get the woman, Cody."
Scott: "I wouldn't try it."
Akins: "Got to. Come too far to turn back now."
Scott: "Don't do it, Ben."

It goes without saying that Akins turns to face Scott and pays with his life.

When Gates is reunited with son and husband, the man turns out to be blind, not a coward as thought. Job done, Scott rides off (as Wayne walked off in that famous closing shot), a lonely figure outlined on a ridge in the scenic splendor of Lone Pine, his quest for his missing wife ongoing, perhaps never-ending, an enigmatic climax, and a moving one also. Westerns don't come more fundamentally simplistic than this one, an apt tribute to the adult-orientated Ranown cycle of Boetticher horse operas and to the undervalued talents of Randolph Scott, who knew deep down in his boots that the genre as he had known it was drawing to a close. A transitional phase was in the pipeline and he wanted no part of it. The hard-bitten range-busting American Western of the '50s was morphing once again into something not so tough; more scatty, often plain silly and softer around the edges. He would team up with another Western veteran, Joel McCrea, for Sam Peckinpah's *Ride the High Country* in 1962 and that would be his swansong, an appropriate one with which to close his long, illustrious career.

In retrospect, the enduring impression given out by the Randolph Scott/Budd Boetticher Westerns, particularly *7 Men from Now*, *The Tall T*, *Ride Lonesome* and *Comanche Station*, is one of a select group of sparse, character-driven studies in revenge, microcosmic in scope, where complex emotions bubble just beneath the surface and where subterfuge and double bluff tied in with a survival of the fittest motif forms the main dramatic thrust. Similarities can be found in Anthony Mann's *The Naked Spur* (MGM 1953) and John Sturges' criminally neglected *The Law and Jake Wade* (MGM 1958); both dealt with a not-so-innocent lawman up against a charming villain in isolated, unforgiving surroundings, a female lead dragged into the plot to provide a catalyst between the warring factors (*The Naked Spur*'s location was Durango, Colorado; *Jake Wade* was shot at Lone Pine). These two pictures could quite easily have been directed by Boetticher, who maybe would have been out of his depth handling *The Searchers*, Howard Hawks' *Rio Bravo* (Warner Bros. 1959) and Edward Dmytryk's *Warlock* (20th Century Fox, 1959), three expensive motion pictures with big-name stars to match, coming in at two-hours plus, which received, in the United Kingdom, major release dates, unlike the majority of the Scott pictures. Boetticher's memorable and highly professional essays in the ethics, codes and practices of the Old West stick in the subconscious—we want to revisit them time and time again, if only to remind ourselves that this is how it *used* to be done; solid, no-nonsense craftsmanship within a tight budget, Scott's iconic weather-beaten features blending in oh so perfectly with that haunting Lone Pine scenery. We mourn the passing of such marvelous pieces of work from the realm of cinema and from the Western genre in particular.

CHAPTER 17
MONTGOMERY: 1956-1959

George Montgomery parted company with Columbia at the end of 1955, the remainder of his output up to 1959 divided between Allied Artists, Warner Bros. and United Artists, plus a solitary effort for soon-to-be-defunct Republic in 1957. He was now on good money—$35,000 to $50,000 a picture, plus a percentage of the profits. Of the nine Westerns he would make, four were in black-and-white, no bad thing in itself but a sign that, quality-wise, his oaters in the latter part of the decade didn't quite match those of the first part; there was a gradual falling-off in excellence, with plots containing a mixture of themes done many times before. It's true to say that there are no George Montgomery classics from this period to equal the caliber of *The Texas Rangers* and *The Lone Gun* (*Gun Duel in Durango* is the exception); nevertheless, their entertainment factor is still high, and that, in the end, is what matters. His first and only outing in the saddle in 1956, Allied Artists' *Canyon River* (aka *Cattle King*), was an easy-on-the-eye Western that contained a bit of gunplay, a bit of romance and a bit of rivalry between friends; nothing to shout from the rooftops about, maybe, but a fine example of a mid-'50s CinemaScope oater in color, beautifully photographed by Ellsworth Fredericks. Scriptwriter Daniel B. Ullman rehashed his *The Longhorn* (Monogram 1951) in a tale of tough Wyoming cattleman Montgomery (as Steve Patrick) heading to Oregon to buy up 1,000 head of Longhorn, which he hopes to breed with Herefords, producing a heavier meat stock. Mortgaging his ranch up to the hilt to obtain the funds, he sets off with partner Peter Graves, unaware that Graves plans to stab him in the back. Graves has cut a deal with cattleman Walter Sande: Rustle the herd at Canyon River, kill Montgomery if necessary, purchase all available ranch land and reap the profits from the new breed. But halfway into their trip, the two cowpokes are waylaid by horse thieves; Graves is seriously wounded and is forced to recuperate in widow Marcia Henderson's cabin while Montgomery pushes on to Oregon, recruiting a gang of ex-convicts to form his team of cow punchers, led by Alan Hale, Jr. When the two first meet, Hale challenges Montgomery to a fight ("Make your play, big man."), is knocked senseless, and agrees to join

George Montgomery and Marcia Henderson in *Canyon River* (1956)

his victor on the drive. Graves, suffering from an attack of guilt through Montgomery's caring for him, joins the drovers along with Henderson and her young son, Richard Eyer (he played the genie in *The 7th Voyage of Sinbad*). Graves has fallen in love with the lass, but she's taken with Montgomery. When Graves catches them canoodling, he flares up and decides to go along with Sande's criminal scheme after all.

As stated, *Canyon River* is undemanding, easygoing and enjoyable (Marlin Skiles' score is a joy), containing several sparky flirtatious scenes between Montgomery and Henderson, showing that he could switch on the charm when required and pull it off. Scowling Robert J. Wilke is the ubiquitous villain, a part he was born to play in countless films, while Graves isn't quite right as the good guy/bad guy, paying for his double-crossing with a bullet. It all ends happily-ever-after, Sande and Wilke both shot dead and the herd safely delivered to a freezing cold Wyoming. Oh yes, and judging by the grin on his face, Eyer could expect to have a brand new father pretty soon!

1957 commenced with Allied Artists' *Last of the Badmen*, and if Daniel B. Ullman's screenplay brings on a sense of déjà vu, audiences would be right: Other adaptations of his story include *Flaming Bullets* (PRC, 1945), *Wanted Dead or Alive* (Monogram, 1951) and Audie Murphy's *Gunfight at Comanche Creek*. Marginally better made than Murphy's 1963 version, Paul Landres' opus is only interesting in patches, weighed down by a Dragnet-style voice-over and lack of a female lead (casino girl Meg Randall makes a fleeting cameo, and that's it). As the plot is fully described in chapter 19, I'll briefly summarize it here: In Colorado of 1875, an outlaw gang led by Douglas Kennedy springs criminals from jail, uses the men in robberies and then murders them, collecting the reward; as the last victim was an operative employed by the Chandler Detective Agency, agent Montgomery (Dan Barton) goes undercover, given a false identity (that of a wanted killer), is jailed, released by Kennedy's henchmen and forced to participate in holdups; Montgomery's contact, Keith Larson, surveys the gang's hideout from a ridge but is caught napping and killed; gang member James Best wrestles with his conscience, falls in with Montgomery but is shot dead by Marshal Willis Bouchy, the brains behind it all; and the villains are all rounded up in the final reel. Montgomery doesn't get to use his guns until the dying seconds and the movie has a tired look about it—even Paul Sawtell's score fails to liven things up. And one question remains unanswered: If every sheriff/marshal/deputy is brutally killed by this mob to prevent them talking (by bullet or knife) when an outlaw is sprung from behind bars, why, when the agency sends Montgomery out on

his mission, don't they get their heads together with the authorities and take measures to safeguard lawmen in future jail breaks?

How to construct a spiffy Western on low finances: Direct and act with a belief in your project; hire an imaginative cinematographer capable of bringing gloss to the black-and-white imagery; bring in a composer to lift the action and take on a scriptwriter who can elicit a punchy screenplay. Step forward, then, director Sidney Salkow, actors Montgomery, Ann Robinson, Bobby Clark and Steve Brodie, photographer Maury Gertsman, composers Paul Sawtell and Bert Shefter (one of their first-ever collaborations) and writer Louis Stevens. Together, these filmmakers turned United Artists' *Gun Duel in Durango* (1957) into a 73-minute gem of a Western; simply told, containing the right mix of gunplay and sentiment, a pared-to-the-bone movie to delight all cowboy fans and become another long-forgotten Montgomery winner. "George Montgomery's name will ensure drawing power," said *The Hollywood Reporter*, and it was true, his name alone could pull in the crowds, as Scott, McCrea and Murphy's names continued to do.

The story is nothing new: Montgomery plays Will Sabre, a notorious gunfighter, bank robber and gang leader who has decided to call it a day and go straight. Trouble is, second-in-command thug Steve Brodie doesn't want him to quit, giving him 30 days to decide his future; either he rejoins his fellow partners in crime, or he's a dead man. Picking up 13-year-old Bobby Clark on the trail, who's trying to bury his dead father

George Montgomery and Bobby Clark (who is trying to bury his father) in *Gun Duel in Durango* (1957)

(Clark was Alan Hale, Jr.'s son in the TV series *Casey Jones*, broadcast in 1957/58), outlaw and boy carry on to Ann Robinson's Lazy K spread; Montgomery hasn't seen his girl for two years and wants to take up where they left off: "Have ta get used to living with people again, too," he tells her. After a disagreement, Robinson agrees to take on the responsibility of Clark's welfare (a delightful performance from the child star) and marry Montgomery if he keeps to his promise of hanging up those twin six-shooters ("Yippee! I'll be the best hand you ever had," yells Clark joyfully). Taking a job in Durango's bank ("You're not going into a bank!" cries Clark to his benefactor, fully aware of his past reputation), Sheriff Frank Ferguson is faintly suspicious of the new member of his community (now calling himself Dan Tomlinson), even though Texas Ranger Denver Pyle assures the lawman that when he and his boys were ambushed by Brodie's bunch, Montgomery was on his side in the gunfight. Meanwhile, up at Boulder Ridge, Brodie is planning a raid on the Wells Fargo express office *and* the bank in Durango, knowing that his old boss is in town, breaking that 30-day agreement.

Salkow constructs the narrative expertly, segueing from family-type drama to shoot-'em-ups with ease. Clark's innocence plays on Montgomery's conscience ("He showed us what human beings are supposed to be like."), the former gunman keeping his revolvers handy in the bank but refusing to shoot when Brodie's gang robs the express office; he's then branded "yeller," Clark given a black eye at school for his association with a someone who won't fire a pistol in times of trouble ("I don't want to use a gun anymore," Montgomery tries to explain to Clark, to no avail). Of course, we all know that George *will* strap on that double holster when push comes to shove, and he does so on the hour after being forced into helping Brodie rob the bank—Clark has been abducted as collateral. Riding over to the hideout at Boulder Ridge, he confronts Brodie on the roof of a shack, both guns firing with deadly accuracy, gunning down two desperadoes and wounding his ex-partner in the leg. Brodie is taken into Durango for sentencing, Montgomery pardoned and Clark adopted by the newly married couple. So ends a minor but deeply satisfying Western all round.

There are three hidden horror connections tied up with Republic's *Pawnee*, also released as *Pale Arrow* in September 1957: Director George Waggner came up with two classic Universal horror movies in 1941, *Man Made Monster* and *The Wolf Man*; producers Jack J. Gross (Grosse on some prints) and Philip N. Krasne, in addition to editor Kenneth G. Crane, drummed up the *Monster from Green Hell* in 1958; and Dabbs Greer starred in *House of Wax*, *The Vampire* and *It! The Terror from Beyond Space*, three undisputed '50s classics. Many have described *Pawnee* as a horror show all in itself, the very worst of Montgomery's Westerns, a belief compounded in the sixth

minute when George rides into camera shot, shocking us with the unexpected—he's an Indian! A white painted streak across his face, stripped to the waist and wearing decorated breechclouts, Montgomery plays Pale Arrow, or just plain Paul Fletcher ("Paul" derived from "Pale" and "Fletcher" from a maker of arrows; I'll spell it out, just as the film does!), raised by the Pawnee from boyhood. Peace-loving Chief Wise Eagle (Ralph Moody) instructs his adopted son to join a wagon train to "learn the heart of the white man" while jealous-as-hell Crazy Fox (Charles Horvath) loiters furtively in the shadows of the wigwams, despising Montgomery and lusting after Dancing Fawn (Charlotte Austin), Montgomery's intended. Donning buckskins, Montgomery enlists as a scout in Bill Williams' wagon train, his job being to guide them to Fort Baxter. Sassy Lola Albright recognizes the scout in his new guise; he saved her uncle's life (Francis McDonald) following a Pawnee ambush, so he can't be all that bad, can he? Besides, Montgomery, shirtless, is a damn sight better proposition than morose Williams, so Albright soon has

George Montgomery, as Pale Arrow, admires Lola Albright in *Pawnee* (1957).

two hunks vying for her attention. In the meantime, Wise Eagle has died, poisoned by Crazy Fox, who is tired of peace treaties and just wants to wade into some good old settler massacring; he also tells Dancing Fawn, "I should grab you by the hair and take you to my tent," a Pawnee version of foreplay guaranteed to freeze any girl's emotions.

It's very easy to pile on the vitriol after sitting through *Pawnee*'s illogical, sometimes incoherent, 80-minute running time. Dramatically speaking, the film is as flat as a pancake and has a stack of shortcomings: Waggner, Louis Vittes and Endre Bohem's script veers from the verbose to the juvenile, occasionally stopping in mid-sentence; Waggner's direction is all over the place, neither one thing nor the other; Hal McAlpin is listed as cinematographer, but there's little evidence, in the countless mismatched scenes, of any expertise in this department; far too many studio-bound shots have wagons trundling past the same old trees and bushes, interspersed with live footage of wagons trundling past the same old rocks (even the town is a stage set); Fox's *Buffalo Bill* is plundered mercilessly for its Indians-on-the-warpath sequences, especially in the final reel where Montgomery, Williams, Albright and company, from a cave entrance, watch 50% of the Battle of War Bonnet Gorge taking place, filched from Fox's actioner—audiences can even spot Joel McCrea at one point! Montgomery drowns Horvath in a river, just as McCrea did to Anthony Quinn in *Buffalo Bill*, and would any cavalry commander worth his salt spring into action on the say-so of a complete stranger who bursts into his office, announces he's Pale Arrow and that the Pawnee are on the warpath, without first checking his credentials? Normally reliable, Dabbs Greer wears a fixed, sour expression, grimacing each time his wagon wheels lurch over a rock, disturbing his heavily pregnant wife, lying comatose in the back; in fact, apart from McDonald, the acting is uniformly lifeless throughout. And repeated views of covered wagons filmed from the ground up against a blue sky show them not to be moving at all! It goes without saying that Albright waltzes off with Montgomery in the end, cold-shouldering nice but dull Williams.

Yes, there's no getting away from it, *Pawnee* is an honest-to-goodness, gold-plated Western clunker, as cheap as they come. But, like most of those guilty pleasures prevalent in the field of horror cinema, it's actually quite congenial for all the wrong reasons. The movie garnered enthusiastic write-ups, *Showman's Trade Review* stating that it was "a good Western ... will grip audience interest." It's only in later years that *Pawnee*'s imperfections become apparent; way back in 1957, paying

customers couldn't have cared less, reckoning that they were getting value for money. Praise be to composer Paul Sawtell in hauling this humdrum disaster out of the mire by conjuring up a raucous soundtrack capable of tickling the aural senses, even if Waggner's cowboy versus Indians turkey fails to tickle the *visual* senses. *Pawnee* deserves a five-star rating just for sheer nerve alone; Scott had his own ground zero moment in the 1950s with *Shoot-Out at Medicine Bend*; so did Murphy and McCrea (*Cast a Long Shadow* and *The Oklahoman*). This, undoubtedly, was Montgomery's.

Hardcore Western buffs would say that things only marginally improved with the last of the star's 1957 Westerns, Warner Bros.' *Black Patch*, written by screen bruiser Leo Gordon. Shot in *noir*-style by producer/director Allen H. Miner, the movie boasted atmospheric monochrome photography courtesy of Edward Colman, an early Jerry Goldsmith score and exemplary performances. It's certainly unconventional in approach for a standard '50s oater, but is it entertaining? The two-minute pre-credit sequence is straightforward cowboy fare and promises much: a lone horse, tethered; two gunshots; black-clad Leo Gordon striding into view, staring at a fresh grave and smiling, riding off, leaving us wondering. But after that, we're plunged into *noir* territory: Gordon is married to Diane Brewster, who once had a serious affair with Marshal Clay Morgan (Montgomery); he's just taken part in a robbery, $40,000 hidden in that grave; youngster Tom Pittman, derisorily nicknamed "Fly-trap" by the locals (the actor tragically died

George Montgomery and Diane Brewster in *Black Patch* **(1957)**

in a car crash a year after completing this picture) moons around Montgomery's office and the saloon, aspiring to be the fastest draw in the West, while no-good hombres Sebastian Cabot and House Peters, Jr. plot to relieve Gordon of the stolen loot. In *Black Patch*, as in all *film noir*, everyone nurses hidden agendas and grievances, Miner filming faces in half-shadow and close-up, townsfolk whispering to one another; there's even a nod in the direction of the vogue of dark '50s detective thrillers, Cabot beating up his mistress, who goes looking to get even with her face badly bruised.

Gordon writes himself out of the scenario after 30 minutes: Imprisoned for the robbery, Peters promises to lend the outlaw a gun to break free if he lets on about the whereabouts of the loot and the proceeds are split down the middle. The plan goes ahead, Gordon is shot twice in the back by Peters while escaping, Montgomery picks up the $20,000 on Gordon's body and is subsequently accused of the killing; he's charged but the verdict is justifiable homicide. From being "Black Patch," he's now "Yellow Patch," a coward shirked by Santa Rita's saintly citizens *and* Brewster. Even Pittman, strapping on Gordon's gun, is ready to shoot his one-time hero anytime he calls it. The second half is devoid of action and begins to pall, umpteen glimpses of Montgomery slumped in a squeaking swivel chair, deep in thought, while Pittman, after Brewster has rejected his fumbling advances (my, how "Fly-trap" has grown up in such a short space of time!) gets drunk and falls in with Cabot; the despot sits in his room playing the harpsichord, Gordon's bank haul hidden among the instrument's innards.

It's all gloom and doom, not helped by a tedious interlude involving a firearms dealer and a limp finale: Pittman calls on Montgomery (*why* does he wear an eye patch, by the way?) to draw, Brewster runs up and informs the kid that Peters shot Gordon dead and the three march off to nab the town's two villains; cue for the end credits to role. "Come on, Carl. We've got a job to do," the marshal says to "Fy-trap" and that's it.

Montgomery thought highly enough of Gordon's screenplay to finance the picture under his own production company, and some flashes of dialogue mirror Gordon's renowned tough screen image, as when he tells picked-upon Pittman, "Someone bothers you, you knock 'em down." But *Black Patch* is too downbeat and oppressive to appeal to a lot of Western fans, with Montgomery looking glum throughout. *Film noir* may have suited some aspects of moviemaking during the 1950s, notably the gangster/detective picture, but in this setting, it seemed at odds with the material. The movie could easily be labeled Montgomery's most unwatchable

Western, whether or not the production values were a notch above most 1957 B-cowboy pictures. It did, however, prove to be a money-spinner at the time and earned backer Montgomery a healthy profit into the bargain.

It was back to widescreen, color and firmly established good old Western practices in Allied Artists' 1958 offering, *Man from God's Country*, directed by Paul Landres. Like the director's previous effort, *Last of the Badmen*, *Man from God's Country* was a talkative affair (script by George Waggner), focusing on strained relationships rather than out-and-out gunfights. It doesn't start out that way: Montgomery (Sheriff Dan Beattie) is first seen throwing a drunk into the street, shouting his favorite line: "Get outta town and stay out." The cowboy goes for his gun and is shot dead. Hauled up in front of a court ("Gun-law is a thing of the past. It's got to go," states the prosecutor), Montgomery is cleared of murder but decides he's had enough of being a lawman if he can't do the job properly. The movie then switches to the well-worn "town against railroad" scenario, with Montgomery joining Gregg Barton's cattle drive and eventually meeting war buddy House Peters, Jr. in Sundown with a view to a ranching partnership. Peters, however, is in the pocket of town boss Frank Wilcox, who is busy preventing ranchers from selling their land to the railroad as this will ruin his freighting commerce. On hand is gunman/bully-boy James Griffith to make sure that anyone crossing his employer and disagreeing with his roughhouse tactics is beaten up or shot in the back.

Man from God's Country is an amiable enough time-passer that doesn't outstay its short 72-minute running time, *Motion Picture Herald* noting that Montgomery was "a key figure in contemporary Western film." Husky voiced song-and-dance dame Randy Stuart turns up as Wilcox's mistress, throwing herself all over Montgomery with wanton abandon. Kim Charney, Peters' young son, hero-worships the ex-sheriff from afar, but Peters falls out with his old pal, unable to break free from Wilcox's clutches, and Griffith lurks and smirks. Waggner conjures up some snappy dialogue, the best of which occurs when Montgomery faces Wilcox and tells him to go for the draw. "I haven't got a gun," says the scared-as-hell businessman. "Why, that's criminal negligence," replies a deadpan Montgomery. The picture culminates in an explosive shoot-out: Griffith and an accomplice are gunned down in Wilcox's saloon while Peters, coming to Montgomery's aid, is wounded and the corrupt town boss receives a bullet from Montgomery, much to the relief of Stuart, whose reward is a proposal from hunky George, which any girl would find difficult to refuse. A decently paced generic B-Western from Allied Artists, which must have looked super-duper in a theater when it was first released in February 1958.

A much-favored Montgomery storyline figured in *The Toughest Gun in Tombstone* (United Artists, 1958), that of a lawman posing as an outlaw to gain access into a gang of no-gooders and bringing them to heel. This time round, he was an Arizona Ranger, Captain Matt Sloane, given the job of busting apart a bunch of desperadoes led by Ike Clanton (Gerald Milton), Johnny Ringo (Jim Davis) and Curly Bill Brosius (Lane Bradford), operating out of Tombstone, Arizona in the 1880s. Arizona is due to become a state, and both the President and Arizona's governor want rid of these varmints who are tarnishing the area with their activities. Montgomery is also bent on avenging the death of his wife, murdered by Clanton in a robbery; his young son (Scotty Morrow) witnessed the killing and is being hunted by the outlaws, getting hit in the arm by a rifle slug at one point. Because Montgomery has to pose as one of the villains he's after, the relationship with the boy reaches breaking point, although blonde Beverly Tyler (last seen in Audie Murphy's *The Cimarron Kid*) does her best to calm things down and mend all the broken fences between father and son.

Earl Bellamy's oater, containing a lively score by Paul Dunlap and another in a long line of decent turns by perpetual co-star Harry Lauter, is standard Montgomery fodder made to please the fans, nothing more, nothing less, as witnessed by *Variety*: "George Montgomery's name will give this picture its strongest momentum." The leading man, dressed in black shirt, black trousers and black wide-brimmed hat, offset by a white neckerchief, looks uncannily like a young Randolph Scott in some sequences, carrying the action on his broad shoulders with dash. Davis and his confederates are rustling cattle across the border, exchanging the herds for Mexican silver and legalizing their profits through the supposedly defunct Barrelhead Silver Mine, the enterprise set up by Tyler's devious father, assayer Don Beddoe. He's shot dead in the last few minutes. There's an all-guns showdown at the mine, and Davis and Milton, riding hard toward Mexico, having abducted Morrow, die at the hands of the ranger captain. Arizona now cleared of its criminal elements and declared a state, Montgomery and Tyler plan to wed and provide a home for cute little Morrow.

Toward the end of 1958, the TV Western began making inroads into areas of mass entertainment, leading eventually to the virtual demise of the Hollywood B-Western second-feature; many of the actors who had graced these once incredibly popular, and profitable, programmers drifted over to the small screen. After completing his next film, *Badman's Country*, Montgomery himself went into television, taking on the role of gun-toting Mayor Matt Rockford in 26 episodes of *Cimarron City*, from September 1958 through April 1959.

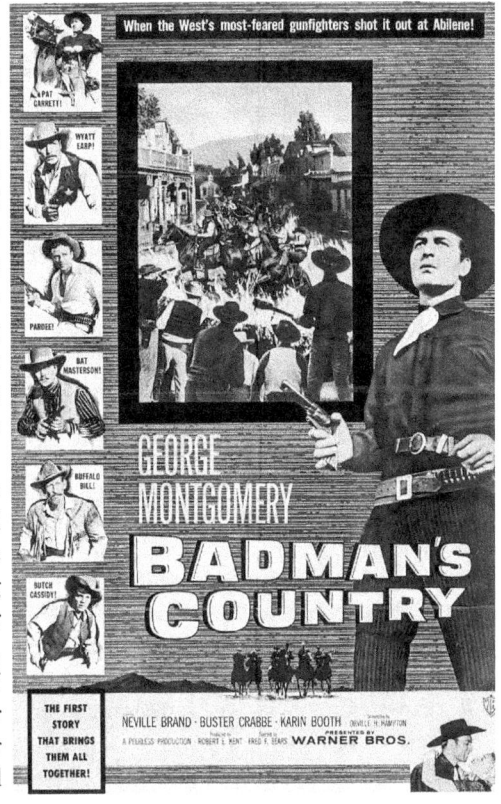

Badman's Country was wrapped up in late 1957 but didn't hit theaters until August 2, 1958; it was one of five films director Fred F. Sears made during 1956/1957 that were released after his sudden death on November 30, 1957 from a heart attack at the age of 44. *Badman's Country*, issued by Warner Bros., had "B-movie" written all over it, as one would expect from Sears and

his long association with quickie producer Sam Katzman (Robert E. Kent produced this picture). Orville V. Hampton's liberty-taking screenplay pitted Pat Garrett (Montgomery), Wyatt Earp (Buster Crabbe), Bat Masterson (Gregory Walcott) and Buffalo Bill (Malcolm Atterbury) against Butch Cassidy (Neville Brand), the Sundance Kid (Russell Johnson), Harvey Logan (Richard Devon) and Black Jack Ketchum (Fred Graham) in Abilene Town. Brand's bunch are planning to grab a half million dollar train shipment while Montgomery, betrothed to Karin Booth, can't make up his mind whether to throw in his badge and head for California for a life of peace or stay put and terminate the outlaws' reign. When timid town marshal Dan Riss begs for Montgomery's assistance in dealing with five desperadoes who have ridden into town, the proclaimed "killer with a badge" does just that, shooting two and placing Johnson, Devon and Graham behind bars. Cowardly mayor Morris Ankrum huffs and puffs, pleading with Montgomery to be the new marshal one minute and despising his deadly use of the gun the next; he then sanctions the release of the three bandits, worried (as are the townsfolk, chicken-hearted to a man) that their presence might draw Brand and his boys into town, but he needn't have worried on that score—aware that Brand has a stooge listening in on the telegraph, Montgomery relays false information, stating that the payroll is in Abilene's bank vault, not on the train, thereby forcing the gang into town where an ambush will be waiting to greet them. The film ends with a smoke-filled gunfight after the bank door has been dynamited, the gang hemmed in by a flaming barricade; Brand is pursued by Montgomery, knocked senseless and arrested. The last word is left to doddery old Buffalo Bill, watching newly wedded Montgomery and Booth speeding off to pastures new: "She said a funny thing. The three of them are going to be very happy," says Booth's father. "That's right," replies Atterbury. "Lorna, Pat and the badge."

A tuneful title theme sung by The Mellowmen (written by producer Kent) sets the tone for this 68-minute stock oater whose cast of B-stalwarts, together with Montgomery and Brand's energetic playing, lift it out of the rut of mediocrity into something worthwhile. One thing that could always be said about these programmers was that the cast, however routine and over-done the material might be, gave it their all, a true mark of their professionalism. But for Montgomery and others of his ilk (apart from the indefatigable Murphy), the last sunset almost beckoned on the horizon; he had one more throw of the dice in the '50s before the decade came to a close, and that was Allied Artists' *King of the Wild Stallions*, released in May 1959.

King of the Wild Stallions was Montgomery's 24th Western of the decade and the last orthodox one he would ever make, an engaging horse opera attractively photographed by Carl E. Guthrie and directed with zest by R.G. Springsteen; the picture featured the same frisky black stallion that had starred in Murphy's *Sierra* and McCrea's *Black Horse Canyon*. Being kiddie friendly meant toning down the gunfights and fistfights, although the climactic punch-up between Montgomery and Emile Meyer was a real bruiser. George seemed to have an affinity with children in his movies—here, young Jerry Hartleben played the son of widow Diane Brewster, whose grazing permit is due to expire. She needs $500 to renew the lease but hasn't the cash. Meyer has given instructions to real estate manager Byron Foulger not to advance her the money so that he can buy up her ranch and land at a rock-bottom price (he's already rustled some of her cattle in

George Montgomery in *King of the Wild Stallions* (1959)

an attempt to ruin her). Then Meyer offers $500 to the man who can bring in Black Lightning, a magnificent wild black stallion running loose among the rocks at Mexican Flats (filming was carried out at the Vasquez Rocks area in California). Montgomery (as Randy Burke), ranch foreman and Brewster's fiancé, and Edgar Buchanan hit upon the idea of roping the mustang and collecting the reward, thus saving her ranch, but Meyer gets wind of their plans, instructing heavies Denver Pyle and Dan Sheridan to thwart their every move. Unbeknown to everyone, Hartleben, with the help of his dog Buzz, has tethered Black Lightning to a tree, using the selfsame rope that Sheridan tried to lasso him with, and gets George to bronco-bust the horse, ride him into town, collect the $500 and prevent Brewster's spread from falling into Meyer's greasy hands.

No one gets killed in *King of the Wild Stallions* (it's not that type of film), only wounded, the baddies herded off to jail in the end, not gunned down in the street. Brewster retains control of her ranch and trots off with Montgomery, Buchanan and Hartleben, with Black Lightning tethered to her buggy. Not a "ride into the sunset" moment, maybe, but as far as George Montgomery's main body of work in the Western genre went, it bore all the hallmarks of being one. Not as wise or as deep as Scott, or as casual as McCrea, or as buoyant as Murphy, Montgomery was, more so than his three compatriots, the personification of the '50s B-Western action hero: A no frills, no fuss, tough-speaking, tough-acting hombre who dispensed with nuances and let his actions speak louder than words, the kind of easily recognizable leading man who, as we have mentioned before, audiences felt comfortable with and kids could ape in their dusty backyards. Glanced over or ignored by many film writers and movie compendiums, George Montgomery came a lot closer to what the paying public expected of their Western heroes than critics give him credit for. In his own unassuming way, he left his mark in the Western Hall of Fame.

Chapter 18
Scott and McCrea at MGM, 1962

Scott was coaxed out of retirement to star in MGM's *Ride the High Country* (aka *Guns in the Afternoon*) after Burt Kennedy gave him N.B. Stone, Jr.'s script to read and it aroused his professional curiosity; he opted to play the bad guy for a change, Gil Westrum. Joel McCrea (as Steve Judd) partnered him, the first time the two had starred together (you can discount that fleeting moment when they were both on the set of 1929's *Dynamite*). The days of the glossy '50s brand of slam-bang, shoot-'em-up, hard ridin' Western, with bulldozing, roughhouse action every few minutes, often comic book in scale, were well and truly over. The myriad of stars who made it all happen—Scott, McCrea, Murphy, Montgomery, Rod Cameron, Rory Calhoun, Jeff Chandler et al.—had more or less decided to call it a day or hung on in there for a few more years, wringing the subject matter dry. Only Murphy forged on ahead, making 15 more oaters between 1960 and 1969. "Gentle" and "restrained" are two words that have been used to describe Sam Peckinpah's reverential journey into Old West nostalgia. We could never describe the stereotypical 1950s horse opera as such; they were more akin to rabid dogs let off the leash, a good reason why the Western from that particular decade is so idolized by diehard aficionados. Therefore, while *Ride the High Country* is a worthy way to end one's 33-year stint in the saddle, it betrays, in some quarters, the less abrasive center that was to afflict the Western genre from 1961 onwards. Westerns underwent a subtle shift in presentation, either lapsing into semi-comical whimsy with silly interludes backed by twee scores or ultra-violence, with no middle ground. Compared to Scott's output of the '40s and '50s and a string of classics including *Abilene Town, Coroner Creek, Return of the Badmen, The Doolins of Oklahoma, The Nevadan, Man in the Saddle, Hangman's Knot* and the Budd Boetticher features, the actor's final Western lacked that "in-your-face" style we were so used to seeing; it's brilliant in parts, not-so-good and rather draggy in others. And for McCrea, too, this would be *his* final testament to the Western if you discount the two forgettable movies he made afterwards.

Fact: In 1952, 85 Westerns were produced by American film companies both big and small; in 1962, 10

Randolph Scott (far left) and Joel McCrea (right) in *Ride the High Country* (1962) in a lobby card using the aborted title, *Guns in the Afternoon*

years later, that figure had shrunk to 18, fully illustrating the public's waning appetite for the Western cycle on top of the studios' disinterest. *Ride the High Country* could therefore be viewed a last-gasp effort to continue with '50s Western values, hoping to attract moviegoers who were now up to their eyes in James Bond gadgetry, British X-rated kitchen-sink dramas and spy/sex thrillers, having become blasé over the whole cowboy and Indians deal. Kicking off in typical 1960s comedic fashion with a camel versus horse race, McCrea canters into town and straightaway puts a business proposition to Scott (that of guarding gold shipments), who is employed in a carnival as sharpshooter "The Oregon Kid." Along for the ride is young Ron Starr, Scott's work buddy, thus forming the youth element in the trio. He's in on Scott's plans to double-cross McCrea in order to get his hands on the gold; Scott reckons he's earned it after all these lean years, whether McCrea likes it or not.

There's an over-emphasis on age both in dialogue and the failing faculties of the two leads in the film's early stages. "I expected a much younger man," the bank manager tells McCrea before hiring him, while Scott (minus his token signet ring and attired in red long johns, but sporting his battered leather jacket) hankers after some "old-time activity" and suffers saddle-soreness. McCrea isn't immune to the aging process, either—he surreptitiously dons reading glasses to peruse his contract, ensuring darn well that his new employer doesn't see him do it. A man's gotta have his pride! Much reminiscing, bickering and remembering of previous places, deeds and people they knew; yep,

Joel McCrea (far left) speaks to Randolph Scott in *Ride the High Country*.

we're on a rite of passage trip here for two worn out saddle tramps, with Starr playing gooseberry, the wet-behind-the-ears upstart who hasn't experienced one iota of what these two grizzled cowhands have in their eventful lifetimes.

The pace slows when they reach R.G. Armstrong's homestead for a rest; the farmer's a bible-thumper, preaching the gospel day in, day out, and forbidding his tomboy daughter (Mariette Hartley) from associating with men. Engaged to be married, she sets her sights on Starr, seeing him as a way out of her repressive existence, thus introducing a love angle, albeit a none-too steamy one: Unlike the oaters of before, Hartley is no glammed-up sexy dame flashing her wares, another nod in the new direction; she's reasonably attractive but certainly no head-turner. After spending the night in a barn, the three ride off into the magnificent California Sierras, brilliantly photographed by Lucien Ballard, George Bassman's Elmer Bernstein–type score far too lush and overbearing in some scenes (gone were the days of the hard-hitting soundtrack by David Buttolph, Mischa Bakaleinikoff, Paul Sawtell and their like). Hartley catches up with them, having walked out on her bullying father, setting the scene for an almighty confrontation when they reach the mining camp; the gal's intent (although petrified) on marrying miner James Drury, one of five loathsome brothers (the Hammonds) whose unwholesome habits would give the desert coyote a bad name.

The movie's lengthy middle section focuses on the squalid camp conditions, dominated by a gaudy brothel, "Kate's Place," the muddy dump run by Edgar Buchanan playing, for the thousandth time in his professional acting career, a drunken judge ("A

Randolph Scott proves that he can ride a camel just as well as a horse, in *Ride the High Country.*

fat-gutted soak," Scott calls him). Hartley, fighting against her fears and revulsion, gets hitched to leering groom Drury in a farce of a wedding ceremony and is almost gang-raped on her wedding night by his grotesque siblings; Scott grabs the license off a hung-over Buchanan at gunpoint and Hartley flees with him, McCrea and Starr ("We're packing gold, not petticoats," complains Scott) and the aggrieved Hammond clan in hot pursuit. Up in the pine-clad hills, Scott casts his eyes lovingly on the gold, knowing that he will have to face his old partner if he wishes to get his hands on it and break their newfound bond. He makes his move but backs down when McCrea pulls a gun on him ("Draw, you damned tinhorn" barks McCrea, as mad as hell). Starr has doubts about the whole enterprise, his mind more on Hartley than the gold; Scott is tied up but let loose when, next morning, the Hammond boys open fire among the rocks. Two brothers are killed, Scott vanishes and we reach the expected showdown at Armstrong's ranch; the farmer lies dead, Drury, Warren Oates and John Anderson waiting in ambush to surprise McCrea and his team.

Peckinpah handles that final showdown with aplomb: "Let's meet 'em head on," McCrea says to Scott, who has turned up to join in the gunfight, charging into the fray on his horse, firing wildly. "Halfway, just like always." "My sentiments exact," grins Scott. The two former marshals walk across the sun-baked yard toward the three brothers, taunting them with insults; bullets fly, Scott is hit in the arm, McCrea receives a fatal chest wound and the Hammonds are slaughtered. Surely Leone must have had this display of bravura in mind when he filmed the seven-minute standoff at the climax to

The Good, the Bad and the Ugly. Likewise, McCrea's dying moments are constructed with dignity. "So long partner," he gasps to Scott who, turning, replies, "See you later," his very final line in his last-ever Western. Levering himself up on one arm, McCrea takes a lingering look at those stunning mountain vistas and sinks to his death out of frame.

Ride the High Country takes on the mantle of a requiem for times past, for Scott, McCrea and those gloriously entertaining, rowdy B-Westerns of the previous three decades which would never, in the way they were conceived and served up to cowboy-hungry audiences, grace the silver screen again. It's an elegiac, mellow picture, not quite up there with the greats, showing two old pros at the end of their working days. Scott quit acting soon afterwards, never bothering with TV or working as a small screen cowboy. He had made his fortune in oil deals over the years and had had enough of the film industry. Old leather face, the model B-Western movie actor of his generation, stayed on his ranch, played golf and avoided, as he always had done, the Hollywood limelight, passing away on March 2, 1987. The legacy left to fans from his 64 Westerns is of inestimable value not only to the history of the cinema, but to the history of Western cinema per se—and they *still* make great viewing. McCrea would go on to star in one inferior picture, *Cry Blood, Apache* (Bronco Films, 1970) and another not-so-bad feature, *Mustang Country* (Universal, 1976). Audie Murphy, in many ways Scott's Universal-International counterpart, carried on up to 1969, bowing out with *A Time for Dying*, while George Montgomery completed his last Western in 1967, A.C. Lyles Productions' low-budget *Hostile Guns*. By 1970, as we have seen in the first chapter of this book, the classic, traditional Western that had enthralled generations of cinemagoers for over half a century was no more, passing like so much tumbleweed in a desert sandstorm—along with the stars, like Randolph Scott, Audie Murphy, Joel McCrea and George Montgomery, who made them.

Essential Scott
Abilene Town
Coroner Creek
Return of the Badmen
The Doolins of Oklahoma
Man in the Saddle
Hangman's Knot
Carson City
7 Men from Now
Ride Lonesome
Comanche Station

Chapter 19
Murphy: 1960-1969

Audie Murphy began his cowboy career in 1950 on a modest budget in *The Kid from Texas*; in 1960, he started the new decade in John Huston's $5,000,000 *The Unforgiven*, another United Artists picture to follow the lusterless *Cast a Long Shadow*. Adapted from Alan Le May's novel by scriptwriter Ben Maddow, Huston's ambitious project, his own personal statement on racial intolerance, was beset with problems on and off set: Audrey Hepburn broke four small bones in her back after falling from a horse (she later suffered a miscarriage as a result); Murphy was almost drowned in a boating accident (America's most decorated war hero couldn't swim); and Huston, when he wasn't arguing with the production's financial backers over what kind of picture this was going to turn out to be and asking for more funds, was busy ferrying contraband art treasures over the Mexican border in Murphy's private plane. But this was an A-production all round; how could it not be, with not only the gamine Hepburn as the female lead but Hollywood heavyweight Burt Lancaster running the show. Lancaster had two expensive and highly successful '50s Westerns under his belt in *Vera Cruz* and *Gunfight at the O.K. Corral*; his was a sure-fire name guaranteed to pull in the punters, or so Huston and his backers thought. Yet the public stayed away. Poor critical reviews had a lot to do with its failure, plus the fact that this was no ordinary Western, rather an extreme example of the issues tackled so magnificently in John Ford's *The Searchers*, also adapted from a Le May novel by Frank S. Nugent. Murphy was to return to Universal and the standard-format Western after this one; until then, audiences had to get used to him playing a hotheaded, hard-drinking, Indian-hating bigot (and with a mustache!) spitting out venomous one-liners, a role he excelled in, giving one of his best-ever screen performances. He jumped at the chance to team up with the fiery director again; Murphy had shone under Huston's guiding hands in *The Red Badge of Courage* nine years earlier and relished the opportunity to repeat the experience. (Kirk Douglas was originally mooted for Murphy's part, reuniting him with Lancaster after their memorable Wyatt Earp/Doc Holliday partnership in *Gunfight at the O.K. Corral*. Huston didn't think it would work, making the leads too top-heavy, so Murphy was hired as second choice.)

Nothing much happens during the first 35 minutes, Franz Planer's vivid photography soaking up the wild Durango vistas in which the drama takes place. Dimitri Tiomkin's grand score does its best to match that arid, sun-scorched Mexican scenery. Lancaster, Hepburn, Murphy, Ma Lillian Gish and young brother Doug McClure join forces with neighbor Charles Bickford's outfit to herd cattle to Wichita. When Bickford's son Albert Salmi is butchered by Kiowa braves after visiting Hepburn and arranging to marry her, the truth comes out: Hepburn, brought into Lancaster's family as a baby after an Indian massacre, is a Kiowa herself and the tribe, led by her brother (Carlos Rivas), wants her back. Old loyalties fall apart: Bickford lays the responsibility for his son's death on Lancaster's family ("A half-breed Injun. Red niggers!" screams his wife at Hepburn), a half-crazed hermit (Joseph Wiseman) is hung after telling all and Murphy, seething with rage at the revelation (Lancaster and Hepburn are making plans to marry—each other!), storms out of his brother's homestead, straight into the arms of man-hungry Kipp Hamilton ("I'm not stayin'. Not for a red-hide nigger!"). Rolling in the hay with

Hamilton, he informs her that, "I've left my Indian lover's family." In a way, his actions are understandable; Murphy's Pa died from a fatal Kiowa spear wound and, ever since, he's hated Redskins. The movie ends in a lengthy Indian raid on the Lancaster ranch in which the body count is extremely high; Gish is killed, Murphy, on his own, comes to the rescue, guns blazing, and Hepburn shoots her brother dead. In the final shot, Huston's camera pans away from the smoking embers of the family ranch, Lancaster, Hepburn, McClure and Murphy framed in a group, facing an uncertain future.

Although painted on a broad canvas and beautiful to look at, Huston later claimed that *The Unforgiven* was the worst film he had ever participated in, while Murphy was dismayed at the marked slump in public enthusiasm. The knives came out, the reception hostile—noted film critic Dwight MacDonald called it, "a work of profound phoniness," while Stanley Kauffmann condemned the picture as "ludicrous." Comparisons with *The Searchers* are inevitable, given the near-identical themes of abduction, mass slaughter and racial disharmony between the white folk and the Indians. Hepburn's character is almost a carbon copy of Natalie Wood's Debbie in the Ford epic as, in a minor way, is Murphy's racist Cash Zachary to John Wayne's Ethan Edwards. But out of the two, *The Searchers* was the more accessible, appealing to a wider audience, plus of course it had Wayne's mighty box-office clout; *The Unforgiven*, a reverse take on *The Searchers*' main plotline, is hard-going in parts, almost surreal (the hunt for half-mad Wiseman during a nocturnal desert storm is especially disturbing). It refused to compromise and by doing so alienated itself from a mass audience. Fifty years on, *The Unforgiven*, faultlessly acted by the entire cast, comes under that well-worn cinematic banner of "flawed masterpiece." It's almost a one-off, as bleak in outlook as the landscape in which the action unfolds. But any fan that discounts a Western that has both Lancaster and Murphy as its two leading men does so at their own cost!

In mid-1959, Murphy struck a deal with Universal to make a series of back-to-basics Westerns with producer Gordon Kay. Each would be budgeted at half a million bucks, shot in a time frame of 18-20 days and feature a hero, a villain and a leading lady. Seven Westerns resulted: *Hell Bent for Leather* (1960), *Seven Ways from Sundown* (1960), *Posse from Hell* (1961), *Six Black Horses* (1962), *Showdown* (1963), *Bullet for a Badman* (1964) and *Gunpoint* (1966). Kay was to Murphy what Harry Joe Brown had been to Scott, their sparse Westerns superficially based on Scott's seven Budd Boetticher outings and looking

all the better for it. For those fans bemoaning the path Murphy had taken since the heady period of *Ride Clear of Diablo* and *No Name on the Bullet*, these Westerns represented a return to the good old days, when Murphy was a straightforward cowboy going about his business with fists and guns. In a decade that saw the gradual decline of the medium-budget Western and the loss of so many actors who had taken part in them, Murphy alone flew the flag, stoically battling on despite dwindling audiences and a general apathy toward the cowboy flick per se. The first two of the seven count among the finest Westerns Murphy ever starred in, streamlined actioners that were far more '50s in approach than '60s: a simple plot, spectacular scenery, plenty of gunplay and the man himself, older, wiser and carrying a certain amount of gravitas etched in those boyish good looks.

Filmed at Lone Pine in the summer of 1959, *Hell Bent for Leather* is a terrific Western that rewards time and time again. Someone at Universal must have been keeping a close eye on what Scott and Boetticher were knocking out; *Hell Bent for Leather* has all the hallmarks of a Boetticher production, expertly directed by George Sherman, who takes full advantage of Lone Pine's towering rock formations (beautifully shot in CinemaScope by Clifford Stine), placing his characters amid this desolate splendor to bestow shape and texture to the narrative. It's a case of wrongful identity for Murphy (as Clay Santell) when he rides into Sutterville after being waylaid in the desert by mass killer Jan Merlin. The townsfolk, attending the funeral of Merlin's latest two victims, reckon that *he's* the killer because he's carrying Merlin's fancy shotgun. Psychotic sheriff Stephen McNally (catch his loony performance in RKO's *Devil's Canyon*, 1953) arrives on the scene; he's been trailing Merlin for an eternity but that's not going to stop him from arresting Murphy, who he knows *isn't* Merlin, and carting him off to a suitable spot to shoot him. By doing this, he can cover himself with glory. He'll be known as the person who has brought the gunman down, even if it's the wrong gunman. What follows is a chase movie, the cast dwarfed by those immense walls of gray rock: Murphy gets free from McNally and pinches a buckboard, hitching up with Felicia Farr, a woman who believes in his innocence; McNally and his posse gallop after the fugitives, demented Merlin one step ahead of both parties. An edgy interlude in Farr's old homestead, where she and Murphy are paid an unwelcome visit from leering Robert Middleton and his two rancid brothers, leads to a dramatic showdown among the boulders; Merlin guns down the crazy sheriff on a ridge and dies from a Murphy dead shot. In the closing

Audie Murphy and Felicia Farr in *Hell Bent for Leather* (1960)

minutes, Sherman pans across the spectacular Alabama Hills as Murphy and Farr leave the accusing makeshift posse to their own guilty deliberations, presumably to head off into the wilderness and play house.

With *Hell Bent for Leather*, Murphy was right back where he belonged, looking at home in the saddle, ably assisted by McNally's sneering, crooked lawman and Farr's feisty heroine (the attractive actress hit it off with Murphy behind the scenes and remains one of the best of his leading ladies). Irving Gertz and William Lava's scintillating score was a treat, adding icing to a very tasty Western cake in which unfathomable, soul-searching undercurrents were replaced by old-fashioned Western thrills and spills.

Seven Ways from Sundown, the last of Murphy's films released in 1960, was just as good. The title refers to his character name, Seven Ways from Sundown Jones, who canters into the town of Buckley minus a sidearm to take up his position as a Texas Ranger. Murphy's a crack-shot with a rifle, though, proving it by shooting a hawk ready to swoop on Venetia Stevenson's pet dog (Murphy carried out a year-long affair with the actress during and after filming). On the orders of Kenneth Tobey, Murphy rides out with grizzled John McIntire to bring in notorious killer Barry Sullivan and be given lessons in handgun shooting by his veteran sidekick. Unbeknown to Murphy, Sullivan shot dead his younger brother, also a Ranger, when Tobey, in on the action, hid behind a rock. Tobey wants Murphy out of the way so that the truth of his cowardice will never be known and is convinced that Sullivan will dispose of him. In an ambush, McIntire is killed but Murphy takes Sullivan prisoner by knocking him clean from his saddle with a single rifle shot. What follows is a lengthy journey through hostile terrain back to Buck-

ley in which the pair form a bond of sorts, mirroring the relationship between Murphy and Dan Duryea in *Ride Clear of Diablo* and also that of Randolph Scott and Claude Akins in *Comanche Station*: All three pictures saw the protagonist, charming and likeable, winning over his captor by force of personality; in the end, villain and hero come to grudgingly appreciate each other's qualities to the extent that by the final reel in *Seven Ways from Sundown*, Murphy is on the point of joining up with Sullivan at his instigation. It's a captivating scenario, wonderfully played by Murphy and Sullivan, who make the most of Clair Huffaker's incisive script, adapted from his novel.

The two play cards, get one over on each other (Sullivan pinches Murphy's gun to find it empty; Murphy is hit, regains consciousness and clubs Sullivan senseless) and banter. "I'm beginning to think that you and me ought to be partners," muses the outlaw. Forced into allowing his captive some leeway, they fend off Apaches and a couple of bounty hunters in Hobbs, where Sullivan has a legion of admirers. "The town comes to life when he's here," says a saloon girl. "He's what every man would like to be but never is." Mowing down Charles Horvath's gang in a skirmish, they reach Buckley and Sullivan is placed behind bars. Murphy tells Stevenson: "I trust him more than any man I know. He's wild and free as a bird." But Tobey lets the killer out on the promise that he won't spill the beans about his own desertion. Sullivan plugs Tobey and rides off, the townsfolk firing wildly. However seduced he has become by Sullivan's charm, Murphy is alarmed when his girl receives a stray bullet but survives. Sullivan returns for a final tete-a-tete, virtually pleading with his young companion to join him in a life of crime: "One last chance to come along with me." It doesn't work. "I've got to stop you, Jim. Turn around." Sullivan does—he really has no alternative—and brings his gun out before Murphy, who takes advantage of the pause and shoots the outlaw. Director Harry Keller allows his camera to pull back from Murphy crouching over Sullivan's still body in the darkened street, reflecting on what has just happened, a downbeat climax but, in the context of what has preceded it, a fitting one to an excellent picture from every point of view; *Variety* called it "A well made oater with high quality acting."

In *Posse from Hell* (1961), set in 1880, Murphy is *meaner* than hell! Playing stopgap lawman-cum-gunfighter Banner Cole, he's a merciless killing machine, intent on exacting retribution on escaped convict Vic Morrow and his group of ruthless gunslingers (Lee Van Cleef among them), who have entered the town of Paradise, having slaughtered four people and the sheriff for kicks, robbed the bank of $11,000 and taken Zohra Lampert hostage, to be used for their pleasure. The movie opens brutally and climaxes violently, Murphy striding toward camera, a look of hate masking his features as he pumps five slugs into Morrow's writhing body. Murphy's ragtag posse includes tenderfoot city banker John Saxon, ex-Union captain Robert Keith, Indian tracker Rodolfo Acosta, Lampert's drink-sodden uncle Royal Dano and young gun Paul Carr. One by one, they fall by the wayside in the pursuit of the four killers until it is left to Murphy and Saxon to finish off the two remaining members of the bunch. After this stormy rite of passage, saddle-sore Saxon now feels more like a man than he ever did dressed up in fancy duds, while romance blossoms on the horizon for new town marshal Murphy and Lampert.

Murphy is uncompromisingly tough in Herbert Coleman's hard-boiled Western. He has little regard for his posse ("None of you are worth a damn.") and even less sympathy for Lampert who, when found, has obviously been subjected to multiple rape ("You're gonna have to live with it," he snarls at the poor girl). When cocksure Carr is found wanting and shot dead, unable to press the triggers of his two Colts and paying with his life, Murphy observes, "Lot of difference between a target and a man." He softens enough in the end to appreciate Saxon's contribution and to think of settling down with Lampert, their final touching scene together in a graveyard giving him time to reflect on his own thoughts and motives.

Joseph Gershenson stitched together a stock score from eight composers' works, mainly from the Universal monster/sci-fi productions of the previous decade, and the strident music played over the credits perfectly establishes the picture's dark tone, sounding just like one of the company's renowned horror themes (the film was classified "A" in Britain). Shot around Lone Pine's Alabama Hills, with a taut script from Clair Huffaker based on his novel, *Posse from Hell* has enough standoffs, gunfights and incidents to appease all Western buffs, in addition to a moral message concerning violence as a way of life. It was Murphy's third outright winner in a row, proving to his detractors that he still had it in him to come up with a classic Western when others of his class were floundering.

Audie Murphy played Tom "Whispering" Smith (right) for one season of *Whispering Smith* in 1961; George Romack played his partner.

Out of his 1960s offerings, *Hell Bent for Leather*, *Seven Ways from Sundown*, *Posse from Hell* and his next, *Six Black Horses*, are as good as anything he made in the early '50s, his flowering period as an actor. They remain outstanding examples of the kind of cowboy picture that will never grace the silver screen again.

Between his busy filming schedules, Murphy found time to star as Tom "Whispering" Smith in 26 episodes of the TV series *Whispering Smith*, aired from May to September 1961 (Alan Ladd had played the character in Paramount's 1948 movie of the same name). By 1962, when *Six Black Horses* was released, Scott had retired (he never delved into the world of the television Western), while McCrea and Montgomery were each to have two more throws of the Western dice. Murphy, among the four champions of the medium-budget Western, was out on his own and still had a few surprises up his sleeve ("I seem to be the only one left," he told a reporter in 1963. "I'll keep on making them until they get wise to me."). Murphy's fourth Gordon Kay production is another deeply rewarding journey into the world of the minimalistic Western, basically centered around a trio of well-rounded characters: Murphy plays drifter Ben Lane, Dan Duryea (their third pairing) a hired gun and Joan O'Brien the feisty woman who hires them to take her across Coyoteras Indian country to meet with her husband in Del Cobre. Director Harry Keller opens with a tremendous tracking shot of Murphy, horseless, lugging his saddle across the striking Utah plains. Roping a wild stallion, he's accused of horse theft by a bunch of homesteaders and saved from a necktie party by gunman Duryea. The two form an unlikely alliance, both rootless and short of a dollar or two, sharing dreams of a better life, until O'Brien appears in the flea-bitten town of Perdido and offers them $1,000 each to guide her across Indian territory to join up with her husband. The trouble is, her husband's dead, shot by Duryea in a gunfight. The black widow wants personal satisfaction and plans to have Duryea killed out on the trip, having failed to nail him in Perdido; her two hired assassins are brought down by Murphy and Duryea in a street fight.

Six Black Horses is similar in execution to Scott's *Ride Lonesome*, almost a companion piece, which isn't surprising: Burt Kennedy was responsible for both screenplays, even doubling up on the scene (and dialogue) in which Murphy is asked by a Coyoteras chief to barter O'Brien for a horse. And note the piece in the beginning when footsore Murphy takes off a boot to inspect his sock—Scott did the selfsame thing in *The Tall T*! Murphy gets to learn about O'Brien's hidden agenda but falls for her anyway, leading to a difference of opinion between the two men over the woman's true intentions. After a highly charged encounter with three scalp-hunters who need fresh mounts and a skirmish with the Indians, the unavoidable showdown takes place, even though neither man wishes it to happen. "I've never gone against anybody I knew before, let alone liked. It's a fact, Ben. I *like* you. I'm beggin' you Ben, catch up your animal." Duryea does his best to avoid a standoff, but Murphy's having none of it. "This is as far as we go, Frank." Duryea is outgunned and Murphy honors his partner's wishes, that he be buried in a hearse drawn by six black horses. The funeral over and done with, Murphy and O'Brien take off for Montana where he plans to build a ranch and raise kids.

All dressed up in Maury Gertsman's gleaming cinematography, taking full advantage of Utah's magnificent canyon country, this great-looking Western was unaccountably slammed by the papers when first released, taking the form of a Murphy backlash. How, for example, the *New York Times*' film critic could label it "pathetic" is beyond belief. If only they could have seen what became of the genre in years to come, they wouldn't have been so unduly harsh in their put-downs. Ignore those barbed comments: *Six Black Horses* is a Western beauty, completing a compulsive quartet of Murphy sagebrush sagas that he wouldn't repeat again (with the exception of 1964's *Bullet for a Badman* and 1966's *Gunpoint*). Akin to the Scott/Boetticher Westerns in so many areas of filmmaking, these

pictures defined Audie Murphy in the 1960s. What came after would never quite match up to them.

Photographed in black-and-white, Murphy's first 1963 entry, *Showdown*, was gritty and dour. The cowboy star kicked up a huge amount of fuss over the lack of color, vowing never to make a non-color movie again. *Variety* backed him up, calling the film "routine ... the lack of color is no help." He didn't, but by then Universal, who cut costs in this production, were losing faith in the Western picture and all that it had stood for; as a result, R.G. Springsteen's effort showed a marked downturn in quality compared to the four crackers that had preceded it. Murphy played Chris Foster, a cowhand who, with his gambling, drinking pal (Charles Drake) is arrested after a saloon fracas. The partners then get caught up in Harold J. Stone's shenanigans after the outlaw and his gang of criminals escape from a novel way to contain lawbreakers—chain them by the neck to a post in the middle of town. Stone (a great huffing and puffing turn from the Hollywood B-heavy) releases Drake on condition he rides back to town and cashes in stolen bonds worth $12,000; Murphy is held prisoner in lieu of the ransom. Drake returns, but without a dollar: He sent the money to girlfriend Kathleen Crowley for cheating on her, so Murphy gallops off to apprehend Crowley; it's now Drake's turn to be kept captive until the cash turns up.

There's no getting away from the fact that for once, the black-and-white format drags the film down, lending it the look and feel of a '40s Western. Also slowing the pace is Crowley's over-emotive performance, particularly in a lengthy scene where she explains to Murphy her past problems with Drake and why she is so mentally unstable. To even the score, Springsteen treats us to a fabulous panoramic shot of a horse-less Murphy (he was always losing his horse in these pictures!) striding across the desert, determined, against the odds, to win the day, the Lone Pine Sierras shimmering in the heat—nearly all Murphy pictures had to include a symbolic few moments, showing him battling alone against the natural elements, and this sequence ranks with the best. The director expertly choreographs the final gunfight between Murphy and Stone, bullets flying in the street before Audie brings the burly killer down with three slugs. At the close, he wanders into the arms of Crowley, her dissolute boyfriend having been blasted in the back by Skip Homeier. Color would have given *Showdown* the extra patina it needed, to make the action more enjoyable. As it is, the final product mirrors Murphy's discontent; good in parts, patchy in others.

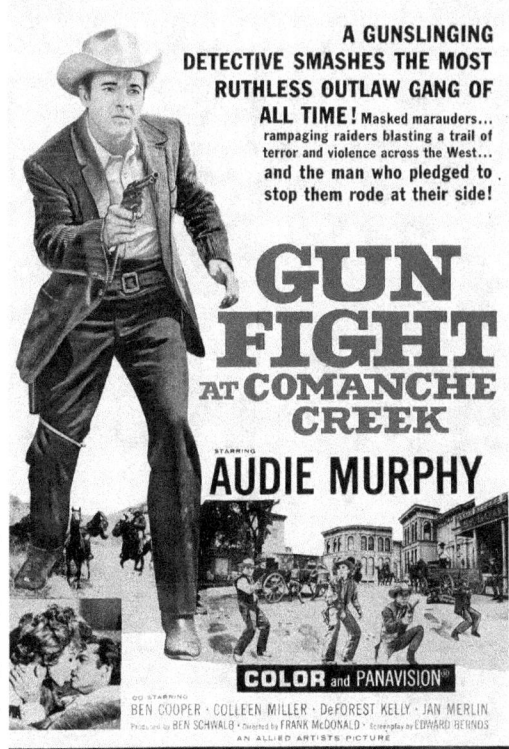

Murphy moved over to Allied Artists for the second of his 1963 releases, *Gunfight at Comanche Creek*, an inferior remake of George Montgomery's 1957 opus, *Last of the Badmen*. "It was a bottom-of-the-bill potboiler," admitted co-star Jan Merlin soon after completion. "We finished the movie, went home and forgot about it." His sentiments would probably sum up what many fans would think about the picture, the first of Audie's outings in this decade to look like a typical '60s Western: Drab color photography, unimaginative score (Miles Skarlin), a so-so script written by B-movie veteran Edward Bernds and the leading man himself looking older, tired and slightly ragged around the edges. Fifties gloss and vibrancy had been replaced by dullness and lethargy, as it would do so from now on; the plot was middling, maybe worth a second airing, but in this case, the execution stayed firmly rooted in mediocrity and Murphy, although acting the part of agent Bob Gifford with assurance, seemed to have lost his boyish charm.

It's 1875: An outlaw gang led by unhinged killer DeForest Kelley (*Star Trek* fame beckoned on the horizon for this excellent actor) has discovered a novel way to rake in the dollars: Bust into jail, release the prisoner, use him for bank jobs and, when the bounty is high, kill him and collect the reward money. Trouble is, their last stooge was a government undercover agent, shot down in the line of duty; Murphy (described as "Someone smart, tough, never loses his head.") and Merlin are tasked by their detective agency to infiltrate the gang and seek redress by bringing them to justice. Murphy, posing as make-believe bank robber Judd Tanner, is jailed, then sprung from behind bars, with Merlin spying on Kelley's hideout, the Circle W Ranch, from an overlooking

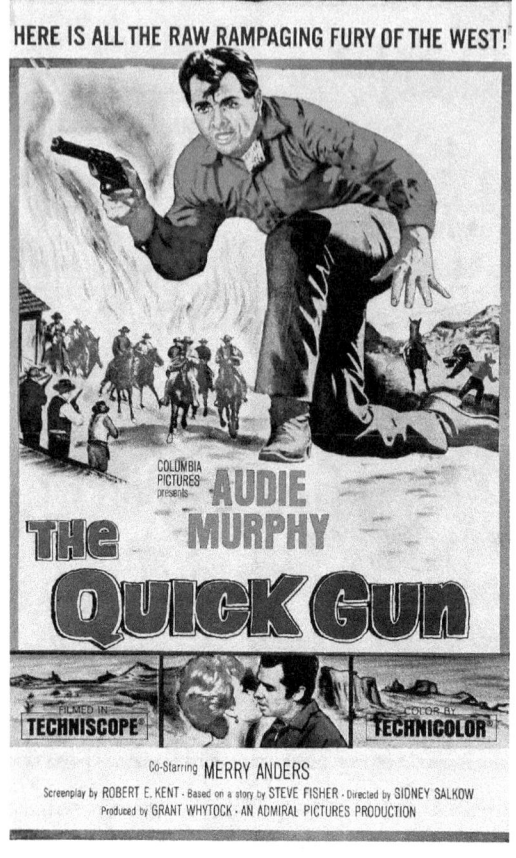

ridge. Unusually for a Murphy oater, there is no female love interest. Colleen Miller plays a saloon owner who womanizing Audie makes a grab for in the film's first half, but this proposed love tryst is abandoned, never to return. After Merlin is caught out and shot dead, Murphy and Michael T. Mikler are forced into robbing Comanche Creek's bank; the resultant gunfight with surrounding agents reveals Marshal John Hubbard as the brains behind the operation. Kelley and Hubbard surrender, and for once, the film closes without any loving arms to embrace our hero.

Reed Hadley narrates in deadpan *Dragnet*-style, lantern-jawed villain Mort Mills stirs up trouble and young outlaw recruit Ben Cooper, wanting out, is murdered by Hubbard to prevent him from upsetting the lawman's corrupt activities. Flatly directed by Frank McDonald, *Gunfight at Comanche Creek* needed far more zing and zest to bring it to life; it was Murphy's first below-average outing of the 1960s and it wouldn't be his last. But all credit to him; he alone was giving the genre his all when many others had simply given up and turned their backs on one of cinema's topmost forms of entertainment. Figuratively speaking, he was giving it his best shot. For that reason alone, we must thank our lucky stars that he was content to crank out substandard fare such as this to keep Western fans happy.

From Allied Artists to Columbia—Sidney Salkow's *The Quick Gun*, released in 1964, was a slight improvement on *Showdown* and *Gunfight at Comanche Creek*. Murphy was back looking refreshed and youthful, and the pleasing color photography added an extra sheen to what was basically a rehash of two previous United Artists' programmers: 1955's *Top Gun* and 1960's *Noose for a Gunman*. Steve Fisher wrote the stories for all three, while producer/writer Robert E. Kent cooperated on *Noose for a Gunman* and *The Quick Gun* (Kent scripted the Murphy remake), with bad guy Ted de Corsia starring in the latter two. Fearsome outlaw leader de Corsia wants ex-gunman Murphy (as Clint Cooper) to hook up with his gang; Murphy, against the idea, kicks ashes in his old boss' face and gallops into Shelby, where he's about as welcome as a tick on an old hounddog. Seems that two years back, he shot dead Walter Sande's two sons after Sande tried to relieve Murphy of his ranch. The town lays the blame on Murphy good and square and, to make matters worse for Audie, his one-time sweetheart Merry Anders is getting hitched

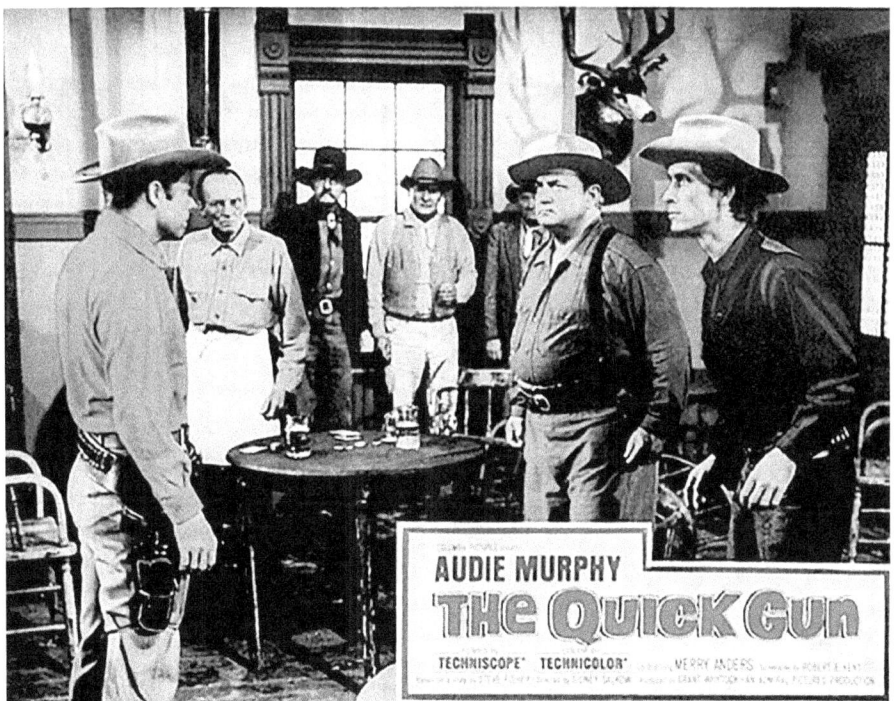

Audie Murphy squares off against Walter Sande and Rex Holman in *The Quick Gun* (1964).

to Sheriff James Best in a couple of weeks. Sande and nephew Rex Holman are also gunning for Murphy, not content to let matters rest over the deaths of Sande's boys. When the shunned cowpoke warns the locals that de Corsia is on his way with over a dozen men to rob the bank, women and children take refuge in the church (most of their men folk are away on a cattle drive) and barricades are erected at both ends of town to prevent access. Night falls, the signal for an attack from the gang; Murphy, after shooting Sande and Holman in self defense, joins in the fray, having hastily been made town sheriff; Best has sacrificed himself to enable Murphy to marry Anders, de Corsia refusing to parley and putting a bullet in him. The whole cast is wiped out in the overwhelming assault and it's left to Anders to shoot villainous Mort Mills in the back at the exact moment Murphy beats de Corsia to the draw. The lovers walk off past the barricade's smoking rubble, bodies strewn among the wreckage (as if in a Shakespearean melodrama) and Murphy stating that no more guns will figure in his future.

In the conditions surrounding the declining state of the Western in the 1960s, *The Quick Gun* just about passes muster, the new Techniscope widescreen process and Murphy's name drawing in the fans. However, the urgency and vibrancy of what Murphy was appearing in a decade back is missing and it shows. That once-fresh pool of talent, elevating the standard trail buster to essential cinema viewing on a Saturday night, was fast becoming stagnant; now and again, the star appeared to be simply going through the motions. He did, however, buck up enough enthusiasm to produce one more minor classic for shrinking audiences, returning to Universal for 1964's *Bullet for a Badman*.

It was just like old times again: The familiar Universal logo, Frank Skinner's raucous music, Joseph F. Biroc's gleaming photography highlighting Utah's Snow Canyon region, an insightful script by Marvin H. Albert and Mary and Willard Willingham and forceful plotting from director R.G. Springsteen. Topped by a splendid cast including Darren McGavin, Ruta Lee, Alan Hale, Jr. and Skip Homeier, *Bullet for a Badman* was a splendid return to former glories for Murphy, a Western with real depth. Many fans rate this picture as his finest '60s oater; certainly, it's one of his most scenic, the rugged Utah hills filmed to absolute perfection. Echoes of the Anthony Mann/James Stewart classics of the early '50s abound in this taut-as-a-bowstring tale of old loyalties put to the test and the morality of violence set against that of greed.

Former gunslinger/Texas Ranger Murphy (playing Logan Keliher) is now a family man, putting aside his .45 in favor of farming and raising his young stepson Kevin Tate with wife Beverly Owen. Short of cash, he rides into town and asks former girlfriend Cece Whitney for a $500 loan at the same time that ex-partner McGavin and his gunmen are robbing the Griffin Bank. In the ensuing gunfight, McGavin's bunch are slaughtered; the leader, wounded, heads for Murphy's ranch. Owen is his ex-wife, Tate his son and McGavin wants Murphy dead—for pinching them from him while he was in jail ("I'm takin' you back," he shouts, grabbing Owen and kissing her hungrily). McGavin leaves with the stolen money, Murphy arrives, learns of his visit and straps on his gun belt ("I was praying you'd never have to use that gun again," Owen says). McGavin finds his way to a remote shack, home to fiery Ruta Lee, who decides to throw in her lot with him for a life in El Paso. But Murphy crashes through the door to upset their plans, and so does a motley posse consisting of gunmen Skip Homeier, Berkeley Harris, Alan Hale, Jr., Edward Platt and grizzled guide George Tobias.

The scriptwriters now present us with a journey back to civilization through hostile terrain, beset with problems. Should Murphy share the proceeds of the $20,000 with the others instead of giving it back to the bank? How will they face up to an Apache war party on their trail? And will wily, smooth-talking McGavin free himself and shoot Murphy dead, even though he doesn't really want to? ("I'm gonna kill you for taking them away from me.") Springsteen utilizes the scenic splendor of Utah's canyon country for cumulative impact as the eight face warring Indians and each other's personal agendas. Holed up in a box canyon, Tobias reminisces about times past, the disappearance of Old West times and the code of violence with Murphy. "Life's sort of passed us by," he muses. "Now fighting Indians, well, that makes us of some use again." After routing the Redskins (Lee and Platt are killed in the raid), Murphy faces up to a furious gun battle among rocks with the others, leaving McGavin with a fatal gunshot wound. Murphy escorts him back to his ranch, where the outlaw saves his ex-partner by taking a bullet from Homeier who, also wounded, has followed them back. "You're doing a good job, Logan, with my, er, your son," he gasps with his dying breath, thus redeeming himself. "Yuh. With our son," responds Murphy, sad at the loss of his double-dealing but eminently likeable old foe. Walking off with his family, we assume that Murphy keeps the loot for himself; after the trials and tribulations he has just gone through, who could honestly blame him.

In 1954, 58 Westerns were produced in America, and one in Mexico. In 1964, when Murphy's third feature of that year, *Apache Rifles*, came out, the total was 23; 16 from America, the remainder from Europe. The traditional American Western was on the verge of extinction, but Murphy was carrying on regardless, almost an anachronism among the soon-to-be-released stylistic violence of *A Fistful of Dollars* and its ilk. 20th Century Fox's cavalry versus Indian saga, set in Arizona, 1879, was yet one more take on those pesky Redskins (in this case the Mescalero Apaches) straying from their reservation and causing no end of trouble en route—if you think you've seen it all before, you have, in George Montgomery's far superior *Indian Uprising*. Murphy played Indian-hating Jeff Stanton, an officer whose father had been cashiered out of the army, charged with disgracing himself in the line of duty by being too friendly with the Indians, leading to a wholesale cavalry massacre. Determined to restore the family reputation, Murphy attempts to make peace with Chief Joseph Vitale and his son, Michael Dante, by driving the miners out of their territory, even though he says of the Redskins, "The only God they know is war." But lowlifes L.Q. Jones, Ken Lynch and Charles Watts have other ideas, having just discovered a rich lode: They murder a prospector, stick an arrow in his back and, before you know it, Murphy is relieved of his post, the army slaughter an Indian settlement and Vitale's warriors are on the warpath.

Directed by veteran William Witney, who clocked up dozens of low-budget Westerns and Republic serials in his prolific career, the main problem with *Apache Rifles* is one

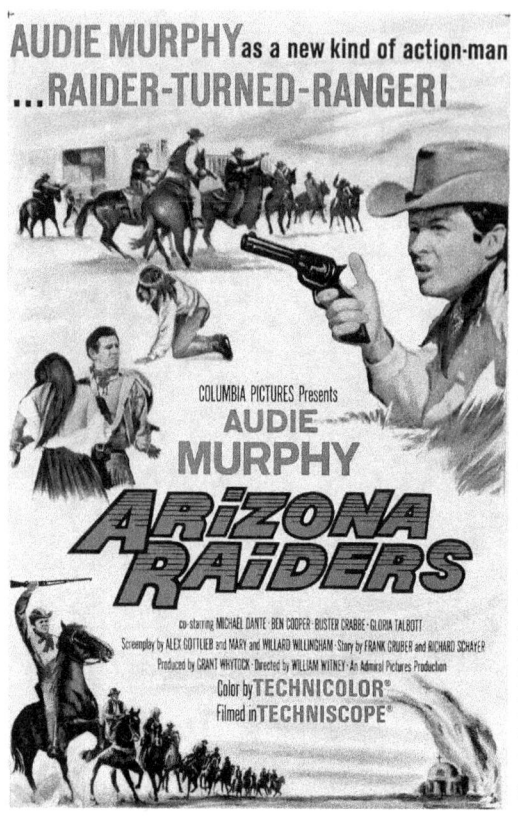

of length: At 92 minutes, it's a good 10 minutes too long. In the movie's central section, the pace drags, with Murphy scurrying here, there and everywhere in an effort to stave off a full-blown Apache war. The love triangle—Dante loves half-Comanche missionary Linda Lawson, who falls for Murphy—doesn't exactly set the screen alight with passion; Murphy gets her in the end after Dante and the tribe journey to a reservation in Texas. The first tightly edited 25 minutes is the best, Murphy ordering the weary troops of B company out into the desolate wilderness to apprehend Vitale, the actors looking minute against Red Rock Canyon's mighty cliff faces (these are the same striking rock formations that featured so prominently in *Drums Across the River*). If only the remainder of *Apache Rifles* had built on that promising opener, this would have been a Murphy effort of some merit. The end result is disappointing, a standard cowboys and Indians flick that runs out of steam well before Dante confers his blessing on the lovers and departs for pastures new.

The same team of Murphy, Witney, producer Grant Whytock and Michael Dante was retained for Columbia's *Arizona Raiders*, released in 1965, another sloppy remake of a key George Montgomery Western, *The Texas Rangers*. We have to express admiration for Murphy for persevering in what had now become very much derivative fare, and *Arizona Raiders* was just that—derivative. We're back with Quantrill's Raiders again, Murphy (Clint Stewart) and Ben Cooper the youngest of the bunch. In a town ambush, Quantrill is wounded and captured, and Murphy and Cooper, also apprehended, receive 20 years hard labor. George Keymas takes over as *de facto* leader of the gang when Quantrill dies, Michael Dante his number two, the pair embarking on a series of gold shipment robberies and setting up camp in a Yaqui village. Into the action steps Texas Ranger Buster Crabbe, who arranges for Murphy and Cooper's release (a faked escape) on condition that they nail Keymas' mob, but is Murphy to be trusted? He can't decide whether to go along with Crabbe's plans or not; however, when his kid brother (Ray Stricklyn), also a Ranger, is gunned down by a member of the outlaws, Murphy swears to get even, vowing to kill Keymas and end his reign of terror.

The influence of the Spaghetti revisionist horse opera, making headway into U.K. and U.S. cinemas, was seeping into the American Western, and it shows here: blood by the bucketful, peaceful Indians gunned down without mercy, close-ups of arrows in

backs and torture by cactus (one scene has the Indians hurling cactus branches down upon the outlaws' heads). Allied Artists' one-time Queen of Horror, Gloria Talbott, turns up as a Yaqui woman terrorized by Keymas, and there's no romantic compensation in store for Audie: After the gang is defeated, he returns to the village, only for Talbott, looking drab and tired, to state that she'll be taking her vows (she also played an Indian lass in McCrea's *The Oklahoman*). "I'll be a good nun," she wanly smiles, dashing any hopes of a roll in the hay for our hero, who promptly turns on his boot heels and gallops off with Crabbe.

One sequence alone underlines the dramatic lulls inherent in this picture: Murphy stalks Keymas across adobe rooftops, a cat-and-mouse episode that should have guaranteed a degree of suspense. Instead, Richard LaSalle's nondescript score fails to inject the right amount of "oomph" needed and the result, along with Witney's haphazard direction, is curiously flat. The Westerns of the previous decade benefited from exciting soundtracks to propel the action along; *Arizona Raiders* cried out for a score to rouse the senses but didn't get one. And as in *Gunfight at Comanche Creek*, an unnecessary voice-over narration also became an intrusion. The widescreen photography is passable, and Murphy's one good scene is with Stricklyn, cradling him as he dies in his arms. Otherwise, his performance is solid and reassuring in a picture that, were he not in it, audiences wouldn't give it a second's thought.

Murphy's very last Universal Western, *Gunpoint*, released in 1966, contained that requisite hard-hitting score missing from *Arizona Raiders*, and it struck with a vengeance. Composer Hans J. Salter, under contract with the company since 1937, produced a stirring soundtrack to send Audie on his way; his lilting song "Far Away" is used as a leitmotif throughout, including the title theme, a lovely tune of the kind sadly missing

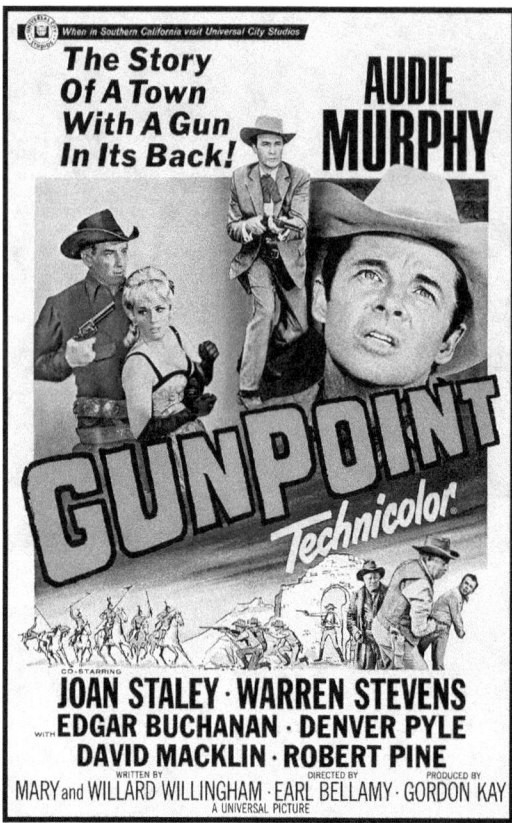

from today's empty-headed blockbusters. Shot against a stunning backdrop of canyons and gorges at St. George, Utah, *Gunpoint* could have been made in 1956, not 1966; it harks back to a time when the cowboy flick dominated the cinema scene, a fitting swansong to Murphy's 16-year career with Universal-International.

The story is nothing new: Murphy (as Sheriff Chad Lucas) and deputy Denver Pyle attempt to stop a train robbery in its tracks (this long opening sequence is filched direct from *Night Passage*; Murphy evens wears the same leather garb as the Utica Kid to ensure the scenes match). Pyle, nursing a grudge because the authorities chose a younger man for sheriff over his older head, shoots Murphy and the robbery, led by bandit Morgan Woodward, proceeds as planned; back in Lodgepole, Colorado, Murphy turns up wounded, unaware that Pyle fired the shot, and forms a posse to hunt down Woodward and his villains, who are holed up just across the New Mexico state line in Warren Stevens' saloon, The Texas Lady. Following a fracas, Woodward and his mob ride off with Stevens' fiancée Joan Staley and the stolen cash; Murphy, Pyle, Stevens and a ragtag posse gallop off in pursuit, meeting en route Edgar Buchanan's trio of murderous trappers, who also want to get their grubby hands on the $20,000 and Murphy (who is Staley's ex-beau from years back) finally gets her to himself after the entire cast is killed in one melee after another.

Writers Mary and Willard Willingham take a familiar plot, aided by Earl Bellamy's brisk direction, and they somehow manage to keep things fresh. There's a lot going on here. Will oily, quick-talking Stevens relinquish his hold on Staley to Murphy without the need to pull a trigger on him? When will embittered Pyle make his move and finish off his young rival ("Passed over in favor of a punk kid," he grumbles). After escaping from the outlaws, does Staley (a vivacious actress not given her worth, becoming stuck in TV work at the expense of film) know more about them than she's letting on (her brother is a gang member)? Against this background of double-cross and deceit, the posse has to struggle up a near-vertical cliff face, an unusual, enthralling sequence directed with dash by Bellamy, and tackle warlike Apaches. The director even throws in a bruising fistfight between Murphy and hulking Kelly Thordsen, one of Buchanan's two sidekicks, Murphy flooring the brute with a series of right hooks and left uppercuts. If you recognize the horse stampede and the nighttime raid on Murphy's camp, you'll be right; they were pinched from *Sierra* and *Gunsmoke* respectively. At one point, Staley says to Murphy, "You're not the man I once knew." "I'm older," he replies. "But you're cold and hard now," she retorts. After playing in Westerns for 16 years, the Murphy persona had indeed hardened, from the tough but softer "Kid" of the '50s to the callous-minded, more experienced individual of the '60s. There were only three more outings to go for Murphy, but *Gunpoint* would have, and should have, been the more fitting picture to bow out on. And when he and Staley hold each other at the end to the sound of Salter's nostalgic-sounding "Far Away," you cannot help feeling a sense of loss at the passing of this type of fare and the stars that made them so appealing.

During the mid-1960s, many American actors were crossing the Atlantic to Europe and appearing in Spaghetti Westerns, following in the successful boot prints of Clint Eastwood. Murphy had a stab at it himself in Columbia's *The Texican* (1966), but whether or not it was worth the effort is open to conjecture; does it rate as one of his worst '60s features, or an honest attempt to depart from the norm and come up with something different? After being used to watching Murphy riding against a Lone Pine or St. George, Utah canvas, it's something of a shock to see him towing a prisoner through the dried-up gulches of Barcelona's Catalonia region, Francisco Marin's rather washed-out color photography lending the sequence a muddy air. Audie plays Jess Carlin, a gunman out to avenge the killing of his newspaper reporter brother, who has been murdered by Rimrock's head honcho, Broderick Crawford, under threat of exposure. That's the story in a nutshell. Murphy, a $500 price tag on his head, deals with a couple of bounty hunters, wins a shoot-out in a windy, dusty street with three gunslingers, has two women (Diana Lorys and Luz Marquez) eying him up, engages in a few violent bar brawls (no stunt doubles were used to save on costs) and puts paid to Crawford in the final reel.

The Spaghetti Western was quirky to say the least, and *The Texican* is no different from the rest: Nico Fidenco's ever-present soundtrack sounds as though the composer borrowed heavily from Ennio Morricone's *For a Few Dollars More* score sheet; there's a myriad of badly dubbed secondary characters up to the kind of facetious shenanigans that sometimes marred these pictures; the plotting is all over the place; and Spanish adobe hovels populated by Spanish/Italian actors stand in for the real Wild West. Lesley Selander directed, the man behind Scott's *Tall Man Riding*, Montgomery's *Dakota Lil* and countless other medium-budget oaters, bowing out in 1968 with *Arizona Bushwackers*. Murphy appears slightly bemused throughout the film's 91-minute running time and too clean-cut (Italian Westerns were renowned for their grubby look), no doubt wondering what on earth was taking place on and off set, while heavy-drinking Crawford barges through the proceedings like a bull in a china shop. There are plenty of lousier Spanish/Italian Westerns out there, made in this fretful period, and, to its credit, Murphy's contribution just about manages to rise above the pack. It's certainly no *Fistful of Dollars* but then, many of these gimcrack Westerns aspired to be as great as Sergio Leone's groundbreaking masterpiece.

Audie Murphy's last Western proper was Columbia's offering *40 Guns to Apache Pass*, veteran William Witney at the helm for what turned out to be a serviceable but tired-looking cavalry versus Indians oater. It's watchable for three reasons: Murphy's in it; co-star Kenneth Tobey, an actor of vast experience, never really given his due in Hollywood, plays a meddlesome, double-crossing army corporal, and location work takes place among Red Rock Canyon's oft-used, but eminently watchable, cliffs, mesas and buttes in California. This was 1967, the year in which the highly profitable British "X" certificate Western, spearheaded by Leone's *A Fistful of Dollars* and *For a Few Dollars More*, dominated the cinema scene. A quick look at the cowboy flicks released that year shows that the traditional American Western was, like its stars, receding into the sunset:

Any Gun Can Play, *Bang Bang Kid*, *A Bullet for the General*, *Johnny Yuma*, *Payment in Blood*, *The Hellbenders*, *Dos Cruses en Danger Pass*, *El Pistolero Desconocido*, *Django*, *Kill* and *The Stranger Returns*. All these were so-called "Euro-Westerns," produced by Spanish and Italian film companies. Clint Eastwood, and a host of Eastwood imitators, was the new icon on the block, appealing to a more adult audience, and as a result, the British U-rated *40 Guns to Apache Pass* which, had it been issued 10 years earlier, would have enthralled the kids, went out with a whimper, not a bang, on the U.K. circuits. Murphy would go on to play a small role in Budd Boetticher's *A Time for Dying* two years later, but as far as full-length Western motion pictures went, this was his final shot.

In 1869, Apache chief Cochise (Michael Keep) has vowed to murder every white man, woman and child in Arizona. As Captain Bruce Coburn, hardened cavalry officer Murphy is rounding up the under-threat palefaces and escorting them to a temporary fort at Apache Wells for protection. En route, he gets involved in a tussle with loud-mouthed Tobey (you'd have thought that the movie's producers would have colored Tobey's stunt double's hair sandy to match his own!) and threatens to bust him down to private if he doesn't behave. Tobey doesn't forget the threat. When a detail of men ("Not exactly the cream of the crop," Murphy drily observes) is ordered to collect 40 repeating rifles from scouts at Hatchet Rock, Tobey volunteers to go, planning on dealing with Murphy and steal the rifles, selling them to Cochise for gold. Along for the ride are rookies Michael Blodgett and Michael Burns. Blodgett's looking forward to the action, but his brother is terrified at the thought of a close encounter with bloodthirsty Injuns. On their first confrontation with Cochise's men, Blodgett is killed, Burns cowering in fright, too scared to assist. Tobey turns the tables on the troops and grabs the rifles, but Murphy steals the rifles back, retaining five and sending Burns (now having proved himself in battle) with

A French poster for *A Time for Dying* (1969)

the rest back to the fort. Audie, with five rifles strategically placed among rocks, now has to deal with Cochise and his marauding bucks single-handed, as well as treacherous Tobey. Reinforcements arrive and the remaining Apaches scatter, leaving Murphy to engage in a bloody shoot-out with Tobey; both are riddled with bullets, but Murphy survives. The last image we see of him is back at the fort, embracing Laraine Stephens under the American flag, a symbolic salute to times past if ever there was one.

Give William Witney his due; the director managed to drum up some energetic action sequences, spoiled to some extent by Jacques R. Marquette's less-than-sparkling photography of the rugged locale, Richard LaSalle's typically '60s lukewarm score and intrusive narration ("Flat and stale," said one critic). *40 Guns to Apache Pass* was one of the very last of the medium-budget sagebrush sagas of the type that had thrilled moviegoers just a few years earlier, a '50s movie in '60s guise. Scott had quit the industry, McCrea had two more movies left in him and Montgomery had bowed out with *Hostile Guns* in 1967. For these once Kings of the Open Range, the crowd-pullers that had intoxicated adults and children alike, their time was almost at an end.

A chaotic muddle, or was this a last-ditch attempt to keep American Western values and myths alive and kicking? Budd Boetticher had little regard for *A Time for Dying*, released by independent outfit Fipco in 1969, produced by Murphy, who featured in a cameo role as Jesse James. Viewed today, it contains everything that made the mid- to-late 1960s American cowboy picture so difficult to watch or stomach, a kind of low-budget take on 1965's *Cat Ballou*, the movie that started the trend in these noisy, spoof semi-comic Westerns: a distinctly modernistic, un-Western score from Harry Betts; hollering cowpokes forever shooting, falling off horses, acting the fool and yelling at each other; a paper-thin plot, scripted by Boetticher; an instantly forgettable lead in Richard Lapp (who only made one other oater after this, 1970's *Barquero*); veteran thespian Victor Jory hamming it up to epic proportions as whiskey-swigging Judge Roy Bean; and a four-minute appearance by the one person fans most wanted to see (the film wasn't distributed until 1972 in some parts of Europe and was hardly ever screened in the United Kingdom. It surfaced in the States in 1982). Lapp arrives in rowdy Silver City, two revolvers strapped to his waist, anxious to prove himself as a gun hawk of some repute. He rescues soon-to-be prostitute Anne Randall in a flapping pink dress from the clutches of the drink-fueled townsfolk, rides to the town of Vinegaroon, is arrested for indecency for spending the night with the gal, then is married to the lass by

Jory, has a drunken wedding ceremony, encounters an aging Jesse James and is finally outgunned by scabby outlaw Bob Random in Silver City because his Colts slip from his sweaty hands. Cue for Randall to gather up her grubby pink skirts and leave, another girl coming in by stage to take her place.

In the 43rd minute, Lapp gets to meet Murphy, playing a paunchy, bearded Jesse James, who imparts a few words of wisdom ("When you get tired of being a farmer, look me up.") and then rides off with his gang after four minutes of screen time, having brought just a little bit of sense and decorum into the shambolic undertaking. Although the movie's only 71 minutes long, the silly antics and sappy music will make even the most dedicated diehards sink into cinematic depression, yearning for past glories, and murmur to themselves, "Where did it all go wrong?" Along with *Cast a Long Shadow*, the prophetically titled *A Time for Dying* marks the low-water level of Murphy's Western career, though his input was minimal. It was also an all-time low for Boetticher as well.

Audie Murphy never had the chance to expand his often-overlooked talents into other areas of cinema; the gods had decreed otherwise. On May 28, 1971, on his way to a business trip, his private plane crashed into the side of a mountain in thick fog, in the Appalachian range, near Roanoke, Virginia, killing him and five others. Murphy was 45, a month away from his 46th birthday. It was a tragic end for the boyish-looking actor who, without too much in the way of performing virtuosity (which he was always the first to admit), had nevertheless managed to star in a string of cowboy movies essential to preserving the genre in the minds of fans and film critics alike. Would he, like so many other American cowboy actors, have chosen to eke out the rest of his career in Spaghetti Westerns (he turned down the offer of playing the psycho in Don Siegel's 1971 *Dirty Harry*). One will never know. Murphy's premature death actually adds a certain degree of poignancy to his movies that the films of Scott, McCrea and Montgomery do not (and could never) possess; after all, he didn't live to see old age like the other three. This writer's lasting impression of the young cowboy star is from the opening few minutes of *Tumbleweed*. That big shiny Universal-International globe, announcing the start of something special; Henry Mancini, Milton Rosen and Herman Stein's incisive title score; Russell Metty's glowing photography; and the "Kid" himself, on horseback and towing a spare mount, making his way slowly over the rocky ground of California's Death Valley, the sun's glare creasing those baby-faced features, one of the Western's most iconic images from the 1950s. *That's* how Audie Murphy should forever be remembered.

Essential Murphy
The Kid from Texas
Kansas Raiders
Gunsmoke
Tumbleweed
Ride Clear of Diablo
Destry
No Name on the Bullet
Hell Bent for Leather
Seven Ways from Sundown
Bullet for a Badman

Chapter 20
Final Roundup:
McCrea and Montgomery, 1965-1976

McCrea got together with son Jody and director Casey Hibbs in 1966 for a possible project based on bronco busting, *The Young Rounders*, but it never got off the ground. Likewise *Sioux Nation*, which McCrea was going to direct in 1970, never saw the light of a projection lamp. But he hadn't quite called it a day yet. Jody cajoled his father out of semi-retirement to make a cameo appearance in Bronco Films' *Cry Blood, Apache*, released in 1970 but not surfacing in Britain until 1974, rated "AA" (in America, it was R-classified). On first viewing, director Jack Starrett's exploitive anti-Western, partly financed by McCrea, Jr., underlines just how far along the road the genre had disintegrated since the heady period of the 1950s. The film opens with the sadistic massacre of an Indian settlement by five disparate cretins and includes several scenes of brutal murder not deemed suitable for a younger audience; a cut-price variation on Ralph Nelson's controversial *Soldier Blue* if ever there was one. Starrett's erratic direction, borrowing heavily from the Spanish/Italian Western influence prevalent at the time, is all close-ups of ugly, snarling faces, while Elliot Kaplan's dissonant score jars the senses, although his title theme is quite tuneful.

Bruce Scott photographs the locations (California's Sequoia National Forest and parts of Arizona) in garish color while McCrea, Sr. bookends the movie, on screen for just under five minutes—four and a bit at the beginning, and 15 seconds at the end. Easy to dismiss, then, as cheap, nasty trash not worthy of the name McCrea, making one hanker for the likes of director Ray Enright, composer David Buttolph and cinematographer Charles Lawton, Jr., true artists of the old Hollywood school who knew how to mold their collective talents into conjuring up a classic Western. Take a second look, though (if you can bear to!) and audiences will discover a passable little oater buried under an avalanche of new-wave Western gross-out.

McCrea (as Old Pitcalin and billed as "Special Guest"), 65 years of age at the time of shooting, rides into view, pausing on a ridge to reflect on the site of an unpleasant incident that occurred in his life many sunsets ago. In flashback, McCrea (now Jody), Robert Tessier, Rick Nervik, Jack Starrett (yes, he acted as well as directed) and Don Henley are busy wiping out an Indian camp, gleefully raping, slaughtering and scalping (bearded oaf Nervik slaps one woman to death). Marie Gahva, a survivor from the atrocity, promises to show the men where a quantity of gold nuggets can be found to save her own skin, so they set off to find it, McCrea forming a close bond with the traumatized girl. Hot on their trail is enraged warrior Dan Kemp, determined to mete out Apache justice to these white scum who killed his wife and child. And that's it. Nervik gets an arrow in the back and dies a slow death, paralyzed from the waist down; Henley is strung upside down above a river and drowns, crying and  screaming for his mother; Tessier has a sack thrown over his head containing a rattlesnake; and Starrett is led away tethered to a horse, reduced to a raving religious lunatic. In a strenuous knife tussle between McCrea and Kemp in the snow, Gahva shoots the Indian (her brother) dead with a flintlock rifle, deciding she's better off with McCrea, and the movie closes with a symbolic shot of a desiccated corpse wedged in the thorny embrace of a bleached cactus.

Ironically, *Cry Blood, Apache* erupts into precisely the kind of excessive violence that McCrea used to publically disavow, so what his views were on seeing the finished product can well be imagined. Take away that awful soundtrack and the histrionic performances and we are left with a dirty-looking '70s version of the once much-loved trail buster that incorporates within its inconsistent arrangement some striking location work and one or two diverting points of interest to genre buffs. Unfortunately, it also demonstrates McCrea, Jr.'s singular lack of screen aura compared to that possessed by his illustrious father—but then, as they always say in these pictures, legends are sometimes very hard to live up to.

Joel McCrea's very last appearance in a motion picture was Universal's *Mustang Country* (1976), a family wilderness-type Western that might well have been produced by the Disney Studios. Filmed amid the magnificent splendor of Alberta's Banff National Park, with its stunning vistas of mountains, woods and lakes, the slight yarn had sheep farmer McCrea (Dan) and passive Indian orphan Nika Mina attempting to capture Shoshawnee, a wild black stallion with a $500 reward on his head. Set in 1925 on the Montana-Canadian border, Patrick Wayne and Robert Fuller guested as two trappers unable to rope the horse, leaving after one scene. Thereafter, McCrea and the scenery carried a picture stacked full of wildlife stock footage to appease the kids (deer, bears, a mountain cat, wolves, raccoons, fish), drama coming in the form of Old Three Toes, a

fierce grizzly who once broke the shoulder of McCrea's pet dog, a Rottweiler named Luke. The youngster forms an attachment with McCrea and doesn't want to leave his side; the old-timer shows his little pal a watch given to him by Buffalo Bill for becoming a rodeo champion, and all efforts to corral the horse fail miserably ("He's too much for us. He's too much for anybody," bemoans McCrea). On the point of quitting ("He's a lost cause."), McCrea's horse Rosie becomes stuck in quicksand and Shoshawnee, enticed by his favorite berries and agreeing to be roped, pulls the mare free; he's now fully tamed! During a stormy night spent in a spooky barn (the nearby ranch burned to the ground, killing its two occupants), Old Three Toes attacks McCrea, badly mauling his left arm, but is shot dead. Patched up in Beaver Creek, McCrea, Mina, Rosie and Shoshawnee are last seen heading toward Great Falls, the picture ending rather abruptly.

McCrea's solid professionalism makes it look all so easy and, in one sequence where he has to bury Luke, savaged to death by the rampaging grizzly, his undisguised grief at losing his pet dog hits the heartstrings. McCrea loved working with animals and brought genuine compassion to the scene. On the technical side, J. Barry Herron's cinematography does full justice to the picturesque locations, while director/producer/writer John Champion is content to let the animals and McCrea simply get on with it. On the downside, composer Lee Holdridge has to insert, in the 25th minute, a syrupy song, "Follow Your Restless Dreams," two minutes of sheer purgatory, ruining what is otherwise a beautifully written score, but many Westerns of the time included out-of-context musical themes in their overall design ("Raindrops Keep Fallin' on My Head" in *Butch Cassidy and the Sundance Kid* is one obvious example), so *Mustang Country* certainly wasn't bucking any trend. And the 76-minute print shown on British TV years ago omitted footage filched from two of McCrea's earlier outings, *Black Horse Canyon* and *Cattle Drive*.

Mustang Country is not in the same league as *Black Horse Canyon* or, for that matter, Murphy's *Sierra* and Montgomery's *King of the Wild Stallions*, three movies whose horse-driven plots were produced in the days when the Western genre was in full swing. But it's a sweet film to go out on, far sweeter than *Cry Blood, Apache* that preceded it, maybe one of the reasons why the actor agreed to the project. McCrea spent the remaining

Joel McCrea as he appeared in 1976 from *Mustang Country*

years of his life on his Thousand Oaks Ranch in California, surrounded by his family and their cherished horses, passing away on October 20, 1990. There's a fetching line of dialogue in *Mustang Country* that he imparts to his young Indian buddy: "Death isn't the end of everything." One likes to imagine McCrea's spirit, or the spirit of what he stood for, roaming those rugged Western wilds on Dollar with all those other Western stars at his side. Fanciful, maybe, but to those who sat through and enjoyed countless oaters rolled out over the golden years, 1930 to the mid-1960s, it's a pleasant thought to have at the back of your mind when McCrea and horse trot past those vivid canyon walls, at one with nature and the elements, elevating, in snapshot moments, the Old West and its values to mythical status.

Essential McCrea
Union Pacific
Colorado Territory
Saddle Tramp
Black Horse Canyon
Wichita
The Tall Stranger
Cattle Empire
Fort Massacre
The Gunfight at Dodge City
Ride the High Country

A foreign poster for *Outlaw of Red River* (1965)

After 1959's *King of the Wild Stallions*, George Montgomery's career fragmented into television and theater; from 1960 to 1963, he trod the boards, touring the States in, among other stage productions, *Toys in the Attic*, *Plain and Fancy*, *The Big Killing* and *A Hole in the Head*. He also set up his own production company, MONT/Winchester, starring in, scripting, co-producing and directing four oddities shot in the Philippines: *The Steel Claw* (1961), *Samar* (1962), *From Hell to Borneo* (1964) and the weirdly titled *Guerillas in Pink Lace* (1964), all distributed by Warner Bros. A ragtag bunch of other feature films included a vignette in Ken Annakin's WW2 blockbuster *Battle of the Bulge* (Warner Bros., 1965). On the home front, he also made the Hollywood headlines in 1963 when his mentally unstable housekeeper, jealous of his association with other women, attempted to shoot him dead and commit suicide—she was arrested before the deed was carried out. Like many American cowboy actors who had made their names pre-1960s, Montgomery was enticed over to the Continent in 1965 by the Spanish to take the lead in *Outlaw of Red River* (*El Proscrito del Rio Colorado*). A typical Euro hybrid Western of the day, this Hispanic-type soap opera, filmed around Almeria, Spain, was as muddy as Manuel Merino's cinematography, a talkative, turgid effort directed by Maury Dexter, doyen of countless B-programmers. Montgomery was fine if a little morose in a sub-Spaghetti horse opera that was low on action, high on chat. If one must lay his hands on a copy, unofficial DVD releases come in at 73 minutes, 16 minutes shorter than the original running time, accounting for numerous jumps in narrative and an overall ragged look. It's hard to sit through, even for Montgomery devotees.

George plays Texan outlaw Ray O'Brien, the underling of General José Nieto, a ranchero feuding with rival Jesus Tordesillas; Nieto's engaged to be married to Tordesillas' bewitching niece, Elisa Montés, with her brother (Ricardo Valle) firmly against the match while trying to bed Nieto's bitchy daughter (Ana Maria Custodio). Wily bandit chief Miguel del Castillo, doing a reasonable impersonation of Eli Wallach's memorable Tuco in *The Good, the Bad and the Ugly*, is making life uncomfortable for everyone. In the opening minutes, Montgomery slings a poncho over his saddle, lulling us into thinking that he's going to be the Clint Eastwood to Castillo's Tuco; unfortunately for all, it doesn't happen. Montgomery is beaten up by Castillo's swarthy-looking cutthroats for refusing to join his gang, Valle is shot dead by persons unknown, Montés gives her lover the cold shoulder and Montgomery, once accused of killing his wife in a raid but innocent all along (a subplot that goes nowhere), turns detective to track down Valle's murderer. The whole topsy-turvy shebang ends in a gunfight; Castillo and his gorillas are wiped out and Tordesillas, the real assassin of Valle, is sprayed with bullets. "Adios" says Montés without an ounce of feeling to the departing Nieto, a forlorn figure on his horse, swiftly turning her attention to unsmiling Montgomery and batting her mascara-laden eyelashes at the handsome gringo.

All the overweight bandits wear those bulky crossover cartridge belts across their expansive chests, the Spanish locations always were a poor substitute for Red Rock Canyon and Lone Pine, the dubbing is dreadful and Manuel Parada's quirky accordion-based soundtrack seems at odds with what's going on, which isn't a lot. There's no doubt about it—*Outlaw of Red River*, not *Pawnee*, is the worst Western George Montgomery ever appeared in. Perhaps we can all count our blessings that it's extremely difficult to obtain a copy of this rarity today.

In 1967, aged 51 and looking fit and healthy, Montgomery starred in his final Western, A.C. Lyles Productions' *Hostile Guns*, released through Paramount. By now, the traditional American cowboy flick was virtually dead in the water, producer Lyles one of the few moviemakers left in Hollywood attempting to keep the genre from fading out of sight; he was responsible for a string of low-budget Westerns in the '60s such as *Apache Uprising* (1965), *Fort Utah* (1967) and *Buckskin (*1968), stocking each with an ensemble of experienced character actors capable of turning hackneyed material into something reasonably pleasurable: Rory Calhoun, John Ireland, Virginia Mayo, Richard Arlen, Barton MacLane, Wendell Corey and Barry Sullivan, among others. *Hostile Guns* had a worthy cast: Apart from Montgomery, we had Leo Gordon, Tab Hunter, Virginia Mayo, Brian Donlevy, John Russell, James Craig, Emile Meyer and, all the way from the 1930s, Fuzzy Knight, lending their unquestionable talents to a film that was 10 years out of date. In 1957, this would have made a smashing little crowd-pleaser, but not in 1967, and again, the main fault lay in the score. As mentioned, Western scores pre-1960 were vibrant affairs, propelling the action along, a major contribution to the

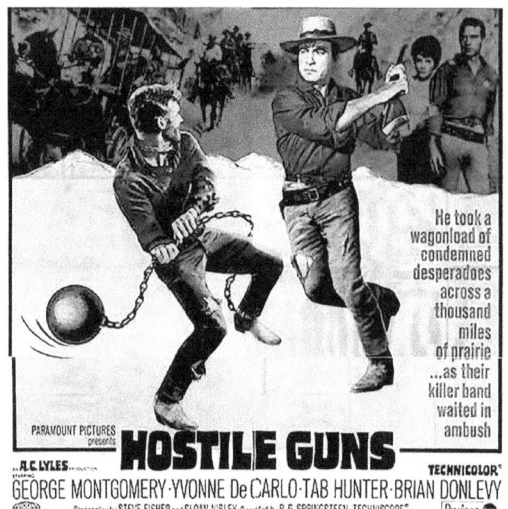

production. Not any more. Jimmie Haskell's music burbled inoffensively in the background, a soundscape to forget. What was urgently needed here was a Paul Sawtell or Hans J. Salter killer soundtrack to pump some life into the flaccid proceedings, preventing customers from dozing in their seats. Director R.G. Springsteen did an efficient job with Steve Fisher and Sloan Nibley's derivative screenplay, but this was 1967, the era of the British "X" certificate gangster and Western movie; audiences were no longer bothered with this redundant U-certified type of cowboy feature. *Hostile Guns* isn't that dreadful, but it would have fared better in the 1950s with, as stated, a far better score.

Montgomery's Sheriff Gid McCool is transporting a prison wagon across the Texas badlands to Huntsville (the Vasquez Rocks area was used for location work), containing killer Leo Gordon (inappropriately named Pleasant, given the actor's snarling screen persona), goat thief Pedro Gonzalez Gonzalez and corrupt official Robert Emhardt. Tailing the wagon are Gordon's two brothers, John Russell and James Craig, determined to set him loose (Gordon has one classic line to mouth: "Anyone laughs at Hank Pleasant loses their teeth!"). On the journey, they pick up Yvonne De Carlo from a stagecoach; she happens to be an old flame of Montgomery, accused of murdering her lover. Deputy Tab Hunter gets fresh with her, is stuck in the back with the others to cool off but released when Russell and Craig make their move. The two outlaws and their boys are shot to pieces, De Carlo confesses her love for Montgomery and the wagon trundles on over the closing credits.

Not a bad film to finish one's Western career with then, but certainly no must-see. Montgomery (he doesn't smile once and wears his shirt with the collar up at the back, as he so often did in other Westerns) carried the picture with his usual assertiveness and masculine screen presence, his veteran co-stars giving their all. But in 1967, queues were forming around the block to catch Sergio Leone's violent revisionist anti-Western, the X-rated *For a Few Dollars More*. Humble efforts like *Hostile Guns* hardly got a look, consigned to second-feature status or never making it onto the circuits. The days of the classic mid-budget and B-oater were drawing to a close: George Montgomery, one of its foremost figures, an athletic, square-jawed leading man of the old school, carried on in cameos and TV work up until 1985, calling it a day after starring as Major Nestorovic in the Russian war drama *Dikiy veter*.

It's a little-known fact among film buffs that George Montgomery was a renowned art collector and sculptor with a passionate involvement in the lore of the Old West. From 1974 onwards, he concentrated on sculpting as a living, creating nearly 50 bronze busts (John Wayne, Randolph Scott, Ronald Reagan, ex-wife Dinah Shore, among

many) and Western figures cast in various poses, opening The George Montgomery Gallery of Western American Art in Palm Springs Desert Museum. His highly prized work (Montgomery's sculpture of Custer's Last Stand at the Little Bighorn is miraculous in its fine detail) can be found in various museums, including the Ronald Reagan Presidential Museum and Library in Simi Valley. Montgomery died on December 12, 2000 after suffering prolonged ill-health symptoms that had been difficult to diagnose. The 31 Westerns he had featured in from 1939 onward defined, simply and effectively, just what the genre was all about during those halcyon days of the 1940s and 1950s; his is a name often overlooked by many, but undeservedly so. Tune in someday to *The Lone Gun* or *The Texas Rangers* and catch a Western every bit as good as a Scott, Murphy and McCrea offering, and even one made by a much bigger name in the film business. In the area of medium-budget Western cinema, George Montgomery shines as an underrated star.

Essential Montgomery
The Cisco Kid and the Lady
Dakota Lil
The Texas Rangers
Indian Uprising
Cripple Creek
Jack McCall Desperado
Gun Belt
The Lone Gun
Masterson of Kansas
Gun Duel in Durango

Chapter 21
Filmography

Film Ratings

Dead shot 🥾🥾🥾🥾🥾
Hits the target 🥾🥾🥾🥾
Finger on the trigger 🥾🥾🥾
Half-cocked 🥾🥾
Firing blanks 🥾

RANDOLPH SCOTT

The Virginian
Paramount 1929; 94 minutes; Producers: B.P. Schulberg and Louis D. Lighton; Director: Victor Fleming
Gary Cooper; Mary Brian; Walter Huston; Richard Arlen; Chester Conklin; Eugene Pallette; E.H. Calvert; Victor Potel (Scott's role was un-credited) 🥾🥾🥾🥾

Heritage of the Desert
aka *When the West Was Young*
Paramount/Unity 1932; 60 minutes; Producer: Harold Hurley; Director: Henry Hathaway
Randolph Scott; J. Farrell MacDonald; Sally Blane; David Landau; Gordon Wescott; Guinn "Big Boy" Williams; Vince Barnett; Fred Burns 🥾🥾🥾

Wild Horse Mesa
Paramount/Favorite Films 1932; 63 minutes; Producer: Harold Hurley; Director: Henry Hathaway
Randolph Scott; Fred Kholer; Sally Blane; Lucille La Verne; George "Gabby" Hayes; Charles Grapewin; E.H. Calvert; Jim Thorpe (Prints not available)

Buffalo Stampede
aka *The Thundering Herd*
Paramount/Favorite Films 1933; 59 minutes; Producer: Harold Hurley; Director: Henry Hathaway
Randolph Scott; Noah Beery; Judith Allen; Raymond Hatton; Blanche Friderici; Buster Crabbe; Barton MacLane; Monte Blue 🥾🥾🥾🥾🥾

Sunset Pass
Paramount/Favorite Films 1933; 61 minutes; Producer: Harold Hurley; Director: Henry Hathaway
Randolph Scott; Harry Carey; Kathleen Burke; Noah Beery; Tom Keene; Leila Bennett; Vince Barnett; Fuzzy Knight (Prints not available)

Man of the Forest
aka ***Challenge of the Frontier***
Paramount 1933; 62 minutes; Producer: Harold Hurley; Director: Henry Hathaway
Randolph Scott; Noah Beery; Verna Hillie; Blanche Friderici; Guinn "Big Boy" Williams; Buster Crabbe; Vince Barnett; Tempe Pigott 🥾🥾

To the Last Man
aka ***Law of Vengeance***
Paramount/Favorite Films 1933; 72 minutes; Producer: Harold Hurley; Director: Henry Hathaway
Randolph Scott; Noah Beery; Jack La Rue; Esther Ralston; Egon Brecher; Gail Patrick; Barton MacLane; Fuzzy Knight 🥾🥾🥾

The Last Round-Up
Paramount/Favorite Films 1934; 61 minutes; Producer: Harold Hurley; Director: Henry Hathaway
Randolph Scott; Monte Blue; Fred Kohler; Barbara Fritchie; Fuzzy Knight; Barton MacLane; Frank Rice; Charles Middleton (Prints not available)

Wagon Wheels
aka ***Caravans West***
Paramount/Favorite Films 1934; 59 minutes; Producer: Harold Hurley; Director: Charles Barton
Randolph Scott; Monte Blue; Billy Lee; Gail Patrick; Raymond Hatton; Olin Howland; Howard Wilson; Jan Duggan 🥾🥾🥾🥾🥾

Home on the Range
aka ***Code of the West***
Paramount/Favorite Films 1935; 54 minutes; Producer: Harold Hurley; Director: Arthur Jacobson
Randolph Scott; Evelyn Brent; Jackie Coogan; Dean Jagger; Fuzzy Knight; Addison Richards; Howard Wilson; Ann Sheridan (Prints not available)

Rocky Mountain Mystery
aka ***The Fighting Westerner***
Paramount/Favorite Films 1935; 63 minutes; Producer: Harold Hurley; Director: Charles Barton
Randolph Scott; Charles "Chic" Sale; George Marion, Sr.; Leslie Carter; Howard Wilson; Willie Fung; Kathleen Burke; James C. Eagles 🥾🥾🥾🥾

The Last of the Mohicans
Reliance/United Artists 1936; 91 minutes; Producer: Edward Small; Director: George B. Seitz
Randolph Scott; Bruce Cabot; Robert Barrat; Henry Wilcoxon; Binnie Barnes; Phillip Reed; Heather Angel; Hugh Buckler 🥾🥾🥾🥾

High, Wide, and Handsome
Paramount 1937; 110 minutes; Producer: Arthur Hornblow, Jr.; Director: Rouben Mamoulian
Irene Dunne; Randolph Scott; Alan Hale; Akim Tamiroff; Charles Bickford; Dorothy Lamour; Raymond Walburn; Elizabeth Patterson 🥾🥾🥾🥾

The Texans
Paramount 1938; 92 minutes; Producer: Lucien Hubbard; Director: James P. Hogan
Joan Bennett; Randolph Scott; Walter Brennan; Robert Cummings; Robert Barrat; May Robson; Raymond Hatton; Francis Ford 🥾🥾

The Road to Reno
aka *The Ranger and the Lady*
Universal 1938; 72 minutes; Producers: Edmund Grainger and Jules Brulatour; Director: S. Sylvan Simon
Randolph Scott; Hope Hampton; Glenda Farrell; David Oliver; Helen Broderick; Alan Marshal; Ted Osborne; Samuel S. Hinds 🥾

Jesse James
20th Century Fox 1939; Technicolor; 106 minutes; Producer: Darryl F. Zanuck; Director: Henry King
Tyrone Power; Henry Fonda; Nancy Kelly; Randolph Scott; John Carradine; Jane Darwell; Brian Donlevy; Henry Hull 🥾🥾🥾🥾

Susannah of the Mounties
20th Century Fox 1939; 79 minutes; Producers: Kenneth MacGowan and Darryl F. Zanuck; Director: William A. Seiter
Shirley Temple; Randolph Scott; Margaret Lockwood; Martin Good Rider; Victor Jory; J. Farrell MacDonald; Lester Matthews; Moroni Olsen 🥾🥾

Frontier Marshal
20th Century Fox 1939; 71 minutes; Producer: Sol M. Wurtzel; Director: Allan Dwan
Randolph Scott; Cesar Romero; Nancy Kelly; John Carradine; Joe Sawyer; Lon Chaney, Jr.; Binnie Barnes; Edward Norris 🥾🥾🥾🥾

Virginia City
Warner Bros. 1940; 121 minutes; Producers: Robert Fellows and Hal B. Wallis; Director: Michael Curtiz
Errol Flynn; Miriam Hopkins; Randolph Scott; Humphrey Bogart; Alan Hale; Guinn "Big Boy" Williams; John Litel; Moroni Olsen 🥾🥾🥾

When the Daltons Rode
Universal 1940; 81 minutes; Produced and Directed by George Marshall
Randolph Scott; Broderick Crawford; Brian Donlevy; Kay Francis; Edgar Buchanan; Andy Devine; George Bancroft; Stuart Erwin 🥾🥾🥾

Western Union
20th Century Fox 1941; Technicolor; 95 minutes; Producer; Harry Joe Brown; Director: Fritz Lang
Robert Young; Randolph Scott; Dean Jagger; Chill Wills; Virginia Gilmore; John Carradine; Slim Summerville; Barton MacLane 🥾🥾🥾🥾

Belle Starr "The Bandit Queen"
20th Century Fox 1941; Technicolor; 87 minutes; Producer: Kenneth MacGowan; Director: Irving Cummings
Gene Tierney; Randolph Scott; Dana Andrews; Chill Wills; Elizabeth Patterson; Shepperd Strudwick; Louise Beavers; Olin Howland 🥾🥾

The Spoilers
Universal 1942; 87 minutes; Producer: Frank Lloyd; Director: Ray Enright
Marlene Dietrich; Randolph Scott; John Wayne; Margaret Lindsay; Richard Barthelmess; Harry Carey; George Cleveland; Samuel S. Hinds 🥾🥾🥾

The Desperadoes
Columbia 1943; Technicolor; 88 minutes; Producer: Harry Joe Brown; Director: Charles Vidor
Randolph Scott; Glenn Ford; Evelyn Keyes; Claire Trevor; Raymond Walburn; Edgar Buchanan; Guinn "Big Boy" Williams; Bernard Nedell 🥾🥾🥾

Belle of the Yukon
International Pictures Inc. 1944; Technicolor; 83 minutes; Produced and Directed by William A. Seiter
Randolph Scott; Gypsy Rose Lee; Dinah Shore; Robert Armstrong; Guinn "Big Boy" Williams; William Marshall; Bob Burns; Charles Winninger 🥾🥾

Abilene Town
United Artists 1946; 89 minutes; Producer: Jules Levy; Director: Edwin L. Marin
Randolph Scott; Rhonda Fleming; Lloyd Bridges; Ann Dvorak; Richard Hale; Edgar Buchanan; Jack Lambert; Dick Curtis 🥾🥾🥾🥾🥾

Badman's Territory
RKO-Radio 1946; 97 minutes; Producer: Nat Holt; Director: Tim Whelan
Randolph Scott; Ann Richards; Nestor Paiva; Richard Hale; Ray Collins; James Warren; Chief Thundercloud; Lawrence Tierney 🥾🥾🥾

Trail Street
RKO-Radio 1947; 84 minutes; Producer: Nat Holt; Director: Ray Enright
Randolph Scott; Steve Brodie; Robert Ryan; Anne Jeffreys; Madge Meredith; George "Gabby" Hayes; Billy House; Jason Robards, Sr. 🥾🥾🥾

Gunfighters
aka ***The Assassin***
Columbia 1947; Cinecolor; 87 minutes; Producer: Harry Joe Brown; Director: George Waggner
Randolph Scott; Dorothy Hart; Barbara Britton; Bruce Cabot; Forrest Tucker; Charles Grapewin; Grant Withers; Steven Geray 🥾🥾🥾

Albuquerque
aka ***Silver City***
Paramount 1948; Cinecolor; 90 minutes; Producers: William H. Pine and William C. Thomas; Director: Ray Enright
Randolph Scott; Barbara Britton; Catherine Craig; Lon Chaney, Jr.; George "Gabby" Hayes; George Cleveland; Russell Hayden; Russell Simpson 🥾🥾🥾

Coroner Creek
Columbia 1948; Cinecolor; 90 minutes; Producer: Harry Joe Brown; Director: Ray Enright
Randolph Scott; George Macready; Marguerite Chapman; Forrest Tucker; Edgar Buchanan; Sally Eilers; Barbara Reed; Wallace Ford 🥾🥾🥾🥾🥾

Return of the Badmen
RKO-Radio 1948; 90 minutes; Producer: Nat Holt; Director: Ray Enright
Randolph Scott; Robert Ryan; George "Gabby" Hayes; Robert Armstrong; Jacqueline White; Ann Jeffreys; Tom Tyler; Robert Clarke 🥾🥾🥾🥾🥾

The Walking Hills
Columbia 1949; 78 minutes; Producer: Harry Joe Brown; Director: John Sturges
Randolph Scott; Arthur Kennedy; Edgar Buchanan; John Ireland; William Bishop; Ella Raines; Russell Collins; Houseley Stevenson 🥾🥾🥾

Canadian Pacific
20th Century Fox 1949; Cinecolor; 95 minutes; Producer: Nat Holt; Director: Edwin L. Marin
Randolph Scott; J. Carrol Naish; Victor Jory; Nancy Olson; Jane Wyatt; Robert Barrat; Walter Sande; Don Haggerty 🥾🥾🥾

The Doolins of Oklahoma
aka ***The Great Manhunt***
Columbia 1949; 90 minutes; Producer: Harry Joe Brown; Director: Gordon Douglas
Randolph Scott; George Macready; Noah Beery, Jr.; Jock Mahoney; Virginia Huston; John Ireland; Louise Allbritton; Dona Drake 🥾🥾🥾🥾🥾

Fighting Man of the Plains
20th Century Fox 1949; Cinecolor/Black-and-White; 93 minutes; Producer: Nat Holt; Director: Edwin L. Marin
Randolph Scott; Barry Kelley; Jane Nigh; Bill Williams; Joan Taylor; Victor Jory; James Millican; Dale Robertson 🥾🥾🥾

The Nevadan
aka *The Man from Nevada*
Columbia 1950; Cinecolor; 81 minutes; Producers: Harry Joe Brown and Randolph Scott; Director: Gordon Douglas
Randolph Scott; Forrest Tucker; George Macready; Dorothy Malone; Jock Mahoney; Frank Faylen; Tom Powers; Jeff Corey 🥾🥾🥾🥾🥾

Colt .45
aka *Thundercloud*
Warner Bros. 1950; Technicolor; 74 minutes; Producer: Saul Elkins; Director: Edwin L. Marin
Randolph Scott; Zachary Scott; Lloyd Bridges; Ruth Roman; Alan Hale; Chief Thundercloud; Charles Evans; Lute Crockett 🥾🥾🥾

The Cariboo Trail
20th Century Fox 1950; Cinecolor; 81 minutes; Producer: Nat Holt; Director: Edwin L. Marin
Randolph Scott; George "Gabby" Hayes; Bill Williams; Karin Booth; Victor Jory; Dale Robertson; Lee Tung Foo; Mary Kent 🥾🥾🥾🥾

Sugarfoot
aka *Swirl of Glory*
Warner Bros. 1951; Technicolor; 79 minutes; Producer: Saul Elkins; Director: Edwin L. Marin
Randolph Scott; Raymond Massey; Adele Jergens; S.Z. Sakall; Gene Evans; Hugh Sanders; Arthur Hunnicutt; Hank Worden 🥾🥾

Santa Fe
Columbia 1951; Technicolor; 86 minutes; Producer: Harry Joe Brown; Director: Irving Pichel
Randolph Scott; Janis Carter; Roy Roberts; Jock Mahoney; Jerome Courtland; John Archer; Chief Thundercloud; Warner Anderson 🥾🥾🥾

Fort Worth
Warner Bros. 1951; Technicolor; 80 minutes; Producer: Anthony Veiller; Director: Edwin L. Marin
Randolph Scott; David Brian; Phyllis Thaxter; Helena Carter; Ray Teal; Emerson Treacy; Bob Steele; Paul Picerni 🥾🥾🥾

Man in the Saddle
aka *The Outcast*
Columbia 1951; Technicolor; 87 minutes; Producers: Harry Joe Brown and Randolph Scott; Director: André De Toth
Randolph Scott; Alexander Knox; Joan Leslie; Guinn "Big Boy" Williams; Richard Rober; John Russell; Alfonso Bedoya; Ellen Drew 🥾🥾🥾🥾🥾

Carson City
Warner Bros. 1952; Warnercolor; 87 minutes; Producer: David Weisbart; Director: André De Toth
Randolph Scott; Raymond Massey; Richard Webb; Lucille Norman; James Millican; Larry Keating; Don Beddoe; George Cleveland 🥾🥾🥾🥾

Hangman's Knot
Columbia 1952; Technicolor; 81 minutes; Producers: Harry Joe Brown and Randolph Scott; Director: Roy Huggins
Randolph Scott; Lee Marvin; Ray Teal; Richard Denning; Donna Reed; Guinn "Big Boy" Williams; Monte Blue; Claude Jarman, Jr. 🥾🥾🥾🥾🥾

The Man Behind the Gun
Warner Bros. 1953; Technicolor; 82 minutes; Producer: Robert Sisk; Director: Felix E. Feist
Randolph Scott; Alan Hale, Jr.; Dick Wesson; Philip Carey; Patrice Wymore; Morris Ankrum; Anthony Caruso; Robert Cabal 🥾🥾

The Stranger Wore a Gun
Columbia 1953; Technicolor; Orig. in 3-D; 82 minutes; Producers: Harry Joe Brown and Randolph Scott; Director: André De Toth
Randolph Scott; George Macready; Joan Weldon; Claire Trevor; Lee Marvin; Ernest Borgnine; Alfonso Bedoya; Clem Bevans 🥾🥾

Thunder Over the Plains
Warner Bros. 1953; Warnercolor; 82 minutes; Producer: David Weisbart; Director: André De Toth
Randolph Scott; Charles McGraw; Phyllis Kirk; Lex Barker; Henry Hull; Elisha Cook, Jr.; Lane Chandler; Trevor Bardette 🥾🥾🥾🥾

Riding Shotgun
Warner Bros. 1954; Warnercolor; 75 minutes; Producer: Ted Sherdeman; Director: André De Toth
Randolph Scott; Joan Weldon; Wayne Morris; William Johnstone; Fritz Feld; James Millican; James Bell; Joe Sawyer 🥾🥾🥾🥾

The Bounty Hunter
Warner Bros. 1954; Warnercolor; 79 minutes; Producer: Samuel Bischoff; Director: André De Toth
Randolph Scott; Dolores Dorn; Ernest Borgnine; Howard Petrie; Harry Antrim; Marie Windsor; Paul Picerni; Robert Keys 🥾🥾🥾

Ten Wanted Men
Columbia 1955; Technicolor; 80 minutes; Producers: Harry Joe Brown and Randolph Scott; Director: H. Bruce Humberstone
Randolph Scott; Richard Boone; Jocelyn Brando; Skip Homeier; Leo Gordon; Lee Van Cleef; Denver Pyle; Dennis Weaver 🥾🥾🥾🥾

Rage at Dawn
RKO-Radio 1955; Technicolor; 87 minutes; Producer: Nat Holt; Director: Tim Whelan
Randolph Scott; Forrest Tucker; J. Carrol Naish; Kenneth Tobey; Mala Powers; Edgar Buchanan; Ray Teal; Howard Petrie 🥾🥾🥾

Tall Man Riding
Warner Bros. 1955; Warnercolor; 83 minutes; Producer: David Weisbart; Director: Lesley Selander
Randolph Scott; Dorothy Malone; Robert Barrat; Peggie Castle; John Baragrey; Paul Richards; William Ching; John Dehner 🥾🥾🥾🥾

A Lawless Street
Columbia 1955; Technicolor; 78 minutes; Producers: Harry Joe Brown and Randolph Scott; Director: Joseph H. Lewis
Randolph Scott; Angela Lansbury; Don Megowan; Warner Anderson; John Emery; Michael Pate; Jeanette Nolan; Ruth Donnelly 🥾🥾🥾

Seven Men from Now
Warner Bros./Batjac 1956; WarnerScope/Warnercolor; 78 minutes; Producers: Andrew V. McLaglen, Robert E. Morrison and John Wayne; Director: Budd Boetticher
Randolph Scott; Gail Russell; Lee Marvin; Walter Reed; John Larch; Donald Barry; John Barradino; Steve Mitchell 🥾🥾🥾🥾🥾

7th Cavalry
Columbia 1956; Technicolor; 75 minutes; Producers: Harry Joe Brown and Randolph Scott; Director: Joseph H. Lewis
Randolph Scott; Barbara Hale; Russell Hicks; Jay C. Flippen; Leo Gordon; Donald Curtis; Harry Carey, Jr.; Denver Pyle 🥾🥾🥾🥾

The Tall T
Columbia 1957; Technicolor; 78 minutes; Producers: Harry Joe Brown and Randolph Scott; Director: Budd Boetticher
Randolph Scott; Richard Boone; Maureen O'Sullivan; Skip Homeier; Henry Silva; John Hubbard; Arthur Hunnicutt; Robert Burton; 🥾🥾🥾🥾🥾

Shoot-Out at Medicine Bend
Warner Bros. 1957; 87 minutes; Producer: Richard Whorf; Director: Richard L. Bare
Randolph Scott; James Garner; Angie Dickinson; Myron Healey; James Craig; Trevor Bardette; Don Beddoe; Robert Warwick 🥾🥾

Decision at Sundown
Columbia 1957; Technicolor; 77 minutes; Producers: Harry Joe Brown and Randolph Scott; Director: Budd Boetticher
Randolph Scott; John Carroll; Karen Steele; Noah Beery, Jr.; John Archer; Valerie French; Ray Teal; Andrew Duggan 🥾🥾🥾🥾

Westbound
Warner Bros. 1958; WarnerScope/Warnercolor; 72 minutes; Producer: Henry Blanke; Director: Budd Boetticher
Randolph Scott; Karen Steele; Michael Dante; Andrew Duggan; Virginia Mayo; Michael Pate; Walter Barnes; Wally Brown 🥾🥾🥾

Buchanan Rides Alone
Columbia 1958; Columbiacolor; 78 minutes; Producers: Harry Joe Brown and Randolph Scott; Director: Budd Boetticher
Randolph Scott; Craig Stevens; Barry Kelley; Manuel Rojas; L.Q. Jones; Tol Avry; Peter Whitney; Robert Anderson 🥾🥾🥾🥾

Ride Lonesome
Columbia 1959; CinemaScope/Eastmancolor; 73 minutes; Producers: Harry Joe Brown and Randolph Scott; Director: Budd Boetticher
Randolph Scott; Karen Steele; Pernell Roberts; James Coburn; James Best; Lee Van Cleef; Roy Jenson; Dyke Johnson 🥾🥾🥾🥾🥾

Comanche Station
Columbia 1960; CinemaScope/Eastmancolor; 74 minutes; Producers: Harry Joe Brown and Randolph Scott; Director: Budd Boetticher
Randolph Scott; Claude Akins; Nancy Gates; Skip Homeier; Richard Rust; Rand Brooks; Dyke Johnson; Foster Hood 🥾🥾🥾🥾🥾

Ride the High Country
aka **Guns in the Afternoon**
MGM 1962; CinemaScope/Metrocolor; 94 minutes; Producer: Richard E. Lyons; Director: Sam Peckinpah
Joel McCrea; Randolph Scott; Mariette Hartley; Ron Starr; Edgar Buchanan; James Drury; R.G. Armstrong; L.Q. Jones 🥾🥾🥾🥾

RANDOLPH SCOTT
IN
THE BOUNTY HUNTER

AUDIE MURPHY

The Kid from Texas
aka ***Texas Kid, Outlaw***
Universal 1950; Technicolor; 78 minutes; Producer: Paul Short; Director: Kurt Neumann
Audie Murphy; Gale Storm; Albert Dekker; Shepperd Strudwick; Ray Teal; Will Geer; Robert Barrat; William Talman 🥾🥾🥾🥾

Sierra
Universal 1950; Technicolor; 83 minutes; Producer: Michael Kraike; Director: Alfred E. Green
Audie Murphy; Wanda Hendrix; Dean Jagger; Richard Rober; Roy Roberts; Houseley Stevenson; Anthony (Tony) Curtis; Sara Allgood 🥾🥾🥾

Kansas Raiders
Universal 1950; Technicolor; 80 minutes; Producer: Ted Richmond; Director: Ray Enright
Audie Murphy; Brian Donlevy; Marguerite Chapman; Richard Long; Tony Curtis; Dewey Martin; James Best; Scott Brady 🥾🥾🥾🥾🥾

The Cimarron Kid
Universal 1951; Technicolor; 85 minutes; Producer: Ted Richmond; Director: Budd Boetticher
Audie Murphy; Beverly Tyler; James Best; Roy Roberts; Hugh O'Brian; Yvette Duguay; Leif Erickson; Noah Beery, Jr. 🥾🥾🥾

The Duel at Silver Creek
aka ***Claim Jumpers***
Universal 1952; Technicolor; 77 minutes; Producer: Leonard Goldstein; Director: Don Siegel
Audie Murphy; Stephen McNally; Faith Domergue; Susan Cabot; Gerald Mohr; Eugene Iglesias; Lee Marvin; James Anderson 🥾🥾🥾🥾

Gunsmoke
aka ***Roughshod***
Universal 1953; Technicolor; 79 minutes; Producer: Aaron Rosenberg; Director: Nathan Juran
Audie Murphy; Susan Cabot; Charles Drake; Paul Kelly; Donald Randolph; Jack Kelly; Mary Castle; William Reynolds 🥾🥾🥾🥾

Column South
Universal 1953; Technicolor; 82 minutes; Producer: Ted Richmond; Director: Frederick de Cordova
Audie Murphy; Robert Sterling; Joan Evans; Dennis Weaver; Ray Collins; Jack Kelly; Palmer Lee; Russell Johnson 🥾🥾🥾

Tumbleweed
Universal 1953; Technicolor; 79 minutes; Producer: Ross Hunter; Director: Nathan Juran
Audie Murphy; Chill Wills; Lori Nelson; Roy Roberts; Russell Johnson; Lee Van Cleef; Ralph Moody; Madge Meredith 👢👢👢👢👢

Ride Clear of Diablo
Universal 1954; Technicolor; 80 minutes; Producer: John W. Rogers; Director: Jesse Hibbs
Audie Murphy; Dan Duryea; Susan Cabot; Paul Birch; William Pullen; Russell Johnson; Abbe Lane; Jack Elam 👢👢👢👢👢

Drums Across the River
Universal 1954; Technicolor; 78 minutes; Producer: Melville Tucker; Director: Nathan Juran
Audie Murphy; Lyle Bettger; Walter Brennan; Jay Silverheels; Lisa Gaye; Hugh O'Brian; Mara Corday; Emile Meyer 👢👢👢👢

Destry
Universal 1954; Technicolor; 95 minutes; Producer: Stanley Rubin; Director: George Marshall
Audie Murphy; Lyle Bettger; Mari Blanchard; Thomas Mitchell; Edgar Buchanan; Lori Nelson; Alan Hale, Jr.; Wallace Ford 👢👢👢👢

Walk the Proud Land
Universal 1956; CinemaScope/Technicolor; 88 minutes; Producer: Aaron Rosenberg; Director: Jesse Hibbs
Audie Murphy; Anne Bancroft; Charles Drake; Patricia Crowley; Robert Warwick; Jay Silverheels; Tommy Rall; Morris Ankrum 👢👢

The Guns of Fort Petticoat
Columbia 1957; Technicolor; 82 minutes; Producers: Harry Joe Brown and (un-credited) Audie Murphy; Director: George Marshall
Audie Murphy; Kathryn Grant; Hope Emerson; Jeff Donnell; Patricia Tiernan; Kim Charney; Nestor Paiva; Ainslie Pryor 👢👢👢

Night Passage
Universal 1957; Technirama/Technicolor; 90 minutes; Producer: Aaron Rosenberg; Director: James Neilson
James Stewart; Audie Murphy; Dan Duryea; Dianne Foster; Elaine Stewart; Brandon De Wilde; Jay C. Flippen; Herbert Anderson 👢👢👢

Ride a Crooked Trail
Universal 1958; CinemaScope/Eastmancolor; 87 minutes; Producer: Howard Pine; Director: Jesse Hibbs
Audie Murphy; Walter Matthau; Gia Scala; Henry Silva; Eddie Little; Joanna Moore; Richard H. Cutting; Mort Mills 👢👢👢

No Name on the Bullet
Universal 1959; CinemaScope/Eastmancolor; 77 minutes; Producers: Howard Christie and Jack Arnold; Director: Jack Arnold
Audie Murphy; Charles Drake; Joan Evans; Willis Bouchey; Simon Scott; Edgar Stehli; John Alderson; Whit Bissell 🥾🥾🥾🥾🥾

The Wild and the Innocent
Universal 1959; CinemaScope/Eastmancolor; 84 minutes; Producer: Sy Gomberg; Director: Jack Sher
Audie Murphy; Sandra Dee; Gilbert Roland; Joanne Dru; Jim Backus; George Mitchell; Peter Breck; Strother Martin 🥾🥾🥾

Cast a Long Shadow
United Artists 1959; 82 minutes; Producers: Walter Mirisch and (un-credited) Audie Murphy; Director: Thomas Carr
Audie Murphy; John Dehner; Terry Moore; Denver Pyle; James Best; Ann Doran; Rita Lynn; Wright King 🥾

The Unforgiven
United Artists 1960; Panavision/Technicolor; 125 minutes; Producers: James Hill, Harold Hecht and Burt Lancaster; Director: John Huston
Burt Lancaster; Audrey Hepburn; Audie Murphy; Lillian Gish; Doug McClure; Charles Bickford; Kipp Hamilton; Carlos Rivas 🥾🥾🥾🥾

Hell Bent for Leather
Universal 1960; CinemaScope/Eastmancolor; 82 minutes; Producer: Gordon Kay; Director: George Sherman
Audie Murphy; Stephen McNally; Felicia Farr; Robert Middleton; Jan Merlin; Bob Steele; Herbert Rudley; Rad Fulton 🥾🥾🥾🥾🥾

Seven Ways from Sundown
Universal 1960; Eastmancolor; 86 minutes; Producer: Gordon Kay; Director: Harry Keller
Audie Murphy; Barry Sullivan; Venetia Stevenson; John McIntire; Kenneth Tobey; Mary Field; Ward Ramsey; Charles Horvath 🥾🥾🥾🥾

Posse from Hell
Universal 1961; Eastmancolor; 89 minutes; Producer: Gordon Kay; Director: Herbert Coleman
Audie Murphy; John Saxon; Vic Morrow; Zohra Lampert; Robert Keith; Rodolfo Acosta; Paul Carr; Royal Dano 🥾🥾🥾🥾🥾

Six Black Horses
Universal 1962; Eastmancolor; 80 minutes; Producer: Gordon Kay; Director: Harry Keller
Audie Murphy; Dan Duryea; Joan O'Brien; George Wallace; Roy Barcroft; Bob Steele; Henry Wills; Charlita 🥾🥾🥾🥾🥾

Showdown
Universal 1963; 79 minutes; Producer: Gordon Kay; Director: R.G. Springsteen
Audie Murphy; Charles Drake; Kathleen Crowley; Harold J. Stone; Skip Homeier; L.Q. Jones; Charles Horvath; Strother Martin 🥾🥾🥾

Gunfight at Comanche Creek
Allied Artists 1963; Panavision/DeLuxecolor; 90 minutes; Producer: Ben Schwalb; Director: Frank McDonald
Audie Murphy; Jan Merlin; DeForest Kelley; Colleen Miller; Mort Mills; John Hubbard; Ben Cooper; Michael T. Mikler 🥾🥾

The Quick Gun
Columbia 1964; Techniscope/Technicolor; 87 minutes; Producer: Grant Whytock; Director: Sidney Salkow
Audie Murphy; Merry Anders; Ted de Corsia; James Best; Mort Mills; Walter Sande; Rex Holman; Gregg Palmer 🥾🥾🥾

Bullet for a Badman
Universal 1964; Eastmancolor; 80 minutes; Producer: Gordon Kay; Director: R.G. Springsteen
Audie Murphy; Darren McGavin; Ruta Lee; Skip Homeier; Beverly Owen; Alan Hale, Jr., George Tobias; Berkeley Harris 🥾🥾🥾🥾🥾

Apache Rifles
20th Century Fox 1964; DeLuxecolor; 92 minutes; Producer: Grant Whytock; Director: William Witney
Audie Murphy; Linda Lawson; Michael Dante; L.Q. Jones; Ken Lynch; John Archer; Joseph Vitale; Robert Brubaker 🥾🥾🥾

Arizona Raiders
Columbia 1965; Techniscope/Technicolor; 88 minutes; Producer: Grant Whytock; Director: William Witney
Audie Murphy; Ben Cooper; Michael Dante; Gloria Talbott; Buster Crabbe; George Keymas; Ray Stricklyn; Fred Graham 🥾🥾

Gunpoint
Universal 1966; Technicolor; 86 minutes; Producer: Gordon Kay; Director: Earl Bellamy
Audie Murphy; Warren Stevens; Joan Staley; Denver Pyle; Edgar Buchanan; Morgan Woodward; David Macklin; Nick Dennis 🥾🥾🥾🥾

The Texican
Columbia 1966; Techniscope/Technicolor; 91 minutes; Producers: John C. Champion, Bruce Balaban and Paul C. Ross; Director: Lesley Selander
Audie Murphy; Broderick Crawford; Diana Lorys; Luz Marquez; Antonio Molino Rojo; Aldo Sambrell; Antonio Casas; Victor Vilanova 🥾🥾

40 Guns to Apache Pass
Columbia 1967; Pathecolor; 95 minutes; Producer: Grant Whytock; Director: William Witney
Audie Murphy; Kenneth Tobey; Laraine Stephens; Robert Brubaker; Michael Burns; Michael Blodgett; Byron Morrow; Michael Keep 👢👢

A Time for Dying
Fipco 1969; DeLuxecolor; 71 minutes; Producer: Audie Murphy; Director: Budd Boetticher
Richard Lapp; Anne Randall; Victor Jory; Audie Murphy; Bob Random; Walter Reed; Casey Tibbs; Ron Masak 👢

AUDIE MURPHY IN THE WOLD AND THE INNOCENT

JOEL MCCREA

Wells Fargo
Paramount 1937; 97 minutes; Produced and Directed by Frank Lloyd
Joel McCrea; Frances Dee; Bob Burns; Ralph Morgan; Mary Nash; Lloyd Nolan; Henry O'Neill; Jack Clark 🥾🥾🥾

Union Pacific
Paramount 1939; 135 minutes; Produced and Directed by Cecil B. DeMille
Barbara Stanwyck; Joel McCrea; Robert Preston; Brian Donlevy; Akim Tamiroff; Lynne Overman; Henry Kolker; J.M. Kerrigan 🥾🥾🥾🥾🥾

The Great Man's Lady
Paramount 1942; 90 minutes; Produced and Directed by William A. Wellman
Barbara Stanwyck; Joel McCrea; Brian Donlevy; Katharine Stevens; Thurston Hall; Frank M. Thomas; Lloyd Corrigan; Etta McDaniel 🥾🥾🥾

Buffalo Bill
20th Century Fox 1944; Technicolor; 89 minutes; Producer: Harry Sherman; Director: William A. Wellman
Joel McCrea; Maureen O'Hara; Anthony Quinn; Edgar Buchanan; Linda Darnell; Thomas Mitchell; Frank Fenton; Moroni Olsen 🥾🥾🥾

The Virginian
Paramount 1946; Technicolor; 90 minutes; Producer: Paul Jones; Director: Stuart Gilmore
Joel McCrea; Barbara Britton; Brian Donlevy; Sonny Tufts; Fay Bainter; Bill Edwards; Tom Tully; Henry O'Neill 🥾🥾

Ramrod
Enterprise/United Artists 1947; 95 minutes; Producer: Harry Sherman; Director: André De Toth
Joel McCrea; Veronica Lake; Preston Foster; Donald Crisp; Don DeFore; Arleen Whelan; Charles Ruggles; Lloyd Bridges 🥾🥾🥾🥾

Four Faces West
aka *They Passed This Way*
Enterprise/United Artists 1948; 89 minutes; Producer: Harry Sherman; Director: Alfred E. Green
Joel McCrea; Frances Dee; Charles Bickford; Joseph Calleia; William Conrad; Dan White; William Garralaga; Raymond Largey 🥾🥾🥾🥾

South of St. Louis
Warner Bros. 1949; Technicolor; 88 minutes; Producer: Milton Sperling; Director: Ray Enright
Joel McCrea; Alexis Smith; Douglas Kennedy; Zachary Scott; Dorothy Malone; Victor Jory; Bob Steele; Art Smith 🥾🥾🥾🥾

Colorado Territory
Warner Bros. 1949; 94 minutes; Producer: Anthony Veiller; Director: Raoul Walsh
Joel McCrea; Virginia Mayo; Dorothy Malone; Henry Hull; John Archer; James Mitchell; Morris Ankrum; Ian Wolfe

The Outriders
MGM 1950; Technicolor; 93 minutes; Producer: Richard Goldstone; Director: Roy Rowland
Joel McCrea; Arlene Dahl; Barry Sullivan; James Whitemoor; Ramon Novarro; Jeff Corey; Ted de Corsia; Claude Jarman, Jr.

Stars in My Crown
MGM 1950; 89 minutes; Producer: William H. Wright; Director: Jacques Tourneur
Joel McCrea; Ellen Drew; Dean Stockwell; James Mitchell; Juano Hernandez; Ed Begley; Alan Hale; Lewis Stone

Saddle Tramp
Universal 1950; Technicolor; 76 minutes; Producer: Leonard Goldstein; Director: Hugo Fregonese
Joel McCrea; Wanda Hendrix; John McIntire; Jeanette Nolan; John Russell; Ed Begley; Jimmy Hunt; Gordon Gebert

Frenchie
Universal 1950; Technicolor; 80 minutes; Producer: Michel (Michael) Kraike; Director: Louis King
Joel McCrea; Shelley Winters; Elsa Lanchester; Paul Kelly; Marie Windsor; John Emery; John Russell; Paul E. Burns

Cattle Drive
Universal 1951; Technicolor; 77 minutes; Producer: Aaron Rosenberg; Director: Kurt Neumann
Joel McCrea; Dean Stockwell; Chill Wills; Leon Ames; Howard Petrie; Henry Brandon; Griff Barnett; Bob Steele

The San Francisco Story
Warner Bros. 1952; 80 minutes; Producer: Howard Welsch; Director: Robert Parrish
Joel McCrea; Yvonne De Carlo; Sidney Blackmer; Onslow Stevens; Richard Erdman; Florence Bates; Lane Chandler; John Raven

The Lone Hand
Universal 1953; Technicolor; 80 minutes; Producer: Howard Christie; Director: George Sherman
Joel McCrea; Jimmy Hunt; Barbara Hale; Alex Nicol; James Arness; Charles Drake; Roy Roberts; Wesley Morgan

Border River
Universal 1954; Technicolor; 80 minutes; Producer: Albert J. Cohen; Director: George Sherman
Joel McCrea; Yvonne De Carlo; Pedro Armendariz; Alfonso Bedoya; Howard Petrie; Ivan Triesault; George J. Lewis; George Wallace 🥾🥾🥾

Black Horse Canyon
aka *Wild Horse Canyon*
Universal 1954; Technicolor; 81 minutes; Producer: John W. Rogers; Director: Jesse Hibbs
Joel McCrea; Mari Blanchard; Race Gentry; Murvyn Vye; John Pickard; Irving Bacon; Ewing Mitchell; Pilar Del Rey 🥾🥾🥾🥾

Stranger on Horseback
United Artists 1955; Ansco Color; 66 minutes; Producer: Robert Goldstein; Director: Jacques Tourneur
Joel McCrea; Kevin McCarthy; Miroslava; John McIntire; Emile Meyer; Nancy Gates; John Carradine; Walter Baldwin 🥾🥾🥾🥾🥾

Wichita
Allied Artists 1955; CinemaScope/Technicolor; 81 minutes; Producer: Walter Mirisch; Director: Jacques Tourneur
Joel McCrea; Vera Miles; Keith Larson; Wallace Ford; Walter Coy; Edgar Buchanan; Carl Benton Reid; Peter Graves 🥾🥾🥾🥾

The First Texan
Allied Artists 1956; CinemaScope/Technicolor; 82 minutes; Producer: Walter Mirisch; Director: Byron Haskin
Joel McCrea; Felicia Farr; Jeff Morrow; William Hopper; Abraham Sofaer; Myron Healey; Jody McCrea; Wallace Ford 🥾🥾🥾

The Oklahoman
Allied Artists 1957; CinemaScope/DeLuxecolor; 80 minutes; Producer: Walter Mirisch; Director: Francis D. Lyon
Joel McCrea; Barbara Hale; Brad Dexter; Gloria Talbott; Michael Pate; Douglas Dick; John Pickard; Anthony Caruso 🥾🥾

Trooper Hook
United Artists 1957; 81 minutes; Producer: Sol Baer Fielding; Director: Charles Marquis Warren
Joel McCrea; Barbara Stanwyck; Earl Holliman; Terry Lawrence; Rudolfo Acosta; John Dehner; Royal Dano; Edward Andrews 🥾🥾🥾🥾

Gunsight Ridge
United Artists 1957; 85 minutes; Producer: Robert Bassler; Director: Francis D. Lyon
Joel McCrea; Mark Stevens; Joan Weldon; Addison Richards; Darlene Fields; Carolyn Craig; L.Q. Jones; Slim Pickens 🥾🥾🥾

The Tall Stranger
aka ***Walk Tall***
Allied Artists 1957; CinemaScope/DeLuxecolor; 81 minutes; Producer: Walter Mirisch; Director: Thomas Carr
Joel McCrea; Virginia Mayo; Barry Kelley; Michael Ansara; George Neise; Ray Teal; Leo Gordon; Whit Bissell 🥾🥾🥾🥾

Cattle Empire
20th Century Fox 1958; CinemaScope/DeLuxecolor; 83 minutes; Producer: Robert Stabler; Director: Charles Marquis Warren
Joel McCrea; Gloria Talbott; Don Haggerty; Phyllis Coates; Bing Russell; Richard Shannon; Paul Brinegar; William McGraw 🥾🥾🥾🥾

Fort Massacre
United Artists 1958; CinemaScope/DeLuxecolor; 80 minutes; Producer: Walter Mirisch; Director: Joseph M. Newman
Joel McCrea; Forrest Tucker; John Russell; Susan Cabot; Francis McDonald; Denver Pyle; Anthony Caruso; George W. Neise 🥾🥾🥾🥾🥾

The Gunfight at Dodge City
United Artists 1959; CinemaScope/DeLuxecolor; 81 minutes; Producer: Walter Mirisch; Director: Joseph M. Newman
Joel McCrea; Nancy Gates; Julie Adams; John McIntire; Don Haggerty; Richard Anderson; Walter Coy; Harry Lauter 🥾🥾🥾🥾

Ride the High Country aka ***Guns in the Afternoon***
MGM 1962; CinemaScope/Metrocolor; 94 minutes; Producer: Richard E. Lyons; Director: Sam Peckinpah
Joel McCrea; Randolph Scott; Mariette Hartley; Ron Starr; Edgar Buchanan; James Drury; R.G. Armstrong; L.Q. Jones 🥾🥾🥾🥾

Cry Blood, Apache
Bronco Films/Liberty 1970; Eastmancolor; 82 minutes; Producers: Jody McCrea and Harold Roberts; Director: Jack Starrett
Jody McCrea; Marie Gahva; Robert Tessier; Jack Starrett; Don Henley; Rick Nervik; Dan Kemp; Joel McCrea 🥾🥾

Mustang Country
Universal 1976; Technicolor; 79 minutes; Produced and Directed by John Champion
Joel McCrea; Nika Mina; Patrick Wayne; Robert Fuller 🥾🥾🥾

George Montgomery

The Cisco Kid and the Lady
20th Century Fox 1939; 74 minutes; Producers: John Stone and Sol M. Wurtzel; Director: Herbert I. Leeds
Cesar Romero; Chris-Pin Martin; Marjorie Weaver; George Montgomery; Robert Barrat; Virginia Field; Harry Green; Ward Bond 🥾🥾🥾🥾

The Cowboy and the Blonde
20th Century Fox 1941; 68 minutes; Producers: Ralph Dietrich and Walter Morosco; Director: Ray McCarey
Mary Beth Hughes; George Montgomery; Alan Mowbray; Fuzzy Knight; Robert Conway; John Miljan; Minerva Urecal; Trevor Bardette 🥾🥾🥾

Last of the Duanes
20th Century Fox 1941; 57 minutes; Producer: Sol M. Wurtzel; Director: James Tinling
George Montgomery; Lynne Roberts; Eve Arden; George E. Stone; Joe Sawyer; Francis Ford; Truman Bradley; William Farnum 🥾🥾🥾

Riders of the Purple Sage
20th Century Fox 1941; 58 minutes; Producer: Sol M. Wurtzel; Director: James Tinling
George Montgomery; Mary Howard; Patsy Patterson; Lynne Roberts; James Gillette; Kane Richmond; Richard Lane; Robert Barrat 🥾🥾🥾

Belle Starr's Daughter
20th Century Fox 1948; 86 minutes; Producer: Edward L. Alperson; Director: Lesley Selander
George Montgomery; Ruth Roman; Rod Cameron; Wallace Ford; William Phipps; Isabel Jewell; Charles Kemper; J. Farrell MacDonald 🥾🥾🥾

Davy Crockett Indian Scout
aka *Indian Scout*
Reliance/United Artists 1950; 71 minutes; Producer: Edward Small; Director: Lew Landers
George Montgomery; Ellen Drew; Phillip Reed; Noah Beery, Jr.; Robert Barrat; Chief Thundercloud; Addison Richards; Erik Rolf 🥾🥾

Dakota Lil
20th Century Fox 1950; Cinecolor; 88 minutes; Producers: Jack Jungmeyer and Edward L. Alperson; Director: Lesley Selander
George Montgomery; Marie Windsor; Rod Cameron; John Emery; Wallace Ford; Jack Lambert; Larry Johns; Walter Sande 🥾🥾🥾🥾

The Iroquois Trail
aka ***The Tomahawk Trail***
Reliance/United Artists 1950; 85 minutes; Producer: Bernard Small; Director: Phil Karlson
George Montgomery; Monte Blue; Brenda Marshall; Sheldon Leonard; Glenn Langan; Paul Cavanagh; Don Garner; Reginald Denny 🥾🥾🥾🥾

The Texas Rangers
Columbia 1951; SuperCinecolor; 74 minutes; Producer: Bernard Small; Director: Phil Karlson
George Montgomery; Gale Storm; Noah Beery, Jr.; William Bishop; John Litel; John Dehner; Douglas Kennedy; Jerome Courtland 🥾🥾🥾🥾🥾

Indian Uprising
Columbia 1952; SuperCinecolor; 75 minutes; Producer: Bernard Small; Director: Ray Nazarro
George Montgomery; Miguel Inclan; Robert Shayne; Douglas Kennedy; Audrey Long; Joe Sawyer; John Baer; Hugh Sanders 🥾🥾🥾🥾

Cripple Creek
Columbia 1952; Technicolor; 78 minutes; Producer: Edward Small; Director: Ray Nazarro
George Montgomery; Jerome Courtland; Richard Egan; William Bishop; Karin Booth; Don Porter; John Dehner; Roy Roberts 🥾🥾🥾🥾

The Pathfinder
Columbia 1952; Technicolor; 78 minutes; Producer: Sam Katzman; Director: Sidney Salkow
George Montgomery; Helena Carter; Jay Silverheels; Walter Kingsford; Stephen Belcassy; Bruce Lester; Elena Verdugo; Rodd Redwing 🥾🥾

Jack McCall Desperado
Columbia 1953; Technicolor; 76 minutes; Producer: Sam Katzman; Director: Sidney Salkow
George Montgomery; Angela Stevens; Douglas Kennedy; James Seay; Jay Silverheels; Eugene Iglesias; William Tannen; John Hamilton 🥾🥾🥾🥾

Fort Ti
Columbia 1953; Technicolor; Orig. in 3-D; 73 minutes; Producer: Sam Katzman; Director: William Castle
George Montgomery; Joan Vohs; James Seay; Howard Petrie; Irving Bacon; Ben Astar; Phyllis Fowler; Lester Matthews 🥾🥾

Gun Belt
United Artists 1953; Technicolor; 77 minutes; Producer: Edward Small; Director: Ray Nazarro
George Montgomery; Helen Westcott; Tab Hunter; John Dehner; William Bishop; Douglas Kennedy; Hugh Sanders; James Millican 🥾🥾🥾

Battle of Rogue River
Columbia 1954; Technicolor; 71 minutes; Producer: Sam Katzman; Director: William Castle
George Montgomery; Martha Hyer; Richard Denning; John Crawford; Michael Granger; Charles Evans; Emory Parnell; Freeman Morse 🥾🥾🥾

The Lone Gun
United Artists 1954; Technicolor; 76 minutes; Producer: Edward Small; Director: Ray Nazarro
George Montgomery; Dorothy Malone; Frank Faylen; Neville Brand; Douglas Kennedy; Robert J. Wilke; Skip Homeier; Douglas Fowley 🥾🥾🥾🥾🥾

Masterson of Kansas
Columbia 1954; Technicolor; 73 minutes; Producer: Sam Katzman; Director: William Castle
George Montgomery; James Griffith; Nancy Gates; William Henry; Bruce Cowling; David Bruce; John Maxwell; Donald Murphy 🥾🥾🥾🥾

Seminole Uprising
Columbia 1955; Technicolor; 74 minutes; Producer: Sam Katzman; Director: Earl Bellamy
George Montgomery; Karin Booth; William Fawcett; Steven Ritch; Ed Hinton; Howard Wright; John Pickard; James Maloney 🥾🥾

Robbers' Roost
United Artists 1955; Eastmancolor; 83 minutes; Producer: Robert Goldstein; Director: Sidney Salkow
George Montgomery; Richard Boone; Peter Graves; Sylvia Findley; Bruce Bennett; Tony Romano; William Hopper; Warren Stevens 🥾🥾🥾

Canyon River
aka ***Cattle King***
Allied Artists 1956; CinemaScope/DeLuxecolor; 79 minutes; Producer: Richard V. Heermance; Director: Harmon Jones
George Montgomery; Marcia Henderson; Peter Graves; Richard Eyer; Alan Hale, Jr.; Walter Sande; Robert J. Wilke; Jack Lambert 🥾🥾🥾

Last of the Badmen
Allied Artists 1957; CinemaScope/DeLuxecolor; 79 minutes; Producer: Vincent M. Fennelly; Director: Paul Landres
George Montgomery; Keith Larson; Douglas Kennedy; James Best; Robert Foulk; Willis Bouchy; Tom Greenway; Michael Ansara 🥾🥾

Gun Duel in Durango
aka **Duel in Durango**
United Artists 1957; 73 minutes; Producer: Robert E. Kent; Director: Sidney Salkow
George Montgomery; Ann Robinson; Bobby Clark; Steve Brodie; Denver Pyle; Don Barry; Frank Ferguson; Henry Rowland 🥾🥾🥾🥾

Pawnee
aka **Pale Arrow**
Republic 1957; Trucolor; 80 minutes; Producers: Jack J. Gross and Philip N. Krasne; Director: George Waggner
George Montgomery; Lola Albright; Bill Williams; Francis McDonald; Dabbs Greer; Charlotte Austin; Charles Horvath; Ralph Moody 🥾🥾

Black Patch
Warner Bros. 1957; 82 minutes; Produced and Directed by Allen H. Miner
George Montgomery; Diane Brewster; Tom Pittman; Leo Gordon; House Peters, Jr.; Sebastian Cabot; Ted Jacques; Strother Martin 🥾🥾

Man from God's Country
Allied Artists 1958; CinemaScope/DeLuxe color; 72 minutes; Producer: Scott R. Dunlap; Director: Paul Landres
George Montgomery; Randy Stuart; Kim Charney; House Peters, Jr.; Frank Wilcox; James Griffith; Susan Cummings; Phillip Terry 🥾🥾🥾

The Toughest Gun in Tombstone
United Artists 1958; 72 minutes; Producer: Robert E. Kent; Director: Earl Bellamy
George Montgomery; Beverly Tyler; Gerald Milton; Jim Davis; Scotty Morrow; Harry Lauter; Don Beddoe; Lane Bradford 🥾🥾🥾

Badman's Country
Warner Bros. 1958; 68 minutes; Producer: Robert E. Kent; Director: Fred F. Sears
George Montgomery; Karin Booth; Neville Brand; Buster Crabbe; Gregory Walcott; Russell Johnson; Malcolm Atterbury; Morris Ankrum 🥾🥾🥾

King of the Wild Stallions
Allied Artists 1959; CinemaScope/DeLuxecolor; 76 minutes; Producer: Ben Schwalb; Director: R.G. Springsteen
George Montgomery; Diane Brewster; Edgar Buchanan; Emile Meyer; Jerry Hartleben; Denver Pyle; Dan Sheridan; Rory Mallinson 🥾🥾🥾

Outlaw of Red River
aka ***Django the Condemned***
Fenix/Harold Goldman Enterprises 1965; Eastmancolor; 89 (73) minutes; Producers: Arturo Marcos and Eduardo Manzanos; Director: Maury Dexter
George Montgomery; José Nieto; Elisa Montés; Jesus Tordesillas; Miguel del Castillo; Ricardo Valle; Gloria Camara; Ana Maria Custodio 🥾

Hostile Guns
A.C. Lyles Prods./Paramount 1967; Technicolor/Techniscope; 91 minutes; Producer: A. C. Lyles; Director: R.G. Springsteen
George Montgomery; Tab Hunter; Leo Gordon; Yvonne De Carlo; John Russell; James Craig; Robert Emhardt; Brian Donlevy 🥾🥾

GEORGE MONTGOMERY IN CRIPPLED CREEK

All those rugged, sun-beaten frontier locations—Lone Pine, Death Valley, Bronson Canyon, the Simi Valley, Red Rock Canyon, the Big Bear Lake area, Arizona's House Rock Canyon, the Vasquez Rocks, Utah's Zion National Park, Mexico's Gallup region, among others—have now reverted to their natural state, the canyons, rocky cliffs, buttes, rivers, mesas, mountains, hills, deserts and woods no longer echoing to the sound of camera crews, gunfire, the gallop of horses' hooves, the cries of Indians on the warpath and the rumble of stagecoaches, wagons and locomotives. RIP the much-loved, much-missed traditional American Western.

Bibliography/Acknowledgment

Below is a list of source references used throughout this book, mainly in the biographies of the four stars. There isn't a great deal of literature on the market dealing with the careers of Randolph Scott, Audie Murphy and Joel McCrea, and even less on George Montgomery. What little there is can be gleaned from the following:

Last of the Cowboy Heroes by Robert Nott (McFarland and Company, 2000). Nott traces the crucial, productive Hollywood years of Scott and McCrea as regards popular output, together with Murphy's films from 1950 onwards, with biographical information spread throughout the book, plus a filmography at the back. Scott and McCrea's earlier work, although briefly mentioned, isn't looked at in great detail.

The Years of George Montgomery by George Montgomery and Jeffrey Millet (Sagebrush Press, 1981). Montgomery self-published his memoirs in this superb, hefty, cloth-bound volume, about the only book available on his childhood and career, both as an actor and sculptor/designer. Each limited edition comes with newspaper cuttings, inscriptions and dedications written by the man himself, plus unique (to each particular book) line drawings (Montgomery, as we have seen, was a talented artist). Expect to pay upwards of $100 for a pristine copy containing hand-written notes by George.

Wikipedia has extensive notes on all four stars (Murphy in particular because of his war record) and **IMDB** contains short biographies.

Online site **https://fifties.westerns.wordpress.com** contains useful snippets of rare information hidden among pages of articles on the Western film and its numerous participants. Boyd Magers' informative online article on George Montgomery's Westerns I found to be helpful.

The Audie Murphy Westerns Collection, a 4-DVD box set, includes short introductions by Ben Mankiewicz on the four films showcased, plus bits and pieces on Murphy as a person. Most high-quality discs contain a smattering of facts relating to the leading man, and the same applies to Scott, McCrea and Montgomery's digital releases.

The publisher would like to thank **Larry Springer** for providing many of the stills used to illustrate this book. The Western movie still collection, begun by Larry's father and carried on by "The Hagerstown Kid," helped to bring this book to vivid life. Thank you for decades of friendship, Larry!

If you enjoyed this book,
write for a free catalog of
Midnight Marquee Press titles
or visit our website at
http://www.midmar.com

Midnight Marquee Press, Inc.
9721 Britinay Lane
Baltimore, MD 21234
410-665-1198
mmarquee@aol.com

www.ingramcontent.com/pod-product-compliance
Lightning Source LLC
Chambersburg PA
CBHW071301110526
44591CB00010B/737